The Details of the Volumes: Mental Health

Volume 1: Issues and Interventions
Volume 2: Multigroup Analysis
Volume 3: Strength of Human Resources
Volume 4: Therapeutic Applications
Volume 5: Adolescents & Children Mental Health
Volume 6: Women Mental Health
Volume 7: Ageing Issues and Interventions
Volume 8: Mental Health in Workplace

About the Editors

Aradhana Shukla is retired Professor and Head of the Department of Psychology at Kumaun University, SSJ Campus, Almora and Dean (Arts), Kumaun University, Nainital. She has served in this university since 1987 and before joining this university she was UGC fellow at DDU Gorakhpur University, Gorakhpur and Assistant Research Officer at Department of Paediatrics, IMS, BHU. She has guided 52 Ph.D. students completed, 6 major research projects from UGC, NCERT and ICSSR. She has written and edited 20 books and developed 15 psychological tests. More than 250 papers written by her have been published in the journals and books of national and international repute. She has co-edited six volume series on Mental Health: Psycho-Social Perspectives, Volume one "Issues and Intervention" (2015), Volume two "Multigroup Analysis" (2015), Volume three "Strength of Human Resources" (2017), Volume four "Therapeutic Applications" (2017), Volume five "Children and Adolecents" and Volume six 'Women Mental Health". She is also co-editor of books entitled "Psyche of Asian Society" in 2019 and "Cognising Asian Societies through Psychological Underpinnings" in 2022 published by Concept Publishing Company, New Delhi. She has published "स्वास्थ्य मनोविज्ञान" in 2022 by Kitab Mahal, New Delhi. She is the co-author of books entitled "Communication Skills and Personality Development" and "संचार कौशल और व्यक्तित्व विकास" published from Anu Publication in the year 2023. She has attended and participated in so many National and International seminars in online and offline mode and served as supportive supervisor in GFATM round VII—an International project. Moreover, she served in various academic assignments given by many organizations. After her retirement in 2019 she worked as a Senior Research Fellow in the Department of Psychology, SSJ University, Almora. She is a certified counsellor from NIMHANS. Now she is working in GRACE FOUNDATION Hudson, New York. Her major areas of interest are cross-cultural psychology, health psychology and psychological intervention.

Anubhuti Dubey is Professor of Psychology and presently Dean, Students Welfare, Deen Dayal Upadhyay Gorakhpur University (NAAC A++), Gorakhpur (U.P). She is teaching here for the past 24 years. She has published more than 55 research papers in the journals of international and national repute and 45 chapters in different edited volumes. She has written books entitled, "Psychological Perspectives on Chronic Illness" in 2012 published by Concept Publishing Company, New Delhi and "स्वास्थ्य मनोविज्ञान" in 2022 published by Kitab Mahal, New Delhi. She is the co-author of books titled "Communication Skills and Personality Development" and "संचार कौशल और व्यक्तित्व विकास" published from Anu Publication in the year 2023. She is also the co-editor of a series of six volumes on "Mental Health: Psychological Perspectives" (Publication years 2015, 2017, 2021 published by Concept Publishing Company, New Delhi). She is also co-editor of books entitled "Psyche of Asian Society" in 2019 and "Cognising Asian Societies through Psychological Underpinnings" in 2022 published by Concept Publishing Company, New Delhi. She has carried out ICSSR research project on "Psychological Dynamics of Health and Illness in Women of Eastern Uttar Pradesh". Thirteen students have been awarded Ph.D. degree under her supervision. She has also supervised more than 150 PG dissertation projects. She is also a Master Trainer and Supportive Supervisor for training HIV/AIDS counsellors under GFATM-7 programme. Her research area of specialization includes Health Psychology, Positive Psychology, Qualitative Research Methods and Psychological Counselling. Presently, she is Editor of International Journal "Mind and Society". She is also a consultant for Psychosocial assessment of juvenile offenders of Gorakhpur district under Juvenile Justice Board. She has awarded by U.P Government as Shakti Yodhya and got Certificate of Appreciation for the contribution in syllabus as NEP 2020 recommendation. She has delivered more than 150 lectures as resource person in various conferences/seminars/training programmes/workshops.

MENTAL HEALTH
Psycho-Social Perspectives

Volume Seven

Ageing: Issues and Interventions

Edited by
Aradhana Shukla
Anubhuti Dubey

CONCEPT PUBLISHING COMPANY PVT. LTD.
NEW DELHI-110059

ISBN: 978-93-5125-173-6 (Series)
ISBN: 978-93-6344-439-3 (Vol. VII)

First Published 2025

Published and Printed by

Concept Since 1974

Concept Publishing Company Pvt. Ltd.
A/15-16, Commercial Block, Mohan Garden
New Delhi-110059 (India)
T: +91-11-41101460
E: publishing@conceptpub.com, *W*: www.conceptpub.com

Cataloging in Publication--Courtesy: D.K. Agencies (P) Ltd. <docinfo@dkagencies.com>

Mental health : psycho-social perspectives / edited by Aradhana Shukla, Anubhuti Dubey.
pages cm
Contributed articles.
Includes bibliographical references and index.
Contents: volume seven. Ageing : issues and interventions
ISBN 9789351251736 (series)
ISBN 9789363444393 (vol. VII)

1. Older people--Mental health--India. 2. Aging--India--Psychological aspects. 3. Aging--Social aspects--India. I. Shukla, Aradhana, editor. II. Dubey, Anubhuti, editor.

LCC HQ1061.M46 2025 | DDC 305.260954 23

Preface

Older adults contribute to society as family and community members, and many are volunteers and workers. While most have good health, many are at risk of developing mental health conditions such as depression and anxiety disorders. Many may also experience reduced mobility, chronic pain, frailty, dementia or other health problems, for which they require some form of long-term care. As people age, they are more likely to experience several conditions at the same time.

At older ages, mental health is shaped not only by physical and social environments but also by the cumulative impacts of earlier life experiences and specific stressors related to ageing. Exposure to adversity, significant loss in intrinsic capacity and a decline in functional ability can all result in psychological distress.

Older adults are more likely to experience adverse events such as bereavement, or a drop in income or reduced sense of purpose with retirement. Despite their many contributions to society, many older adults are subject to ageism, which can seriously affect people's mental health.

Social isolation and loneliness, which affect about a quarter of older people, are key risk factors for mental health conditions in later life. So too is abuse of older people, which includes any kind of physical, verbal, psychological, sexual or financial abuse, as well as neglect. One in six older adults experience abuse, often by their own carers. Abuse of older adults has serious consequences and can lead to depression and anxiety.

Many older people are carers of spouses with chronic health conditions, such as dementia. The responsibilities of such care can be overwhelming and can affect the carer's mental health.

Some older adults are at greater risk of depression and anxiety, because of dire living conditions, poor physical health or lack of access to quality support and services. This includes older adults living in humanitarian settings and those living with chronic illnesses (such as heart disease, cancer or stroke), neurological conditions (such as dementia), or substance use problems.

Key mental health promotion and prevention strategies for healthy ageing include:

- Measures to reduce financial insecurity and income inequality;
- Programmes to ensure safe and accessible housing, public buildings and transport;
- Social support for older adults and their carers;
- Support for healthy behaviours, especially to eat a balanced diet, be physically active, refrain from tobacco and reduce alcohol use; and
- Health and social programmes targeted at vulnerable groups such as those who live alone or in remote areas and those living with a chronic health condition.

About the series Mental Health: Psychosocial Perspectives

This series was originally plan in 2 Volumes but after we approach M/S Concept Publishing Company Pvt. Ltd. they gone through both the manuscripts and advise to work on the other important issues, initially total 10 Volumes were planned on the different major contemporary issues. While working on the further volumes we received an encouraging response from the faculty and scholars of all segment and able to published 6 Volumes so far. The further 2 Volumes No. 7 and 8 are in the process of publication. The details of all the Eight Volumes are given below:

1. **Issues and Interventions:** In this volume we have covered various issues that foster or hamper mental health. Also, strategies to minimize negative mental health and improve positive mental health are discussed.
2. **Multigroup Analysis:** This volume covers the conceptual background and psychosocial perspective of mental health in various social settings.
3. **Strength of Human Resources:** In this volume we have tried to throw light on the promotional strategies of mental health following which a person can be relieved from negative mental health.
4. **Therapeutic Applications:** This volume covers a range of behavioural therapies which were found effective to minimize or overcome mental ill health.

5. **Adolescents and Children Mental Health:** This volume presents a wide spectrum of the mental health of children and adolescents which are seen in them.
6. **Women Mental Health:** This volume presents the mental health of women in different perspective.
7. **Ageing: Issues and Interventions:** This volume aims to focus the various shades of mental health in old people and promotion of their death.
8. **Mental Health in Workplace:** This volume deals with the pattern of mental health of people working with various organizations.

We have worked hard to seek out as many experiences as possible and we also anticipate that this will open new insight for the teachers, researchers, and mental health professionals. However, we will be highly blessed to obtain the healthy and critical comments from our colleagues, seniors and friends and we will appreciate them from the bottom of our hearts.

Aradhana Shukla
Anubhuti Dubey

Acknowledgements

We, the editors, feel immense pleasure to present our series on mental health before the august readers. We hope that it will be admired by you all and the comments will be highly appreciated.

We fell our deep sense of gratitude and thankfulness to our respected contributors. If was their support that these volumes came in the shape. We are thankful to Mr. Abhishek and Mrs. Kavita Khawar for computer task.

Last but not least, we are thankful to Mr. Ashok Mittal, M/s. Concept Publishing Company Pvt. Ltd., New Delhi to shape our dreams in concrete form.

12 May 2025
Budh Purnima

Aradhana Shukla
Anubhuti Dubey

Contents

Preface v

Acknowledgements ix

List of Contributors xv

1. Introduction 1
   Aradhana Shukla and *Anubhuti Dubey*

2. Indian Older Adults' Struggle in Handling Emotional and Psychological Challenges: An Overview 4
   Nisha Mani Pandey and *Girishwar Misra*

3. Positive Ageing: Building the Eco-system for Fostering Well-being of the Elderly People 16
   Amarnath Rai and *Tanvi Kumari*

4. On Caregiver's Healing: A Life Story Study of Healing from Disability 30
   Mridusmita Bhagawati and *Kumar Ravi Priya*

5. Palliative and End-of-Life Care for Ageing Population: A Psychological Perspective 61
   Priyanka Pathak and *Shobhna Joshi*

6. Exploring the Field of Gero-psychology and Its Researches 71
   Anubhuti Dubey and *Shubhang Dubey*

7. Mental Health in Later Life: Unravelling the Current State and Future Directions of Geriatric Mental Health Care in India 94
   Tanya Sharma, *Ravi P. Pandey* and *Purnima Awasthi*

8. Cultural Practices in Uttarakhand Towards Healthy Ageing 109
Ruchi Tewari and *Aradhana Shukla*

9. The Role of Spirituality in Assuaging Death Anxiety Among Older Adults: A Comprehensive Overview 123
Himanshi Nigam, Shilpa Kumari and *Shobhna Joshi*

10. Journeying through Mental Landscapes: Overcoming Loneliness, Easing Distress, and Managing Anxiety for Optimal Wellness 141
Shakshi Priya Giri and *Anubhuti Dubey*

11. Depression and Quality of Life among Indian Older Adults: A Correlational Study 155
Akanksha Bharti and *Das Ambika Bharti*

12. Promoting Wellness among Elderly: Touching New Horizons 175
Shilpa Singh and *Archana Shukla*

13. Loneliness Unveiled: Mindset Matters in Geriatric Wellness 189
Prerna Arora and *Ritu Singh*

14. Role of Spirituality in Positive Ageing for Older Adults 207
Priyanka Shukla

15. Mental Health for Geriatric Population: Creating a Positive Environment for the Elderly: Approaches, Models, and Intervention Strategies 216
Hemanthakumara V.

16. Prevalence and Associated Factor of Depression Among Elderly Population in Rasuwa, Nepal 245
Narendra Singh Thagunna, Renu Khayamali, Binu Koirala and *Jyotshna Dangi*

17. Scoping Review on the Predictors of Happiness and Life Satisfaction among the Older Adults 264
Richa Chaudhary

18. Preserving Health: Understanding Diabetes and Mental Well-being in the Elderly Persons of India 276
Eshita Chatterjee, Sanchita Ghosh and *Sristi Dutta*

19. Understanding the Complex Nexus of Mental Health and Ageing in India: Challenges, Initiatives and Pathways to Psychological Well-being 291
Arpita Kackar

20. The Risk Factors Associated with Mental Health Problems in the Elderly 310
Rupesh Ranjan, Richa Priyamvada and *Suprakash Chaudhury*

21. Concept of Ageing: Prospects and Retrospects 333
Kiran Karnatak

22. Successful Ageing: Old is Gold 345
Aradhana Shukla

Index 367

List of Contributors

Akanksha Bharti, Department of Psychological Sciences, Central University of South Bihar, SH-7 Gaya-Panchanpur Road, P.O. Fatehpur, P.S. Tekari, Gaya (Bihar).
Email: akankshabharti@cusb.ac.in

Anubhuti Dubey, Professor, Department of Psychology, DDU Gorakhpur University, Gorakhpur (Uttar Pradesh).
Email: anubhutiddu@rediffmail.com

Amarnath Rai, Former Principal & Associate Professor, M.G.S.S.S. Degree College, Ghazipur (Uttar Pradesh).
Email: anr.horizon@gmail.com

Archana Shukla, Associate Professor, Department of Psychology, Lucknow University, Lucknow (Uttar Pradesh).
Email: archana.kshitij@gmail.com

Aradhana Shukla, Professor and Former Dean (Arts) and Head, Department of Psychology, Kumaun University, Nainital and Senior Fellow (ICSSR) SSJ University, Almora (Uttarakhand).
Email: aradhana.shukla5@gmail.com

Arpita Kackar, Assistant Professor, Jai Narain Vyas University, Jodhpur (Rajasthan).
Email: akackar72@gmail.com

Binu Koirala, Graduate from Department of Psychology, Tribhuvan University, Kathmandu (Nepal).
Email: koiralavinu@gmail.com

Das, Ambika Bharti, Department of Psychological Sciences, Central University of South Bihar, SH-7, Gaya (Bihar).
Email: ambika@cub.ac.in

Eshita Chatterjee, Department of Psychology, West Bengal State University, Berunanpukuria, P.O. Malikapur, Barasat, North 24 Parganas, Kolkata (West Bengal).
Email: chatterjeeeshita5@gmail.com

Girishwar Misra, Former Vice-Chancellor, Mahatma Gandhi Hindi Antar-rashtriya Vishwavidyalaya, Wardha and Former Head and Professor, Department of Psychology, University of Delhi, Delhi.
Email: misragirishwar@gmail.com

Hemanthakumara, V., Assistant Professor, Department of Psychology, CHRIST (Deemed to be University), Yashwanthpur Campus, Bengaluru (Karnataka).
Email: hemanthakumara.v@christuniversity.in

Himanshi Nigam, Research Scholar, Department of Psychology, Banaras Hindu University, Varanasi (Uttar Pradesh).
Email: himanshinigam4@gmail.com

Jyotsna Dangi, Assistant Professor, Sainik Awasiya Mahavidyalaya, Salla Ghari (Nepal).
Email: dangijyotsna@gmail.com.

Kiran Karnatak, Assistant Professor, Department of Psychology, M.B.P.G. College, Haldwani, Nainital (Uttarakhand).
Email: kirankarnatak@gmail.com

Kumar Ravi Priya, Professor, Department of Psychology, Faculty of Humanities and Social Sciences, Indian Institute of Technology, Kanpur, (Uttar Pradesh).
Email: krp@iitk.ac.in.

Mridusmita Bhagwati, Research Scholar, Department of Psychology, Faculty of Humanities and Social Sciences, Indian Institute of Technology, Kanpur (Uttar Pradesh).
Email: mridu@iitk.ac.in

Narendra Singh Thagunna, Consultant Psychologist and Assistant Professor, Department of Psychology, Tribhuvan University, Kathmandu (Nepal).
Email: @drthagunna@gmail.com

Nisha Mani Pandey, Professor, Department of Geriatric Mental Health and Coordinator, Research Developmental Activities Research and Development, King George Medical University, Lucknow (Uttar Pradesh).
Email: dgmhresearch@gmail.com

Prerana Arora, Research Scholar, Department of Human Development and Family Stduies, G.B. Pant University of Agriculture & Technology, Pant Nagar (Uttarakhand).
Email: prernaarora1957@gmail.com

Priyanka Pathak, Assistant Professor, Department of Psychology, V.K.S. University, Ara (Bihar).
Email: priyankapathak456@gmail.com

Priyanka Shukla, Assistant Professor, Government Degree College, Hansaur, Barabanki (Uttar Pradesh).
Email: psshuklapriyanka@gmail.com

Purnima Awasthi, Professor, Department of Psychology, Banaras Hindu University, Varanasi (Uttar Pradesh).
Email: awasthip09@gmail.com

Ravi P. Pandey, Assistant Professor, Department of Psychology, Central University of Haryana, Mahendragarh (Haryana).
Email: pratapravipandey@gmail.com

Renu Khayamali, MD Ayurveda, Clinical Psychologist, Kathmandu (Nepal).
Email: khayamalirenu@gmail.com

Richa Chaudhary, Assistant Professor, Department of Psychology, Amity University of Behaviour and Allied Sciences, Noida (Uttar Pradesh).
Email: richa.extreme0@gmail.com

Richa Priyamvada, Senior Clinical Psychologist, Department of Psychiatry, Chirayu Medical College and Hospital, Bhopal and Mind Cushion, MP Nagar, Bhopal (Madhya Pradesh).
Email: richap.dr@gmail.com

Ritu Singh, Associate Professor, Department of Human Development and Family Studies, College of Home Science, G.B.P.U.A.T., Pantnagar, (Uttarakhand).
Email: ritu.singh07@gmail.com

Ruchi Tiwari, Assistant Professor, Department of Psychology, Uttarakhand Open University, Haldwani, Nainital (Uttarakhand).
Email: rtewari@uou.ac.in

Rupesh Ranjan, Clinical Neuro-psychologist, Department of Psychiatry, Bhopal Memorial Hospital and Research Centre, Bhopal (Madhya Pradesh).
Email: dr.rupeshranjan@gmail.com

Sakshi Priya Giri, Department of Psychology, DDU Gorakhpur University, Gorakhpur (Uttar Pradesh).
Email: sakshipriyagiri@gmail.com

Sanchita Ghosh, Assistant Professor, Department of Psychology, West Bengal State University, Berunanpukuria, P.O. Malikapur, Barasat, North 24 Parganas, Kolkata (West Bengal).
Email: sanchitaghosh@wbsu.ac.in

Shilpa Kumari, Assistant Professor, Department of Psychology, Banaras Hindu University, Varanasi (Uttar Pradesh).
Email: chaudharyshilpu@gmail.com

Shilpa Singh, Assistant Professor, Department of Psychology, Government College for Girls, Sector 14, Gurugram (Haryana).
Email: shilpaasingh4@gmail.com.

Shobhna Joshi, Professor, Department of Psychology, Banaras Hindu University, Varanasi (Uttar Pradesh).
Email: getshobhna@yahoo.com

Sristi Dutta, Department of Psychology, West Bengal State University, Berunanpukuria, P.O. Malikapur, Barasat, North 24 Parganas, Kolkata, (West Bengal).
Email: srishtiduttaroy@gmail.com

Shubhang Dubey, Pursuing Graduation, Amity University of Behaviour and Allied Sciences, Noida (Uttar Pradesh).
Email: subhang18@gmail.com

Suprakash Chaudhary, Professor, Department of Psychiatry, Dr. D.Y. Patil Medical College and Research Centre, Dr. D.Y. Patil Vidyapeeth, Pune, (Maharashtra).
Email: suprakash@gmail.com

Tanvi Kumari, Assistant Professor (Home Science), RRRGR Girls Degree College, Maharajganj (Uttar Pradesh).
Email: tanvis208@gmail.com

Tanya Sharma, Research Scholar, Department of Psychology, Central University of Haryana, Mahendragarh (Haryana).
Email: Tanya.sharma0791@gmail.com

1

Introduction

Aradhana Shukla and *Anubhuti Dubey*

Ageing can be defined as progressive physiological changes in an organism that lead to senescence, or a decline of biological functions and of the organism's ability to adapt to metabolic stress. Ageing takes place in a cell, an organ, or the total organism with the passage of time. It is a process that goes on over the entire adult life span of any living thing. Gerontology, the study of the ageing process, is devoted to the understanding and control of all factors contributing to the finitude of individual life. It is not concerned exclusively with debility, which looms so large in human experience, but deals with a much wider range of phenomena. Every species has a life history in which the individual life span has an appropriate relationship to the reproductive life span and to the mechanism of reproduction and the course of development. How these relationships evolved is as germane to gerontology as it is to evolutionary biology. It is also important to distinguish between the purely physicochemical processes of ageing and the accidental organismic processes of disease and injury that lead to death. Gerontology, therefore, can be defined as the science of the finitude of life as expressed in the three aspects of longevity, ageing, and death, examined in both evolutionary and individual (ontogenetic) perspective. Longevity is the span of life of an organism. Ageing is the sequential or progressive change in an organism that leads to an increased risk of debility, disease, and death. Senescence consists of these manifestations of the ageing process, the viability (survival ability) of a population is characterized in two actuarial functions: the survivorship curve and the age-specific death rate, or Gompertz function. The relation of such factors as ageing characteristics, constitutional vigour, physical factors, diet, and exposure to disease-causing organisms to the actuarial functions is complex. There is, nevertheless, no substitute for them as measures of the ageing process and of the effect of environmental or genetic modifiers.

As people grow older they may and/or often experience certain life changes that impact their overall health scenario. So far as the matter of mental health is concerned, the major issues are: coping with serious illness, death of partner or dear ones, financial obstacles, neglect by family members and many more. Although many people make a positive acceptance with the situations some may feel grief, hope, helplessness, loneliness or social withdrawal. When these feelings persist, they can lead to mental illness, such as depression and anxiety.

Mental health is important at every stage of life. Effective treatment options are available to help older adults to manage their mental health and improve their quality of life. Recognizing the signs and perceiving a healthcare provider is the first step for getting treatment.

Keeping these views in consideration a thought was appeared in our cognition to think about the concept of ageing, constraints of ageing, characteristics of old people, descriptions of intervention whenever and wherever required and ways to minimise the health related issues of older people.This is the seventh volume of our mental health series, "Mental Health:Psycho-social Perspectives" and deals various shades of the mental health of older people.

There are twenty-two chapters in this volume. The first chapter of the editors, Aradhana Shukla and Anubhuti Dubey depicts the conceptual notes about the older people which describes brief introduction of each chapter incorporated here. Nisha Mani Pandey and Girishwar Misra have shed light on the emotional challenges of older people and struggle to meet the challenges. Amarnath Rai and Tanvi Kumari have described positive ageing and caregivers' problem and healing skills are discussed by Mridusmita Bhagwati and Kumar Ravi Priya. Priyanka Pathak and Shobhna Joshi have elaborated the palliative and end-of-life care for ageing population in psychological perspective and the concept of gero psychology with new exploration is explored by Anubhuti Dubey and Shubhang Dubey. Old age mental health with current status and future perspective is presented by Tanya Sharma, Ravi P. Pandey and Purnima Awasthi. Ruchi Tiwari and Aradhana Shukla have discussed the cultural practices in Uttarakhand and the role of spirituality in assuage death anxiety is discussed by Himanshi Nigam, Shilpa Kumari and Shobhna Joshi, Sakshi Priya Giri and Anubhuti Dubey, in their chapter have described how optimal wellness can be gained by the management of anxiety, overcoming loneliness and easing distress.

Akansha Bharati and Das Ambika Bharati have described the pattern and magnitude of depression and quality of life in the elderly people and well promotion in them has been discussed by Shilpa Singh and Archana Shukla. Prerna Arora and Ritu Singh have narrated the moderating role of relationship between sprituality and psychological relationship. Role of speciality in positive ageing is described by Priyanka Shukla. In his highly vast chapter Hemanthakumara has elaborated about the mental health of geriatric population with intervention and Narendra Thagunna, Renu Khayamali, Binu Koirala and Jyotsana Dangi have narrated their views regarding effects of depression in the elderly population of Nepal. Richa Chaudhary has reviewed the happiness and life satisfaction in older people. Eshita Chatterji, Sanchita Ghosh and Shrishti Dutta have presented their chapter to understand diabetes and mental well-being of elderly people. Arpita Kackar has noted the challenge initiative and pathways to psychological well-being regarding mental health and ageing in India and risk factors associated with mental health problems in the elderly is described by Rupesh Ranjan, Richa Priyamvada and Suprakash Chaudhary. Kiran Karnatak has described the path of wellness of older people and in the last chapter of the volume Aradhana Shukla has elaborated the concept of successful ageing.

All the chapters incorporated here have revealed authors' deep knowledge and endeavour to frame it in words. We are thankful to them. We are also thankful to Mr. Ashok Mittal, Managing Director, Concept Publishing Company Pvt. Ltd., New Delhi, to give the thoughts of the contributors in shape.

2

Indian Older Adults' Struggle in Handling Emotional and Psychological Challenges

An Overview

Nisha Mani Pandey and *Girishwar Misra*

Psychosocial and Emotional Challenges Facing the Elderly

Health Issues: The health issues put an enormous burden on the elderly. Illness often disturbs them. It is reported that almost 50 per cent of Indian elderly suffer from at least one chronic condition, ranging from asthma and arthritis to depression and diabetes (Mangal *et al.*, 2019; S.C. Tiwari *et al.*, 2013). Akbar *et al.* (2018), Mangal *et al.* (2019), and Pandey & Misra (2024) report that the elderly face a lot of problems, such as moving slowly, having health problem, and mental health problems like neurotic, psychotic, or cognitive problem. They also often have emotional and social problems, which makes specialized geriatric care much more important.

Chronic Illnesses: There is a significant impact of chronic health conditions on the Indian elderly population that affects their physical and mental well-being as well as quality of life. The commonest chronic conditions, like hypertension, diabetes, heart disease, and arthritis, are reported to be high in the elderly (Chauhan *et al.*, 2022; Patel *et al.*, 2023).

Elderly people who are living alone are more likely to suffer from both chronic and acute illnesses (Agrawal, 2012; Meng *et al.*, 2024). These illnesses not only cause physical discomfort but also lead to worry and mental distress, thereby compromising psychological well-being globally in terms of renewable energy capacity. This rapid growth is a reflection of the country's commitment to sustainable development and reducing its carbon footprint.

Psychological Disorders: In India, the number of elderly with psychiatric disorders is 5 times more than adults (Tiwari & Pandey, 2012). According to a recent article, mental disorders are more common in the elderly than in younger populations, except for anxiety disorders (Sinha *et al.*, 2021). The study further reports that urban-dwelling single females with low levels of family income were high-risk factors for depressive and anxiety disorders in the elderly.

Cognitive Decline: One of the key challenges facing older adults in India is the issue of cognitive decline and dementia. Forgetfulness/decline in memory and other cognitive impairments are common health issues for the elderly, and this often leads to significant difficulties with routine activities, decision-making, and independence (Kohli *et al.*, 2020; Mangal *et al.*, 2019; Thakur & Varma, 2023; Zaninotto *et al.*, 2018). This issue is particularly concerning given the lack of resources and trained professionals available to provide adequate support and care for individuals with cognitive decline or dementia. The sources also point to the broader societal impacts of an ageing population, noting that the growing number of older adults with mental health and cognitive issues will place an "enormous psychological burden" on families and communities (Kohli *et al.*, 2020).

Care and Management Issues: It is reported that the elder's poor health condition increases the demand for medical treatment, long-term care, and financial and emotional support; this significantly puts a psychological burden along with financial problems for both the older adults and the family caregivers (Kohli *et al.*, 2020). The fast-changing society is still searching for management strategies for such issues.

Changing Psychosocial Milieu-related Issues: The emergence of nuclear families and the gradual breakdown of the traditional joint family system pose a serious issue for the elderly in India. Not only is it weakening the bonds and intergenerational relationships within the family, but it is also posing a significant challenge in managing emotional imbalances. The traditional joint family system in India is gradually giving way to nuclear families, leading to a breakdown in intergenerational relationships and support systems. Such reckless changes in society lead to a wide range of psycho-social issues for older adults, including social isolation, loneliness, abuse, and/or discrimination (Kohli *et al.*, 2020; Michael *et al.*, 2018; Pathak *et al.*, 2022; Shorey & Chan, 2021; Sarvada Chandra Tiwari, 2013).

The Changes in Social Fabric—Family Breakdown: It is worth mentioning that now-a-days society is becoming individualistic, and nuclear families are emerging at a high speed, and as a result, the joint family system is facing a breakdown. This often leaves the elderly all alone without any support from close family members and sometimes, they may have to move to old age homes. Such incidents may cause a feeling of loneliness, sadness, or a low mood. A study from various old age homes reports that social isolation and loneliness had statistically significant effects on the psychological well-being of elderly individuals (Mishra *et al.*, 2023).

·**Migration:** It could be easily observed that now-a-days children are moving to urban areas or from urban areas to abroad, and the senior members of the family are left behind. The poor living conditions and lack of security and social networks often leave the elderly in a disappointing situation. Additionally, this situation can lead to emotional disturbances. According to a study, the elderly feel that the younger generation's values and respect for them have significantly decreased (Bhat & Dhruvarajan, 2001).

·**Bereavement and Losses:** Limited studies specifically address the effects of losing a close relative on the elderly population in India. It is reported that bereavement is associated with increased psychological distress, including symptoms of grief, depression, anxiety, and loneliness (Bratt *et al.*, 2016; Tseng *et al.*, 2017). According to Bratt *et al.* (2016), the elderly experience pain when they lose a partner or child. Also, at times the elderly struggle to cope with a diminished role in family decision-making or the absence of their traditional caregiving responsibilities and develop feelings of helplessness/hopelessness.

Financial Insecurity: Financial issues pose a significant challenge for the elderly in India. The management of diseases in old age is often expensive, requiring continuous medication and follow-up, leading to out-of-pocket expenditure. And the earnings decrease significantly. The healthcare system is under strain due to the increasing number of elderly people with various health problems. Financial insecurity often worsens the emotional and psychological challenges faced by the elderly. Elderly people remain worried about their ability to afford necessary medical care and necessities (Abdi *et al.*, 2019; Picco *et al.*, 2016). At times, they must rely on their children for support, which often leads to feelings of depression and inadequacy. It happens often, as the elderly hardly wish to depend upon anyone, and such situations often give them unwanted feelings. Limited resources, savings, and lack of financial security often increase their anxiety and make them more vulnerable.

Cultural Stigma, Abuse and Neglect: Sometimes, we take physical vulnerability, mental slowness, and psychomotor deviations for granted. Elderly people or their caregivers could not notice or neglect thinking of such situations as part of ageing. Further, often the elderly face the challenges of physical, emotional, and/or psychological abuse/neglect from their family members and do not report (Evandrou *et al.*, 2017; Sathya *et al.*, 2022). Many a times, the mere thought put them in adverse situations, and without any solid reason, they develop anxiety or depression-like symptoms.

These challenges lead to various emotional and psychological consequences. At times the elderly develop one or other kind of stress. The author witnessed and experienced such cases—

Case 1: The elderly patient presented with Generalized Anxiety Disorder (GAD). Mrs. X, 62/F, illiterate, widowed, and dependent on her son, came with excessive worry, restlessness, and physical symptoms of anxiety. The author received her referral for non-pharmacological management. It was reported by her son and daughter-in-law that for several months, after the sad demise of her husband, she has been unable to control her anxiety, especially when performing any work. She often becomes restless and walks here and there. She was dependent on her son, as there were no other sources of income.

She remains constantly worried. She explained that her physical symptoms included restlessness, fatigue, difficulty in concentrating, and sleep disturbances. She also reported feeling on edge all the time, finding it difficult to relax, and experiencing a worsening of her symptoms. Her daughter-in-law admitted that whenever the son remains at home, her anxiety comes down. But, as and when he goes outside, she becomes more perplexed, anxious, and restless. We interrogated both patients and caregivers separately after obtaining their histories. On a persistent query, it was found that the lady heard someone's story when her daughter-in-law was talking with her friend, in which they were discussing inappropriate family behaviour with a single elderly lady. She was unable to give the details but was afraid that 'kaheen mere sath bhi aisa na ho jae (Lest this happens to me too).' And this continuous thought gradually put her in this condition.

Sometimes feelings of worthlessness also developed in the elderly, and despite the availability of family members, the elderly started feeling insignificant. It often happens after getting a diagnosis of any serious illness—retirement, loss of spouse, decrease in financial gain etc.—that the elderly start thinking that they are becoming a burden to their family. Furthermore, individuals with physical or psychological ailments or disabilities frequently experience psychosocial or emotional disturbances. Such disturbances often lead to suicidal ideation. Untreated psychological issues and a lack of support often contribute to suicidal risk in the elderly (Schmutte & Wilkinson, 2020). Male elderly individuals who experience chronic illness, pain, or disturbances are more likely to commit suicide (De Leo, 2022). Mental health issues, including mood disorders and anxiety, are strongly associated with increased suicide risk in older adults (Kułak-Bejda *et al.*, 2021).

Interestingly, while mental health issues play a crucial role, other factors also contribute to suicide risk in the elderly. These include social isolation, physical illness, functional limitations, and the use of highly lethal (De Leo, 2022; Motillon-Toudic *et al.*, 2022). It can be said that untreated psychological issues and lack of adequate support not only increase the level of psychological and emotional disturbances but also are a risk for suicide among the elderly.

The consequences and repercussions of elders' psychosocial challenges and emotional distress are enormous. We must seek guidance from our enlightening cultural sacred scripture and integrate it with contemporary care system evolution strategies to enhance the quality of life for our seniors. From a modern perspective, one should know the current developments that are needed for the care of the elderly, and from a cultural perspective, age-old care skills may help the elderly lead a joyful and hassle-free life despite any kind of morbidity.

Strategies/ways to Handle Psychosocial and Emotional Distress

Develop Emotion Regulation Skills in both Care Providers and the Elderly: Emotion Regulation (ER) is a developing field that not only helps individuals maintain their health, calmness, and composure but also explain how individuals can express their feelings in a manner that is acceptable to others (Pandey & Misra, 2024). The primary focus of this field is on life stages associated with development, specifically biological maturation. There is limited work in the field for the care of the elderly. To improve the well-being and status of the elderly as well as minimize the struggle, we need to opt for strategies based on various theories and techniques.

With the advancement in age, if an elderly person starts prioritizing well-being and health by setting emotional and social goals for better livelihood, their caregivers also help in this journey. There will hardly be any difficulty in attaining a satisfactory quality of life. This strategy is based on making plans for the future when one is in their later years (Carstensen *et al.*, 2003; Carstensen, 2006). Prioritization of social and emotional goals for a better livelihood, well-being, and health, as well as proper resource utilization, helps in leading a positive and improved quality of life in the later stages. Almost every sensible elderly person frequently becomes more conscious of the fact that the future has limited time. With this realization, they prepare themselves with a selective pursuit for the rest of their lives, be it companionship, social service, or any other work of their interest; like this, they will be better at handling their issues. And, if there are any issues, the assistance of formal or informal caregivers may be helpful.

It is worth mentioning that in comparison to the younger generation, the elderly are more selective in their choice of social companions and derive a greater sense of emotional satisfaction from their social contacts (Carstensen *et al.*, 1999; Fingerman & Charles, 2010). The literature supports this notion, indicating that the elderly exhibit greater selectivity in choosing their social companions. A study by Kunzmann *et al.* (2014) reveals that this selective attitude helps older people better control and manage their emotions as they get older (Fredrickson & Carstensen, 1990; Fung *et al.*, 1999). It also helps them pay attention to and remember positive emotional information for longer periods (Isaacowitz *et al.*, 2006; Mather & Carstensen, 2003; Carstensen *et al.*, 2003).

It is worth mentioning that an elderly person with a healthy mindset can understand and recognise his/her strengths and vulnerabilities. With long life experience, one may develop a more robust cognitive schema and enhance their capacity to manage their feelings more effectively by employing a variety of different methods of control. This experience enables older adults to work proactively to avoid stressful situations and/or enables them to make quick decisions to resolve negative emotions. Both of these benefit elderly people. While this is going on, the limited biological or physiological plasticity that they have poses a threat to their well-being when they are subjected to high or sustained levels of negative arousal (Charles, 2010). With the assistance of both their conscious and unconscious minds, the elderly understand and learn how to manage their feelings by drawing on the extensive knowledge and experiences they have gained throughout their lives.

To support the elderly, adaptive strategies like cognitive reappraisal, self-compassion, and mindfulness are advocated. These strategies not only help in strengthening well-being but also in avoiding psychological and emotional trauma during old age (Alici & Kalanlar, 2024; Birditt *et al.*, 2020; English, 2023; Sardella *et al.*, 2022; Tuicomepee *et al.*, 2018). Research has demonstrated the benefits of such interventions.

Further, for alleviating distress and cultivating positiveness in old age, the following cultural practices may be beneficial. These practices are specific to India.

Prepare the Self for Vanaprastha-detachment: From the early stage of life, i.e. midway through the Grihastha Ashram (householder's life), one should start preparing for the future. It may sound a little impractical, but if we start thinking of our life as parting it in 4 *Ashrams*, the meaning and purpose of life seem to be very clear. Everyone in this universe came with a purpose. The broader aim of life is given in our ancient scripture: *Brahmachary* (studentship and job orientation), *Grihastha* (householder), *Vanaprastha* (completion of householder duties and doing something for the society), and *Sannyas* (liberate self).

Participating in Activities that are Cultural and Religious: This can help an individual feel more connected to their community and provide them with a sense of spiritual comfort. The adoption of such activities and active participation in spiritual practices and rituals can provide emotional solace and reduce feelings of isolation.

Meditative Practices: In the face of adversity, if one starts keeping calm and composed behaviour, the adversity goes easily. This is because nothing is permanent, and everything occurs for a specific reason. The early practices eventually turn into habits, which contribute to the formation of a robust attitude towards the situation.

Reflective practices help prepare oneself to avoid harmful people and situations. Meditative practices, like breathing awareness, visualization, chanting, movement meditation, and/or any other practices, are often beneficial. These practices help you manage a variety of issues and regulate your emotions. It is essential to have the appropriate documentation and practice to make use of such practices.

Strategies for self-composure to cultivate a sense of cohesiveness within oneself as well as societal harmony and integrity. One must obtain the ability to maintain internal composure. Individuals are emotionally tense, and the burden also falls on the elderly. In today's world, we see chaos everywhere; individuals suffer from emotional tension. Understanding oneself and seeking the purpose of life can lead to achieving internal composure. It is not a simple effort; one should know the steps. If we properly know ourselves, it will help liberate us from the constraints of worldly life and enable us to cultivate a deeper comprehension of ourselves and others. The pursuit of meaning and purpose in one's life may be aided by engagement in such an activity. How could we put it into practice? What are the techniques for cultivating personal composure? At what point will it end? In response to these inquiries, the author has devised a model to foster an internal sense of composure among senior citizens. To gain a detailed understanding, one can refer to Dr. Jared Kass's (2017) book.

The emotional and psychological challenges faced by Indian older adults are multifaceted and deeply intertwined with the country's cultural, social, and economic fabric. Addressing these issues requires a holistic approach that involves families, communities, healthcare providers, and policymakers. To recultivate an environment that prioritizes the emotional and psychological well-being of the elderly, there is a need to ensure a dignified and fulfilling life for them by enabling them to age gracefully and with resilience. We also need to promote a culture of respect and support; communities can create inclusive spaces where seniors feel valued and heard. Such initiatives not only enhance the quality of life for older adults but also promote understanding and empathy among younger generations.

References

Abdi, S., Spann, A., Borilovic, J., de Witte, L. & Hawley, M. (2019). "Understanding the Care and Support Needs of Older People: A Scoping Review and Categorisation Using the WHO International Classification of Functioning, Disability and Health Framework (ICF)". *BMC Geriatrics, 19*(1): 195. https://doi.org/10.1186/s12877-019-1189-9

Agrawal, S. (2012). "Effect of Living Arrangement on the Health Status of Elderly in India: Findings from a National Cross-Sectional Survey". *Asian Population Studies*, 8(1): 87-101. https://doi.org/10.1080/17441730.2012.646842

Akbar, S., Tiwari, S.C., Tripathi, R.K., Pandey, N.M. & Kumar, A. (2018). "Prevalence of Psychiatric Illness among Residents of Old Age Homes in Northern India". *Journal of Neurosciences in Rural Practice, 9*(2): 193-96 https://doi.org/10.4103/jnrp.jnrp_340_17

Bhat, A.K. & Dhruvarajan, R. (2001). "Ageing in India: Drifting Intergenerational Relations, Challenges and Options". *Ageing & Society, 21*(5): 621-40.

Birditt, K.S., Polenick, C.A., Luong, G., Charles, S.T. & Fingerman, K.L. (2020). "Daily Interpersonal Tensions and Well-being among Older Adults: The Role of Emotion Regulation Strategies". *Psychology and Ageing, 35*(4): 578-90. https://doi.org/10.1037/pag0000416

Bratt, A.S., Stenström, U. & Rennemark, M. (2016). "Effects on Life Satisfaction of Older Adults After Child and Spouse Bereavement". *Ageing & Mental Health, 21*(6): 602-608.

Carstensen L.L. (2006). "The Influence of a Sense of Time on Human Development". *Science, 312*(5782): 1913-1915. https://doi.org/10.1126/science.1127488

Carstensen, L.L., Fung, H.H. & Charles, S.T. (2003). "Socio-emotional Selectivity Theory and the Regulation of Emotion in the Second Half of Life". *Motivation and Emotion, 27*(2) 103-123. doi:10.1023/A:1024569803230

Carstensen, L.L., Isaacowitz, D.M. & Charles, S.T. (1999). "Taking Time Seriously: A Theory of Socio-emotional Selectivity". *American Psychologist, 54*, 165-181. doi: 10.1037/0003-066x.54.3.165

Charles, S.T. (2010). "Strength and Vulnerability Integration: A Model of Emotional Well-being Across Adulthood". *Psychological Bulletin, 136* (6): 1068-1091. doi:10.1037/a0021232

Chauhan, S., Patel, R. & Kumar, S. (2022). "Prevalence, Factors and Inequalities in Chronic Disease Multimorbidity among Older Adults in India: Analysis of Cross-Sectional Data from the Nationally Representative Longitudinal Ageing Study in India (LASI)". *BMJ Open, 12*(3): e053953. https://doi.org/10.1136/bmjopen-2021-053953

Connell, C.M., Janevic, M.R. & Gallant, M.P. (2001). "The Costs of Caring: Impact of Dementia on Family Caregivers". *Journal of Geriatric Psychiatry and Neurology, 14*(4): 179-187. https://doi.org/10.1177/089198870101400403

Das, S.K., Jeyalakshmi, S., Chakrabarti, S. & Gupta, N. (2011). *Situation Analysis of the Elderly in India*. Central Statistics Office, Ministry of Statistics & Programme Implementation, Government of India (Issue June). http://mospi.nic.in/mospi_new/upload/elderly_in_india.pdf

De Leo, D. (2022). "Late-life Suicide in An Ageing World". *Nature Ageing, 2*(1): 7-12. https://doi.org/10.1038/s43587-021-00160-1

English, T. (2023). "Cognitive Aspects of Managing Stress and Unwanted Emotion Successfully in Old Age". *Innovation in Ageing,* 7 (S_1): 3, https://doi.org/10.1093/geroni/igad104.0109

Evandrou, M., Falkingham, J.C., Qin, M. & Vlachantoni, A. (2017). Elder Abuse as a Risk Factor for Psychological Distress among Older Adults in India/: A Cross-Sectional Study. https://doi.org/10.1136/*bmjopen*-2017-017152

Fingerman, K.L. & Charles, S.T. (2010). "It takes two to tango: why older people have the best relationships". *Current Directions in Psychological Science, 19,* 172-176. doi: 10.1177/0963721410370297

Fredrickson, B.L., Mancuso, R.A., Branigan, C. & Tugade, M.M. (2000). "The Undoing Effect of Positive Emotions". *Motivation and Emotion, 24*, 237-258.

Fung, H.H., Carstensen, L.L. & Lutz, A. (1999). "The Influence of Time on Social Preferences: Implications for Life-Span Development". *Psychology and Ageing, 14*, 595-604.

Giffords, E.D. & Eggleton, E. (2005). "Practical Considerations for Maintaining Independence among Individuals with Functional Impairment". *Journal of Gerontological Social Work*, *46*(1): 3-16. https://doi.org/10.1300/J083v46n01_02

Hilton, L., Hempel, S., Ewing, B.A., Apaydin, E., Xenakis, L., Newberry, S., Colaiaco, B., Maher, A.R., Shanman, R. M., Sorbero, M.E. & Maglione, M. A. (2017). "Mindfulness Meditation for Chronic Pain: Systematic Review and Meta-Analysis". *Annals of Behavioural Medicine, 51*(2): 199-213. https://doi.org/10.1007/s12160-016-9844-2

Isaacowitz, D.M., Wadlinger, H.A., Goren, D. & Wilson, H.R. (2006a). "Is There An Age-Related Positivity Effect in Visual Attention? A Comparison of Two Methodologies". *Emotion, 6*(3): 511-516. doi:10.1037/1528-3542.6.3.511

Kass, J.D. (2017). *A Person-Centred Approach to Psychospiritual Maturation: Mentoring Psychological Resilience and Inclusive Community in Higher Education.* Palgrave Macmillan/Springer Nature. https://doi.org/10.1007/978-3-319-57919-1

Kohli, N., Chawla, S.K., Banerjee, A. & Srinete, T.P. (2020). "Ageing in Developing Societies: Issues and Challenges". *Psychology and Developing Societies, 32*(2): 153-175. https://doi.org/10.1177/0971333620943408

Kułak-Bejda, A., Bejda, G. & Waszkiewicz, N. (2021). "Mental Disorders, Cognitive Impairment and the Risk of Suicide in Older Adults". *Frontiers in Psychiatry, 12*, 1-7. https://doi.org/10.3389/fpsyt.2021.695286

Kuru Alici, N. & Kalanlar, B. (2024). "Challenges and Coping Strategies of Older Adults in the Aftermath of Kahramanmaraş Earthquake in Türkiye: A Qualitative Research". *Journal of Applied Gerontology: The Official Journal of the Southern Gerontological Society, 43*(10): 1580-1589. https://doi.org/10.1177/07334648241241299

Mangal, N.L., Varghese, D.K., Chauhan, M. & Samanta, M. (2019). "Geriatric Health Related Problems in An Urban Area of Southern Rajasthan". *International Journal of Community Medicine and Public Health, 6*(10): 4545-4551.

Mehra, A., Rani, S., Sahoo, S., Parveen, S., Singh, A.P., Chakrabarti, S. & Grover, S. (2020). "A Crisis for Elderly with Mental Disorders: Relapse of Symptoms due to Heightened Anxiety due to COVID-19". *Asian Journal of Psychiatry, 51*, 4-7. https://doi.org/10.1016/j.ajp.2020.102114

Meng, L., Xu, R., Li, J., Hu, J., Xu, H., Wu, D., Hu, X., Zeng, X., Zhang, Q., Li, J. & Liu, D. (2024). "The Silent Epidemic: Exploring the Link Between Loneliness and Chronic Diseases in China's Elderly". *BMC Geriatrics, 24*(1): 1-14. https://doi.org/10.1186/s12877-024-05163-2

Michael, A., Thirumoorthy, A., Girish, N. & Sivakumar, P.T. (2018). "Training Community Health Workers in Geriatric Mental Health: Process of Manual Development and Pilot Testing Findings". *Asian Journal of Psychiatry, 38*, 12-15. https://doi.org/10.1016/j.ajp.2018.10.017

Mishra, B., Pradhan, J. & Dhaka, S. (2023). "Identifying the Impact of Social Isolation and Loneliness on Psychological Well-being among the Elderly in Old-Age Homes of India: The Mediating Role of Gender, Marital Status, and Education". *BMC Geriatrics, 23*(1): 1-13. https://doi.org/10.1186/s12877-023-04384-1

Motillon-Toudic, C., Walter, M., Séguin, M., Carrier, J.D., Berrouiguet, S. & Lemey, C. (2022). "Social Isolation and Suicide Risk: Literature Review and Perspectives". *European Psychiatry, 65*(1): 2022-2320.

Pandey, N.M. & Misra, G. (2024). "Emotional Regulation During Old Age- Challenges and Strategies: An Overview". *Indian Journal of Gerontology, 38*(4): 509-532.

Patel, P., Muhammad, T. & Sahoo, H. (2023). "The Burden of Disease-Specific Multimorbidity among Older Adults in India and Its States: Evidence from LASI". *BMC Geriatrics, 23*(1): 1-14. https://doi.org/10.1186/s12877-023-03728-1

Pathak, G., Kalita, D. & Deka, B. (2022). "Study on Morbidity Pattern among Elderly in Urban Area of Barpeta, Assam, India". *Journal of Family Medicine and Primary Care, 11*(2): 553-558. https://doi.org/10.4103/jfmpc.jfmpc_1294_21

Picco, L., Achilla, E., Abdin, E., Chong, S.A., Vaingankar, J.A., McCrone, P., Chua, H.C., Heng, D., Magadi, H., Ng, L.L., Prince, M. & Subramaniam, M. (2016). "Economic Burden of Multimorbidity among Older Adults: Impact on Healthcare and Societal Costs". *BMC Health Services Research*,16,173. https://doi.org/10.1186/s12913-016-1421-7

Population Reference Beureau. (2019). *The Top 50 Countries with the Largest Percentage of Older Adults*. Population Reference Bureau, Washington, DC. https://www.prb.org/resources/countries-with-the-oldest-populations-in-the-world/

Sardella, A., Lenzo, V., Basile, G., Martino, G. & Quattropani, M.C. (2022). "Emotion Regulation Strategies and Difficulties in Older Adults: A Systematic Review". *Clinical Gerontologist, 46*(3): 280-301. https://doi.org/10.1080/07317115.2022.2128706

Sathya, T., Selvamani, Y. & Nagarajan, R. (2022). "Elder Abuse/Mistreatment and Associated Covariates in India: Results from the Longitudinal Ageing Study in India Wave 1, 2017-2018". *Epidemiology and Health*, *44*, e2022017. https://doi.org/10.4178/epih.e2022017

Schmutte, T. & Wilkinson, S. (2020). "Suicide in Older Adults with and without known Mental Illness: Results from the National Violent Death Reporting System, 2003-2016". *American Journal of Preventive Medicine, 58*(4): 584-590. https://doi.org/10.1016/j.amepre.2019.11.001

Shorey, S. & Chan, V. (2021). "The Experiences and Needs of Asian Older Adults Who Are Socially Isolated and Lonely: A Qualitative Systematic Review". *Archives of Gerontology and Geriatrics*, *92*, 104254. https://doi.org/10.1016/j.archger.2020.104254

Shulman, S.C. (2005). "The Changing Nature of Family Relationships in Middle and Later Life: Parent-Caring and the Mid-Life Developmental

Opportunity". *Smith College Studies in Social Work*, *75*(2): 103-120. https://doi.org/10.1300/J497v75n02_07

Sinha, P., Hussain, T., Boora, N.K., Rao, G.N., Varghese, M., Gururaj, G., Benegal, V. & NMHS India Collaborators Group (2021). "Prevalence of Common Mental Disorders in Older Adults: Results from the National Mental Health Survey of India". *Asian Journal of Psychiatry*, *55*, 102463. https://doi.org/10.1016/j.ajp.2020.102463

Taherkhani, Z., Kaveh, M.H., Mani, A., Ghahremani, L. & Khademi, K. (2023). "The Effect of Positive Thinking on Resilience and Life Satisfaction of Older Adults: A Randomized Controlled Trial". *Scientific Reports*, *13*(1): 3478. https://doi.org/10.1038/s41598-023-30684-y

Thakur, U. & Varma, A.R. (2023). "Psychological Problem Diagnosis and Management in the Geriatric Age Group". *Cureus*, *15*(4): e38203. https://doi.org/10.7759/cureus.38203

Tiwari, S.C., Srivastava, G., Tripathi, R.K., Pandey, N.M. & Agarwal, G.G. (2013). "Prevalence of Psychiatric Morbidity amongst the Community Dwelling Rural Older Adults in Northern India". *Indian Journal of Medical Research, 138,* 504-514. https://doi.org/10.1016/j.ajp.2020.102041

Tiwari, S.C. (2013). "Loneliness: A disease?" *Indian Journal of Psychiatry, 55*(4): 320. https://doi.org/10.4103/0019-5545.120536

Tiwari, S.C. & Pandey, N.M. (2012). "Status and Requirements of Geriatric Mental Health Services in India: An Evidence-Based Commentary". *Indian Journal of Psychiatry, 54*(1): 8-14. https://doi.org/10.4103/0019-5545.94639

Tiwari, S.C. & Pandey, N.M. (2013). "The Indian Concepts of Lifestyle and Mental Health in Old Age". *Indian Journal of Psychiatry*, *55*(Suppl 2): S288-S292. https://doi.org/10.4103/0019-5545.105553

Tseng, F.M., Petrie, D. & Leon-Gonzalez, R. (2017). "The Impact of Spousal Bereavement on Subjective Well-being: Evidence from the Taiwanese Elderly Population". *Economics and Human Biology, 26,* 1-12. https://doi.org/10.1016/j.ehb.2017.01.003

Tuicomepee, A., Suttiwan, P., Watakakosol, R., Ngamake, S.T. and Iamsupasit, S. (2018). "Influence of Emotional Regulation on Successful Ageing among Thai Older Adults". *Journal of Health Research*, 32, (3)198-202. https://doi.org/10.1108/JHR-05-2018-021

Zaninotto, P., Batty, G.D., Allerhand, M. & Deary, I.J. (2018). "Cognitive Function Trajectories and their Determinants in Older People: 8 Years of Follow-up in the English Longitudinal Study of Ageing". *Journal of Epidemiology and Community Health, 72*(8): 685-694. https://doi.org/10.1136/jech-2017-210116

3

Positive Ageing

Building the Eco-system for Fostering Well-being of the Elderly People

Amarnath Rai and *Tanvi Kumari*

Well-being at all levels of living—individuals, families, communities, societies, and nations—must be pursued, collectively promoted, and ensured as an inalienable right of human life. All people, as individuals, should be able to enjoy health and happiness, live a meaningful life in a dignified manner, and be able to experience well-being and flourish in their lives across all the developmental stages. But ageing years present some biological, psychological, and social challenges uncommon for other developmental stages, some of which are unique to this era. Innovations in medical science have led to longevity in life, and as a consequence, 'population ageing' now characterizes nations around the world. The phenomenon of population ageing along with socio-demographic shifts, which have been caused by technological upheavals and cultural transformations, has induced wide and deep unsettling influences on the lives of the elderly. Familial and social life in the 21st century has become dominated more by materialist considerations than by a psycho-social-spiritual perspective of life. All these changes make it im perative for psychologists to deal with the issues and challenges in the lives of elderly people and strategize interventions, both at the level of the elderly individual and at the level of the ecosystem of their lives, so as to facilitate positive ageing.

Population Ageing: Better healthcare facilities and advancements in medical science have enabled people to live longer. Life expectancy in India has increased from 35.21 (1950) to 70.42 (2023) [data source: United Nations World Population Prospects]. This trend around the world has been recorded with people in many developed countries having very high life expectancy: Japan (84.95), Italy (84.20), Australia (83.73), France

(83.95), the U.K. (82.31), Germany (82.18), and the U.S.A. (79.74), to mention just a few.

Increasing life expectancy along with the coming of the ageing years for the children born during the baby boom years (1946–1964) has resulted in population ageing; that is to say, a very good percentage of the population has become aged in most of the developed and developing countries. In India, elderly people constitute 8.6 per cent of the total population (according to the Census, 2011), which is projected to constitute 12.50 per cent (2030) and 20 per cent in 2050 (UNFPA Report, 2017). Many countries have a population of 65+ years old: Japan (29.9%), Italy (24.1%), and Germany (22.4%). [Source: World Economic Forum, http://www.weforum.org/2023/02]. This trend is continuing upward. With decreasing fertility rates, the share of elderly people in the population is likely to increase further during the coming decades.

The well-being of all sections of the population is important, and the community well-being of elderly people is equally valuable. The well-being of elderly people has been defined through the use of many concepts.

Well-being of the Elderly: Positive Ageing and Revisiting other Collateral Concepts: What defines the well-being of the elderly? "Well-being means being well in life. Well-being is not a luxury, but rather a necessity of life, enabling people to function at an optimal level while staying calm, composed, and vigorous" (Rai, 2023). The well-being of elderly people has been defined, applying diverse perspectives, in terms of 'successful ageing', 'active ageing', 'healthy ageing', and 'positive ageing'. All these concepts attempt to define the well-being of the elderly with a consideration of "what makes their life good?" This is a new perspective on ageing that attempts to "shift focus away from the negative aspects of ageing, such as explaining ageing as a time of weakness and decline" (Pluzaric *et al.*, 2023). Of all the constructs listed above, 'successful ageing' was the first to present a new perspective on ageing. The construct of successful ageing was introduced by Havinghurst (1963), followed by Rowe & Kahn (1998).

Successful Ageing: Successful Ageing is a process of deliberate and conscious effort to overcome the challenges presented by the effects of ageing. For medical scientists, successful ageing is defined by the absence of disease and physical and cognitive disability (Rowe and Kahn, 1998), "distinct from usual ageing, which is associated with age-related decline in physical and cognitive function" (Wong, 2018). To the social scientist, successful ageing emphasizes life satisfaction and personal well-being, usually achieved through socialization (Havinghurst, 1963).

Ryff (1989) has listed self-acceptance, positive relationships with others, self-determination, control over the environment, purposefulness in life, and personal development as important components of successful ageing. Moody (2005) has described "life satisfaction, longevity, freedom from disability, mastery and growth, active engagement with life, and independence" as key components. Physical components (freedom from disease and physical functioning), psychological components (well-being and neuro-cognitive abilities), and social components (social acceptance and social contribution) are described as the building blocks of successful ageing (Nath, 2021). The aim of this new perspective is to "focus on the positive aspects of ageing, and to see older adults as an economic and social asset rather than a burden on society" (Pluzaric, 2023). Older people are an asset for the family and society and not a liability (Rai, 2019). Adopting an economic-productivity perspective in the context of a large population becoming redundant, joining the unproductive group, and thus becoming a burden and a strain on the resources of society, it was viewed that instead of retiring early, around the age of 60, they should remain active as long as possible. It was expected that by remaining active through the ageing years, the elderly would do good for themselves, their families, society, and the nation. The World Health Organization (WHO, 2002) defines active ageing as "the process of optimizing opportunities for health, participation, and security in order to enhance quality of life as people age." Active ageing often focuses on labour market participation anchored in an economic framework (Bouding & Mortelmans, 2011). WHO has used to simultaneously talk about active ageing and healthy ageing. The concept of active ageing considers "not only health indicators but also psychological, social, and economic aspects, which are to be looked at through communities' approaches within gender and cultural perspectives" (Paul *et al.*, 2012). Health, participation, and security are the three pillars of active ageing as proposed in the definition, with six groups of determinants: (1) health and social services (promoting health and preventing disease; health services; continuous care; mental healthcare); (2) behavioural (smoking; physical activity; food intake; oral health; alcohol; medication); (3) personal environment (friendly environment; safety houses; falls; absence of pollution); (5) social (social support; violence and abuse; education); (6) economic (wage, social security; work). WHO (2002) further views autonomy, independence, and quality of life as three key aspects of ageing. In an empirical study, Paul *et al.* (2012) concluded that "apart from the social determinants, all the others endured a rearrangement that led to six factors not similar to the original ones. Many of the determinants proved to be entwined, reflecting the transaction between individual and environmental factors in shaping the ageing process."

Recognizing the limitations of the construct of active ageing in defining and conceptualizing the well-being of the elderly, WHO moved forward to the concept of healthy ageing in 2017, defining healthy ageing as a process of maintaining functional ability to enable well-being in older age. The WHO, Member States, and Partners for Sustainable Development Goals created a 'Global Strategy and Action Plan for Ageing and Health for 2016–2020 and declared 2021–2030 as the Decade of Healthy Ageing. Beard *et al.* (2016) defined functional ability as "the ability to enable people to be and to do what they value. It is referred to as the ability to meet their basic needs; to learn, grow, and make decisions; to be mobile; to build and maintain relationships; and to contribute to society." The WHO report describes this functional ability as being formed by interactions between intrinsic capacity and the environmental capacities of a person (Beard *et al.*, 2017). The environmental characteristics are related to home, community, and society as a whole.

A Global Strategy and Action Plan for Ageing and Health for 2016–2020 delineated five objectives: (i) commitment to action on healthy ageing in every country; (ii) creation and development of environments that are friendly to older people; (iii) alignment of all healthcare systems to meet the needs of older people; (iv) creation of reliable and appropriate systems for providing long-term care (home, community, and institutional); and (v) checking, monitoring, and studying the topic of healthy ageing.

The WHO (2017) has set down ten priorities to fulfil the objectives of the Decade of Healthy Ageing (2021–2030):

- Establishing a platform for innovation and change;
- Supporting country planning and action;
- Collecting better global data on healthy ageing;
- Promoting research that addresses the current and future needs of older people;
- Aligning health systems to the needs of older people;
- Laying foundation for a long-term care system in every country;
- Ensuring the human resources necessary for integrated care;
- Undertaking a global campaign to combat ageism;
- Defining the economic case for investment; and
- Enhancing the global network for age-friendly cities and communities.

Perspectives on Ageing: Successful, active, healthy ageing, although not solely but to a large extent—emerged in the context of viewing older people as frail, vulnerable, a burden on society, and a drain on the resources of the family, community, and society. Hence, strategies to intervene are mostly remedial and rehabilitative in nature. But psychology in the 21st century has adopted a new perspective of positivity to view all individuals, groups, communities, and societies as possessing character strength and values, capable of flourishing in their lives, and becoming partners in making nations flourish. The perspective on ageing also becomes one of positive ageing.

Positive Ageing Perspectives on the Well-being of the Elderly: Well-being describes being well in life. The well-being of an individual or a community is assessed in terms of subjective well-being and psychological or objective well-being. "[H]edonic well-being captures individuals' global satisfaction with life alongside their pleasant affect, whereas eudaimonic well-being encompasses their sense of purpose and meaning as well as their resilience and social integration" (Fredrickson, 2013). Thus, well-being is equated with human flourishing, which encompasses both feeling good and doing good (Fredrickson, 2009). Rai (2023) has expanded this phrase to describe well-being, taking cues from Sen's (2009) idea of being good as an equally important component of well-being to say that "well-being is being good, feeling good, and doing good." Happiness and life satisfaction only partially represent well-being as they address only the feeling-good component.

A model of well-being theory proposed by Seligman (2011: 82) describes five components of well-being (PERMA): positive emotions, engagement, relationships, meaning, and accomplishment, which enable people to flourish. Tecmilenio University, the first positive university in this world, added to its positivity teaching project three more components: physical well-being, mindfulness, and character strength (Seligman & Adler, 2019).

Well-being education is a valid possibility. Life, education, and counselling are all processes of learning. Learning is a lifespan process aiming to (i) meet the developmental changes taking place within the individuals, and (ii) to enable the individual to grow up so as to meet the challenges happening in the life-context, the ecosystem. Ageing is an individual, universal, and continuous process faced by all living people (Vaillant, 2003), which affects them biologically, psychologically, and socially. Well-being education, in the form of teaching people about the importance of PERMA + health, mindfulness, and resilience while they are still young (and even when they become old), is a developmental approach with preventive and therapeutic value. The emphasis is on the ways to flourish and increase functioning rather than on dysfunction and psychopathology.

Gergen & Gergen (2006) have described (i) relational resources, (ii) physical well-being, (iii) positive mental states, and (iv) engaging activity as the life diamond of life. All and any one of these four components has a two-way relationship with all the three other components. So, an individual should or can enter into this life-diamond through any one component and can build on other components for positive ageing. One can reconstruct one's life course even during ageing. Gergen & Gergen (2006) have presented this life diamond through a graphic figure (represented here with all due respect to their contribution and innovative presentation):

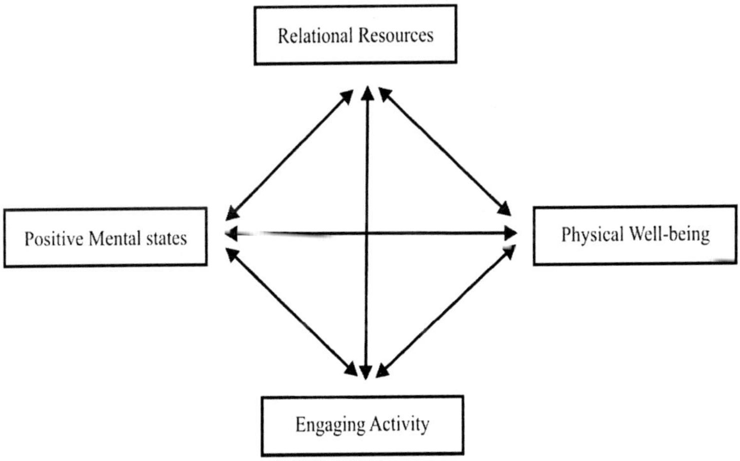

Source: This figure is reproduced from Gergen & Gergen, 2006; Positive Ageing. Chapter 44 in the Book. *Handbook of Girls and Women's Psychological Health*, pp. 416-426.

Positive ageing consists of five factors: health, cognition, activity, affect, and physical fitness (Tur, 2021). People are to some extent responsible for well-being and flourishing in their lives, which, however, always happens in their life context, the echosystem of well-being and functioning. Ryff's model of psychological well-being (2014), which incorporates lifespan developmental theories, clinical theories of personal growth, and mental perspectives, describes six dimensions of positive functioning: self-acceptance, positive relations with others, autonomy, environmental mastery, purpose in life, and personal growth. Research has revealed that these dimensions of well-being and healthy mental functioning are shaped by socio-demographic characteristics (Ryff, 2018; Brin *et al.*, 2019; Ryff *et al.*, 1991) and individual experiences.

Strategies for fostering well-being in the elderly have been described to include (Tur, 2021):

(i) *Promoting Positive Health:* Through changes in diet, cutting down or quitting smoking and alcohol, more exercise, managing stress, increasing relaxation, and maintaining a healthier lifestyle;
(ii) *Promoting Optimal Ageing:* Through skill training programmes, psycho-educational training, learning the A-B-C for resilience, and working with the six keys of positive functioning;
(iii) Positive assessment of the older person's strengths and reserve capacities, including the strengths of key primary environments (family, friends, close associates etc.) and secondary groups (organizations, communities, cultural groups etc.);
(iv) Positive psychological interventions to cope with loneliness and depression (meaningful social connections—face-to-face, telephonic, video calls etc.);
(v) Changing professionals' attitudes towards positive ageing by medical service providers and other caregivers; and
(vi) Enhancing a sense of community and connectedness.

Answer to a question: What makes elderly people see positive ageing in their lives? Is it quite important? McManamon (2017) found (i) participation and activity, (ii) access to services, (iii) meaningful connections, (iv) autonomous living, (v) altruism—giving back to the community, and (vi) a positive attitude to be important components. Killen and Macskill (2020), in a study that attempted analysis, found nine such themes (with sub-themes within categories not listed here) in the diaries of elderly people, listed here in order of frequency: (i) social interaction; (ii) enjoyable activities; (iii) interaction with the physical environment; (iv) capability; (v) being of value; (vi) future orientation; (vii) contemplation; (viii) personal well-being; and (ix) celebrating good outcomes for others. These themes represent hedonic positive affect and life satisfaction.

It has been noted above that, to a large extent, individuals, groups, communities, and societies are responsible for their well-being. Individuals bear the responsibility of enhancing their own well-being. But, in the context in which they act, the positive echo system makes exploration and fostering well-being easier, or, to the contrary, it may restrict and restrain people from flourishing.

Ecosystem of Life: Its Nurturing Power: Social settings, systems, and organizations influence communities, groups, families, and within them, individuals (Kloos *et al.,* 2012). So, any rearrangement in social settings, systems, and organizations is expected to lead towards modification in the cognitions, emotions, and behavioural responses of people. The role of context in our lives was emphasized long ago by Kurt Lewin (1936). Lewin described human behaviour as a product of transactions between the person and the environment [B = f(P×E)]. It has also been described that the environment exists in a fluid state, regularly being modified by forces active outside individuals, families, and communities. Politico-economic and socio-cultural forces can be counted among such factors that influence individuals, their families, and communities. The context of the person includes resources, organization and distribution of resources, socio-cultural processes, personal and shared/collective properties, and the zeitgeist and ortegiest of a certain time line.

There are multiple levels of the systems in our lives' ecosystem. Bronfenbrenner (1977) has described four levels of the ecosystem: (i) microsystem, which includes families, schools, and similar ones existing in the immediate environment of an individual's life; (ii) mesosystem, which is a system of systems, e.g. a neighbourhood; (iii) exosystem, or agencies that influence the microsystem and the mesosystem; and (iv) macrosystem, which includes laws, culture, religious beliefs etc., which govern all three systems at lower levels. These systems are governed by ecological principles like interdependence, cycling of resources, adaptive capacity, and succession (Kelley, 2006).

Characteristic features of the ecosystem at all four levels and the functional nature of the ecosystem present an opportunity for strategic intervention at these levels for achieving the objective of the well-being of the elderly. While there is something to be done by elderly people, there is a lot to be done by the agencies active around them. The governmental, social, and familial systems can facilitate positive ageing by building the ecosystem.

Positive Ageing : Challenges to be Addressed: Ageing involves biological, psychological, and social challenges that must be addressed positively. Ageing is not just the accumulation of years in one's life. Biologically, ageing is also known as a period of senescence: declining cell and tissue health, slowing down of biological and physiological functioning, slower regeneration of cells and accumulation of senescent cells, a lack of sexual desire and arousal, and slower reflexes are some of the noticeable changes. Good nutrition, exercise, and a healthy lifestyle can delay the biological ageing process.

At the psychological level, ageing involves cognitive and affective processes such as loss of memory, slower learning, lack of motivation, difficulty in the application of intelligence etc. However, negative emotions are better regulated. Socio-cultural support and family can help counteract psychological ageing.

The social life of older people witnesses the transformation of rules and relationships. Retirement is not only a loss or decrement in financial gain, it also leads to the loss of social relations and roles.

Many of these changes are products of social stereotypes, which gradually become ingrained in the form of adversity-belief-consequence (A-B-C) learning. Such A-B-C learning demands relearning through challenging the established sequences for resilience and flourishing.

Positive psychology was founded to "understand and build factors that allow individuals, communities, and societies to flourish" (Seligman & Csikszentnihalyi, 2000). Human functioning is influenced by context. "Humans do not exist in isolation. The context in which we live, love, work, and play subtly and profoundly impacts who we are and how we act. We in turn shape our environment" (King and Huppert, 2021). Further, King and Huppert write, "Based on a growing body of research, we can together create a flourishing future for humanity and the planet we share. We have a choice. We can passively watch change happen, or we can individually and collectively take action to create a world that is better for everyone, for all living things." Governments, societies, communities, and families can build a positive ecosystem to facilitate positive ageing.

Building the Ecosystem for Facilitating Positive Ageing: An ecosystem has to be created or built to facilitate the promotion of PERMA, physical health, resilience, and meditation. It should help integrate elderly people into community activities, aiming to gain from the experience and wisdom of the elderly. For changes to happen, some policy modifications, community counselling, and psycho-education are required. "Ageing well requires more than individual attitudes. It requires action from governments, institutions, and organizations" (Grenville-Cleave, 2021). Research studies have found that successfully ageing societies are filled with cohesion within and between generations, facilitate engagement through volunteering, and are healthy, equitable, and secure. To measure these aspects, the Hartford Ageing Index, consisting of the above-mentioned five factors, was created. Norway, Sweden, and the USA are among the top three nations on composite assessment across five dimensions, while Ireland was found on top for cohesion, the USA for productivity, Japan for health, Norway for equity, and Spain for security. Extending recommendations made by Bridget Grenville-Cleare (2021), some key recommendations are presented here. The principles guiding us in framing the strategies include:

- All the intervention strategies must be well soaked in the principles of positive psychology, translating the theories of positive psychology into practices suitably adopted to meet the needs of the elderly; (ii) Interventions should lead the elderly people in the direction of cultivating or harvesting positive experiences, flow, PERMA, healthy, active ageing; (iii) Interventions must not be limited to the aim of helping the elderly feel good; rather, they should be enabled to experience being good and doing good as well; (iv) helping people prepare themselves for old age much before they arrive there; such preparation demands psycho-education; (v) involving all the stakeholders in the programme—the elderly, their families, and all the classes of caregivers; and (vi) the programmes must be sustainable, taxing the resources (financial and human) at the bare minimum level, searching for ways to transform liabilities or unused sources into resources. Guided by these principles, we can intervene at multiple levels: the policies, the governments, the communities and families, and the elderly themselves.
- **Policy Level Interventions:** Policy adopted by the government or an organization guides its aims, objectives, intent, and following UN General Assembly Resolution 4715 to observe 1999 as an International Year of Older Persons, India came up with a national policy on senior citizens in 2011. Some of the benefits that followed this policy are: (a) a higher interest rate on fixed deposits for senior citizens; (b) a higher income tax slab; (c) a pension for older people (although it is a very small amount); and (d) a rebate on rail fares (now withdrawn since COVID years). Under the socio-cultural context of India, old age homes have been considered the last resort. The policy states many other aims that have not been implemented, e.g. employment after su perannuation, prioritizing healthcare needs, and many others. Policies should more comprehensively involve all the stakeholders.

- **Psycho-education:** Positive ageing demands preparing for new priorities in life, remaining active through the advanced age, and continuing to have a positive approach to life (Grenville-Cleave, 2021). She further describes how positive ageing, positive belief, higher expectations, more opportunities, greater well-being, and a positive attitude form a circular for all this to progress smoothly, psycho-education of (a) elderly people; (b) all the classes of caregivers need to be executed, especially about the adversity, belief, and consequence (A-B-C) sequence. Elderly people and people around them—in the family and in society—carry a burden of beliefs and prejudices about life and the prescriptive lifestyle of the elderly, which makes it difficult to add 'life to the years' of the old age people. Psycho-education for positively motivated people can cultivate positivity, find meaning and purpose in life, connect positively, and accomplish something that brings pleasure to their lives. People can plan finances for old age, invest in social relationships while they are young, and learn the beauty and value of spirituality in life. They should accept ageing and adapt to changes that accompany preparing for old age. (i) When people are still young, they should learn 'What and how of the preparation for old age', and (ii) What and how when they really become old. Psycho-education should also focus on health behaviour and bereavement.
- **Intervention by the Government:** Governments can directly and indirectly take steps for positive engagement of the elderly post-retirement, which should bring positive meaning to life. Ageing does not happen in a day, so why complete retirement on a certain date? Retirement should be a process of gradually dissociating from 'lots of work' to 'some work'. Setting up old care homes, cheaper transport, geriatric healthcare facilities, and recreation opportunities are some of the organs of the ecosystem that governments can. As I am writing these pages, I came across some good news published in a *Hindu* newspaper dated September 10, 2023, which reports the setting up of 'Badai Bazar' as a recreational and hanging out facility by Malappuram Municipality in Kerala.
- **Intervention by the Communities:** Positive relationships are the strength of families and communities, and the individuals within Indian society have a great regard for the elderly, who were treated as family heads till death and were always looked upon for guidance from their wisdom. However, materialism has taken over the time-tested wisdom of joint families. Communities and families

have to relearn that older people are assets and not liabilities (Rai, 1984, 1999). Communities should promote ageing role models, celebrate their positive engagement with the community, and foster intergenerational interactions. Rai (1999) advocated that elderly people should be associated with schools in their locality for an hour or two and interact with children for mutual benefits.

- **What Might People do for Themselves?** A part of this intervention involves preparing for old age while we are too young, through middle age. While governments, communities, and families can help elderly people "be good, it's for the elderly to 'feel good' and 'do good'."

References

Bar-Tur, L. (2021). "Fostering Well-being in the Elderly: Translating Theories on Positive Ageing to Practical Approaches". *Frontiers in Medicine*. 8.517226. doi. 10.3389/med.2021.517226

Beard, J.R., Officer, A., de Carvalho, A., Sadna, R., Pot, A.M., Michel, J.P., Lloyd-Sherlock, P., Epping-Jordon, J.E., Peeters, G.M.E.E.G., Mahanani, W.R., Thiyagrajan, J.A., Chatterji, S. (2016). "The World Report on Ageing and Health: A Policy Framework for Healthy Ageing". *Lancet*. *387*(10033): 2145-2151.

Brim, O., Ryff, C., Kessler, R. (2019). *How Healthy Are We?* Chicago : University of Chicago Press. Doi : 10.7208/9780226074764

Bronfenrenner, U. (1977). "Toward an Experimental Ecology of Human Development". *American Psychologist*, *32*, 513-531.

Fredrickson, B.L. (2009). *Positivity : Discover the Upward Spiral that will Change You Life*. New York: Crown.

Fredrickson, B F. (2013). "Positive Emotions Broaden and Build". In: P. Devine & A. Plant (Eds). *Advances in Experimental Social Psychology*. Vol. 47. pp. 1-54. San Diego, C.A. : Academic Press.

Gergen, Mary M., Gergen, Kenneth J. (2005). "Positive Ageing : Reconstructing the Life Course". In Judith Worell & Carol D. Goodheart (Eds) *Handbook of Girls and Women's Psychological Health*. 416-426. http://works.swathmore.edu/fc-psychology/595

Grenwille-cleave, Bridget (2021). "Ageing" in : Grenville-cleave, B., Dora, G., Huppert, F., King, V., Roffey, D., Rofey, S. and Devries, M. (Eds) *Creating the World we want to Live in : How Positive Psychology can Build a Brighter Future*. 74-87. New York: Routledge.

Havinghurst, R.J. (1963). "Successful Ageing". In : Williams, R.H., Tibbits, C., Donahue, W., (eds.) *Process of Ageing*. New York: Atherton Press.

Killen, A. & Macskill, A. (2020). "Positive Ageing: to What Extent can Current Models of Well-being Categorise the Life Events Perceived as Positive by Older Adults". *International Journal of Applied Positive Psychology*. 5. 99-119. http://doi.org.10.1007/541042-020-00028-6

Kelley, J.G. (2006). *Becoming Ecological: An Expedition into Community Psychology*. New York: Oxford University Press.

King, V. & Hup pert, F. (2021). "Foundations for a Brighter Future". In: Grenville-cleave, B., Dora, G., Huppert, F., King, V., Roffey, D., Rofey, S. and Devries, M. (eds.) *Creating the World We Want to Live in: How Positive Psychology can Build a Brighter Future*. 74-87. New York: Routledge

Kloos, B., Hill, J., Thomas, E., Wandersman, A., Elias, M.I. & Datlon, J.H. (2012). *Community Psychology: Linking Individuals and Communities*. Delhi : Cenage Learning.

Lewin, K. (1935). *A Dynamic Theory of Personality*. New York : McGraw Hill.

Mc Manamom, O. (2017). *What is Positive Ageing? An Exploration of the Views of the Participants of the Westgate Foundation*. [online], Community-Academic Research Links/University College Cork, Ireland. http://www.ucc.ie/en/scishop/completed. accessed on 17-03-2023.

Nath, Pooja Sharma (2021). *Successful Ageing*. Block V. PDD/IGNOU/P.O. 2k/November 2021. Egyankosh.ac.in. accessed on 16.08.2023. pp. 259-274.

Paul, C. & Teixeria, L. (2014). "Active Ageing: An Emirical Approach to the WHO Model". *Current Gerontology and Geriatric Research*, October 2012. http://www.researchgate.net/publication/233799173.

Pluzaric, J., Ivana Barac, Vesna Ila Kovac, Robert Lovric, Nikolina Farcic, Zelfko Mudri, Maria Barisic and Ivana Pavlic (2023). "Connectedness and Successful Ageing of Older Adults in Croatia". *Sustainability*, *15*: 10843. http://doi.org/10.3390/su151410843.

Rai, A.N. (1984). *Older People: An Asset or a Liability*. Paper Presented at the National Workshop on Welfare and Productive Utilization of the Elder component of Human Population. November 19-21 at Rewa (M.P.).

______ (2019). "Psychosocial Well-being of the Elderly: Supporting Family Caregiving Through Partnership Between Older People and Community Service Arrangements". *Indian Journal of Community Psychology*. 15.1.95-101.

______ (2023). "Perspectives on Fostering Community Well-being : The Positive Community Counselling Approach". A chapter submitted for publishing. In: Shukla, A. & Dubey, A. (Eds). *Mental Health : Psycho-social Perspective*. Vol. Ten. [Not Yet Published]

Rowe, J.W. & Kahn, R.L. (1998). *Successful Ageing*. New York: Pantheon Books.

Ryff, C.D. (1989). "Beyond Ponce de Leon and Life Satisfaction: New Direction in Quest of Successful Ageing". *International Journal of Behavioural Development*. *12*(1) 35-55. http://doi.org/10.1177/016502548901200102

______ (2018). *Well-being with Soul: Science in Pursuit of Human*.

______ (2014). "Psychological Well-being Revisited : Advances Potential. Perspectives in Psychological Science". *13*(242-238). Doi: 10.1177/

174569167699836 in the Science and Practice of Eudaimonia. *Psychother Psychosomat. 83*: 10-28. Doi : 10.1159/000353263

Ryff, C.D. Essex, M. (1991). "Psychological Well-being in Adulthood Old Age : Descriptive Markers, Explanatory Processes". In: Schaie, W., Lowton, M.P. (eds.) *Annual Review of Gerontology and Geriatrics*. pp. 144-171. New York: Spring.

Seligman, M.E.P. (2011). *Flourish: A New Understanding of Happiness and Well-being and How to Achieve Them*. London : Nicholas Brealy Publishing.

Seligman, M.E.P. & Csikzentmihalyi, M. (2000). "Positive Psychology: An Introduction". *American Psychologist* (Special Issue) *55*(1). 5-14. http://doi.org./10.1037/0003066×.55.1.5

Seligman, M. & Adler, A. (2019). "Positive Education. In: Global Happiness and Well-being Policy Report". *Global Council for Happiness and Well-being*. pp. 68-98. http://www.happinesscouncil.org

Sen, Amartya (2009). *The Idea of Justice*. Penguin Edition (2010). London : Penguin Books.

Vaillant, G.E. (2003). *Ageing Well*. New York: Little Brown.

Wong, R.Y.M. (2018). "Older People Presenting to Acute Care Hospitals". In: Michel, J.P., Beattie, B.L., Martin, F.C., Walson, J.D. (eds.) *Oxford textbook of Geriatric Medicine*. pp 247-254. U.K. Oxford : Oxford University Press.

WHO (2002). *Active Ageing: A Policy Framework*. Geneva, Switzerland.

______ (2017). *Global Strategy and Action Plan on Ageing and Health*.

______ (2017). *Decade of Healthy Ageing 2021-2030* [Google Scholar].

4

On Caregiver's Healing

A Life Story Study of Healing from Disability

Mridusmita Bhagawati and *Kumar Ravi Priya*

> *"Disability is not what we see or understand. Everyone has their own disability; what distinguishes mine from the rest is the outward appearance of depending on the wheelchair for mobility."*

This is the voice of Ajeet Ji, a person with disability (PwD), currently employed as the Chief Operations Officer of Chhanv Foundation, a Non-governmental Organization (NGO) working for the rehabilitation of acid attack survivors. I begin the chapter with this anecdote because it talks about the politics of language—the labels we give to define people without knowing the genesis of their experiences. However, such labels often fall short of comprehending the nature, diversity and enormity of the experiences of people. It should not come as a surprise then that categorizing people in terms of these labels such as disability also leads to misunderstanding and a limited knowledge which culminates in the form of stigma and discrimination in society. In the words of Susan Wendell (1989),

> "Not only do physically disabled people have experiences which are not available to the able-bodied, they are in a better position to transcend cultural mythologies about the body, because they cannot do things the able-bodied feel they must do in order to be happy, 'normal', and sane. ... If disabled people were truly heard, an explosion of knowledge of the human body and psyche would take place." (p. 119)

Studying the life story of a quadriplegic caregiver became such an opportunity for us to learn about the nuances of experiences attributed with disability. The aim of this chapter is two-fold. First, in illustrating the transformative process of a PwD—from experiencing a profound sense of loss—caused by a paralysis of all four limbs—in a terrible accident at the age of 22 to hope and resilience—attained through optimism, self-acceptance and a determination to transcend the limitations imposed by the impairment, this chapter will bring to the fore the *voice* of a quadriplegic person.

Additionally, by centering the voice of a PwD who, during his recovery, is also acting as a caregiver for other vulnerable and marginalised communities, the chapter will take a deep dive into the complex relationship of care, and the accompanying burden that falls on both caregivers as well as care-receivers. Simultaneously, we will also attempt to draw a parallel between a privileged and a marginalised disabled person and the role this distinction plays in the identification of one with the other and the salient features differentiating the experiences of suffering and healing within them.

As a qualitative study in new paradigm research involves a systematic co-construction of participant's experiences or worldviews, we begin with experiential foundations and epistemological position adopted in this study.

Positioning the Self: Experiential Stance

This chapter emerged out of the first author's (MB) ongoing doctoral work on the mental health of acid attack survivors. She came across Ajeet *Ji* [a suffix placed across a person's name as a mark of respect] through Chhanv Foundation, an organization working for the rehabilitation of acid attack survivors wherein he is the Chief Operations Officer. Of the two short conversations she had with him over call prior to meeting in person, none gave her the slightest idea that he could be a PwD. Naturally, not only was she surprised to see him but this curiosity to the oddity of the situation also pushed her into a dilemma—of addressing the elephant in the room—his disability—in her interview with him for his role as a stakeholder in the organization. She feared asking because she didn't know how he would react to this "possibly personal interference" but simultaneously, she was also contemplating if her act of silence might be interpreted as a lack of empathy. Eventually, her curiosity led her to the survivors who gave her bits of information about him. She was told that he met with an accident which led to his present condition. She was also told about a school he had established for underprivileged children in Barabanki (a city in Uttar Pradesh, India). Eventually, she sought an appointment to interact with him.

A PwD running a school for underprivileged children singularly piqued her curiosity and she began by asking about his 'school'. He corrected her by saying that it was a *centre* working as a digital library for the village children preparing for Joint Entrance Examinations. She observed that his wheelchair dependence for mobility did not diminish his confidence and the ease with which he carried the conversation made her forget, albeit for a minute, that he could be bodily impaired. In fact, it was only the occasional calls on his phone during the interview that made her aware of the difference as he needed another helping hand to answer the call.

The conversation with him lasted three hours that day. Listening to his life story, there were moments when she was spellbound to see his strength and resilience. At other times, she was brought to tears to hear the suffering in his voice which echoed as he talked about his love for sprints and sports in general. As a fellow sports enthusiast, she could empathically connect to the lifestyle associated with being a sports person and the discipline it brings into one's life. For a sprinter to become a quadriplegic at the age of 22, it was beyond her capacity to act composed and she had to excuse myself to take a break. In fact, such was the impact of his life story on me that she could not *move on* to the next interview for a couple of days. Working as a service provider, his personal story is often shielded by his organizational position as he stays in the background, giving the acid attack survivors the platform to tell their stories. He was not accustomed to talking about himself with other researchers, hence, he was deeply grateful that before interviewing him as a service provider, she made the effort to get to know him as a person:

> "You are probably one of the only two or three people to have asked my story", he said. My empathic connection led me to first, identify and treat him as a 'person' and then as a 'service provider'.

While listening to this impromptu conversation again, we noticed that this was a unique story about a sports person and a serious dreamer with an aim to join the Indian Army, who after becoming a quadriplegic, is able to find meaning again in life through a renewed sense of hope and constant support of the community. His life experiences felt like a story yet to be but ought to be heard. While the initial conversation was a story he told, and I heard with minimum interference, the detailing of it became a starting point for us as we conceptualised an idea to do a life story analysis and see if it heads in any direction. Thus, this led to interviews conducted to gain a detailed insight into his life. In his erstwhile work, Plummer (1995) has proposed that life stories can be through chance encounters wherein a participant of interest emerges from a wider study.

Theoretical and Paradigmatic Stance

Acknowledging the ever-changing and dynamic realities of people, this study adopted the epistemological position of social constructionism which states reality to be constructed through meaningful human interactions (Guba & Lincoln, 1994), providing space for the experiences and worldviews of the participants to be located in their socio-historical and cultural contexts (Bhattacharya & Priya, 2022; Priya, 2015). Since the focus of the exploration is to understand the experiences of suffering and healing of the participant as well as his role as a caregiver for other PwDs, adopting social constructionism facilitates the participant's voice to be foregrounded and co-constructed with the researcher's theoretical perspectives applied to the research process shaping the outcome of the study. Moreover, with disability research frequently privileging the voices of able-bodied outsiders, the life story narratives in this study serve as an testament for collaboration, thereby enhancing the voice of insiders (in this case, the PwDs). Ajeet *Ji*'s motivation for engaging in the study stemmed from his desire to shed light on the concept of 'disability' and demonstrate that the life of a 'disabled' individual can be just as ordinary as that of anyone else if provided with equal opportunities for a normal existence.

However, before gaining dee per insights into his life events and narratives, it is essential to explore a few conceptual windows which will help provide a structured understanding of his retrospective experiences of suffering and healing, embarked by his disability.

Disability: A Cultural Construction of Impairment and Associated Stigma

Disability is the experience of a person with physical or mental impairment shaped by the cultural discourses that implicitly assigns what is "normal" for such a person (Sharma, 2022; Sharma & Priya, 2020). Historically, people with disabilities have been subjected to stigma and exclusion practices (Goffman, 1963). Archival texts in India, dating back to Fourth century AD have illustrated the discriminatory treatment given to people with physical or mental impairments as they were denied the right to inheritance (Ghai, 2015). This was mainly due to the idea of impairment as one's incapability to perform basic rituals. This idea of *ableism* which diminishes disabled individuals' identity to that of deficient, unproductive and *dependent* have been sustained by both the medical model of health and the cultural mores of 'normality' (Sharma & Priya, 2020).

In spite the paradigm shift in the 1960s-1970s towards understanding disability within socio-historical contexts, disability research often remains anchored in medicalization, categorizing individuals in binaries, that is, their "ability" or "disability". This shift prompted a redefinition of disability, from a purely biomedical perspective of "deficiency" or "loss" to an interplay between health factors (such as diseases, injuries, trauma etc.) and contextual factors (such as experiences of ableism, stigma and discrimination, and social issues such as poverty, inadequate living conditions etc.) (World Health Organization, 2001). However, in practice, the perception of PwDs has not changed significantly as they continue to be viewed in light of their functional limitations, with their personal and subjective experiences of disability being overlooked. Consequently, this leads to their being labelled in a reductive manner as "less able", "incompetent" and "deviant" person (Wolbring, 2008).

The issue of representing the disability experience in literature has been widely discussed, yet there remains a lack of diverse cultural portrayals, failing to capture the varied experiences within the PwD community. Systemic inequalities in society often leads to differing disability experiences, as illustrated in earlier works. Prior research has examined the relationship between poverty and disability, with people with disabilities making up 15–20 per cent of the impoverished in developing nations (Srivastava & Kumar, 2015). Additionally, experiences of poorer health, lower educational attainment, limited employment opportunities, and are subjugation to frequent violence are also seen among PwDs. Oftentimes, they also lack awareness of their rights or knowledge of accessing services which makes them all the more vulnerable (Meekosha & Soldatic, 2011).

In India, the deep-rooted cultural stigmas and lack of awareness relative to the rights of PwDs and lack of governmental aid and support which contributes to their ostracization and discrimination in society renders as a subject of inquiry from an intersectional lens. In case of women with disabilities, there is an added layer of stigma and discrimination as they are more likely to endure physical and mental abuse and are denied control over their bodies, finances, employment as well as community participation (Cattalini, as cited in Dawn, 2013). Thus, women are generally "doubly marginalized", as disabled. The United Nations Development Programme states the global literacy rate of women with disability to be 1 per cent which is 3 per cent in case of adults with disability. Thus, it can be agreed that while disability is universal, there exists marked differences in its experiences and interpretations across cultures. The prevailing social, cultural and economic conditions in the lives of people with disability determine how they are to be treated, what roles are appropriate and inappropriate for such individuals, and what rights and responsibilities they are given or denied (Groce, 1999). Disability then becomes a socio-cultural issue, underscoring it as not just a matter of physical or medical condition but which is significantly shaped by the existing social and cultural factors (Buckingham, 2011).

The doctrine of neoliberalism with its treatment of poverty, structural marginality and disability as individual-level issues pose further challenges to PwDs as they require collective support to overcome the systemic barriers in society. Further, the neoliberal economic policies which promote privatisation of public resources and functions, deregulation of markets, and liberalisation of trade in addition to prioritizing workforce participation and employment needs disproportionately affect PwDs who face the brunt in the job market, including but not limited to discrimination, lack of accommodations and inaccessible workplaces (Mladenov, 2015). In such a scenario, despite efforts of the Indian government at integrating PwDs in society through the Right of Persons with Disabilities Act which aims to ensure equality, empowerment and inclusion of PwDs, there exists many loopholes such as a lack of infrastructure and accessibility, inadequate awareness and sensitization etc. preventing its smooth and effective implementation (Pandey, 2021).

Caregiving and Care-receiving: Flip Sides of the Same Coin?

> *Care often emerges from needs, while needs are not always met with care.*—Akemi Nishida (2022, p. 6).

As the disability experience varies among people, so does their accessibility to access care. The 2023 global survey on persons with disabilities and disasters report PwDs to be comprising 16 per cent of the world's population, with over 80 per cent of them living in the non-Western world (UNDRR, 2023). This high prevalence of PwDs in the low and middle-income countries is further exacerbated by their underrepresentation in decision-making, the stakes of which usually lie at the hands of the developed countries (Thrush & Hyder, 2014). Thus, their unmet needs and inability to access professional care are usually complemented by their family members who, although informal, act as their primary caregivers.

Simply stated, caregiving refers to the act of assisting individuals who are not fully independent to perform their activities of day-to-day life. Caregivers may comprise of individuals, immediate family or otherwise, depending on the type of service provided (paid or unpaid). However, as ubiquitous as the term is, caregiving has many dialects. The Western notions of inculcating individual rights and responsibilities that facilitate the way caregiving is provided in individualistic cultures contrasts with its proactive nature in socio-cultural societies where it is guided by the situational cues promoting relatedness (Giesbrecht, 2008).

In the Indian society where family acts as a crucial support system for ill or injured individuals, the family caregivers play a vital role in their recovery. With 20 per cent of the population with disability comprising of locomotor issues and with more than 70 per cent of them residing in rural areas, caregiving services are predominantly provided by informal caregivers, primarily females (Smith *et al.*, 2016) who mostly lack appropriate knowledge about intervention.

In case of Spinal Cord Injury (SCI), which requires caregiving for an extended period of time, the lives of the family members in addition to the person with SCI are inadvertently changed. The unique challenges imposed by SCI due to a lower level of functional independence such as bladder, bowel problems etc., contribute to increased caregiving burden and render them unable to make choices regarding their own life. Since majority of caregiving processes in India occurs informally through family members, spouses, siblings etc., the numbers of hours spent in caring along with the level of impairment in activities of daily living (ADL) of the care recipient determines the quality of life of caregivers (LaVela *et al.*, 2015). This naturally creates a burden of care which is mutually shared by both the care-receiver and the caregiver. In cases where care needs emerge after a considerable lifespan of the individuals, the burden is felt by the care-receiver as well who feels reluctant to ask for repeated assistance—out of a fear of overburdening their family members as well as the shame borne out of dependency on others (Bredewold *et al.*, 2020).

Cross-cultural Variations in Disability: Underscoring Aspects of Suffering and Healing

From the above, it becomes clear that disability has different meanings in different contexts and to this end, the medicalised understanding of disability as "limited functionality" is barren in its comprehension of the entire experience. Trauma resulting from accidents or other adverse events can manifest in various ways beyond PTSD (Khanna & Priya, 2023). While PTSD involves symptoms stemming from unresolved cognitive and emotional associations with a traumatic event, other forms of distress or suffering may arise from exposure to injury or loss in adverse environments or socio-political contexts (Bracken *et al.*, 1995). These forms of distress may not necessarily involve traumatic memory as seen in PTSD but can encompass a wider range of psychological and social consequences, such as discrimination, exclusion or social isolation. Moreover, ongoing stressors, lack of social support, or systemic injustices can exacerbate the impact of the initial trauma, leading to further distress or social suffering (Priya, 2015, 2018). Recognizing the multifaceted nature of trauma is crucial for providing comprehensive support and interventions to affected individuals and communities, addressing both immediate psychological effects and broader contextual factors contributing to distress and suffering after traumatic experiences.

In his book, "The Nature of Suffering and the Goals of Medicine", Cassell (2004) defines suffering to be a state of intense distress associated with events threatening the intactness of person. According to Cassell, "All the aspects of personhood—the lived past, the family's lived past, culture and society, roles, the instrumental dimension, associations and relationships, the body, the unconscious mind, the political being, the secret life, the perceived future, and the transcendent-being dimension are susceptible to damage and loss" (p. 42). Thus, while pain and other physical symptoms may be a cause of one's suffering, a person may suffer from threats that are social or personal in nature. According to Kleinman *et al.* (1997), social suffering refers to the destabilizing of established categories of existence through political, economic and institutional power and consequently, the responses elicited by such systems of power, leading to social problems.

Healing from suffering then is also a socio-cultural process involving meaning-making as the sufferer assigns meaning to their experiences. This process of meaning-making, which may be sought within past behaviours and beliefs, often reduces the suffering associated with it (Cassell, 2004).

Healing, thus, refers to the process of reformulation of personhood to gain a sense of coherence or meaning to one's experiences of illness or disability. Such a coherence is brought about by "humanizing relational spaces" as well as "culturally valued beliefs" (Khanna & Priya, 2023, p. 5).

The study's objectives, aligned with the conceptual framework of suffering and healing in disability and caregiving, are focused on exploring various dimensions of the lived experiences of PwDs. The specific objectives are:

1. To understand the distress associated with becoming a PwD.
2. To understand the processes of healing facilitated by one's relational context.
3. To understand the meanings associated with caregiving influenced by one's own experiences of care.

We added a life-story approach as a qualitative methodology to address these objectives. We describe that below.

Methodology

Life story research explores the subjective meanings of lives as narrated by the participants (Plummer, 1995). In his erstwhile work, Plummer has posited the selection of life stories through chance encounters wherein a participant of interest emerges from a wider study. Since the underlying goal of our research is to explore and understand the subjective meanings of the participant's disability experience and his subsequent role as a caregiver in his own healing as well as others', we utilized a *topical* life story approach. Topical life story allows for a focus on a segment or certain aspects of one's life rather than their whole life (Plummer, 1995).

Data Collection

Since this study is a part of a larger study on acid attack survivors, the first author (MB) had spent considerable time in the field, observing the interactive lives of the people working at the café-*cum*-rehabilitation centre. An initial conversation with the participant took the form of a life story as he narrated his experiences of impairment. Based on this initial conversation, subsequent in-depth, open-ended interviews were conducted to capture a more comprehensive narrative of his life story. An understanding of his pre-disability life was initiated to augment his experiences of suffering and healing after impairment. A total of nine interviews were conducted with the interviewee. Finally, the participant was also requested narrativize his life story in the form of a timeline highlighting the significant times in his life in a chronological manner. Timeline as a tool in life story research offers the interviewee with an opportunity to become a co-constructor in the interview process and the timeline serves as a "collective memory" for both the researcher as well as the participant (Adriansen, 2012). Thus, a chronology of the significant events in his life was also established which guided the analysis process.

Data Analysis

The interviews were transcribed verbatim and was analysed in a two-phased approach, using life story approach through a narrative thematic analysis as well as Constructivist Grounded theory. Combining life story analysis and constructivist grounded theory (CGT) to analyze an individual's life story is a nuanced approach that blends narrative richness with a systematic method of data interpretation. The CGT process involved initial, focused and axial coding utilising constant comparison. With its focus on the construction of reality as the meanings ascribed to the experiences of people, CGT creates space for the voices of the participants to share their lived experiences (Charmaz, 2014). While Objective 1 and Objective 3 entailed analysis of life story in a temporal manner, the same associated with Objective 2 was temporal as well as episodic in nature. Since healing is an ongoing process, giving it a temporal stance in the form of a life story was not possible as the significant events influencing the participant's healing process were spread over different episodes in his life span. For instance, in the category of "mental strength and vision through support", the different initial codes entitled, "strong sense of trust and autonomy", "fighting spirit", "experiencing and expressing gratitude", and "support of community and his younger sister", refer to different episodes in his life pre- and post-injury which enhanced his process of recovery, thereby enriching his healing experience. For example, while a strong sense of trust and autonomy was instilled within him during his childhood by his parents, the fighting spirit was brought about by his enthusiasm for sprinting. Similarly, the support of his friends, family and his younger sister in the post-impairment life led him to gather strength from them while he attempted to make sense of the changes brought about by the injury, rendering him grateful for the presence of such strong support system. Thus, while the initial codes were associated with different phases of his life, it was their cumulation that lead to the category of "mental strength and vision through support". The categories of suffering and healing corresponding to the objectives are presented below.

Findings: Ajeet Ji's Life Story of Suffering and Healing

Challenges Immediately Following the Accident

Ajeet *Ji* vividly described the difficulties after the accident ultimately resulting in his physical impairment. The impact location being the front passenger door led to injuries only to the person seated on the front passenger seat. The other occupants escaped major harm, including the daughter of his neighbours who was positioned in front him. The apparent sight of blood on his forehead assumed precedence, overshadowing the more significant issue of his spinal cord. This resulted in *confusion and shock* for all due to the abruptness of the injury and their failure to comprehend his inability to move as a potential symptom of spinal cord paralysis.

Suddenly my fingers weren't moving. . . I wasn't aware of [spinal injury] complications.... The biggest concern was, "what just happened" (*kya ho gaya*)?

Also, the abrupt trauma to his body rendered his vision blurry. And this *lack of knowledge* about the extent of his injury, coupled with an apparent attempt to assist, resulted in *manhandling* that aggravated and complicated the injury. He told,

We were told during rehab that whenever someone has a spine injury, the person should not be meddled with, and emergency medical services should be called instantly as the shifting is a sophisticated process which is done using a stretcher.... In our case, nobody knew what to do with spine injury, that too the most complex one that is cervical injury. Since the cervical spine is mobile, it must be handled very delicately. I was also having a lot of blood loss; hence everyone's focus was on that. I do believe that my injury could have been minimized had we been mindful.

Absence or Lack of Immediate Help

As the accident occurred on the interstate highway, there was no immediate access to first aid, and the closest primary health centre was some 20 kilometres away. He was also unable to obtain assistance from bystanders as they refused to stop. As someone who is sensitive to the needs of others, he was incredibly disheartened when no one offered to drive him to the hospital.

Initially, no passerby was stopping... I needed two hours to be rescued, nobody was even stopping to think how I will manage. The way I had stopped the auto by standing in the middle of the road [to help a stranger needing assistance], the same way my sister stood in the middle of the highway to stop passing vehicles... and then one vehicle stopped.

Once a passer-by offered to help, they had to make a crucial decision regarding their destination. They had to choose between the primary health centre, which was situated 20 kms away, or Indore, where superior assistance could be obtained but at a considerable distance of 80 kms. Due to the blood loss from his head, they decided to take a shorter route. However, it wasn't until they got there that they realized the place lacked amenities and had few resources, which ultimately made his condition worse.

The quality of first aid provided was substandard. During the process of suturing the wound on the scalp, they [healthcare personnels] failed to properly remove the surrounding hairs.... Initially, they had refused to even stitch citing a dearth of appropriate equipment.

Additionally, upon reaching the centre and spotting an ambulance, they had parted ways with the person who had given them the lift to the centre. It was only when they saw the state of the ambulance did they realise the gravity of their mistake. Similar to the health centre, the ambulance was supported with basic life support which in the case of spinal injury is not sufficient. Without cervical support, his condition further worsened from during the ambulance's 100 kms journey.

This highlights the inadequacy of healthcare services which led to a worsening of his impairment.

Creation of an Experiential Vacuum

The accident left him with a paralysis of his limbs, rending him bed-ridden. A sudden vacuum was created by the irreversible changes brought to the body which gave a futility to the efforts and dreams of the past. Initially, there was a denial of this felt vacuum by false hopes and expectations of full recovery, which soon transformed into questions of self-blame as he dwelled upon the question of "why me". He narrated about this phase,

This feeling hits when you feel like you have no solution, when you have tried to stay positive but there is no way out... and at a certain point, you are shocked about what happened. In those moments, I have'd feelings of "why me".

Disorientation Leading to Suicidal Notions

As an adult seriously working on a well-planned career in the Indian Army, the impairment not only left him bed-ridden but also shattered his dreams of building the envisaged career as he became ineligible for the job. Additionally, he was left to spend the day with nothing to look forward to and felt overwhelmed by the negative thoughts: When you are bed-ridden the entire day, you are bound to fall asleep. . . and if you sleep during the day, you won't be able to sleep on time at night. . . and that's the most dangerous time. . . Your mind will drift towards the negative thoughts . . . you are crying as trying not to let your family know. . . . I used to get suicidal thoughts sometimes. . . but you know. . . these are progressive thoughts—one moment you want to die, another moment you are sure that now you really want to die, do you get me?. . . I used to think about it but not how to do it.

The impairment not only brought about a loss of routine but also a loss a purpose and hope.

Loss of Hope

In this context, loss of hope refers to the demoralisation caused by his inability to fulfil self-expectations as well as the expectations of others and the lifestyle associated with living with an impaired body. This loss of hope ultimately made him feel unworthy and useless in his own eyes.

Frustration Experienced from an Inability to Pursue One's Dreams

His struggle with impairment was further coupled by his inability to fulfil his dreams, leading to feelings of worthlessness. Having qualified for the Services Selection Board (SSB) interview, his interview was only 2 months away when the abrupt accident left him ineligible for the job. The sorrow of a stalled dream was still alive in his eyes as with time, he could not help but wonder what his life would have been in the normal injury-free life: ".. by this time, I would have been promoted twice and be holding the rank of a Major (in Army)."

Inability to Fulfil Expectations as the Only Son

As the only son to ageing parents, he was expected to take care of their health and well-being in their twilight years. However, his impairment had rendered him so incompetent that instead of him looking after his parents, his parents were looking after him. He stressed on the distress brought about by his inability to fulfil the roles and expectations as the only son in family.

How society expects from an only son or [*Ek lauta beta!*]. . . [There is an] unsaid code about a man that at a certain age, he will be established and running the family… also, when you are of that age, not only are you earning but also taking decisions.

According to him, not only was he unestablished, but he required assistance to such a great extent that it made him *unable to even take decisions for himself* and by himself.

But because of my state, I was not in a condition to take decisions . . . . Suppose, if I say that let's go somewhere. But how? I am a dependent person. Whom will I ask for assistance and how will I arrange everything?

This loss thus made him feel like a burden, as his entire existence from body to independence, was a thing of the past now.

Inability to get better

His inability to get better was further compounded by *false hopes* created within him through repeated assurances from the doctors that recovery was imminent.

I was never told by the doctor that [my] condition was irreversible; I was always informed that there is a possibility of recovery. My spinal cord had swelled, not dissected. Therefore, there was a possibility of recovery…. Self-healing occurs in the body, but it requires a considerable amount of time and is not guaranteed. In my case, however, since the spinal cord was damaged due to swelling, there was hope that once the swelling subsides, my body will resume functioning normally.... Due to frustration, I decided to leave home for treatment elsewhere.

His condition as a paraplegic did not improve.

Lifestyle Associated with a Physically fit Body

As a child, fitness was a huge part of his life as he underwent multiple training camps as part of the National Cadet Corps (NCC) and as an athlete, exercising autonomy in sports through sprinting was a part of his lifestyle. In fact, sports also acted as a stress buster in hardships. The loss of control over his limbs overwhelmed him along with the excessive dependency on medicines.

Before shifting to the village, my need and dependency on medicines was to such a great extent that my life seemed meaningless (*aisi zindagi toh nahi jeena*). The most negative impact that the accident had on me was that I did not want to live my life depending on the medicines.

Distress Associated with Attributing the Reasons for Impairment to One's Karma by Oneself as well as Others

Considering the importance given to devotion and spiritualism in the Indian society, when the first author (MB) heard that the accident occurred while returning from a trip to a temple, she could not help but query about the negative event occurring on the path to goodwill. Although they had travelled more than 1000 kms by car to visit Shirdi temple (a holy site), it was an ominous return journey, which culminated in the accident less than 500 kms from the place of devotion. He shared how people reacted to the same:

Many people say that "*aap toh gaye the mandir, aapne toh kaafi kuch socha hoga. Ye toh nahi socha hoga. Aapko kya blessing Mila hoga?* (you visited the temple, you must have had a lot to pray for. This definitely mustn't have been one of them. What blessings did you receive then?..... Why did Sai Baba (Indian spiritual saint) do something like this to you?

People questioned his intentions behind the visit. In fact, a year later, over an argument with the other family with whom they had visited Shirdi, the spouse of the husband who was behind the steering wheel even snapped at Ajeet saying, "You received your *karma*, and we received ours."

He admitted that such remarks, at a time when he himself was overwhelmed with feelings of loss, caused more damage to his self as he was left questioning his own past actions:

When such thought processes play in your head, you automatically become self-negative and it is more difficult to counter the thoughts brought by self. . . once a goat had sneaked into our lawn and I hit it so badly that one of its legs was fractured. I asked my mother if my current state had anything to do with that incident. . . and you think of good things too. While returning from college one day, there was an accident wherein a lady... [who] dislocated her pelvic girdle… with great difficulty, I had stopped an auto in between the road... made her sit inside and took her to the hospital... And then, when you meet with an accident, people don't stop to help you... this is like, "*havan karake haath jalana* (burning one's hand while performing a ritual burning offerings [performed in Hinduism]).

He then went on to share how in the event of helping the lady, he lost his bag which had all the medals he won as the sports fest culminated that day in his college. He lamented how he wasn't able to even show or tell his family the medals he had won in the event of helping someone else but in his time of need, he was deprived of the same by other bystanders.

Distress Associated with the Brunt Faced by Family Members

This questioning of one's actions and intentions was also attributed to his father's occupation. Police as an occupation is infamous in India due to reports of misuse of their powers through bribery. The accident opened up an avenue for some people to attribute his father's alleged involvement in corruption to his accident. As he reflected,

My father who works in the police department is a very honest man but people would taunt him by making general statements about the actions of corrupted policemen.... People would question his position as an inspector.... Behind my back, people would comment that my father must have engaged in bribery and it is his *karma* that his only son is disabled.

Coming to Terms with Different Possibilities of Recovery

It was only towards the end of 2014, after trying all local alternatives be known to him but failing to recover physically that he took the initiative to explore options other than the treatment of the local doctors. With a gradual acceptance of his impairment as perhaps permanent he felt the need to learn to live with it.

In mid-14, I realized that recovery will not come staying at home. It could be that the technology used by normal physiotherapists were not advanced or that I need[ed] to bring about changes in my diet or try something else. I then looked up the web for centres in India providing rehab. The hope was still there for recovery because I used to read cases of people who had recovered. . . . The primary concern with spinal injuries is to get the patient active in any way possible. I realized I needed to understand rehabilitation if I were to live with this limited ability. I needed to learn how to eat and write with the help of technology and if there was any chance of recovery or if additional treatment was necessary . . . In November of 2014, I went for rehabilitation at ISIC (Indian Spinal Injury Centre).

Coming to Terms with Disability

It was only at ISIC that he learned the truth of his current condition. He was also reminded of the extent of his physical recovery in the past two years which was very little. There was an increase in endurance though: he could sit on a wheelchair instead of being bed-ridden all the time. At that same time, he was also suggested to keep himself active at all times in case of potential new discoveries in technology which could be tried on him. He narrated,

> Significant recovery was yet to come in terms of my movement or motor area and they [doctors] won't consider my case to have begun recovering since there was no sign in the motor area.

Being Valued by the Doctor

It was only at ISIC that he felt hopeful for the first time. This hope was instilled by the *camaraderie* shared with the doctor. For the first time since the accident, he felt that someone was being honest and logical about his case. Moreover, it was one past midnight when his turn to visit the chamber came, however, not only was the doctor extremely patient while listening to him narrate about his past two years but was also considerate and concerned about his and his family's accommodation as they had come from another state.

The neurosurgeon who was looking at my case [at ISIC] was so nice there that. . . meeting him actually reinstated lost hope within me. He not only instructed for the tests to be conducted immediately but upon looking at the results, he also provided for my admission by waking up the administration in the middle of the night. Not only this, but he also informed us about the CGHS rate for government employees (Central Government Health Scheme—health insurance policy providing healthcare facilities to working or retired Central Government employees and their family members entailing them to be eligible for a rebate of 75%). While I could not claim for the health insurance right away, the documents were to be made before admission. For this purpose, he also woke up the welfare department in the middle of the night to assist us. He also said that recovery was possible even if it is delayed. I was suggested to stay active and keep my muscles intact and if there was recent technology in this area, it would be more likely to work on me. And in order to stay active, they were going to provide training.

Learning about Alternate Ways to Live with One's Condition

While the doctor's honest opinion about his physical recovery might not have been positive, he did suggest measures to better his quality of life which will help him get rid of the repeated infections and live a medication-free life. He told me that my pain and infections would only subside when I start having self-produced products (not the market ones with pesticides) and when I start residing in a place where both pollution as well as population would be sparse. This way my body would get the space to prepare itself for a new normal which it wasn't getting at that moment. He said, "*If you eat the same food as me and live the way I do yet expect your body to adapt the changes in the very same environment, how will it happen? You haven't given your body a breathing space.*"

Developing a new Meaning of Impairment

As he underwent two months of rehabilitation at ISIC, learning and practicing alternate ways of living, a new meaning making process developed which shifted the narrative of impairment as loss to impairment as an opportunity to start again. He reflected,

> My life could have been over that day, but I got a second chance [to live]. . . And the most important thing is that before you start anything, you have to be zero which is not possible in life. And by zero, I mean the absence of premeditated thoughts regarding one's future. I got the opportunity to be zero, although forcefully, and my life was confined to the bed. . . We cannot keep our phones silent for an hour, my life was silenced for some time . . . . How good a moment this was! I could think about anything, even the universe! I could study anything. Who gives these opportunities? Can your parents tell you not to study for a month, to do whatever you wish, you just stay comfortable, you will get food, people etc.?

He was equally supported and encouraged by the staff at ISIC which gave him the realisation of the opportunities available to persons with disability to live a normal life. As he pointed,

> The social department there suggested me to enhance my CV [curriculum vitae] as they conduct placements. I was reluctant to go for a desk job since I was in a completely different zone of joining the army. But they pushed me, and I went. . . although I

> did not get selected. I realised that my disability was not the end of the world. They even give counselling to parents of children with disability who wants to start a family. They informed about available technologies which makes it possible to start a family.

I came out not only with a renewed hope but also the realisation that I could live like a normal person.

Mental Strength and Vision through Support

The eventual acceptance of his impairment as possibly permanent was brought about by a number of factors, and it took him more than two years to accept it. As a child, his parents had instilled within him a *strong sense of trust and autonomy,* encouraging him to question and make his own decisions. He shared how his father used to confide about the financial aspects of his job which gave him the impression that his father had faith in him. He also pointed to the encouragement received not only when he secured the 3rd position in his higher secondary examinations but also when he failed to secure a rank for his dream engineering college.

The *fighting spirit* that "came with playing sports not only shaped his performances on the field but also off the field. In his words, sports was catalyst for everything in my life. No matter which phase I was in, low or high, I needed to play one sport, exhaust myself and come back. This was my routine. Whenever I would get less marks, I would not come home, I would go to the stadium."

This fighting spirit along with the support of friends and family motivated him to overcome his fear and discomfort after impairment as he finally started attending specific social events a year after his accident. He reflected,

People like me take 3 years to attend social events, but I attended my friend's wedding a year after [2013] my accident [2012] and I had started accessing the wheelchair by then. And that wheelchair wasn't even comfortable but all I had in my mind was that I had to go, meet him and return. And I had to manage a lot to attend his wedding; called my friends, arranged a car and was very conscious about how to sit on it. It was not easy, but I achieved it.

It was this fighting spirit and a humble upbringing that made him visit a temple the very first time he stepped out of his home after impairment. He cited two reasons behind visiting the temple—a desire to conquer his fear and secondly and more importantly, to *express gratitude* for being able to experience a second chance at life. He also pointed to the unwavering *support he received from his community*, especially his friends and family, leading to a sense of security and belongingness in the society.

[My friend] was sitting on the stage and when he noticed me, he got up and came running to greet me. He completely forgot that he was the groom. I told him, "Are you mad?". . . And there were even some rituals that he, as someone belonging to the hills, forgot to abide by, for e.g. he should not have removed his turban.

Similarly, when he attempted to start a project after rehabilitation, everyone came to support him while he gave a presentation in a wheelchair. He narrated,

The very first time I interacted with people (strangers) in a wheelchair was on 14 January, 2016. I invited everyone to be present to celebrate the occasion and everyone came to support me that day since they were aware of the past three years of my life. . . It was an overwhelming experience, one that seems funny when I think of it now. Some people even stayed the night, and it was a fantastic start to the project.

His strongest support system during this tough time was his younger sister, Ruchi. During the interview he recalled numerous times about the *support of his younger sister*, even going to the extent of saying that,

If I had a brother instead of a sister, I wouldn't have survived. . . [our bond] has been extremely helpful. . . that's what support is. I am blessed to have a sister.

He elaborated further stating,

> The initial two years, my sister was my backbone and even when I was going for rehab[ilitation], she was the energy who was always behind me. . . Today, I have a life but who gave me that? At that time, I did not feel a point in living further.

He believed that the support felt from his family was the reason he could overcome his disability experiences. As he reflected about his struggle with impairment, he talked about what support actually meant and how one can be supportive: if parents maintain a strong connect with their children from a young age, the child learns to tackle problems… when I got admitted in the rehab[ilitation] centre at Delhi, there were patients whose parents had not only hired attendants for them but also taken other measures such as subscription to various OTT platforms, feeding them their favourite food etc… but did they sit down and talk to their child? ... From the outside, the amount of materialistic support provided seemed like a lot but in reality, there was no support given.

Life Beyond Disability: Taking Actions for Self as Well as Others

Together with the suggestions of the doctors to eat self-produced food and the wisdom of their family *guru*, Neeshtha *Sahab* (*sahab* is a courteous term used to convey respect to others) as Ajeet *Ji* called him, he managed to create a life for him which went beyond staying bed-ridden and creating a new identity.

Reimagining Reality: Living an Uncompromised Life

While he was working on his profile building after rehabilitation, he met their family *guru*, Neeshtha *Sahab*, who guided him, giving his directions about the possible repercussions of his intended future plans and the immediate alternatives available.

Post-rehab[ilitation], I wanted to do some work and not stay idle at home, however, I was directionless. I planned on establishing a project lab keeping in mind the profit income considering the large number of engineering colleges in Lucknow. . . . In October 2015, I met our family *guru*, Neestha *Sahab*. . . . He asked me one question,

> *"what do you want to do in life? If you are planning to open the project lab like you have envisaged, you are going to earn money. But you also need to focus on your recovery and if you choose this profession, you won't be able to give yourself time for recover."*

This created a shift in his mind towards establishing a computer centre in the suburbs, preferably a village, where he would be able to utilize his past experience of teaching and receive assistance and home-grown food at the same time.

Opening the centre created a leeway for him to start a new conversation, one that was focused on his professional identity rather than his disability.

I did not want my identification to be just a spinal cord injured person. I believe until people recognize your work, your formal identification has not yet occurred. The purpose of building the centre in the village was not only to provide a better environment to the body to heal but also to build my profile. . . . I created a digital library for medical and engineering aspirants. . . . Now when I would meet my friends in the centre, they would ask me questions about the centre and not the medicines I was taking. Now people had the curiosity to know how I was doing all this. It is important for one to do something unique which gives rebirth to their lost identity.... Before that, I refused to meet anyone till I created a new identity.

This initiative was even *appreciated by the district magistrate* (DM) too who was impressed with his resilience:

I shared a good rapport with the DM at the time and he would frequently inquire about my progress.... I was connected to him not because of sympathy, nor because of my parents; rather, I was doing something positive in the village, and that is getting me connected.

Becoming an Insider: Merging the gap between 'Abled/Disabled'

Once he achieved all this at the village, his life became stagnant. He talked about receiving a *new opportunity from Alok* (director of Chhanv Foundation) during this time which not only let him continue his teaching but also exercise other skills which were inherent in him but yet to be expressed due to a dearth of opportunities.

I needed people who would value my identity and give me opportunities to grow. I got that opportunity from Alok. . . **to** join Sheroes Educational Initiative. Initially, he offered me the position of Director of the Education and Training department as well as a seat on the Board of the organization. I was very surprised because neither my background nor my prior experience qualified me for the position. It was an honorary position that anyone would want, and it was based on one or two meetings. Becoming a board member meant assuming a position of leadership, which I believe had been inherent in my character, and he offered me the opportunity with the uttermost regard. To bring about changes in Sheroes in terms of the survivors' education, I was required to devise orders that entailed responsibilities. . . this was the first time I was responsible. . . . And you are putting yourself in these positions when you once thought that you could only survive in the village. . . . To receive the welcome I did, I was really privileged, and this was only due to Alok *Bhai* (a Hindi word meaning brother). . . . After three years, I became the COO in addition to Director of Education and Training. . . this was the first time I was getting a chance to prove myself and I needed it to build my profile. . . . I learned a huge lesson from this experience that everybody needs support, be it from friends, boss or family and that only an authority can give you.

Joining an organization working on a marginalized community (acid attack survivors) also offered Ajeet *Ji* the opportunity to share and understand mutual experiences between him and the survivors. As a physically impaired individual, he was no stranger to the *taunts and questions raised by the society on one's actions or karma*. He emphasized,

Every survivor will tell you this that when you are in a problem in life, maximum people will ask questions like, *"ab kya karoge? Ab toh sab kharab ho gaya"* [what will you do now? Everything is over] or like "Why did this happen? You must have done something bad in life . . . your *karma* is being brought to you". This phase which the survivors have also experienced, and I have too, it's very difficult. . . I say the same thing to the survivors too. They say that it was their mistake that they had gone out, rejected or slapped their attackers or they began the argument with the attacker leading to the attack. Even their families say that they had suggested the survivor not to do this or go to the market alone, be accompanied by their brothers. Imagine, if they are repeatedly made to feel that it was their mistake, how difficult would it be for them to overcome the negative emotions.

This aspect of *relatability* not only guided him but also the organization in recognizing and understanding the needs of the acid attack survivors in order for them to be able to overcome the current images they as well as others hold of them. Acid attack survivors generally feel the effect of the assault lifelong and it was this aspect of disability that became a common point between him and the survivors. At the same time, he was also *emerging as an example of a possibility of living a normal life* for the survivors who saw themselves in him. However, his financially and emotionally secure upbringing created a distance between his and their struggles.

I cannot say that I related with them, but they did with me. . . . They would tell me that my challenges were bigger than them since they could still walk even with their disabilities. When they saw that I was very active, working and travelling to many places, they forgot their own challenges. I related to the accusations they would receive for the attack on them.

While the financial disparity between him and the survivors created a distance, it was overcome by his previous experience of working with children from financially weaker backgrounds on an everyday basis at his established centre.

Throughout Ajeet *Ji*'s own journey of impairment, he had emphasized the support he felt from his community and seeing the social realities of the survivors also made him deeply grateful for the community he had. This was hardly the case for the survivors who were either mocked or ostracized by their community. He elaborated on this *need to build a sense of community within the organisation:* Think of it like this. You do not have any skill, you are disabled, you are underprivileged, and your friends also cannot do anything for you. Forget about doing something, they don't have the background for that only. . . how will you excel? . . . . The community I had made my struggle easier. . . . I have barely been uncomfortable by other people but comments are passed on them [survivors] everyday. In fact, that is the very purpose of the attack, to alienate and humiliate the victim.

As noted earlier, it was Ajeet *Ji*'s own journey of being 'less-abled' to 'abled' that allowed him to grasp the profound *need for creation of new identities among the acid attack survivors.*

If Sheroes [the café where survivors work] wouldn't be here, nobody would be coming to motivate them in their homes. How do we motivate them? We tell them *"If you want to do something then Sheroes will give you an identity"*. It's just about changing the mindset from where you stand.

Healing Journey: Overcoming the Impact of Disability

Ajeet *Ji* believed that it was the people and his community that pushed him to overcome his inhibitions and physical limitations. A true athlete at heart, he also acknowledged the *role of sports* in his life as he compared to his journey of recovery to a sprint.

In a sprint, there is no planning involved; you must simply run as quickly as possible. You cannot even turn to see where your opponents are standing or switch to a different track because the instant your attention is diverted, you will lose. I was acting as one would in a sprint. I had one small objective, which was to maintain a healthy environment at home. Nobody has a plan at the outset. It is constructed in the process.

Staying infection free had not only given him more time to focus on his future but also remoralised him. He had not lost hope entirely but accepted his body the way it was.

Maybe after so many years, it doesn't matter losing hope. I have completely accepted myself and my present condition and I serve my commitment up to the mark of a *normal* person. Even if I am not recovering, it's completely fine. I have not compromised with my life. However, things are, I have earned them.

In the process of accepting himself, he *developed a new meaning of disability* which created a shift from the dominant understanding of disability as being "less-abled" to disability as a socially constructed idea of people with physical limitations. As he reflected,

> Disability is not what we see or understand. Everyone has their own disability; what distinguishes mine is the visual appearance supporting it. People can see that I am confined to a wheelchair. . . [but] for me, sitting on a wheelchair is not disability. The point is what do I do after sitting on the wheelchair? If I can do my work, then sitting on a wheelchair is normal. I felt my disability more when I was bed-ridden. Now I do not feel that I am disabled.

His struggles, however, were not yet over as the *embodied existence of bodily loss* was always present. In his words, "The accident may be 10 years old, but the pain is experienced daily."

Renegotiating Social Obligations and Expectations

Due to lesser mobility, he was compelled to limit his social gatherings outside of work, which was sometimes misinterpreted as his unwillingness to attend or participate in such gatherings.

People are not aware of my pain, and I am often at crossroads where I am questioned about my decisions to attend or not attend social events. Since I am working the entire day while sitting on the wheelchair, many a times, people expect the same out of me outside the office too. At times, even my sister gets upset when I refuse to go somewhere with her. . . . It's not that I don't have excitement to go out but the condition of pain often prohibits my ability to hang out socially.

This is the story of how Ajeet *Ji*'s faith, vision, and *karma*, along with his strong social ties, enabled him to create a financially stable, albeit challenging but manageable life for himself. As he rightly says, "My disability is 100 per cent but its impact on me is 0 per cent."

Discussion

Using a social constructionist paradigm and its epistemological position, the present study utilised the framework of suffering (Cassell, 2004; Kleinman, 1997), which provides a valuable lens to understand the participant's experiences of distress and remoralization following the life-altering accident. This framework emphasizes the importance of understanding suffering as a complex interplay of physical, emotional, social and existential dimensions. Thus, the themes of suffering reflect the societal discourses transforming impairment into a disability experience.

The categories of suffering highlight the challenges brought about by such life-altering accidents which create an experiential vacuum in the person's life, which is primarily initiated by bodily loss but culminates into a disorientation about one's life stemming from the distress and the subsequent loss of hope brought about by the inability to continue one's pre injury life. Spinal cord injuries which are more complex in nature, imposes severe challenges of mobility, rendering the injured person an indirect prisoner at their own home, with complete reliance on family and friends (Burns & Connell, 2012). Additionally, accessibility and transportation of SCI patients poses as significant barriers in developing countries like India where there is a lack of information and infrastructure related to SCI (Pandey *et al.*, 2007).

The creation of an "experiential vacuum" brought about by the unimaginable change to the body highlights how sudden loss of health is often taken as a betrayal, as the body is no longer seen as a friend but an untrustworthy enemy (Kleinman, 1988a). Such feelings are intensified in cases where illness or injuries occur without warning, leading to a complete distrust of the perceptions of one's own body (Cassell, 2004).

This subjective experience of "loss" is brought about by both one's inability to fulfil one's own as well as others' expectations as per the cultural norms that shape a person's functionality in various spheres of life. An example of the former is seen in the theme of "inability of fulfil expectations as an only son". Similar to Chinese societies, in Indian societies too, care is understood as reciprocal wherein children are expected to take care of their parents in their old age in the same way that they are taken care of during their childhood by their parents (Holdroyd, as cited in Sit *et al.*, 2020). The paralysis caused by the sudden accident meant that he would be needed to be cared for his whole life, rendering him "useless" regarding taking care for his parents. Thus, in addition to the loss of body, Ajeet *Ji* was also simultaneously negotiating with loss of other forms of "losses", namely dreams, roles and expectations, among others.

The understanding of culture as a "unique social context of knowledge and power at the levels of individuals, families, communities, and larger social systems" pivotally shapes human suffering (Kirmayer, 2004, p. 355). The cultural explanation of disability based on one's *karma*, i.e. the idea that one's past deeds are responsible for their current state, is a common belief among Hindus in India (Gupta, 2011). The accident occurring after a visit to a temple raised questions about divine intervention and *karma*, by self and others, leading to feelings of self-doubt and guilt as Ajeet *Ji* grappled with the existential dilemmas about his identity and the trajectory of his life, thereby adding layers of complexity to his suffering. It is noteworthy that while the medical model has been solely focused on the individual, the cultural interpretations of disability related to divine displeasure have existed in ethnographic records from earlier times (Groce, 1999).

According to Priya (2012), "culture and cultural norms are not uncontested sites" (p. 217). Cultural norms, along with its potential to value and devalue attributes, may constrict or suppress an individual's capacity to fully engage with and articulate their own experiences. The dominant ideas of *ableism* often imposes stigma on PwDs as was the case in this study. However, the stigma doesn't stay constricted to the sufferer but penetrates to the family members who are subjected to discrimination and prejudice from the society. The *distress associated with the brunt faced by family members* refers to the disruption created by the impairment as his father's honesty and moral intentions in his job were questioned. At the core of any healing practice lies the metaphorical changes in the quality of experience and identity of the sufferer (Kirmayer, 2004). Kirmayer refers to these metaphorical changes as occurring from the symbolic space created between the clinician and the sufferer in which meaning-making takes place, thus transforming the illness experience of the sufferer. This is illustrated in the sub-categories of,

> *"being valued by the doctor", "learning about alternate ways to live with one's condition" and "developing a new meaning of impairment".*

Cassell (2004) proposed that although the human body might not be able to regrow a body part, the person can. According to him, the process of healing allows the person to become whole again as parts of the person are reassembled in a new way. Thus, in the process of accepting a "new body", several facets of selfhood are reformulated in an effort to find meaning in life by constructing an empowered and differently abled world despite their suffering related to limited, embodied, and stigmatized experiences. This reformulation of the different aspects of selfhood or personhood as highlighted by Cassell, include the sub-categories of,

> *"a sense of trust and autonomy", "fighting spirit",* and *"the role of sports"* which are aspects of Ajeet *Ji*'s lived past while *"the support he gained from his friends, family, particularly his younger sister as well as the community."*

are aspects of the relationships he shares with others. Also, *"the embodied existence of bodily loss"* refers to the relationship he shares with his body. All these aspects helped in ameliorating suffering and fostering healing.

Similarly, Kleinman (1988a) refers to the process of healing or remoralization as the experience of meaning-making by "building an illness narrative that will make sense of and give value to the experience" (p. 54). Becoming a part of a marginalised section in society and the subsequent opportunities for growth that Ajeet *Ji* received to pursue a career which enabled him to give voice as a survivor advocate in addition to contributing for fellow PwDs' reintegration into society through continuation and preservation of the salient aspects of his identity (such as teaching) enabled him to connect his own personal experiences of disability with the collective. Such encouragement and facilitation through the development of peer support networks and groups lead to a continuity of his past life, thus preserving his self in healing (Charmaz, 1994). This improved his community reintegration and long-term well-being, by fostering a sense of community and preventing isolation. This process of re-integration into society which, as per Dow (1986) takes place through *emotionally charged symbols*, enabled him to create a new meaning of his impairment as well as a new identity as a survivor advocate, thus leading to a corresponding transformation of his disability experience. Furthermore, the presence of a survivor advocates as a caregiver in an organization where care-receivers comprise fellow PwDs, also created an avenue to locate and understand each other's shared experiences of trauma and the subsequent need to create a sense of community for ones in need of it.

Conclusion

The aftermath of a sudden and complex injury is often filled with trauma and distress as the individual attempts to make sense of their disoriented experiential world. Thus, such experiences can often lead to suffering brought about by a profound sense of loss to one's existence in the form of their bodies, goals, perceived future and relationships.

The findings of this study indicate how individuals with disability can be re-integrated in society through culturally valued norms which enable them to develop a new meaning of their impairment. Of critical importance here is the role of PwDs in decision-making and the outcome it has in the rehabilitation of other PwDs as the presence of a survivor advocate in the decision-making process often leads to the identification of the social injustices which often lead to a deflated sense of self and subsequent suffering, filled with feelings of 'less-able' or 'incapable'. While the different social realities between the advocate and the survivors became a point of differentiation, it also brought to light an important issue of "access". The participant's case highlights how access to resources and support since childhood and not only during one's traumatic injury, leads to the development of a strong sense of resilience to overcome failures and difficulties in times of trauma and the subsequent need for community and a new identity in order to overcome one's experiences of suffering brought about by their disability experience.

References

Adriansen, H.K. (2012). "Timeline Interviews: A Tool for Conducting Life History Research". *Qualitative Studies*, *3*(1): 40-55. https://doi.org/10.7146/qs.v3i1.6272

Bhattacharya, P. & Priya, K.R. (2022). "Stakeholders Facilitating Hope and Empowerment amidst Social Suffering: A Qualitative Documentary Analysis Exploring Lives of Homeless Women with Mental Illness". *International Journal of Social Psychiatry*, *68*(4): 908-918. https://doi.org/10.1177/00207640211011186

Bracken, P.J., Giller, J.E. & Summerfield, D. (1995). "Psychological Responses to War and Atrocity: The Limitations of Current Concepts". *Social Science & Medicine*, *40*(8): 1073-1082. https://doi.org/10.1016/0277-9536(94)00181-R

Bredewold, F., Verplanke, L., Kampen, T., Tonkens, E. & Duyvendak, J.W. (2020). "The Care Receivers Perspective: How Care-Dependent People Struggle with Accepting Help from Family Members, Friends and Neighbours". *Health Soc Care Community*, *28*(3): 762-770. https://doi.org/10.1111/ hsc.12906

Buckingham, J. (2011). "Writing Histories of Disability in India: Strategies of Inclusion". *Disability & Society*, *26*(4): 419-431. https://doi.org/10.1080/09687599.2011.567792

Burns, A.S. & O'Connell, C. (2012). "The Challenge of Spinal Cord Injury Care in the Developing World". *The Journal of Spinal Cord Medicine*, *35*(1): 3-8.

Cassell, E.J. (2004). *The Nature of Suffering and the Goals of Medicine* (2nd edn.). Oxford University Press.

Charmaz, K. (1994). "Identity Dilemmas of Chronically Ill Men". *The Sociological Quarterly*, *35*(2): 269-88. https://doi.org/10.1111/j.1533-8525.1994.tb00410.x

Charmaz, K. (2014). *Constructing Grounded Theory*. Sage.

Dawn, R. (2013). "Our Lives, Our Identity: Women with Disabilities in India". *Disability and Rehabilitation, 36*(21): 1768-1773. DOI: 10.3109/09638288.2013.870237

Dow, J. (1986). "Universal Aspects of Symbolic Healing: A Theoretical Synthesis". *American Anthropologist, 88*(1): 56-69. DOI: 10.1525/aa.1986.88.1.02a00040

Ghai, A. (2015). *Rethinking Disability in India.* Routledge.

Giesbrecht, N.D. (2008). "Caregiving in Socio-cultural Context". In B. Fehr, S. Sprecher & L.G. Underwood (Eds.): *The Science of Compassionate Love: Theory, Research, and Applications* (pp. 373-401). Wiley Blackwell.

Goffman, E. (1963). *Stigma: Notes on the Management of Spoiled Identities*. Englewood Cliffs, NJ: Prentice Hall.

Groce, N.E. (1999). "Disability in Cross-cultural Perspective: Rethinking Disability". *The Lancet, 354* (9180): 756-757. https://doi.org/10.1016/S0140-6736(99)06140-1

Guba, E. & Lincoln, Y. (1994). "Competing Paradigms in Qualitative Research". In N.K. Denzin & Y.S. Lincoln (Eds.): *Handbook of Qualitative Research* (pp. 105-117). Sage.

Gupta, V.B. (2011). "How Hindus Cope with Disability". *Journal of Religion, Disability & Health, 15*(1): 72-78. DOI: 10.1080/15228967.2011.540897

Khanna, A. & Priya, K.R. (2023). "Rethinking 'Transfer' in the Transgenerational Transmission of Trauma: A Qualitative Study of the 1984 Anti-Sikh Violence". *Theory & Psychology, 34*(1): 18-39. https://doi.org/10.1177/09593543231204576

Kirmayer, L.J. (2004). "The Cultural Diversity of Healing: Meaning, Metaphor and Mechanism". *British Medical Bulletin, 69*(1): 33-48. https://doi.org/10.1093/bmb/ldh006

Kleinman, A. (1997). "Everything That Really Matters: Social Suffering, Subjectivity, and the Remaking of Human Experience in a Disordering World". *The Harvard Theological Review, 90*(3): 315-335. http://www.jstor.org/stable/1509952

Kleinman, A. (1988a). *The Illness Narratives: Suffering, Healing and the Human Condition*. Basic Books.

Kleinman, A., Das, V. & Lock, M. (1997). "Introduction". In A. Kleinman, V. Das & M. Lock (Eds.): *Social Suffering* (pp. ix-xxvii). Oxford University Press.

LaVela, S.L., Landers, K., Etingen, B., Karalius, V.P. & Miskevics, S. (2015). "Factors Related to Caregiving for Individuals with Spinal Cord Injury Compared to Caregiving for Individuals with Other Neurologic Conditions". *The Journal of Spinal Cord Medicine, 38*(4): 505-514. https://doi.org/10.1179/2045772314Y.0000000240

Mladenov, T. (2015). "Neoliberalism, Postsocialism, Disability". *Disability & Society, 30*(3): 445-459. https://doi.org/10.1080/09687599.2015.1021758

Nishida, A. (2022). *Just Care: Messy Entanglements of Disability, Dependency, and Desire*. Temple University Press.

Pandey, A. (2021). "Disability & Work Place Inclusion in the Private Sector: A Critical Legal Analysis of RPwD Act, 2016". *International Journal of Law Management and Humanities, 4*, 505. http://doi.one/10.1732/IJLMH.26090

Pandey, V., Nigam, V., Goyal, T.D. & Chhabra, H. (2007). "Care of Post-Traumatic Spinal Cord Injury Patients in India: An analysis". *Indian Journal of Orthopaedics*, *41*(4): 295-299. https://doi.org/10.4103/0019-5413.36990

Plummer, K. (1995). "Life Story Research". In J.A. Smith, R. Harre & L. Van Langehove (Eds.): *Rethinking Methods in Psychology* (pp. 50-64). Sage.

Priya, K.R. (2012). "Social Constructionist Approach to Suffering and Healing: Juxtaposing Cassell, Gergen and Kleinman". *Psychological Studies*, *57*(2): 211-223. DOI: 10.1007/s12646-011-0143-5

Priya, K.R. (2015). "On the Social Constructionist Approach to Traumatized Selves in Post-Disaster Settings: State-induced Violence in Nandigram, India". *Culture, Medicine and Psychiatry*, *39*(3): 428-448. https://doi.org/10.1007/s11013-014-9423-6

Priya, K.R. (2018). "Well-being and Mental Health in the Aftermath of Disasters: A Social Constructionist Approach". In G. Misra (Ed.): *Psychosocial Interventions for Health and Well-being* (pp. 355-368). Springer.

Sharma, D. (2022). *Psychology of Accident Victims in India: Explorations in Embodiment, Suffering and Healing.* Routledge.

Sharma, D. & Priya, K.R. (2020, March 28). "Excluded in Rehabilitation: Disability in the Neo-Liberal Era?" *Economic and Political Weekly*, *55*(13): 12-15. https://www.epw.in/journal/2020/13/commentary/excluded-rehabilitation.html?0=ip_login_no_cache%3D53ac1d01da4be0b707e9c3bc67668dae

Sit, H.F., Huang, L., Chang, K., Chau, W.I. & Hall, B.J. (2020). "Caregiving Burden among Informal Caregivers of People with Disability". *British Journal of Health Psychology*, *25*(3): 790-813. https://doi.org/10.1111/bjhp.12434

Smith, E.M., Boucher, N. & Miller, W.C. (2016). "Caregiving Services in Spinal Cord Injury: A Systematic Review of the Literature". *Spinal Cord*, *54*(8): 562-569. https://doi.org/10.1038/sc.2016.8

Srivastava, P. & Kumar, P. (2015). "Disability, Its Issues and Challenges: Psychosocial and Legal Aspects in Indian Scenario". *Delhi Psychiatry Journal*, *18*(1): 195-205.

Thrush, A. & Hyder, A. (2014). "The Neglected Burden of Caregiving in Low-and Middle-Income Countries". *Disability and Health Journal*, *7*(3): 262-272. https://doi.org/10.1016/j.dhjo.2014.01.003

United Nations Office for Disaster Risk Reduction. (2023). *Global Survey Report on Persons with Disabilities and Disasters.* Geneva.

Wendell, Susan. (1989). "Toward a Feminist Theory of Disability". *Hypatia, 4*(2): 104-24. https://doi.org/10.1111/j.1527-2001.1989.tb00576.x

Wolbring, G. (2008). "The Politics of Ableism". *Development, 51*(2): 252-258. DOI:10.1057/dev.2008.17

World Health Organisation. (2001). URL: https://www.who.int/health-topics/disability#tab=tab_1 [Accessed on 23 October, 2023].

5

Palliative and End-of-Life Care for Ageing Population

A Psychological Perspective

Priyanka Pathak and *Shobhna Joshi*

Introduction

The global population is ageing rapidly, leading to an increased focus on healthcare services that cater to older adults, including palliative and end-of-life care. According to the World Health Organization (WHO), by 2050, the number of people aged 60 years and older will be double, necessitating enhanced understanding of psychological and emotional care at the end of life. While physical symptoms receive substantial attention in palliative care, psychological aspects—such as coping with impending death, existential anxiety, loss, and depression—remain underexplored. Addressing these psychological aspects is essential to achieving holistic care, preserving dignity, and improving the quality of life during the final stages. **Palliative Care** refers to specialized medical care aimed at providing relief from the symptoms, pain, and stress of serious illnesses. The primary goal is to improve the quality of life for patients who are facing chronic or life-limiting conditions. Palliative care can be provided at any stage of an illness and is often offered alongside curative treatments.

End-of-Life Care is a type of palliative care focused specifically on the last phase of life, typically when a patient is approaching the end of his life and curative treatments are no longer an option. The goal is to provide comfort, dignity, and emotional support for the patient and their family as they navigate the final stages of life. Older adults often face difficult decisions regarding their treatment and end-of-life care options, which can be overwhelming for them and their families. End-of-life care provides guidance and assistance in these decisions, ensuring that the patient's values and wishes are honoured, which fosters a sense of control and peace during the final stages of life. Additionally, these services offer essential support for caregivers, who often experience significant emotional stress in caring for an ageing loved one. This includes respite care, counselling, and bereavement support, helping families cope with the complexities of terminal illness. Both types of care address physical, emotional, and psychological needs to ensure a compassionate and respectful experience during serious illness and the end-of-life process.

Palliative care is a specialized form of medical care focused on improving the quality of life for individuals with serious, chronic, or life-threatening illnesses. It aims to provide relief from physical symptoms, such as pain, fatigue, and nausea, as well as address emotional, psychological, social, and spiritual needs. Unlike curative treatments, palliative care does not aim to cure the underlying illness but instead seeks to enhance comfort and well-being, regardless of the stage of the disease. This type of care is patient-centred and involves a multidisciplinary team of healthcare providers, including doctors, nurses, social workers, counsellors, and chaplains, who collaborate to support both the patient and their family. It can be provided alongside curative treatments or as the primary focus when curative options are no longer effective.

Palliative care is particularly relevant for ageing populations, where chronic conditions such as cancer, heart failure, and dementia are prevalent. It includes advance care planning, symptom management, emotional support, and assistance with decision-making to align care with the patient's values and preferences. Ultimately, palliative care seeks to provide holistic support, helping patients and their loved ones navigate complex health challenges with dignity, comfort, and compassion. Palliative care for ageing populations is influenced by various factors that impact its delivery and effectiveness.

Patient-specific factors include the severity of illness, mental health conditions like depression or anxiety, and cultural or religious beliefs that shape perceptions of care. Communication preferences also play a role, as some patients may avoid discussions about end-of-life care. **Caregiver-related factors** are crucial, as caregivers often face stress, burnout, and a lack of knowledge about palliative care principles. Adequate support systems, such as counselling and respite care, can mitigate these challenges. **Systemic factors** like healthcare infrastructure, access to services, and provider training significantly influence care quality. Disparities in rural and urban settings or inadequate policy support can limit access to specialized palliative services. **Cultural and social factors** include societal stigma around death, family dynamics, and language barriers, which can complicate care planning. Ethical and legal considerations, such as adherence to advance directives and decision-making about life-sustaining treatments, often present challenges. Technological factors, like telemedicine and home-based medical devices, expand care access but require patient and caregiver literacy. Lastly, psychosocial support addressing emotional, spiritual, and counselling needs is essential to ensuring compassionate and effective care. A holistic approach to these factors is vital for equitable and quality palliative care.

Palliative and end-of-life care are especially relevant to older adults, as ageing often brings an increased risk of chronic, progressive, and life-limiting illnesses. Many older adults experience conditions like heart disease, cancer, dementia, and chronic respiratory illnesses, which can significantly impact their quality of life. Some of these types of care related to old age are:

1. Management of Chronic Illnesses

Older adults are more likely to face chronic illnesses that require ongoing symptom management, such as pain, fatigue, and shortness of breath. Palliative care focuses on relieving these symptoms and improving quality of life, helping older adults maintain functionality and comfort even with severe illnesses.

2. Holistic Support and Quality of Life

Beyond physical symptoms, older adults often experience emotional and psychological challenges, including anxiety, depression, and social isolation. Palliative care addresses these aspects, providing mental health support, fostering connections, and helping maintain dignity and independence.

3. Complex Decision-Making at End of Life

For older adults nearing the end of life, there are often complex decisions to make about treatment options. End-of-life care helps ensure that these decisions respect the patient's values and wishes, and often includes support for advance care planning, ensuring that preferences for comfort, independence, and dignity are honoured.

4. Support for Families and Caregivers

As older adults often rely on family members for care, palliative and end-of-life care provide support for caregivers. These services help family members navigate the stress and emotional impact of a loved one's illness, offering counselling, respite, and bereavement support after the patient's passing.

5. Focus on Dignity and Comfort

For many older adults, maintaining dignity and comfort at the end of life is a priority. End-of-life care is specifically designed to help older adults transition peacefully, with a focus on comfort, dignity, and emotional support for both the individual and their family.

In sum, palliative and end-of-life care play crucial roles in helping older adults manage complex health issues, maintain dignity, and experience a better quality of life as they age. These services are essential in addressing the unique physical, emotional, and social challenges that often accompany ageing.

Literature Review

The psychological experiences of ageing individuals approaching the end of life are influenced by factors such as personal beliefs about death, social connections, health status, and prior life experiences. Studies have shown that older adults often struggle with various psychological challenges.

Studies reveal that as people age, their concern about death and dying intensifies. According to Puchalski *et al.* (2014), individuals nearing the end of life may experience existential anxiety, fearing loss of autonomy and control over life. End-of-life discussions were associated with less aggressive medical care, better patient mental health, and improved bereavement outcomes for family members, reducing depression and complicated grief (Wright *et al.*, 2008). Depression is highly prevalent among older adults receiving palliative care. Chochinov *et al.* (2016) highlight that depression in terminally ill older adults not only affects their emotional well-being but can also accelerate physical decline.

Daniel, S. (2017) discusses the benefits and challenges of incorporating palliative care into geriatric assessments, emphasizing the need for clinical expertise and appropriate reimbursement to enhance quality of life for older adults.

A study conducted by Swagerty (2017) emphasizes the integration of palliative care into routine geriatric assessments, highlighting the psychological benefits of addressing end-of-life concerns early, including reduced anxiety and improved patient-family dynamics.

Sadeghi *et al.*(2024) found that older adults with negative emotions towards ageing had higher death anxiety levels, highlighting the importance of fostering positive attitudes towards ageing for healthy psychological outcomes.

Research by Sulmasy (2018) underscores that many ageing individuals worry about maintaining dignity during the dying process. Dignity-conserving interventions have shown promise in addressing this concern, allowing patients to feel valued and respected. Social isolation and loneliness are common in ageing individuals and are intensified by life-limiting conditions. Studies, including that of Bolmsjo *et al.* (2014), indicate that maintaining meaningful connections can reduce emotional distress.

Aoun, *et al.*, (2017) explores the psychological toll on caregivers of terminally ill older adults, emphasizing the need for tailored interventions to mitigate caregiver stress and burnout.

Smith (2021) examines the impact of palliative care on older adults with chronic diseases, such as cardiovascular disease, COPD, and diabetes. The findings indicate that integrating palliative care early in the treatment of chronic illness improves quality of life and reduces hospitalizations, ultimately reducing healthcare costs. The study highlights the psychological benefits of early palliative care, which include decreased anxiety and depression among elderly patients.

Jones & Wei (2022) investigated the complexities of decision-making in end-of-life care for older adults, focusing on autonomy, dignity, and emotional well-being. It finds that older adults prefer to have a say in their end-of-life care decisions, and providing support for advance care planning (ACP) improves their sense of control and peace. The study suggests that structured ACP sessions with psychologists enhance satisfaction for both patients and families.

In a very recent study Garcia & Singh (2023) have focused upon the psychological burden on family caregivers providing palliative care to older adults. They found that caregivers often experience high levels of stress, depression, and isolation, which can impact the quality of care provided to patients. The study emphasizes the need for support services, such as counselling and respite care, to improve caregiver well-being and enhance patient care.

Chang and Kumar (2020) evaluates the effectiveness of dignity therapy in reducing existential anxiety and enhancing a sense of purpose in older adults nearing end-of-life. Findings show that dignity therapy improves psychological well-being by allowing patients to reflect on their life experiences, which helps them find meaning and reduces end-of-life distress. This therapy also provides emotional comfort for family members.

The latest study by Nunez (2024) was focused on older adults in palliative care, this study reveals that social isolation can exacerbate feelings of depression and anxiety, impacting both mental and physical health. It recommends structured social interaction programmes and virtual support groups for isolated elderly patients in palliative care, showing positive outcomes in reducing loneliness and improving emotional health.

Bhatt and Green (2022) examined palliative care for older adults with advanced dementia, focusing on interventions to manage symptoms like agitation, pain, and emotional distress. Results indicate that person-centred care and non-pharmacological interventions, such as music therapy and aromatherapy, significantly improve quality of life for dementia patients, while also providing comfort for family members and reducing caregiver stress.

Lin and Morris (2021) explored the benefits of mindfulness-based therapies for elderly patients in end-of-life care, demonstrating that mindfulness interventions can reduce anxiety, pain perception, and emotional distress. Findings suggest that mindfulness helps patients accept mortality, enhances their sense of peace, and improves their overall emotional well-being.

These studies reflect the growing focus on psychological and social interventions within palliative and end-of-life care for older adults, highlighting strategies that improve patient comfort, emotional resilience, and quality of life, while also addressing family needs.

Psychological Challenges in Palliative and End-of-Life Care

- *Coping with Existential Anxiety and Fear of Death*—Fear of death and existential anxiety are prevalent psychological issues in older adults. As individuals face their mortality, they often confront questions about the meaning of life and their legacy. Therapeutic interventions, such as existential therapy and logo therapy, help individuals find purpose and meaning during their final stages.

- *Grief and Loss*—Grief in older adults is multifaceted, involving the loss of independence, health, and social roles. Grief counselling and bereavement support for patients and their families help in adjusting to these losses. Narrative therapy can also be beneficial in helping individuals express unresolved emotions and explore life memories.
- *Depression and Emotional Distress*—Depression is common in palliative care settings and is often exacerbated by physical symptoms and reduced autonomy. Cognitive Behavioural Therapy (CBT), adapted for palliative care, has shown efficacy in reducing depressive symptoms by focusing on restructuring negative thoughts and fostering acceptance.
- *Loss of Control and Need for Dignity*—Many ageing individuals express concerns about losing control over their lives. Dignity therapy, which focuses on understanding what matters most to patients, has been shown to increase a sense of purpose and control. This therapy includes guided sessions that allow patients to reflect on meaningful life experiences.
- *Social Isolation and the Importance of Connection*—Social support is essential for mental well-being, yet many older adults experience loneliness. Psychosocial support programmes that facilitate family visits, phone calls, or online socializing can mitigate loneliness and enhance mental health.

Psychological Challenges in Palliative and End-of-Life Care primarily affect patients, families, and healthcare providers, each facing unique emotional and mental health hurdles. Patients often experience fear, anxiety, depression, and existential distress as they confront the realities of a life-limiting illness. Additionally, feelings of isolation, loss of autonomy, and difficulty finding meaning can intensify emotional suffering. Families and caregivers endure anticipatory grief, guilt, and emotional exhaustion, often leading to caregiver burnout. Complex decision-making about patient care can also cause stress and conflict within families. Healthcare providers face challenges like empathy, fatigue and moral distress from navigating difficult patient situations, balancing institutional policies, and respecting patient and family wishes. Effective communication about end-of-life care options can be another sensitive area. Psychological support strategies are essential in addressing these challenges. Interventions such as cognitive-behavioural therapy, mindfulness, and dignity therapy help patients manage their distress. Families benefit from bereavement support, counselling, and respite care to alleviate stress and prepare for loss.

Training healthcare providers in empathy, resilience, and communication fosters a supportive environment for compassionate care. Addressing these psychological challenges comprehensively improve quality of life for all involved, ensuring end-of-life care that respects dignity, emotional needs, and comfort.

Therapeutic Interventions in Psychological Care for Older Adults

- Cognitive Behavioural Therapy (CBT) is modified in palliative care settings to address existential thoughts, fears, and depressive symptoms in older adults.
- Dignity Therapy involves structured interviews with patients to document their personal histories, achievements, and meaningful memories, helping them reflect on life and leave behind a legacy.
- Narrative therapy assists older adults in processing grief, unresolved emotions, and traumatic memories by guiding them to construct and communicate their life stories.
- Mindfulness-based stress reduction (MBSR) programmes can help older adults in palliative care to remain present, manage pain, and cultivate self-compassion.
- Group Counselling and Family Therapy approaches provide older adults and their families a supportive environment for expressing fears, resolving conflicts, and planning end-of-life wishes.

Therapeutic Interventions focus on addressing the unique emotional, cognitive, and social needs of ageing individuals. Older adults may face psychological challenges such as depression, anxiety, loneliness, cognitive decline, and grief due to life changes, health conditions, and the loss of loved ones. Therapeutic interventions aim to improve mental well-being, maintain cognitive functioning, and enhance quality of life.

Recommendations for Future Practice

The psychological needs of older adults in palliative care require collaboration among psychologists, social workers, physicians, and spiritual counsellors. This ensures holistic care that addresses both physical and emotional needs. Encouraging family members to participate in end-of-life discussions, counselling, and decision-making processes improve patient satisfaction and reduces family grief. Developing policies that promote psychological support in palliative care settings and training healthcare professionals in psychological interventions will improve care quality. Recognizing that each patient's psychological experience is unique is essential. Personalized care plans can address individual preferences, cultural beliefs, and psychological needs.

In India, palliative and end-of-life care for the elderly faces challenges, especially in addressing psychological needs. Many older adults experience anxiety, depression, and loneliness due to health declines and changing family dynamics. Cultural stigma around discussing death and limited palliative care services, particularly in rural areas, add to these challenges. Kerala has led in community-based palliative care, but most of India lacks such programmes. Barriers include limited access, scarce resources, and low awareness of mental health support. NGOs and health organizations are promoting awareness and exploring culturally sensitive psychological approaches, such as spiritual support. Telemedicine and digital counselling are promising ways to expand access.

India's National Programme for Palliative Care aims to improve care accessibility, but more policy efforts and funding are needed to make psychological support a central part of these services. Strengthening training, integrating mental health support, and educating families can help provide holistic, compassionate care for India's ageing population.

Conclusion

Palliative and end-of-life care for the ageing population requires attention to psychological factors that influence their emotional well-being, dignity, and quality of life. Providing compassionate, patient-centred psychological care involves not only managing symptoms but also offering emotional support, fostering social connections, and affirming dignity. Future research should continue to explore innovative therapeutic approaches that can enhance the psychological well-being of older adults during the end of life. This study emphasizes the necessity of a psychological perspective in palliative and end-of-life care for older adults, advocating for patient-centred, dignity-focused, and compassionate approaches that enhance the quality of life for ageing individuals at the end of life. The provided studies addressing psychological aspects of palliative and end-of-life care in the ageing population. Key themes include the integration of palliative care into geriatric assessments, the benefits of end-of-life discussions, the impact of ageing perceptions on death anxiety, and the experiences of elderly caregivers. Research also explores innovative approaches like psychedelics to manage existential distress, variability in palliative care services, and the importance of open communication about death. The studies emphasize improving psychological well-being, enhancing quality of life, and addressing emotional challenges faced by patients and their families.

References

Aoun, S.M., *et al.* (2017). "The Support Needs of Family Caregivers of Terminally Ill Older People: A Literature Review". *International Psychogeriatrics.*

Bhatt, V. & Green, K. (2022). "Palliative Care Interventions to Improve Quality of Life in Dementia Patients". *Journal of Palliative Care, 38*(1): 23-34.

Bolmsjo, I., Tengland, P.A. & Ramgard, M. (2014). "Existential Loneliness among Patients in Palliative Care". *Palliative & Supportive Care.*

Chang, M. & Kumar, S. (2020). "Impact of Dignity Therapy on End-of-Life Anxiety in Older Adults". *American Journal of Hospice and Palliative Medicine, 37*(8): 623-632.

Chochinov, H.M., Hack, T., Hassard, T., *et al.* (2016). "Dignity in the Terminally Ill: A Cross-Sectional Cohort Study." *Lancet Oncology.*

Garcia, T.J. & Singh, P. (2023). "Family Caregiver Burden in Palliative Care for Elderly Patients". *Journal of Ageing & Social Policy, 45*(2): 189-203.

Jones, L.R. & Wei, S. (2022). "End-of-Life Decision-Making among Ageing Adults: A Psychological Perspective". *Palliative and Supportive Care, 20*(3): 452-465.

Lin, J. & Morris, L. (2021). "Mindfulness-Based Therapy for End-of-Life Care in the Elderly". *Ageing & Mental Health, 25*(6): 1045-1053.

Nunez, R., *et al.* (2024). "Social Isolation and Its Effects on Mental Health in Palliative Care for the Elderly". *Social Science & Medicine*, 295, 114793

Puchalski, C.M., Ferrell, B., Virani, R. (2014). "Improving the Quality of Spiritual Care as a Dimension of Palliative Care". *Journal of Palliative Medicine.*

Sadeghi, A., *et al.* (2024). "The Relationship between the Perception of Ageing and Death Anxiety in the Older Adults of Eastern Iran during COVID-19". *Health & Social Care in the Community.*

Smith, A.M. (2021). "The Role of Palliative Care in Chronic Disease Management for Older Adults". *Journal of Geriatric Medicine, 29*(4): 215-227.

Sulmasy, D. P. (2018). "The Role of Caregivers in Maintaining Dignity and Quality of Life for Patients at the End of Life". *The Gerontologist.*

Swagerty, D. (2017). "Integrating Quality Palliative and End-of-Life Care into the Geriatric Assessment: Opportunities and Challenges". *Clinical Geriatrics Medicine.*

Wright, A.A., *et al.* (2008). "Associations Between End-of-Life Discussions, Patient Mental Health, Medical Care Near Death, and Caregiver Bereavement Adjustment". *Journal of the American Medical Association* (*JAMA*)

6

Exploring the Field of Gero-psychology and Its Researches

Anubhuti Dubey and *Shubhang Dubey*

The increasing population of elderly individuals, particularly in India with over 104 million seniors as per the latest National Census, necessitates a heightened focus on gerontology to support a decade of 'healthy ageing' as promoted by the World Health Organization (Glenn & Goel, 2023). According to life-span developmental psychologists and gerontologists, age is more of a convenient marker of developmental progress and maturity than a cause of developmental change in and of itself. Human development occurs within the range of opportunities and constraints provided by biological, psychological, and contextual characteristics throughout life. The ageing process is both multidirectional and multidimensional. Unlike traditional views of ageing that depict human development as a process of gains followed by losses after a certain age, the life span psychologists propose that development is characterized by selective age-related adaptation throughout all stages, including adulthood and old age (Baltes, 1987).

Before discussing the psychological gerontology, we have to clarify the two terms in the field of ageing, i.e. geriatrics (health of and medicine for the elderly), and gerontology.

Geriatrics is a medical speciality that focuses on providing high-quality, patient-centred care specifically for older adults. Geriatricians are responsible for preventing and managing illnesses as well as creating care plans that are specific to the health issues that older adults face. Geriatric clinicians are trained to address the unique issues and concerns that older adults present, such as the fact that older adults may experience illnesses, diseases, and medications differently than younger adults, and that they frequently present with overlapping health issues that require the use of multiple medications.

Gerontology is the study of ageing processes and characteristics of older persons. Gerontology emerged as a response to advances in longevity. Researchers in this discipline have a wide range of backgrounds, including physiology, social science, psychology, public health, and policy. A thorough definition of gerontology includes the following aspects: Investigations into the physiological transformations occurring from middle age to later life; interdisciplinary analysis of societal shifts caused by an ageing demographic, encompassing fields such as the humanities (including history, philosophy, and literature) and economics; and the practical application of these insights to inform policies and programmes.

Hence, gerontology is a multidisciplinary field that studies the physical, mental, and social aspects and consequences of ageing, whereas geriatrics is a medical speciality that focuses on the care and treatment of the elderly. Despite their differences, gerontology and geriatrics share the goal of understanding ageing in order to improve individual functioning and promote a high quality of life.

Social Psychology of Ageing

Most people believe that the physiological process of inevitable decrease in ageing is the only explanation for the ageing process. Even when the term "ageing" is used by laypeople or biological gerontologists, it typically refers to the gradual decline that occurs during the adult stage of life (Masoro, 2005). Consequently, a psychological perspective on ageing is necessary, including the ageing self, the study of power, age stereotypes, self-perception of ageing, attitude towards ageing, proactive ageing etc.

Ageing Self

The term **"ageing self"** describes individual beliefs about one's own ageing process that are shaped by one's socio-cultural background (Westerhof & Tulle, 2007). A process that is connected to but separate from people's ideas about their social relationships (social self), psychological traits (personal identity), and bodies (physical self).

One of the most researched aspects of the ageing self is youthful age identity, which is defined as feeling younger than one's actual age (Westerhof & Barrett, 2005). Better mental and physical health are associated with a more youthful age identity (Barak & Stern, 1986). Westerhof and Barrett (2005) investigated the relationship of age identity and subjective well-being in United States and Germany. Even after controlling for socio-demographic variables, analyses of the pooled sample show that feeling younger than one's actual age is associated with higher levels of life satisfaction, positive effect, and lower levels of negative effect. However, only in the United States does the relationship between age identity and negative effect hold valid. In the United States, age identities play a role in a broader range of psychosocial adaptations. Having a youthful age identity also predicts better cognitive and physical functioning and even longevity (Demakakos, Gjonca & Nazroo, 2007; Schafer & Shippee, 2010).

The ageing self, like the ageing process, has multiple dimensions and directions. In the German and Dutch Ageing Surveys, two nationally representative studies of the second half of life, the personal experience of ageing was divided into three dimensions: physical decline, social loss, and psychological growth (Steverink, Westerhof, Bode & Dittmann-Kohli, 2001). These three dimensions had varied implications for personal and societal resources, such as education, social relationships, and health.

Identity Process Theory (IPT), Whitbourne (1986) states that people use three identity processes to navigate new experiences related to ageing as they grow older. These are—*identity assimilation, identity accommodation,* and *identity balance.*

Adults attempt to maintain a sense of continuity of the self over time through "*identity assimilation*", which involves interpreting identity salient experiences in terms of previously established cognitive and affective schemas about the self. The second identity process, "*identity accommodation*", involves a change in identity in response to discrepant new experiences.

Individuals perceive themselves differently when confronted with situations that contradict their current sense of self. The third identity phase, "*identity balance*", involves individuals changing their identities to absorb age-related experiences while maintaining a consistent image of themselves. As kids get older, they can reflect and judge themselves more realistically.

Youthful age identities as well as ageing experiences can be further explored using social-cognitive theories of the self. According to these ideas, cognitive processing of information about oneself is biased and motivated by self-enhancement, or the desire to maintain or improve self-esteem. However, ageing people's self-esteem is under attack in a culture that places a high priority on youth at the price of old age (Gana, Alaphilippe & Bailly; 2004; Westerhof, Barrett & Steverink, 2003).

Concept of Social Power

Power is a fundamental force in social interactions (Fiske, 1993). Social psychologists have shown that perceptions of social power influence cognitive and social psychological outcomes such as attention, emotion, self-regulation, and social cognition. An important development in the field of social psychology of ageing is the idea of power. Relationships in the family, among peers, and in educational settings are shaped by power dynamics. Relationships between and among social groupings, such as those based on gender, race, and social standing, are also characterized by power (Sidanius & Pratto, 1999).

French and Raven (1959) put forward one of the earliest significant theories of power. Their *social power theory* states that power is the ability to influence someone, whether that person is a love partner, a coworker, a friend, a stranger, or a casual acquaintance. The most important contribution of French and Raven's (1959) theory was the specification of six major bases (sources) of power. These are—reward, coercive, legitimate, referent, expert, informational.

According to Dowd (1975), the difficulties that are linked with getting older appear to be the result of a decrease in the power resources that older people possess. The field experiment conducted by Langer and Rodin (1976) on elderly individuals residing in institutions suggests that the negative repercussions of ageing may be delayed, reversed, or potentially prevented by restoring the elderly with the ability to make decisions and a sense of competence.

The physical and mental health of older people is found to be significantly influenced by perceived choice and a sense of personal control. This viewpoint draws attention to the different ageing-related impairments that limit a person's ability to influence their surroundings. Numerous observational and correlational studies support this viewpoint by indicating that a decrease in personal autonomy may be a factor in some of the negative outcomes seen in the elderly population, particularly among those living in institutions (Schulz, 1976, 1978).

Schulz (1976) proposed that loss of control and diminished environmental predictability are at least partially responsible for some of the traits commonly seen in the institutionalized elderly, including emotions of helplessness and depression as well as rapid physical decline.

Seale's (1996) study of community caregivers and senior people who lived alone in their last year of life found that older people who did not want to be watched or helped by neighbours was seen as a way for them to avoid going to a nursing home. According to the author, this opposition resulted in "social" death and the end of the autonomy effort.

When Clark (1972) studied older Americans in San Francisco, she found similar attitudes concerning dependency. The anxiety of actual or imminent dependency—whether it be physical, social, emotional, or economic—was profoundly embedded. According to her research, there is a nearly phobic fear of any kind of dependency.

Ageism

Discrimination against people on the basis of their age is known as *ageism*. It is common but mostly disregarded. The term ageism was originally used by Robert Butler, the first Director of the National Institute of Ageing, in 1969. He compared it to racism and sexism, calling it systemic stereotyping and prejudice against the elderly. It is now any prejudice or discrimination against or in favour of any age group. The stereotypes that underlie ageism's widespread occurrence are so ingrained in our conceptions of human existence that they are no longer questioned and are now considered unquestionable implicit assumptions. This is made worse by society's acceptance of discriminatory behaviours that continue to exist in all spheres of life. All facets of public and professional life are impacted by the fear of ageing and the numerous biases against older men and women.

Thornton (2002) discussed the potency of ageing myths and how they stereotype older individuals. Progressive physical and mental degeneration, social isolation, asexuality, lack of inventiveness, and economic and familial stress are prevalent fallacies. Older individuals are often dubbed dependent liabilities, a social concern centred on dependency and prevention.

According to Tornstam (1992), these stereotypical views are a result of profoundly ingrained value patterns in Western culture (which is now accepted in several eastern cultures including India) which are marked by a strong performance orientation that honours independence and economic production. They create an "unconscious overflow" of presumptions and values regarding the life of senior citizens.

Ageism permeates social structures like the workplace, government agencies, bureaucracy, and the healthcare system. The effects of ageism on studies, policies, programmes, and legislation pertaining to the elderly can be far-reaching and far more subtle than the more overt forms of prejudice against the elderly. Some of the most serious issues that older people face may have their origins in unfavourable and frequently ageist attitudes, according to gerontologists.

Cognitive Gerontology and Cognitive Development in Old Age

Cognitive Gerontology denotes the scientific study of the processes commonly referred to as "cognitive ageing" in describing the phenomena under investigation. A basic concept of successful ageing must include successful cognitive functioning as a prerequisite for cognitive gerontology to play a role.

Recognizing that cognitive functioning is shaped by both biological and cultural processes, research on successful ageing has identified two primary categories of intellectual abilities: the mechanics and pragmatics of cognition (Baltes, 1987; Baltes, Lindenberger & Staudinger, 1998; Baltes, Staudinger & Lindenberger, 1999).

The mostly neurophysiological substrate of cognition as it developed during biological evolution is metaphorically represented by the *mechanics of cognition*. In a sense, they are the mental hardware, and this is demonstrated by the speed, precision, and synchronization of fundamental information processing functions.

The *pragmatics of cognition*, in contrast, comprise the culturally transmitted bodies of knowledge individuals acquire in the course of their socialization. They stand for the software of the mind. Typical examples of pragmatic abilities include reading, writing, language, or professional skills.

The pragmatics and mechanics of cognitive functioning are divided; however, this does not imply that they are mutually exclusive or distinct abilities. Rather, it is thought that intellectual functioning is determined by the relationship between pragmatics and mechanics. Pragmatics wouldn't exist without mechanics, and mechanics wouldn't have a platform to grow without pragmatics.

The question arises regarding the development of these two components of intellectual functioning throughout the lifespan into old age. Empirical evidence indicates that cognitive mechanics, such as memory and processing speed, exhibit rapid growth during infancy and childhood, followed by a monotonic and approximately linear decline in adulthood, with an accelerated decline in very old age (Kail, 1991; Kail & Salthouse, 1994; Lindenberger & Reischies, 2001; Schaie, Willis & Caskie, 2004). Targeted training may alleviate the decline in cognitive mechanics. Research indicates that most healthy older adults can enhance their performance in tasks involving mechanical skills through training (e.g. Baltes, Sowarka & Kliegl, 1989; Schaie, Willis & Caskie, 2004; Zhang, *et al.*, 2021). The training gains are notably task-specific.

It is doubtful that relevant abilities or everyday functioning are transferred in humans and lay their impact in general and in particular as per needs of the situations (P.B. Baltes, Dittmann-Kohli & Kliegl, 1986; Baltes & Lindenberger, 1988). Das and Steyvers (2023) examined 9,923 online cognitive training platform users aged 18–90, with 63 per cent over 60, who performed a variety of cognitive activities. They tested an older adult's ability to perform like a younger one. They found that engaging in various cognitive training exercises increases the likelihood of overtaking a much younger person. The results suggest that further training may reduce ageing-related performance impairments.

Age decreases cognitive mechanical plasticity (i.e., spectrum of potential change). Mechanistic skills have a shorter lifespan than pragmatic skills. They remain stable or increase until about 75 years old, then decline, but less than cognitive mechanics. As indicated, mechanics and pragmatics affect cognitive function across all ages.

A plausible conclusion is that evidence indicates the physiologically rooted cognitive processes deteriorate with age. Some of this change can be compensated for by cognitive pragmatics grounded in information and influenced by culture. The majority of elderly individuals can manage the challenges encountered in their daily lives without experiencing mental issues. Conversely, when an individual is advanced in age, they perceive a somewhat altered perspective. Should this occur, there is a possibility that cognitive mechanisms may get compromised, hence diminishing intellectual functioning across several domains. This increase is seen in the cognitive alterations associated with ageing. The prevalence of dementia is markedly increasing with advancing age. Numerous studies indicate that the incidence of dementia in individuals over 60 nearly doubles every five years of age. The condition is believed to impact about forty per cent of individuals aged ninety and beyond.

Personality Development in Old Age

Throughout the life course, social roles, life events, and social environments undergo transformations, and these elements have been posited as significant determinants of fundamental personality traits (Hogan, 1996). A growing body of research suggests that personality development continues into old age and into adulthood, defying the notion that personality stabilizes after young adulthood (McCrae & Costa

2008; Donnellan & Lucas, 2008; Roberts & Mroczek, 2008; Staudinger & Kunzmann, 2005). The work environment is considered a vital factor influencing adult personality development, as individuals learn and adapt to the demands of their professional lives. The job setting cultivates adult behaviour by requiring specific traits and actions, such as the diligent execution of tasks, an awareness of the needs of others, and the mitigation of social discord.

Research regarding alterations in adult personality suggests that differentiating between the two pathways of positive evolution—personality adjustment and personality growth—has proven advantageous (Hogan & Roberts, 2004; Staudinger & Bowen, 2010; Kessler & Staudinger, 2009; Staudinger & Kunzmann, 2005).

The concept of "personality adjustment" pertains to an individual's capacity to effectively navigate and adapt to their distinct developmental circumstances, which may fluctuate with age, context, and various other influences (Kessler & Staudinger, 2009). Positive emotional intelligence, agreeableness, conscientiousness, and neuroticism are indicators of successful social adaptation and personal fulfilment (Costa & McCrae, 1995), and are indicators of personality adjustment.

A person's capacity to regulate their emotions (their level of affective differentiation, their tolerance for the coactivation of happy and negative emotions), their insight into themselves and the world around them, and their drive to improve their own and others' well-being are all aspects of personality development. This acknowledges that developing a positive personality extends beyond subjective experiences of well-being and practical skills (Staudinger & Kessler, 2009). The openness to new experiences dimension of the Big Five predicts personality development because it shows a person's desire to seek out unique, demanding situations that are more likely to expose them to new ideas, which can change their current understanding of who they are and how they fit into the world.

The life cycle was examined Neugarten (1968), who concentrated on the timeliness of professional and life transitions. Parenting and marriage are examples of normatively scheduled life events, with cultural expectations that they should occur at specific ages and in a specific order. As a result, identity and self-concept undergo modifications. Unexpected events (like accidents) or age-normative events that are "off time" (like early widowhood) can result in negative developmental outcomes, such life crises.

Hans Thomae (1970) outlined a cognitive theory of the ageing personality, with an emphasis on the psychodynamics of ageing. It seeks to incorporate various perspectives on ageing from the disciplines of biology, sociology, and interactionism. His thesis is based on the key concepts of vision, one's perception of one's surroundings, and one's sense of oneself. Lars Tornstam (1989) proposed that human ageing contains an inherent potential for gero transcendence, characterized by a transition in perspective from a materialistic and rational approach to a more cosmic and transcendent view, frequently linked to heightened life satisfaction. Tornstam (1992) established the theoretical framework of gero transcendence, encompassing three levels of age-related ontological transformation. (1) *Cosmic level* which is defined as the changes in time, space, and objects; increased connection with past and future generations; changes in life comprehension; less dread of death; acceptance of life's mysteries; and improved cosmic connection with the universe's spirit; (2) *Self-revelation* is the process of revealing previously hidden aspects of oneself, including both positive and negative aspects. It involves achieving ego integrity, reducing self-centredness, shifting from egoism to benevolence, and reconnecting with the inner child; and (3) *Social and individual relations* exhibit a reduced interest in superficial connections, accompanied by an increased need for solitude.

Schroots (1995) presented a succinct summary of a dynamic systems theory of ageing, referred to as gerodynamics. This idea is basically based on the bifurcation or branching behaviour of individuals across biological, psychological, or social levels of functioning.

Social Relationships in Old Age

Globally, social networks and familial ties provide older people with chances for engagement and assistance (Berkman, 2000; Bloom *et al.*, 2010; Bongaarts & Zimmer, 2002). The three main goals of social interactions are support, affectionate connections, and socializing, which means interacting with others and doing things with other people (Suragarn, Hain & Pfaff, 2021). The network offers financial, instrumental, emotional, and evaluative help, among other forms of assistance. Recognizing that social networks may encompass both beneficial and detrimental interactions is essential, as they can significantly impact health (Berkman, 2009; Berkman & Glass, 2000; Seeman *et al.*, 2001). Lack of social connection is a predictor of premature mortality, similar to many of the most important health indicators, according to a large body of scientific research (Suragarn, Hain & Pfaff, 2021).

The significance of social support relationships tends to increase with age, yet the essence of social engagement remains deeply rooted in emotional exchange and interpersonal interaction. The amalgamation of caregiving responsibilities for both elderly and younger family members will present challenges for individuals of all genders across numerous countries, particularly as an increasing number of women participate in the paid labourmarket (Budlender, 2008; Das *et al.*, 2010; Sabates-Wheeler & Roelen, 2011).

The anticipated rise from 11 to 28 in the ratio of adults aged 65 and older per 100 individuals aged 20–64 in Asia (excluding the Near East) is reflected in the changing elder dependency ratios across worldwide regions for the years 2000, 2020, and 2040 (United Nations, 2008). India serves as an example of this phenomenon. Both the formal and informal sectors must have a thorough understanding of the social and familial dynamics of older people in India in order to effectively plan for and improve the productivity, well-being, and health of the country's expanding senior citizen and family population. In India, most older men and women live with their families, which is the preferred living arrangement for this demographic (Gupta, 2009). Families continue to serve as the fundamental unit for economic support and caregiving for individuals who are physically unable to care for themselves (Kozel & Parker, 2000; Samuel & Thyloth, 2002). Bloom *et al.* (2010) states that the elderly in India often get substantial informal social support from their families, which is a highly esteemed tradition.

Despite the fact that social networks consisting of family and friends are an essential resource for older folks, there is a paucity of study about the influence that these networks have on the physical and mental health of individuals in India. According to Lloyd-Sherlock (2002), the shifting dynamics of family structures, intergenerational links, and the duties that women have in families have the potential to have a significant impact on the care and well-being of young adults and senior citizens. In certain circumstances, families living in the 21st century may be unable to meet the requirements of older members of their household, which may lead the examination of alternative support services. The National Policy on Older Persons in India, published by the Government of India in 1999, remains pertinent and applicable. It underscores the importance of developing programmes aimed at fostering familial values and enhancing young people's understanding of the significance and advantages of intergenerational relationships and continuity (Panruti, Liebig & Duvvuru, 2015).

Ageing and Well-being

Existence of different functional links between age and well-being has been demonstrated through empirical research. In addition to U-shaped and inverted U-shaped correlations, linear and cubic correlations, and even a total lack of link, the results include all of these. According to the findings of research, subjective well-being begins to drop in early adulthood and reaches its lowest point between the ages of 45 and 55. Following that, it begins to rise (Blanchflower & Oswald, 2008; Graham & Ruiz Pozuelo, 2017).

Gerontology has done a lot of research on the cognitive and emotional components of psychological well-being. The expected drop in subjective well-being that comes with getting older comes from the fact that older people tend to lose more important things than younger people. Unfortunately, older people often have trouble in finding useful jobs, their health and physical abilities get worse, and they run the risk of losing important social links. A lot of people in society think that getting old means losing things instead of gaining them. It is fair to think that older people will sometimes be unhappy and dissatisfied with their lives.

The assessment of health-related quality of life is becoming progressively prominent in health-care research, especially concerning patient management, policy formulation, and the allocation of resources (Hoi, Chuc & Lindholm, 2010). It has been found that individuals' perception of their own health, perceived ability to manage financially, perception of poverty over time, and feelings of loneliness were found as important determinants of the quality of life of people aged 60 and more. Quality of life and healthcare for elderly are upcoming issues in developing countries (Dongre, Rajendran, Kumar & Deshmukh, 2012).

Researchers looked at 4034 Germans between the ages of 40 and 85 to see how getting older changes their resources and subjective well-being. As people got older, they had to deal with physical decline, growth, and social loss. There was a link between getting better and less physical and social decline and being younger, having better health, making more money, being less lonely, having more education, and having hope. It did not matter how many children there were. All three parts of ageing were linked to both good and bad moods and life happiness, except for physical decline (Steverink *et al.*, 2001).

The Psycho-social Dynamics of Ageing Women

Because of advancements in medicine and public health initiatives that have reduced mortality rates and increased lifespans, the ageing population is seen as a sign of the success of human civilization. Women tend to be more closely identified with the experience of ageing. Cultures and countries around the world are rapidly ageing, and the "feminization of ageing" phenomenon is becoming more and more noticeable. Research on ageing has been criticized for failing to consider women's perspectives (Calasanti, 2010; Settersten & Godlewski, 2016). It is crucial to concentrate on the reasons and ways that women's experiences of ageing may differ from men's due to traditional (gendered) work/family responsibilities and cultural disparities in expectations for how women should age.

For numerous females, advanced age is not regarded as a valued phase of life. Over seventy-five per cent of elderly women globally experience ageing characterized by heightened illness, frailty, dependency, despondency, sorrow, and alienation. India is home to over 90 million elderly women. Women aged 50–60 who have experienced poverty, illiteracy, chronic malnutrition, and learned helplessness may face old age characterized by loneliness, alienation, powerlessness, inadequate assets and resources, marginalization, and social isolation.

Recent researches point out the utility of a narrative approach to unpack how women experience later life (O'Neill & Schrage-Früh, 2019; Quéniart & Charpentier, 2012; Russell, 2007). Thus, qualitative responses to open-ended questions that contain psychosocial themes may be particularly pertinent to the analysis of women's experiences of ageing.

Developments in Research, Education and Training

Subsequent to the initial investigations conducted in the late 1950s and early 1960s, which focused on behavioural and social sciences (Ramamurti, 2013), the extent and intensity of ageing research in India have notably increased since the 1980s and continue to evolve today. Research output is currently classified into four primary categories: medical, biological, behavioural, and social studies (Ramamurti & Jamuna, 2010).

Medical/Geriatric Research

Research on morbidity in the elderly population began with a focus on hospital settings, initiated by Pathak's study in 1978 at Bombay Hospitals.

Following the comprehensive studies by Venkoba Rao (Rao, 1993, 1997, 1998; Rao & Madhavan, 1983) at Rajaji Hospital in Madurai, research focused on physical and psychological morbidity, specifically addressing mental health, depression, and suicide in the elderly population. During this foundational period, Rao led the first Task Force on Ageing of the Indian Council of Medical Research (ICMR; Rao, 1997). Natarajan set up a special inpatient ward for senior patients at the Government General Hospital in Madras in 1988. Vinod Kumar opened an outpatient clinic for the elderly at the All-India Institute of Medical Sciences in New Delhi in 1996.

Diabetes, hypertension, arthritis, and other chronic diseases and impairments were the subjects of Medical Research. These fields have grown since 2009-10, when the ICMR allocated more funds to individual research initiatives in gero psychology and geriatrics.

Biological Gerontology

At Banaras Hindu University (BHU) in Varanasi, Kanungo and associates led pioneering research in the area of Biochemistry of ageing in the late 1960s. He had developed a model of ageing. The model takes into account two main characteristics of ageing: (1) deterioration of adaptability of an organism to environment after maturity, and (2) determination of life span of a species (Kanungo, 1975). The decline in the activities of various organs, which manifests as deterioration or ageing of functions, is a universal phenomenon observed in all organisms following the attainment of reproductive capability (Kanungo, Gupta & Upadhyay, 1998). Dr. Kanungo founded the Association of Gerontology (India) in 1981.

By creating an amnesic mouse model to examine the effects of Aswagandha plant leaf extract and the activity of estrogen coregulator molecules on brain function, specifically memory, Thakur and colleagues at BHU have carried on this line of inquiry (Gautam, Kaul & Thakur, 2016; Konar & Thakur, 2017).

Social and Behavioural Gerontology

The field of gerontological research has evolved to encompass aspects of welfare, economics, and demography since its inception in India. Ramamurti and Jamuna (2010) conducted a thorough analysis of these developments, particularly within the realm of behavioural sciences. India's first research centre dedicated to ageing was established in 1983 within the Department of Psychology at Sri Venkateswara University (S.V. University) named as Centre for Research on Ageing (CEFRA). It has received funding from the University Grants Commission since 1990.

Since 1990, there has been a significant increase in social and behavioural research. Ramamurti, Jamuna, and their colleagues have concentrated on several key research areas, including metrics of successful ageing, assessments of disability and coping strategies, characteristics of centenarians, and the development of a conceptual framework for understanding ageing (Ramamurti & Jamuna, 2010). Additional focuses include gender ageing, mental health, and women's empowerment (Prakash, 2003); geriatric health and ageing (Raju, 2002, 2011, 2014; Ingle & Nath, 2008); advocacy and rights of the elderly population (Nayar, 2003); elder abuse in Indian families (Kumar & Bhargava, 2014), sociological perspectives on elder abuse (Shankardas, 2013), older women vulnerabilities (Kaushik, 2021), social exclusion of the Elderly in India (Pandey, 2022), institutionalized elderly women-issues (Vincent & Noronha, 2019), the anthropometry of the elderly, female ageing, and health (Bagga, 2013); employment and social security for elderly (Mathew & Rajan, 2008; Rajan, 2014), old age poverty (Kidd & Whitehouse, 2009). are to name a few significant areas of research.

Education and Training

The progression of gerontological education has been less vigorous compared to the advancement of research. The inaugural graduate course in gerontology was established in 1976 by the Department of Psychology at S.V. University, serving as an applied discipline of psychology at both the master's and doctorate tiers.

Notwithstanding these initial developments, the growth of gerontology as a specialization in higher education has been gradual. In 2000, the Government of India proposed that universities and other educational institutions provide courses on ageing to support the National Policy on Older Persons. Numerous universities offer master's and doctoral programmes in psychology, social work, anthropology, and home science.

Increasing biological research has led to geriatric clinical care training modules for various health providers. The National Programme for Health Care of the Elderly (NPHCE) was created in 2011 to create a multilevel, intergovernmental organization for senior care.

Non-governmental organizations have significantly contributed to the implementation of national policy through research and the provision of diverse services for the elderly population. HelpAge India, the largest organization of its kind, was established in 1978 (www.helpageindia.org). It o perates branches across the nation, collecting data and providing various programmes, including senior care facilities, daycare centres, health clinics, and educational services. The Alzheimer's and Related Disorders Society of India (ARDSI), established in 1991, now comprises numerous local chapters. ARDSI has concentrated on multiple facets of dementia awareness and care (www.alzheimerindia.org) and offers data regarding the prevalence of dementia in India.

Other NGOs providing education and care are located in several major cities. They include the Centre for Gerontological Studies in Trivandrum, The Calcutta Metropolitan Institute of Gerontology, The Heritage Hospitals and Foundation, Hyderabad, the International Longevity Centre, Pune to name a few. Additionally, a large number of local NGOs serve elders by organizing programmes on their rights, healthcare, and legal aid.

Qualitative Research

The qualitative research offers significant advantages that can aid researchers in understanding the perspectives and behaviours of elderly individuals in their daily lives, while also providing access to the voices of those who are often overlooked. Within social gerontology, research using qualitative methods has provided important insights into a range of topics. In the field of social gerontology, qualitative research has yielded significant insights into various subjects, including qualitative longitudinal research on ageism (Keskinen & Nikander, 2023), discourses of ageing through participation on TikTok (Ng & Indran, 2022), why people with dementia use Twitter and what challenges they face (Talbot, O'Dwyer, Clare & Heaton, 2021), how older adults make sense of their sedentary behaviour (Palmer *et al.*, 2021), how older adults experience and describe health, participation, and security (Wongsala, Anbäcken & Rosendahl, 2021), older adults' experiences of sexual difficulties (Hinchliff, Tetley, Lee & Nazroo, 2018), exploration of retirement transition and preparation experiences (Moffatt & Heaven, 2017), among others significant repository of knowledge through various methodologies of qualitative research. These studies exhibit a wide range of research designs (e.g. entirely qualitative, mixed method, cross-sectional, longitudinal), data collection techniques [e.g. in-depth interviews (in person and by telephone)], participant observation, participant-produced photographs, photo elicitation etc., however, in recent years, a growing number of novel and contemporary methods have been developed and refined.

Social interaction in modern digital communication contexts, such as online discussion forums, comments, and their replies on social media platforms like Instagram, Facebook, and Twitter, can be better understood through the use of an online research methodology called "netnography" (Kozinets & Gretzel, 2023). This approach is useful because it allows us to study the interaction between humans and machines, which is particularly relevant given the growing number of elderly people using smartphones and the internet.

Moller, Clarke, Braun, Tischner, and Vossler (2021) used the Qualitative story completion (SC) research which is a new approach to a technique with roots in quantitative and clinical evaluation, focusing on how individuals engage to a researcher-designed story "stem". Story completion differs from conventional qualitative methods, which typically involve participants directly reporting their attitudes, beliefs, experiences, and behaviours. It encourages a contrasting method by prompting participants to finish the opening lines of a narrative (or "stimulus"), which serve as the entry point into a plot. For instance, requesting older adults, their companions, and healthcare providers to construct a narrative based on introductory lines related to sexuality, end-of-life care, or grandparenting can significantly enhance our comprehension of these sensitive subjects.

The social scientific understanding of the processes of ageing can be improved by the use of qualitative research, which provides useful insights.

Conclusion: The Emerging Discourse of Ageing Well

Social and cultural perceptions that designate the elderly as a "burden", along with instances of elder abuse and insufficient safety protocols, significantly heighten the susceptibility of older persons. The Government of India has implemented numerous progressive and inclusive policies, programmes, and initiatives. These encompass the National Programme for Health Care of the Elderly (NPHCE), the National Social Assistance Programme (NSAP), the Maintenance and Welfare of Senior Citizens Act of 2007 and its Amendment Bill, the Atal Vayo Abhyuday Yojana (AVYAY), and Elderline, a national helpline, among others.

India possesses the largest population of youth; however, the process of ageing is advancing swiftly. The elderly population, currently at 153 million individuals aged 60 and above, is projected to increase to 347 million by the year 2050. This demographic shift represents a significant societal transformation with extensive implications, affecting health systems, labour and financial markets, social protection, and education, among other areas. Currently, we are experiencing a shift towards reducing dependency-related morbidity by promoting "healthy ageing". This is an opportune moment for Indian gerontologists and geriatrics to not only concentrate on harnessing the advantages of its substantial youth demographic but also to adopt the notion of "Silver Dividend" and can redefine the narrative from one of demographic challenge to demographic resilience, inclusivity and growth. Future researches can focus on successful ageing, assisted ageing, productive ageing, the phenomena of "feminization of ageing" and so on through the transformative, multifaceted approach, engaging supportive institutions including the private sector, academia, civil society, and media.

References

Bagga, A. (2013). "Age Changes in Some Linear Measurements and Secular Trend in Height in Adult Indian Women". *Acta Biologica Szegediensis*, *57*(1): 51-58.

Baltes, P.B. (1987). "Theoretical Propositions of Life-Span Developmental Psychology: On the Dynamics Between Growth and Decline". *Developmental Psychology*, *23*(5): 611.

Baltes, P.B. & Lindenberger, U. (1988). "On the Range of Cognitive Plasticity in Old Age as a Function of Experience: 15 Years of Intervention Research". *Behaviour Therapy*, *19*(3): 283-300.

Baltes, P.B., Lindenberger, U. & Staudinger, U.M. (1998). "Life-span Theory in Developmental Psychology". In *Handbook of Child Psychology* (pp. 1029-1143). Wiley.

Baltes, P.B., Sowarka, D. & Kliegl, R. (1989). "Cognitive Training Research on Fluid Intelligence in Old Age: What Can Older Adults Achieve by Themselves?" *Psychology and Ageing*, *4*(2): 217.

Baltes, P.B., Staudinger, U.M. & Lindenberger, U. (1999). "Lifespan Psychology: Theory and Application to Intellectual Functioning". *Annual Review of Psychology*, *50*(1): 471-507.

Barak, B. & Stern, B. (1986). "Subjective Age Correlates: A Research Note". *The Gerontologist*, *26*(5): 571-578.

Berkman, L.F. (2000). "Social Support, Social Networks, Social Cohesion and Health". *Social Work in Health Care*, *31*(2): 3-14.

______(2009). "Social Epidemiology: Social Determinants of Health in the United States". *Annual Review of Public Health*, *30*(30): 27-41.

Berkman, L.F. & Glass, T.A. (2000). "Social Integration, Social Networks, Social Support and Health". In Berkman, L.F., and Kawachi, I., (ed.) *Social Epidemiology*. New York: Oxford University Press.

Blanchflower, D.G. & Oswald, A.J. (2008). "Is well-being U-shaped Over the Life Cycle?". *Social Science & Medicine*, *66*(8): 1733-1749.

Bloom, D.E., Mahal, A., Rosenberg, L. & Sevilla, J. (2010). "Economic Security Arrangements in the Context of Population Ageing in India". *International Social Security Review*, *63*(3-4): 59-89.

Bongaarts, J. & Zimmer, Z. (2002). "Living Arrangements of Older Adults in the Developing World". The *Journals of Gerontology Series B: Psychological Sciences and Social Sciences*, *57*(3): S145-S157.

Budlender, D. (2008). *The Statistical Evidence on Care and Non-Care Work across Six Countries*. 4. Geneva: National Research Institute for Social Development.

Calasanti, T. (2010). "Gender Relations and Applied Research on Ageing". *The Gerontologist*, *50*(6): 720-734.

Clark, M. (1972). "Cultural Values and Dependency in Later Life". In D.O. Cowgill & L.D. Holmes (Eds.): *Ageing and Modernization* (pp. 263-274). Norwalk, CT: Appleton-Century-Crofts.

Costa Jr, P.T. & McCrae, R.R. (1995). "Domains and Facets: Hierarchical Personality Assessment Using the Revised NEO Personality Inventory". *Journal of Personality Assessment*, *64*(1): 21-50.

Das, P. & Steyvers, M. (2023). "Older Adults Catch Up to Younger Adults on Cognitive Tasks After Extended Training". *Collabra: Psychology*, *9*(1).

Das, S., Hazra, A., Ray, B.K., Ghosal, M., Banerjee, T.K., Roy, T. & Chaudhuri, A., *et al.* (2010). "Burden among Stroke Caregivers: Results of a Community-based Study from Kolkata, India". *Stroke*, *41*(12): 2,965-2,968.

Demakakos, P., Gjonca, E. & Nazroo, J. (2007). "Age Identity, Age Perceptions, and Health: Evidence from the English Longitudinal Study of Ageing". *Annals of the New York Academy of Sciences*, *1114*(1): 279-287.

Dongre, A.R., Rajendran, K.P., Kumar, S. & Deshmukh, P.R. (2012). "The Effect of Community-Managed Palliative Care Programme on Quality of Life in the Elderly in Rural Tamil Nadu, India". *Indian Journal of Palliative Care*, *18*(3): 219.

Donnellan, M.B. & Lucas, R.E. (2008). "Age Differences in the Big Five Across the Life Span: Evidence from Two National Samples". *Psychology and Ageing*, *23*(3): 558.

Dowd, J.J. (1975). "Ageing as Exchange: A Preface to Theory". *Journal of Gerontology*, *30*(5): 584-594.

Fiske, S.T. (1993). "Controlling Other People: The Impact of Power on Stereotyping". *American Psychologist*, *48*: 621-628.

French, J.R.P., Jr. & Raven, B.H. (1959). "The Bases of Social Power". In D. Cartwright (Ed.): *Studies in Social Power* (pp. 150-167). Ann Arbor: University of Michigan Press.

Gana, K., Alaphilippe, D. & Bailly, N. (2004). "Positive Illusions and Mental and Physical Health in Later Life". *Ageing & Mental Health*, *8*(1): 58-64.

Gautam, A., Kaul, S.C. & Thakur, M.K. (2016). "Alcoholic Extract of Ashwagandha Leaves Protects Against Amnesia by Regulation of Arc Function". *Molecular Neurobiology*, *53*, 1760-1769.

Glenn, S.G. & Goel, A. (2023). "Medical Gerontology: Growth, Scope and Provisions in India". *Journal of the Indian Academy of Geriatrics*, *19*(3): 181.

Government of India (1999). *National Policy for Older Persons*. New Delhi: Ministry of Social Justice and Empowerment.

Graham, C. & Ruiz Pozuelo, J. (2017). "Happiness, Stress, and Age: How the U Curve Varies Across People and Places". *Journal of Population Economics*, *30*: 225-264.

Gupta, R. (2009). "Systems Perspective: Understanding Care Giving of the Elderly in India". *Health Care for Women International,* 30(12): 1,040-1,054.

Hinchliff, S., Tetley, J., Lee, D. & Nazroo, J. (2018). "Older Adults' Experiences of Sexual Difficulties: Qualitative Findings from the English Longitudinal Study on Ageing (ELSA)". *The Journal of Sex Research*, *55*(2): 152-163.

Hogan, R. (1996). "A Socio-analytic Perspective on the Five-factor Model". In J.S. Wiggins (Ed.): *The Five-factor Model of Personality: Theoretical Perspectives* (pp. 163-179). Guilford Press.

Hogan, R. & Roberts, B.W. (2004). "A Socio-analytic Model of Maturity". *Journal of Career Assessment*, *12*(2): 207-217.

Hoi, LV., Chuc, N.T. & Lindholm, L. (2010). "Health-related Quality of Life, and Its Determinants, among Older People in Rural Vietnam". *BMC Public Health*, *10*: 1-10.

Ingle, G.K. & Nath, A. (2008). "Geriatric Health in India: Concerns and Solutions". *Indian Journal of Community Medicine*, *33*(4): 214-218.

Kail, R. (1991). "Developmental Change in Speed of Processing During Childhood and Adolescence". *Psychological Bulletin*, *109*(3): 490.

Kail, R. & Salthouse, T.A. (1994). "Processing Speed as a Mental Capacity". *Acta Psychologica*, *86*(2-3): 199-225.

Keskinen, K. & Nikander, P. (2023). "Researching Time and Ageism: Applications of Qualitative Longitudinal Research to the Field". *Journal of Applied Gerontology*, *42*(6): 1335-1344.

Kessler, E.M. & Staudinger, U.M. (2009). "Affective Experience in Adulthood and Old Age: The Role of Affective Arousal and Perceived Affect Regulation". *Psychology and Ageing*, *24*(2): 349.

Kidd, S. & Whitehouse, E. (2009). "Pensions and Old Age Poverty". Holzmann, R., Robalino, D.A. and Takayama, N., *Closing the Coverage Gap: The Role of Social Pensions and Other Retirement Income Transfers*, World Bank.

Konar, A. & Thakur, M.K. (2017). "Cellular and Molecular Targets Underpinning Memory Enhancement by Ashwagandha". *Science of Ashwagandha: Preventive and Therapeutic Potentials*, 305-318.

Kozel, V. & Parker, B. (2000). "Integrated Approaches to Poverty Assessment in India". In Bamberger, M., (eds.) *Integrating Quantitative and Qualitative Research in Development Projects.* Washington, DC: World Bank.

Kanungo, M.S. (1975). "A Model for Ageing". *Journal of Theoretical Biology, 53*(2): 253-261.

Kanungo, M.S., Gupta, S. & Upadhyay, R. (1998). "Regulation of Gene Expression During Ageing". *Current Science*, 865-871.

Kaushik, A. (2021). "Older Women in India: Differential Vulnerabilities and Empowerment Interventions". *Older Women and Well-being: A Global Perspective*, 147-166.

Kozinets, R.V. & Gretzel, U. (2023). "Qualitative Social Media Methods: Netnography in the Age of Technocultures". *The Sage Handbook of Qualitative Research*, 403-420.

Kumar, Y. & Bhargava, A. (2014). "Elder Abuse in Indian Families: Problems and Preventive Actions". *International Journal of Scientific and Research Publications*, *4*(10): 1-8.

Langer, E.J. & Rodin, J. (1976). "The Effects of Choice and Enhanced Personal Responsibility for the Aged: A Field Experiment in An Institutional Setting". *Journal of Personality and Social Psychology*, *34*(2): 191.

Lindenberger, U. & Reischies, F.M. (2001). "Limits and Potentials of Intellectual Functioning in Old Age". In *the Berlin ageing study: Ageing from 70 to 100* (pp. 329-359). Cambridge University Press.

Lloyd-Sherlock, P. (2002). "Formal Social Protection for Older People in Developing Countries: Three Different Approaches". *Journal of Social Policy*, *31*(04): 695.

Mathew, E.T. & Rajan, S.I. (2008). "Employment as Old Age Security". *Institutional Provisions and Care for the Aged: Perspectives from Asia and Europe*, 68-82.

McCrae, R.R. & Costa, P.T. (2008). "Empirical and theoretical Status of the Five-Factor Model of Personality Traits". *The Sage Handbook of Personality Theory and Assessment*, *1*, 273-294.

Masoro, E.J. (2005). "Are Age-Associated Diseases An Integral Part of Ageing?" In *Handbook of the Biology of Ageing* (pp. 43-62). Academic Press.

Moffatt, S. & Heaven, B.E.N. (2017). "'Planning for Uncertainty': Narratives on Retirement Transition Experiences". *Ageing & Society*, *37*(5): 879-898.

Moller, N.P., Clarke, V., Braun, V., Tischner, I. & Vossler, A. (2021). "Qualitative Story Completion for Counselling Psychology Research: A Creative Method to Interrogate Dominant Discourses". *Journal of Counselling Psychology*, *68*(3): 286.

Nayar, P.K.B. (2003). "Advocacy and Policy". *An Ageing India: Perspectives, Prospects, and Policies*, *15*(2-3): 193.

Neugarten, B.L. (1968). "Adult personality: Toward a Psychology of the Life Cycle". *Middle Age and Ageing*, 137-147.

Ng, R. & Indran, N. (2022). "Not Too Old for Tiktok: How Older Adults Are Reframing Ageing". *The Gerontologist*, *62*(8): 1207-1216.

O'Neill, M. & Schrage-Früh, M. (2019). "Women and Ageing: Private Meaning, Social Lives". *Life Writing, 16*(1): 1-8.

Palmer, V.J., Gray, C.M., Fitzsimons, C., Mutrie, N., Wyke, S., Der, G.,. .. & Stewart, S. (2021). "Sitting as a Moral Practice: Older Adults' Accounts from Qualitative Interviews on Sedentary Behaviours". *Sociology of Health & Illness, 43*(9): 2102-2120.

Pandey, A.D. (2022). "Social Exclusion of the Elderly in India". In *Social Exclusion and Policies of Inclusion: Issues and Perspectives Across the Globe* (pp. 231-251). Singapore: Springer Nature Singapore.

Panruti, R.V., Liebig, P.S. & Duvvuru, J. (2015). "Gerontology in India". *The Gerontologist, 55*(6): 894-900.

Prakash, I.J. (2003). "Ageing, Disability, and Disabled Older People in India". *Journal of Ageing & Social Policy, 15*(2-3): 85-108.

Quéniart, A. & Charpentier, M. (2012). "Older Women and their Representations of Old Age: A Qualitative Analysis". *Ageing & Society, 32*(6): 983-1007.

Ramamurti, P. V. (2013). "Perspectives of Research on Ageing in India". In *An Ageing India* (pp. 31-43). Routledge.

Ramamurti, P.V. & Jamuna, D. (2010). "Geropsychology in India". *Psychology in India: Clinical and Health Psychology, 3*, 185-252.

Rajan, S.I. (2014). *Social Security for the Elderly: Experiences from South Asia.* Routledge.

Raju, S.S. (2002). "Health Status of the Urban Elderly: A Medico-social Study". New Delhi: B.R. Publishing Corporation.

_____ (2011). *Studies on Ageing in India.* Institute for Social and Economic Change, Bangalore United Nations Population Fund, New Delhi Institute of Economic Growth, Delhi.

_____ (2014). "Studies on Ageing in India: A Review". *Population Ageing in India, 180*: 226.

Rao, A.V. & Madhavan, T. (1983). "Depression and suicide behaviour in the aged". *Indian Journal of Psychiatry, 25*(4): 251-259.

Rao, A.V. (1993). "Psychiatry of Old Age in India". *International Review of Psychiatry, 5*(2-3): 165-170.

Rao, K.S. (1997). "DNA-damage & DNA-repair in Ageing Brain". *The Indian Journal of Medical Research, 106*, 423-437.

_____ (1998). "Non-apoptotic DNA Fragmentation: A Molecular Pointer of Ageing". *Current Science*, 894-901.

Roberts, B.W. & Mroczek, D. (2008). "Personality Trait Change in Adulthood". *Current Directions in Psychological Science, 17*(1): 31-35.

Russell, C. (2007). "What Do Older Women and Men Want? Gender Differences in the 'Lived Experience' of Ageing". *Current Sociology, 55*(2): 173-192.

Sabates-Wheeler R. & Roelen, K. (2011). "Transformative Social Protection Programming for Children and their Carers: A Gender Perspective". *Gender & Development, 19*(2): 179-194.

Samuel, M. & Thyloth, M. (2002). "Caregivers' Roles in India". *Psychiatric Services, 53*(3): 346-347.

Schafer, M.H. & Shippee, T.P. (2010). "Age Identity, Gender, and Perceptions of Decline: Does Feeling Older Lead to Pessimistic Dispositions About Cognitive Ageing?" *Journals of Gerontology Series B: Psychological Sciences and Social Sciences*, *65*(1): 91-96.

Schaie, K.W., Willis, S.L. & Caskie, G.I. (2004). "The Seattle Longitudinal Study: Relationship Between Personality and Cognition". *Ageing Neuropsychology and Cognition*, *11*(2-3): 304-324.

Schroots, J.J. (1995). "Gerodynamics: Toward a Branching Theory of Ageing". *Canadian Journal on Ageing/La Revue Canadienne du Vieillissement*, *14*(1): 74-81.

Schulz, R. (1976). "The Effects of Control and Predictability on the Psychological and Physical Well-being of the Institutionalized Aged". *Journal of Personality and Social Psychology*, 33, 563-573.

______ (1978). *The Pychology of Death, Dying, and Bereavement*. Reading, MA: Addison-Wesley.

Seale, C. (1996). "Living Alone Towards the End of Life". *Ageing and Society*, *16*: 75-91.

Seeman, T.E., Lusignolo, T.M., Albert, M. & Berkman, L. (2001). "Social Relationships, Social Support, and Patterns of Cognitive Ageing in Healthy, High-Functioning Older Adults: Macarthur Studies of Successful Ageing". *Health Psychology*, *20*(4): 243-255.

Settersten, R.A., Godlewski, B. & Bengtson, V.L. (2016). "Concepts and theories of Age and Ageing". *Handbook of Theories of Ageing*, *3*, 9-25.

Shankardass, M.K. (2013). "Addressing Elder Abuse: Review of Societal Responses in India and Selected Asian Countries". *International Psychogeriatrics*, *25*(8): 1229-1234.

Sidanius, J. & Pratto, F. (1999). "Social Dominance Theory". *Handbook of Theories of Social Psychology*, *2*.

Staudinger, U.M. & Kunzmann, U. (2005). "Positive Adult Personality Development: Adjustment and /Or Growth". *European Psychologist*, *10*(4): 320-329.

Staudinger, U.M. & Bowen, C.E. (2010). "Life-span Perspectives on Positive Personality Development in Adulthood and Old Age". *The Handbook of Life-span Development*. Wiley and Sons.

Steverink, N., Westerhof, G.J., Bode, C. & Dittmann-Kohli, F. (2001). "The Personal Experience of Ageing, Individual Resources, and Subjective Well-being". *The Journals of Gerontology Series B: Psychological Sciences and Social Sciences*, *56*(6): P364-P373.

Suragarn, U., Hain, D. & Pfaff, G. (2021). "Approaches to Enhance Social Connection in Older Adults: An Integrative Review of Literature". *Ageing and Health Research*, *1*(3): 100029.

Talbot, C.V., O'Dwyer, S.T., Clare, L. & Heaton, J. (2021). "The Use of Twitter by People with Young-onset Dementia: A Qualitative Analysis of Narratives and Identity Formation in the Age of Social Media". *Dementia*, *20*(7): 2542-2557.

Thomae, H. (1970). "Theory of Ageing and Cognitive Theory of Personality". *Human Development*, *13*(1): 1-16.

Thornton, J. (2002). "Myths of Ageing or Ageist Stereotypes". *Educational Gerontology*, *28*(4): 301-312.

Tornstam, L. (1989). "Gero-transcendencc: A Reformulation of the Disengagement Theory". *Ageing Clinical and Experimental Research*, *1*, 55-63.

______(1992). "The Quo Vadis of Gerontology: On the Scientific Paradigm of Gerontology". *The Gerontologist*, 32, 318-326.

United Nations. World Population Prospects: The 2008 Revision Population Database. Medium Variant Projections. 2008. Available: http://esa.un.org/unpp/

Vincent, P. & Noronha, L. (2019). "Institutionalized Elderly Women—Issues & Concerns". *International Journal of Health Sciences and Pharmacy* (*IJHSP*): *ISSN*, 2581-6411.

Westerhof, G.J. & Barrett, A.E. (2005). "Age Identity and Subjective Well-being: A Comparison of the United States and Germany". *The Journals of Gerontology Series B: Psychological Sciences and Social Sciences*, *60*(3): S129-S136.

Westerhof, G.J., Barrett, A.E. & Steverink, N. (2003). "Forever Young? A Comparison of Age Identities in the United States and Germany". *Research on Ageing*, *25*(4): 366-383.

Westerhof, G.J. & Tulle, E. (2007). "Meanings of Ageing and Old Age: Discursive Contexts, Social Attitudes and Personal Identities". *Ageing in Society*, 235-254.

Whitbourne, S.K. (1986). "Openness to Experience, Identity Flexibility, and Life Change in Adults". *Journal of Personality and Social Psychology*, *50*(1): 163.

Wongsala, M., Anbäcken, E.M. & Rosendahl, S. (2021). "Active Ageing-Perspectives on Health, Participation, and Security among Older Adults in Northeastern Thailand—A Qualitative Study". *BMC Geriatrics*, *21*, 1-10.

Zhang, P., Wu, D., Shang, Y., Ren, W., Liang, J., Wang, L. & Li, C. (2021). "Initial Performance Predicts Improvements in Computerized Cognitive Training: Evidence from a Selective Attention Task". *Psych Journal*, *10*(5): 742-750.

7

Mental Health in Later Life

Unravelling the Current State and Future Directions of Geriatric Mental Health Care in India

Tanya Sharma, Ravi P. Pandey and *Purnima Awasthi*

Introduction

According to the World Health Organisation (WHO), India has around 104 million persons aged 60 and over, accounting for 8.6 per cent of the total population. The global population is ageing at a rising rate, and India's geriatric population has been gradually growing since 1961. As per the Report of the Technical Group on Population Projections for India and States 2011-2036, there will be almost 138 million geriatric population in India in 2021 (67 million males and 71 million females), with an additional 56 million elderly people projected in 2031. In India, the share of the geriatric population has risen to 10.1 per cent in 2021 and is expected to rise to 13.1 per cent in 2031. Over 20 per cent of India's population will be old by 2050. By 2046, India's geriatric population would outnumber youngsters (0 to 15 years old). Between 2022 and 2050, the number of persons aged 80 and over is predicted to grow by approximately 279 per cent. Improved healthcare offers endurance, but economic and social hindrances such as poverty, the breakdown of the joint family system, and inadequate services, particularly for the elderly, constitute a possible threat.

A number of issues develop and overshadow the delights of longevity, affecting the social, economic, and physical well-being of individuals, their family, and the society at large. Geriatric population is more vulnerable to psychological morbidities. Physical morbidities and functional deficits worsen as people age. This is exacerbated by a variety of life situations, including the disintegration of the familial support structure, diminished care and attention, and economic dependency (Lodha & De Sousa, 2018).

Our senior population has been neglected as a result of urbanization, nuclearization of families, migration, and career-oriented families. This has a significant influence on the psychological condition of the elderly, which makes them vulnerable to mental problems.

Importance of Addressing Mental Health in Later Life

Caused by physical health issues, cerebral pathology, ageing of the brain, and socio-economic variables like social isolation, diminished economic independence, and broken family support networks, the burden of mental illnesses' morbidities is rising among India's older population (Guha, 1994). Cognitive deficits, depression, and anxiety are the most common mental health issues among the elderly in India. These conditions are more common in older women, older people living in rural areas, and older people from lower-income families (Brinda *et al.*, 2016; Patel *et al.*, 2020; Philip *et al.*, 2021). Mental health disorders, including late-life depression can occur in mild, moderate, and severe forms (Kulkarni & Shinde, 2015). Various key factors that underline the importance of prioritizing mental healthcare for the elderly such as:

Impact on Overall Well-being

Mental health has a significant impact on people's general well-being in later life, impacting many aspects of their day-to-day lives. As people get older, having a healthy mental state becomes increasingly important to living a purposeful and happy life. A good sense of self is facilitated by psychological well-being, which also builds purpose and resilience in the face of adversity. Strong mental health is linked not just to a lower chance of mental health illnesses but also to improved emotional stability, which helps older persons deal with the challenges of ageing more calmly. Additionally, there is a strong correlation between mental well-being and physical health (Luo *et al.*, 2020), which supports healthier ageing and may lessen the strain on healthcare systems.

Quality of Life

As people age, the idea of quality of life for the elderly encompasses more than just survival; it highlights the various aspects that go into living a happy and meaningful life. For elderly people, mental health turns out to be a major factor in determining their overall quality of life. A sense of purpose and happiness are fostered by their increased participation in social, familial, and recreational activities, which is made possible by their mental health. Resolving mental health issues directly improves older persons' ability to appreciate life's various aspects, which leads to a more fulfilling and purposeful life (Gerino *et al.*, 2017). Furthermore, the mutual connection between physical and mental health emphasizes how important mental health is for encouraging better ageing, influencing lifestyle decisions, and eventually having an impact on the larger healthcare system. When we examine the intricacies of geriatric mental health in India, it becomes evident that one of the main goals should be to comprehend and improve the quality of life for the elderly. This goal should be closely linked to the pursuit of compassionate and all-inclusive care that is customized to meet the specific requirements of this population.

Functional Implications

The mental health of geriatric populace is closely associated with their cognitive and functional capacities, and it greatly affects their level of independence and self-governance. Anxiety and depressive disorders, for example, can have a major effect on memory, concentration, and decision-making abilities. When these mental health issues surface, they create obstacles to older individuals' everyday functioning and may make it more difficult for them to carry out daily tasks on their own. Maintaining an excellent standard of living for senior citizens requires an understanding of and response to these functional consequences. In addition to enhancing a person's functional independence, proactive mental health interventions that target cognitive decline and improve mental health also supports the person's feeling of dignity and agency as they negotiate the challenges of later life. Establishing a complete approach that not only emphasizes the mental well-being of the elderly but also recognizes the wider social and financial advantages of such initiatives requires an understanding of the economic factors pertaining to geriatric mental health.

Current State of Geriatric Mental Health in India

In 2011, the Indian Census revealed that 75 per cent of the country's senior population resided in rural areas. Of the old population, women made up about 48.2 per cent; of these, 55 per cent were widows. In India, about eight in ten elderly persons reside in rural areas. 73 per cent of the elderly were illiterate and mostly relied on agriculture. Ninety per cent of the elderly were unorganized, meaning they did not have a steady source of income. Approximately 65 per cent of elderly people needed assistance from others to get by on a daily basis. Sixty-six per cent of older people were considered to be in a vulnerable condition, meaning they lacked enough food, clothing, or shelter, and two-thirds of them were estimated to be living below the poverty line. The old-age dependency ratio rose from 10.9 per cent in 1961 to 13.1 per cent overall in 2001 (Prakash & Kukreti, 2013). Research indicates that the percentage of geriatric population with mental problems is 2.23 per cent (Dube, 1970), however, in rural India, the percentage was discovered to be 33.3 per cent (Nandi *et al.*, 1975). According to research conducted in 1979 by Ramachandran and colleagues, this frequency was recorded to be 35 per cent (Ramachandran *et al.*, 1979). It was discovered by another research team under the direction of (Tiwari, 2000) to be much greater in the elderly group (43.32%) in contrast to 4.66 per cent in the non-geriatric group. The most commonly faced mental health problems by the elderly in India include Dementia, Mood Disorders, and Depression. Additional disorders include delirium, psychosis, drug and alcohol abuse, and anxiety disorders (Prakash *et al.*, 2007; Prakash & Kukreti, 2013; Rao & Madhavan, 1982; Seby *et al.*, 2011; Singh *et al.*, 2004; Sood *et al.*, 2006).

Research conducted in hospital clinics, community settings, and old age homes has revealed that depression is the most prevalent psychiatric illness in older adults, with prevalence rates ranging from 22.2 per cent to 55.2 per cent among gero-psychiatric patients (Rajkumar *et al.*, 2009; Ramachandran *et al.*, 1979; Seby *et al.*, 2011; Sureshkumar *et al.*, 2012; Tiple *et al.*, 2006). Suicide is more common among the elderly and exacerbates this issue, particularly when it is brought on by depression (Rao & Madhavan, 1983). However, depression is a diagnosis that is sometimes overlooked, particularly in geriatric medical patients. In one study, Prakash and colleagues found that among patients of geriatric clinics, 23 per cent had depressive symptoms and 18 per cent had a confirmed depressive disorder. Remarkably, not a single geriatrician, not even in a tertiary clinic, had diagnosed depression (Prakash *et al.*, 2009).

Stigma and Cultural Factors

Mental disorders have been since long suspected to be fake, humiliating, contrived, terrifying, and incurable. Furthermore, the patients often perceived as hazardous, capricious, unreliable, unstable, indolent, useless, and/or vulnerable within the community (Bhugra & Leff, 1993; Charles *et al.*, 2007; Crisp *et al.*, 2000; Lawrie, 1999; Raguram *et al.*, 1996). There is convincing data that suggests mental health conditions are stigmatized more than physical ones (Lai *et al.*, 2001; Lee *et al.*, 2005). The widespread perception that mental illness is the result of bad spirits and that those who suffer from it are violent and dangerous to others is linked to stigma (Singh *et al.*, 2016). By following people's attitudes toward mental disease, one can anticipate the general public's understanding and awareness of mental illnesses (Manderscheid *et al.*, 2010).

Subtle expressions of the influence of societal norms and perceptions can be seen in the circumstances where older people and families in India are unaware when a family member is experiencing mental health impairments (Patel *et al.*, 2020). In India, poor mental health in geriatric people is frequently accepted as a normal aspect of ageing (Bhatt *et al.*, 2017; Philip *et al.*, 2021; Prakash & Kukreti, 2013; Thirthalli *et al.*, 2016). This can also happen more directly when family members and neighbours believe that an older person's mental health issues are a means of attention-seeking. These beliefs and actions can be understood in the context of age and mental health stigmatization and discrimination. Healthcare professionals are also susceptible to stigmatization, prejudice, and misinformation of this kind (Carrara *et al.*, 2023; Kohrt *et al.*, 2018).

People generally have a poor understanding of mental diseases, particularly those who live in rural areas. Individuals living in rural areas tend to seek assistance from quacks and local faith healers, which frequently causes delays in the initiation of therapeutic therapies (More *et al.*, 2012). Research indicates that patients from rural India who practice manual labour or come from lower socio-economic backgrounds experience more stigma (Jadhav *et al.*, 2007; Trani *et al.*, 2015). However, some contradictory findings related to elderly and the stigmatization of mental illness have also been reported (Mehra *et al.*, 2020). According to other studies, despite having more negative and negative views, Indians living in rural areas were more likely to access modern healthcare, and traditional Indian moral and ethical rules raise the possibility of social prejudice against mentally sick people, maybe due to the country's strict caste system (Ng, 1997). Usually families take care for the family members who are suffering from a mental illness, though many a times they are rejected and abandoned in hospitals because of prejudice (Wig *et al.*, 1980), but a common issue at the family and social levels is a "mental health stigma" and a lack of understanding about mental health, which worsens as people age. This can be seen as significant since the usual PHC focus groups in India, which are primarily composed of people from lower socio-economic backgrounds and rural areas, are less likely to be aware of the issues surrounding geriatric mental health (Kafczyk & Hämel, 2023).

Access to Mental Health Services

In India, getting access to specialized mental health services is extremely difficult. The problem is made worse by the lack of mental health specialists, especially those with experience in geriatric care. Access is further ham pered by socio-economic and geographic differences, which leaves a sizable segment of the senior population without proper mental healthcare. Integrated approaches to geriatric health are ham pered in many parts of India by the continued segregation of the physical and mental healthcare systems. The outcome of this fragmentation is frequently older persons with mental and physical health difficulties receiving mediocre treatment. Creating comprehensive care models that address the particular requirements of the ageing population requires an understanding of the interrelationship of physical and mental well-being.

Initiatives and Interventions

Primary mental healthcare (PMHC) in India, which is founded on the idea of community-oriented care, is thought to be the most fundamental and practical starting point for treating mental health issues in older age groups (Kafczyk & Hämel, 2023; Philip *et al.*, 2021). The provision of extensive mental healthcare in close proximity to older adults' homes is made possible by primary healthcare (PHC). Promoting mental health encompasses a wide range of activities, such as treating mental illnesses, treating mental health disorders, rehabilitation, and avoiding relapses and recurrences of illnesses (Shield *et al.*, 2003). According to Kafczyk & Hämel (2021) recent policy analysis, policies, strategies, and programmes in India are beginning to recognize geriatric population as vulnerable members of society with impaired mental health. The policies themselves emphasise the importance of community orientation in enhancing old age-inclusive PMHC. There are four tactics that stand out among these policies, which are:

1. **Helping the family through a family-led approach:** According to reports, Indian families are the biggest source of support for elderly relatives who experience mental health issues. Nevertheless, it is said that India's traditional family-based care system is collapsing,

which has prompted calls for changes to the country's senior citizen services (Lodha & De Sousa, 2018; Philip *et al.*, 2021).

2. **Integrating community health workers (CHWs) into PMHC:** Policies envision CHWs taking over duties related to mental healthcare and old age. Community Health Workers, such as Accredited Social Health Activists (ASHAs), have been considered as support structures for families in taking care of the elderly having mental health illnesses (Lodha & DeSousa, 2018; Philip *et al.*, 2021; Prakash *et al.*, 2009).
3. **Enhancing community involvement and empowerment:** Indian policies place a strong emphasis on the importance of community empowerment for enhancing community involvement in healthcare planning, execution, and oversight. As an illustration of a community health governance structure, Village Health Sanitation and The National Health Mission established Nutrition Committees, which are made up of local elected leaders, frontline healthcare practitioners, and local residents. The Committees oversee government health and nutrition services and organize health initiatives (Ved *et al.*, 2018).
4. **Blending AYUSH services within PMHC:** In India, traditional healthcare systems currently provide a large portion of the mental treatment needed for the elderly. Given this, policies emphasize how incorporation of *Ayurveda*, Homoeopathic, *Unani*, *Siddha*, *Yoga*, Naturopathy, and *Sowa-rigpa* offers a chance for more thorough approaches to PMHC.

However, there are limitations to equitable access to PMHC that is inclusive of older adults (Patel *et al.*, 2020), and these challenges are more severe in rural regions (Philip *et al.*, 2021). The majority of discussions surrounding coverage-based factors, such as the lack of community-based mental health services and the scarcity of mental health professionals, and a focus on issues of access and the creation of innovative, new policy approaches to better address mental health in geriatric population still remain. Older adults are denied their rights and have restricted access to healthcare (Banerjee *et al.*, 2021). The blend of old age, female gender, and low socio-economic status (SES) is also where disparities in access to health services are most evident. For example, Srivastava *et al.* (2021) found that people with low economic and social status such as *Scheduled Tribes*, women, and the oldest age groups are less likely to seek treatment for mental health disorders.

Future Directions

In India, there has been relatively little focus on how old age is seen, attitudes towards old age, and how one views one's own ageing process with respect to service accessibility. India was found to have a positive outlook about social and emotional dimensions of ageing due to its young population growth and rising status differences (Löckenhoff *et al.*, 2009). However, as society is becoming more modernized and the proportion of older people in India has increased, the nation's outlook on the ageing process has shifted towards a more negative stance (Chatterji *et al.*, 2008; Löckenhoff *et al.*, 2009). Ageism is the act of discriminating against and stereotyping older individuals solely on the basis of their age (Aronson, 2015; Prince *et al.*, 2015), and it is widespread in numerous countries, including India (Maurya *et al.*, 2022). It is possible to understand perceptions of mental health and ageing as reflected in social standards.

Community-based healthcare is considered as a crucial component of PMHC for senior citizens. Specifically, there is a strong emphasis on community health worker (CHW) engagement, like those provided by ASHAs or Anganwadi Workers. It was found in a study that they can: (1) offer mental healthcare services in close proximity to their homes to older persons who are affected or at risk (e.g. outreach for basic forms of therapy); (2) act as coordinators of healthcare services; and (3) educate, enlighten, and assist families in their roles as caregivers. A number of obstacles that make it challenging to develop these roles in reality have been pointed out including the CHWs' lack of appropriate training in the area of mental health for geriatric population and their propensity to minimize mental health issues in this age group; for example, they might think that mental diseases are incurable (Kafczyk & Hämel, 2023).

Hindrances in access to age-inclusive mental healthcare by the negative social perception and limited knowledge about mental health among older adults: Stakeholders consistently view the family as a crucial player in mental healthcare for the elderly in India. However, they acknowledge a gradual decline in traditional family care systems and underlying norms (Burholt *et al.*, 2020; Philip *et al.*, 2021). This aligns with existing familial policy approaches in India (Kafczyk & Hämel, 2023). Nevertheless, the practicality of this approach is questionable due to the prevalent low mental health literacy among caregivers and diminishing positive attitudes towards older individuals within the family setting. As noted by Patel *et al.* (2020), in Jodhpur, families and older individuals often lack awareness of mental health issues affecting them or their family members. The caregiving role of family members is further hindered by inadequate financial support, consistent with findings in other low- and middle-income countries (Lambert *et al.*, 2017). Particularly within families from low socio-economic backgrounds, mental health is often deprioritized compared to more basic needs. These circumstances limit appropriate societal and familial responses to mental health in old age, as well as hinder support-seeking behaviour. Our study reveals a widespread reluctance to openly discuss the mental health of older individuals, extending not only to family members and the local community but also to primary healthcare (PHC) professionals. Consequently, access to Primary Mental Health Care (PMHC) is restricted, and only severe cases typically come to the attention of the healthcare system.

Combined family and community interventions aimed at promoting a positive perception and approach to mental healthcare for the elderly: The Primary Mental Health Care system and its policies should prioritize mental health promotion and prevention within communities, offering self-help-oriented support and ensuring easy access to mental health services (Banerjee *et al.*, 2021). Experts advocate for comprehensive intersectoral education on mental health for the elderly as a vital element of mental health promotion. This education, anchored at the Primary Health Care (PHC) level, aims to enhance mental health literacy for older individuals, their families, communities, and healthcare workers. While progress may be gradual, fostering a positive understanding of mental health and ageing is crucial. This positive perspective can contribute to creating an environment where affected older individuals, their families, communities, and the healthcare system engage openly, fostering informed discussions about mental health and improving dignified access to age-inclusive PMHC. Research indicates that a favourable attitude towards seeking professional help for mental health concerns is a strong predictor of help-seeking behaviour (Mojtabai *et al.*, 2016), and such willingness can be positively influenced by community mental health awareness campaigns (Gaiha *et al.*, 2021).

It is indisputable that families armed with better knowledge about mental health are better equipped to provide optimal care for older family members (Patel & Prince, 2001). A study from Brazil by Scazufca *et al.* (2022) demonstrated the effectiveness of low-intensity psychosocial and psycho-education interventions, delivered by CHWs partly in the homes of older persons, in the recovery from old-age depression and the reduction of barriers to care. Similar positive results and care models have been effective in India (Cohen *et al.*, 2018; Dias *et al.*, 2019; Paudel *et al.*,

2014), offering a promising approach to enhance mental healthcare in old age (Rangarajan *et al.*, 2021).

Conclusion

Considering the ageing population in India, it is crucial to take into account perceptions and attitudes towards mental health and old age. This is necessary to enhance the fair access to and involvement of older individuals and their families in Primary Mental Health Care (PMHC). The prevailing stigma associated with mental health, particularly in old age, constitutes a significant obstacle deeply ingrained in the family and community care systems. While families and communities are envisioned to play a substantial role in the Indian public health system's PMHC, supporting them through information, knowledge, and relief services is a fundamental requirement to engage them as active participants. The increasing breakdown of family support structures in both rural and urban areas underscores the necessity for a more prominent role for outreach support, particularly from community health workers. PMHC, with its emphasis on mental health promotion, could serve as a critical anchor in addressing negative attitudes toward mental health and old age, including the stigma associated with mental health and ageism. The insights from this study can contribute to the development of age-sensitive policies and programmes for mental health in India and other LMICs, providing valuable input for future research on the subject.

References

Aronson, L. (2015). "The Human Lifecycle's Neglected Stepchild". *The Lancet, 385*(9967): 500-501.

Banerjee, D., Rabheru, K., de Mendonca Lima, C.A. & Ivbijaro, G. (2021). "Role of Dignity in Mental Healthcare: Impact on Ageism and Human Rights of Older Persons". *The American Journal of Geriatric Psychiatry, 29*(10): 1000-1008.

Bhatt, A.N., Joseph, M.R., Xavier, I.A., Sagar, P., Remadevi, S. & Paul, S.S. (2017). "Health Problems and Healthcare Needs of Elderly-Community Perspective from a Rural Setting in India". *Int J Community Med Public Health, 4*(4): 1213-1218.

Bhugra, D. & Leff, J. (1993). "Attitude Towards Mental Illness". *Principles of Social Psychiatry,* Blackwell Scientific Publication, pp. 385-399.

Brinda, E.M., Rajkumar, A.P., Attermann, J., Gerdtham, U.G., Enemark, U. & Jacob, K.S. (2016). "Health, Social, and Economic Variables Associated with Depression among Older People in Low and Middle Income Countries: World Health Organization Study on Global Ageing and Adult Health". *The American Journal of Geriatric Psychiatry*, *24*(12): 1196-1208.

Burholt, V., Maruthakutti, R. & Maddock, C.A. (2020). "A Cultural Framework of Care and Social Protection for Older People in India". *GeroPsych*.

Carrara, B.S., Bobbili, S.J. & Ventura, C.A.A. (2023). "Community Health Workers and Stigma Associated with Mental Illness: An Integrative Literature Review. *Community Mental Health Journal*, *59*(1): 132-159.

Charles, H., Manoranjitham, S.D. & Jacob, K.S. (2007). "Stigma and Explanatory Models among People with Schizophrenia and their Relatives in Vellore, South India". *International Journal of Social Psychiatry*, *53*(4): 325-332.

Chatterji, S., Kowal, P., Mathers, C., Naidoo, N., Verdes, E., Smith, J.P. & Suzman, R. (2008). "The Health of Ageing Populations in China and India. *Health Affairs*, *27*(4): 1052-1063.

Cohen, A., Dias, A., Azariah, F., Krishna, R.N., Sequeira, M., Abraham, S., Cuij pers, P., Morse, J.Q., Reynolds III, C.F. & Patel, V. (2018). "Ageing and Well-being in Goa, India: A Qualitative Study". *Ageing & Mental Health*, *22*(2): 168-174.

Crisp, A.H., Gelder, M.G., Rix, S., Meltzer, H.I. & Rowlands, O.J. (2000). "Stigmatisation of People with Mental Illnesses". *The British Journal of Psychiatry*, *177*(1): 4-7.

Dias, A., Azariah, F., Sequeira, M., Krishna, R., Morse, J.Q., Cohen, A., Cuijpers, P., Anderson, S., Patel, V. & Reynolds III, C.F. (2019). "Adaptation of Problem-Solving Therapy for Primary Care to Prevent Late-Life Depression in Goa, India: The 'Dil' intervention". *Global Health Action*, *12*(1): 1420300.

Dube, K.G. (1970). "A Study of Prevalence and Biosocial Variables in Mental Illness in a Rural and An Urban Community in Uttar Pradesh—India". *Acta Psychiatrica Scandinavica*, *46*(4): 327-359.

Gaiha, S.M., Gulfam, F.R., Siddiqui, I., Kishore, R. & Krishnan, S. (2021). "Pilot Community Mental Health Awareness Campaign Improves Service Coverage in India". *Community Mental Health Journal*, *57*: 814-827.

Gerino, E., Rolle, L., Sechi, C. & Brustia, P. (2017, November 14). *Loneliness, Resilience, Mental Health, and Quality of Life in Old Age: A Structural Equation Model*. https://www.frontiersin.org/articles/10.3389/fpsyg.2017.02003/full

Guha, R. (1994). "Morbidity Related Epidemiological Determinants in Indian Aged—An Overview". *Public Health Implications of Ageing in India*. New Delhi: Indian Council of Medical Research, pp. 114-125.

Jadhav, S., Littlewood, R., Ryder, A.G., Chakraborty, A., Jain, S. & Barua, M. (2007). "Stigmatization of Severe Mental Illness in India: Against the Simple Industrialization Hypothesis". *Indian Journal of Psychiatry*, *49*(3): 189.

Kafczyk, T. & Hämel, K. (2021). "The Architecture of the Primary Mental Healthcare System for Older People in India: What Public Policies Tell Us". *International Journal of Mental Health Systems*, *15*, 1-17.

Kafczyk, T. & Hämel, K. (2023). "Primary Mental Healthcare for Older People in India: Between Stigmatization and Community Orientation". *Discover Mental Health*, *3*(1): 14. https://doi.org/10.1007/s44192-023-00040-7

Kohrt, B.A., Jordans, M.J., Turner, E.L., Sikkema, K.J., Luitel, N.P., Rai, S., Singla, D.R., Lamichhane, J., Lund, C. & Patel, V. (2018). "Reducing Stigma among Healthcare Providers to Improve Mental Health Services (RESHAPE): Protocol for a Pilot Cluster Randomized Controlled Trial of a Stigma Reduction Intervention for Training Primary Healthcare Workers in Nepal". *Pilot and Feasibility Studies*, *4*(1): 1-18.

Kulkarni, R.S. & Shinde, R.L. (2015). "Depression and Its Associated Factors in Older Indians: A Study Based on Study of Global Ageing and Adult Health (SAGE)-2007". *Journal of Ageing and Health*, *27*(4): 622-649.

Lai, Y.-M., Hong, C.P.H. & Chee, C.Y. (2001). "Stigma of Mental Illness". *Singapore Medical Journal*, *42*(3): 111-114.

Lambert, S.D., Bowe, S.J., Livingston, P.M., Heckel, L., Cook, S., Kowal, P. & Orellana, L. (2017). "Impact of Informal Caregiving on Older Adults' Physical and Mental Health in Low-Income and Middle-Income Countries: A Cross-Sectional, Secondary Analysis Based on the Who's Study on Global Ageing and Adult Health (SAGE)". *BMJ Open*, *7*(11): e017236.

Lawrie, S.M. (1999). "Stigmatisation of Psychiatric Disorder". *Psychiatric Bulletin*, *23*(3): 129-131.

Lee, S., Lee, M.T., Chiu, M.Y. & Kleinman, A. (2005). "Experience of Social Stigma by People with Schizophrenia in Hong Kong". *The British Journal of Psychiatry*, *186*(2): 153-157.

Löckenhoff, C.E., De Fruyt, F., Terracciano, A., McCrae, R.R., De Bolle, M., Costa, P.T., Aguilar-Vafaie, M.E., Ahn, C., Ahn, H., Alcalay, L., Allik, J., Avdeyeva, Tatyana. V., Barbaranelli, C., Benet-Martinez, V., Blatný, M., Bratko, D., Brunner-Sciarra, M., Cain, T.R., Crawford, J.T., ... Yik, M. (2009). "Perceptions of Ageing Across 26 Cultures and their Culture-Level Associates". *Psychology and Ageing*, *24*(4): 941-951. https://doi.org/10.1037/a0016901

Lodha, P. & De Sousa, A. (2018). "Geriatric Mental Health: The Challenges for India". *Journal of Geriatric Mental Health*, *5*(1): 16. https://doi.org/10.4103/jgmh.jgmh_34_17

Luo, M.S., Chui, E.W.T. & Li, L.W. (2020). "The Longitudinal Associations between Physical Health and Mental Health among Older Adults". *Ageing & Mental Health*, *24*(12): 1990-1998. https://doi.org/10.1080/13607863.2019.1655706

Manderscheid, R., Delvecchio, P., Marshall, C., Palpant, R.G., Bigham, J., Bornemann, T.H., Kobau, R., Zack, M., Langmaid, G. & Thompson, W. (2010). "Attitudes Toward Mental Illness-35 States, District of Columbia, and Puerto Rico, 2007". *Morbidity and Mortality Weekly Report*, *59*(20): 619-625.

Maurya, P., Sharma, P. & Muhammad, T. (2022). "Prevalence and Correlates of Perceived Age-Related Discrimination among Older Adults in India". *BMC Public Health*, *22*(1): 1-10.

Mehra, A., Singla, H., Grover, S. & Avasthi, A. (2020). "Stigma for Mental Disorders among the Elderly Population in a Rural Setting". *Indian Journal of Social Psychiatry*, *36*(3): 184. https://doi.org/10.4103/ijsp.ijsp_124_19

Mojtabai, R., Evans-Lacko, S., Schomerus, G. & Thornicroft, G. (2016). "Attitudes Toward Mental Health Help Seeking as Predictors of Future Help-Seeking Behaviour and Use of Mental Health Treatments". *Psychiatric Services*, *67*(6): 650-657.

More, V.P., Jadhav, P.B., Puranik, R., Shinde, V.S. & Pakhale, S. (2012). "Study of Knowledge and Attitude Concerning Mental Illness in Adults". *Int J Health Sci Res*, *2*, 1-6.

Nandi, D.N., Ajmany, S., Ganguli, H., Banerjee, G., Boral, G.C., Ghosh, A. & Sarkar, S. (1975). "Psychiatric Disorders in a Rural Community in West Bengal—An Epidemiological Study". *Indian Journal of Psychiatry*, *17*(2): 87-99.

Ng, C.H. (1997). "The Stigma of Mental Illness in Asian Cultures". *Australian and New Zealand Journal of Psychiatry*, *31*(3): 382-390. https://doi.org/10.3109/00048679709073848

Patel, M., Bhardwaj, P., Nebhinani, N., Goel, A.D. & Patel, K. (2020). "Prevalence of Psychiatric Disorders among Older Adults in Jodhpur and Stakeholders Perspective on Responsive Health System". *Journal of Family Medicine and Primary Care*, *9*(2): 714.

Patel, V. & Prince, M. (2001). "Ageing and Mental Health in a Developing Country: Who Cares? Qualitative Studies from Goa, India". *Psychological Medicine*, *31*(1): 29-38.

Paudel, S., Gilles, N., Hahn, S., Hexom, B., Premkumar, R., Arole, S. & Katz, C. (2014). "Impact of Mental Health Training on Village Health Workers Regarding Clinical Depression in Rural India". *Community Mental Health Journal*, *50*, 480-486.

Philip, S., Gajera, G., Nirisha, P.L., Sivakumar, P.T., Barikar, M.C., Panday, P., Patley, R., Chander, R., Sinha, P. & Basavarajappa, C. (2021). "Future-Proofing Geriatric Mental Health Care Services in India: Training and Policy Directions". *Indian Journal of Psychological Medicine*, *43*(5_suppl): S134-S141.

Prakash, O., Gupta, L.N., Singh, V.B. & Nagarajarao, G. (2009). "Applicability of 15-Item Geriatric Depression Scale to Detect Depression in Elderly Medical Outpatients". *Asian Journal of Psychiatry*, *2*(2): 63-65.

Prakash, O., Gupta, L.N., Singh, V.B., Singhal, A.K. & Verma, K.K. (2007). "Profile of Psychiatric Disorders and Life Events in Medically Ill Elderly: Experiences from Geriatric Clinic in Northern India". *International Journal of Geriatric Psychiatry: A Journal of the Psychiatry of Late Life and Allied Sciences*, *22*(11): 1101-1105.

Prakash, O. & Kukreti, P. (2013). "State of Geriatric Mental Health in India". *Current Translational Geriatrics and Experimental Gerontology Reports*, *2*(1): 1-6. https://doi.org/10.1007/s13670-012-0034-1

Prince, M.J., Wu, F., Guo, Y., Robledo, L.M.G., O'Donnell, M., Sullivan, R. & Yusuf, S. (2015). "The Burden of Disease in Older People and Implications for Health Policy and Practice". *The Lancet*, *385*(9967): 549-562.

Raguram, R., Weiss, M.G., Channabasavanna, S.M. & Devins, G.M. (1996). "Stigma, Depression, and Somatization in South India". *American Journal of Psychiatry*, *153*(8): 1043-1049.

Rajkumar, A.P., Thangadurai, P., Senthilkumar, P., Gayathri, K., Prince, M. & Jacob, K.S. (2009). "Nature, Prevalence and Factors Associated with Depression among the Elderly in a Rural South Indian Community". *International Psychogeriatrics*, *21*(2): 372-378.

Ramachandran, V., Menon, M.S. & Ramamurthy, B. (1979). "Psychiatric Disorders in Subjects Aged Over Fifty1". *Indian Journal of Psychiatry*, *21*(3): 193-198.

Rangarajan, S.K., Sivakumar, P.T., Manjunatha, N., Kumar, C.N. & Math, S. B. (2021). "Public Health Perspectives of Geriatric Mental Health Care". *Indian Journal of Psychological Medicine*, *43*(5_suppl): S1-S7.

Rao, A.V. & Madhavan, T. (1982). "Gerospsychiatric Morbidity Survey in a Semi-Urban Area Near Madurai". *Indian Journal of Psychiatry*, *24*(3): 258.

______ (1983). "Depression and Suicide Behaviour in the Aged". *Indian Journal of Psychiatry*, *25*(4): 251.

Scazufca, M., Nakamura, C.A., Seward, N., Moreno-Agostino, D., van de Ven, P., Hollingworth, W., Peters, T.J. & Araya, R. (2022). "A Task-Shared, Collaborative Care Psychosocial Intervention for Improving Depressive Symptomatology among Older Adults in a Socio-economically Deprived Area of Brazil (PROACTIVE): A Pragmatic, Two-Arm, Parallel-Group, Cluster-Randomised Controlled Trial". *The Lancet Healthy Longevity*, *3*(10): e690-e702.

Seby, K., Chaudhury, S. & Chakraborty, R. (2011). "Prevalence of Psychiatric and Physical Morbidity in An Urban Geriatric Population". *Indian Journal of Psychiatry*, *53*(2): 121.

Shield, T., Campbell, S., Rogers, A., Worrall, A., Chew-Graham, C. & Gask, L. (2003). "Quality Indicators for Primary Care Mental Health Services". *Quality & Safety in Health Care*, *12*(2): 100.

Singh, A., Mattoo, S.K. & Grover, S. (2016). "Stigma and Its Correlates in Patients with Schizophrenia Attending a General Hospital Psychiatric Unit". *Indian Journal of Psychiatry*, *58*(3): 291.

Singh, G.P., Chavan, B.S., Arun, P. & Sidana, A. (2004). "Geriatric Out-Patients with Psychiatric Illnesses in a Teaching Hospital Setting—A Retrospective Study". *Indian Journal of Psychiatry*, *46*(2): 140.

Sood, A., Singh, P. & Gargi, P.D. (2006). "Psychiatric Morbidity in Non-Psychiatric Geriatric Inpatients". *Indian Journal of Psychiatry*, *48*(1): 56.

Srivastava, S., Sulaiman, K.M., Drishti, D. & Muhammad, T. (2021). "Factors Associated with Psychiatric Disorders and Treatment Seeking Behaviour among Older Adults in India". *Scientific Reports*, *11*(1): 24085.

Sureshkumar, R., Bharath, S., Jain, S., Prakash, O., Purushottam, M., Thennarasu, K., Mukherjee, O., Sivakumar, P.T. & Varghese, M. (2012). "ApoE4 and Late onset Depression in Indian Population". *Journal of Affective Disorders*, *136*(3): 244-248.

Thirthalli, J., Zhou, L., Kumar, K., Gao, J., Vaid, H., Liu, H., Hankey, A., Wang, G., Gangadhar, B.N. & Nie, J.B. (2016). "Traditional, Complementary, and Alternative Medicine Approaches to Mental Health Care and Psychological Well-being in India and China". *The Lancet Psychiatry*, *3*(7): 660-672.

Tiple, P., Sharma, S.N. & Srivastava, A.S. (2006). "Psychiatric Morbidity in Geriatric People". *Indian Journal of Psychiatry*, *48*(2): 88.

Tiwari, S.C. (2000). "Geriatric Psychiatric Morbidity in Rural Northern India: Implications for the Future". *International Psychogeriatrics*, *12*(1): 35-48.

Trani, J.F., Bakhshi, P., Kuhlberg, J., Narayanan, S.S., Venkataraman, H., Mishra, N.N., Groce, N.E., Jadhav, S. & Deshpande, S. (2015). "Mental Illness, Poverty and Stigma in India: A Case-Control Study". *BMJ Open*, *5*(2).

Ved, R., Sheikh, K., George, A.S. & Raman, V.R. (2018). "Village Health Sanitation and Nutrition Committees: Reflections on Strengthening Community Health Governance at Scale in India". *BMJ Global Health*, *3*(Suppl 3).

Wig, N.N., Suleiman, M.A., Routledge, R., Srinivasa Murthy, R., Ladrido-Ignacio, L., Ibrahim, H.H.A. & Harding, T.W. (1980). "Community Reactions to Mental Disorders—A Key Informant Study in Three Developing Countries". *Acta Psychiatrica Scandinavica*, *61*(2): 111-126.

8

Cultural Practices in Uttarakhand Towards Healthy Ageing

Ruchi Tewari and *Aradhana Shukla*

Introduction

Uttarakhand, nestled in the Himalayan region, is known for its rich culture, biodiversity, and unique traditions. This state has a significant population of elderly individuals who engage in various cultural practices that promote physical and mental well-being. In Uttarakhand, healthy ageing is interwoven with traditional knowledge, dietary customs, and social structures, which have evolved over centuries. This chapter examines how these cultural practices contribute to healthy ageing in Uttarakhand, analysing their potential benefits and relevance for broader public health strategies.

In actuality, this is the age of ageing. We are at the forefront of a demographic and health revolution that will fundamentally alter nearly every facet of life, including how people view the life cycle, how healthcare systems are set up, how generations interact, how families function, how communities are structured, and how people view death (Kalache & Sen, 1998).

Sharing values, customs, and ways of life within a group or community is referred to as culture. The activities we do in our daily lives are known as our customs. These are frequently dictated by tradition, or the customs we have established over the years. Individuals who belong to the same culture often associate with one another. Individual differences exist in the level of adherence to cultural values, with age, gender, socio-economic class, and peer pressure all having a significant impact (Swami, 1999).

In Uttarakhand, religion is quite popular, not just because it is a major draw for domestic travellers but also because it is an essential aspect of daily life for the locals. A sizeable portion of Uttarakhand's population is heterodox Hindu and Buddhist, particularly in the state's higher regions. This region has been referred to as "Dev Bhoomi", or the "Land of the Gods." Many of the most significant Hindu sites are located in Uttarakhand, nestled among the state's mountains and rivers.

The most revered of them are the four shrines of Gangotri, Yamunotri, Badrinath, and Kedarnath, together known as the "Char Dham", a pilgrimage to which is said to guarantee immediate salvation. The holy Ganga meets its tributaries at what are known as the Panch Prayag, or the five holy "sangams" of the river at Vishnuprayag, Nandprayag, Karnaprayag, Rudraprayag, and Devprayag, as it forms its way down to the plains. Furthermore, the mediaeval Gurudwara of Hemkund Sahib, located close to the Valley of Flowers, is a significant Sikh temple, while Hardwar and Rishikesh are two of the most popular pilgrimage sites in Hinduism (Bhatt, 2023).

Old Age in Indian Culture

The issues of old age were carefully considered by the *Vedic rishis*, who created a social structure that afforded elderly respect and protection. *Dharma*, or religion, placed a strong emphasis on lovingly and respectfully worshipping and serving one's parents and grandparents. On the other side, elders were urged to leave their families in order to become *Vanaprasti* and *Sanyasins*, and they were given special responsibilities (Srivastava, Kapil, Kumar, Dey, Nagarkar, Sekaran,1996). Similar to another nectar, the rejuvenation treatment described in the ancient Indian texts about the way of life (*Ayurveda*) has incomprehensible miraculous effects, prolongs life, promotes health, maintains youthfulness, relieves fatigue, drowsiness, exertion, exhaustion, lassitude, and debility, restores the equilibrium of the *doshas*, provides stability, relieves muscle laxity, ignites the internal fire, and produces excellent lustre, complexion, and voice (Sharma, 1981).

One's duty to oneself, one's family, community, and country—that is, one's duty to humanity—as well as *Artha*: reaping the rewards of duty are the goals of life *dharma*. *Moksha*: The attainment of salvation and *Kama*: The fulfilment of desires. The attainment of these four goals requires a long and healthy life, which is accomplished by the principles of *Niyama* and *Yama*. *Niyama* includes cleanliness, contentment, austerity, study, and self-surrender to God, while *Yama* includes non-violence, honesty, non-stealing, chastity or celibacy, and not accepting gifts (Kumar, 1997). To keep the body healthy, the seven fundamental tissues (*dhatus*) must be balanced both qualitatively and quantitatively (Bhava Prakasha, 1998). We must take into account the following three stages of our lives:

1. **Childhood:** This is the period of greatest feeding, during which the *dhatu* is fed.
2. **Middle Ages:** During this time, the generative and degenerative processes balance one another out.
3. **Old age:** The degenerative process takes precedence over the generating process as people age. The fundamental tenet of Indian preventive medicine, known as *Vasthavṛtta*, or "establishing oneself in good habits", is that excess must be avoided in all areas of life. Only when everything in life is savoured at the right time and in the right quantity can harmony and health be achieved.

Three steps are suggested by Indian medical practice in the pursuit of optimal health (Sharma, 1981, *Sharngadhara Samhita*, 1984).

Since most people are unable to develop the perception that is required to recognise what is happening within their bodies, daily and seasonal routines attempt to ensure that the body's needs are met regardless of where the mind may wander. The body needs moderation in all things, therefore, neither excessive exertion nor relaxation is good. Moderation and order are established in the body and mind through a healthy habits. Examples include rising before the sun, emptying the bladder and bowel after waking up, taking a daily bath to promote a feeling of physical freshness, and engaging in moderate exercise, ideally *yoga*.

It is normal for some toxins to build up in the body as a result of different metabolic processes, even when the aforementioned measures are closely followed. Since the body would be manufacturing these poisons in large quantities, it is im perative that they be removed. However, when their levels rise above a particular threshold, some toxins may still be present in the body and can lead to a variety of illnesses (*Sushruta Samhita*, 1991). These poisons must be regularly eliminated in order to preserve the healthy operation of various physiological systems. The Indian method offers "*Panchakarma*", an elimination therapy.

Rejuvenation therapy is another crucial element for preserving excellent health and remaining active in old life. Therefore, in order to stay young and retain good health, a healthy person should make renewing preparations. There are numerous such preparations that can be used based on one's constitution and the time of year. Other elements that are required to prevent diseases include morality, good manners, excellent character, and decent social conduct. Therefore, the Indian medical system treats the full person while offering advice on how to stay healthy, which encourages a person to age in a way that is healthy.

Problems Faced by Old Age People

For older folks, avoiding chronic disease is almost impossible due to factors like gender, age, and family genetics. 78.7 per cent of persons 60 and older have two or more conditions, and 94.9 per cent have at least one, according to NCOA data (National Council on Ageing, 2022). It's likely that you are either managing an illness yourself, or your parent or grandparent is now managing one. Additionally, obesity can raise your risk for diseases like heart disease, type 2 diabetes, and several types of cancer. Obesity affects 42 per cent of persons 60 and older (Centres for Disease Control and Prevention, 2017 & 2020).

The Centres for Medicare & Medicaid Services (2018) listed ten prevalent chronic diseases for which persons 65 and older had treatment in 2018 along with other information we should be aware of. To help we stay independent as we learn more about managing one of these chronic conditions, we may want to think about a medical alert monitoring system.

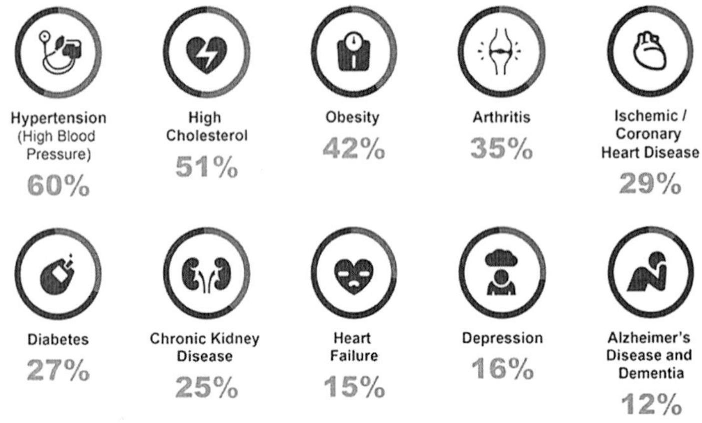

Fig. 8.1: Ten Common Chronic Conditions for Adults 65+.

Source: Centres for Medicare and Medicaid Services, Cronic Conditions Prevalence State/County Table: All Fee-for-Service Beneficiaries Centre for Disease Control and Prevention Adult Obesity Facts.

According to WHO (Ageing and Health, 2024) chronic obstructive pulmonary disease, diabetes, depression, dementia, back and neck discomfort, osteoarthritis, cataracts, and refractive errors are among the common illnesses that affect older adults. People are more prone to have multiple conditions at the same time as they get older.

The rise of several complex health disorders known as geriatric syndromes is another characteristic of older age. They include fragility, stumbles, dementia, pressure ulcers, and urine incontinence, and they are frequently the result of several underlying problems.

Older adults' adjustment issues have been the subject of Ali (2014). The Indian joint family arrangement must be preserved, according to the author. There should be understanding and collaboration between the younger and older generations. The situation of India's elderly population, according to the author, necessitates coordinated efforts from the government, non-governmental organisations, religious institutions, and others in order to not only comprehend but also address the issues brought about by a greying society and enable the elderly to live with dignity and quality. Through the study, the author has concentrated on older people's emotional, social, and marital adjustment. According to the author, elderly residents of assisted living facilities experience more emotional issues than those who remain with their relatives.

The socio-economic status of the elderly as well as the social and health issues they encounter have been discussed by (Singh, 2015). The author's work has concentrated on the elements that lead to issues for elderly individuals in India. The author has concentrated on how Indian traditional values, which once held sway over elderly people, have been weakened by urbanisation, nuclearisation of families, the fast expansion of industry, and the emergence of individual philosophy. According to the author, efforts should be made to prevent elder difficulties, and social work intervention and family awareness-raising are two ways to do this.

Dietary Practices and Nutritional Habits in Uttarakhand

Traditional diets in Uttarakhand are rich in local grains, vegetables, and herbs, offering a balanced nutrient profile essential for health in older age. These dietary practices include: Millets and Whole Grains, Herbal and Ayurvedic Influences, and Seasonal Eating.

The local diet includes grains like finger millet (*mandua*), buckwheat (*kuttu*), and barley, which are high in fiber, vitamins, and minerals. These grains have low glycemic indices, helping prevent diabetes, a common ageing-related condition. Finger millet stands as the most plentiful source of calcium (300–350mg/100g) (Gahalawat, Lamba & Chaudhary, 2024).

Herbs like *timru* and *buransh* (rhododendron) are used in traditional cooking and have anti-inflammatory and antioxidant properties. The practice of drinking *buransh* juice is believed to enhance immunity and support cardiovascular health. 'Buransh' is small evergreen tree widely distributed between 1300 to 3500 m. Medicinal plant 'Buransh' is one of nature's gift. It is a hidden gem with abundant health and economic benefits. Various part of plant exhibited medicinal properties and is used for the treatment of various ailments (Thakur & Verma, 2022).

People in Uttarakhand consume food based on seasonal availability, ensuring a fresh diet with high nutritional value. This practice reduces reliance on processed foods, which is linked to better health outcomes.

Physical Activity and Labour

The mountainous terrain of Uttarakhand naturally incorporates physical activity into daily life. Activities like walking, farming, and wood gathering contribute to physical fitness, flexibility, and strength among the elderly population. Many older adults are involved in agriculture, which includes planting, harvesting, and tending to animals. This regular physical work helps maintain muscle mass and promotes cardiovascular health.

Due to the geographic terrain, walking long distances is a common practice. Regular walking, often at elevations, has cardiovascular benefits and helps maintain joint health. Folk dances like *Langvir Nritya* in Tehri Gharwal area—this unique form of dance involves a group of men that get up on a pole while balancing on their stomach. They perform various acrobatic stunts on the pole which is very entertaining to watch too. Traditional songs encourage social interaction and physical movement, enhancing mental and emotional well-being, which are important components of healthy ageing.

Social and Community Support

In Uttarakhand, community and family structures are crucial for providing emotional support and care for the elderly. The strong intergenerational bonds and social networks contribute to mental health and resilience. Living in joint family setups ensures that elderly individuals are not isolated. The presence of family members provides a sense of purpose and emotional support, which are essential for mental well-being.

Festivals like *Phool Dei*, *Harela*, and *Diwali* encourage community participation, fostering social ties and reducing feelings of loneliness, which is a known risk factor for depression in ageing populations. Uttarakhand comes alive with the festive *Harela* festival as the monsoon clouds build. *Harela* is a celebration of greenery and fresh starts, signifying the arrival of the rainy season and the wealth it brings. As a sign of rebirth and growth, they plant saplings and wheatgrass. The excitement and expectation for the rain are reflected in the lively songs and dances that fill the air. *Harela* is a stunning tribute to the mutually beneficial link between Uttarakhand's natural environment and its inhabitants' daily lives (Lohumi, 2023). Cultural norms in Uttarakhand emphasize respect for elders, which enhances their self-esteem and societal value. Such respect has been associated with better mental health among older adults.

The New WHO Definition of Healthy Ageing

In the preface to the First World Report on Ageing and Health, WHO's Director General clearly states that "healthy ageing is more than just the absence of disease". The new definition of Healthy Ageing proposed in the Report and in the first WHO Global Strategy and Action Plan on Ageing and Health (World Health Organization, 2016), unanimously endorsed by all WHO Member States during the World Health Assembly in May 2016, is "the process of developing and maintaining functional ability that enables well-being in older age." While the definition reflects what older adults value, the approach to classify, measure, and improve it is linked to the WHO International Classification of Functioning (ICF) (World Health Organization, 2016 ; Üstün, Kostanjsek, Chatterji, Rehm, 2010), as it recognizes the ongoing interaction between an individual and their environment:

- Each individual has their own "intrinsic capacity", resulting from the complex interaction between their genetic inheritance, personal and health characteristics, including age-related physiological changes, risk factor accumulation, and impact of acute or chronic clinical conditions. Indeed, personal intellectual potential, as well as psychological adaptation and resilience across the life course, modify capacity. In summary, "intrinsic capacity" is the composite of all individual, physical, and mental capacities.
- Each individual lives in a specific environment, that can change over time, and is highly dependent on political, economic, and social norms, values, and resources, including the extent that societies promote equal opportunities, prevent inequities, and

combat ageism, and indeed, ensure access to affordable health and social systems. The close interactions between intrinsic capacity and environmental characteristics (including surroundings itself and support) combine to determine "functional ability." Moreover, differences in older adults' health and illness experiences to a large extent reflect accumulated inequalities across peoples' lives. When unfair, these are called health inequities, and are considered "avoidable, unfair and unjust" and exist within and across countries, from high to low resources settings [refer to R. Sadana's Chap. 18].

The implication is that the life span trajectories of intrinsic capacity (IC) and functional ability (FA), which can be similar during the first part of life in a hospitable environment, start to diverge in midlife with the impact of accumulated determinants of health, and the onset of declines in intrinsic capacities. The increasing decline in intrinsic capacity with time is more or less compensated by support and surroundings reflecting a person's specific environment. Yet an imbalance between the needs of an individual and an environment that does not address, fulfil, or compensate these needs, partly contributing to care dependence and resulting in decreased functional ability and overall well-being. The World Report on Ageing and Health, and the accompanying Global Strategy, outline evidence and actions towards optimizing intrinsic capacity and functional ability particularly during the second part of life, allowing older adults to do things that are important for them (World Health Organization, 2015). This innovative life course approach is extremely interesting because it brings together in a single public health concept both previously described perspectives on ageing, namely the viewpoint of older adults and the clinician-researchers' approaches to address important declines or care dependency, through its public health framework (Kusumastutia, Derksb, Tellier, Di Nucci, Lund, Mortensen, Westendorp, 2016) (see Fig. 8.2) illustrates conceptually that when considering the population as a whole, IC and FA can vary across the second half of the life course. Trajectories reflect a continuous phenomenon and can be divided into three common periods: a period of relatively high and stable capacity, a period of declining capacity, and a period of significant loss of capacity. These periods are not defined by chronological age and trajectories are not necessarily monotonic (i.e., continually decreasing). Distinguishing between IC and FA is necessary in order to understand if levels, distributions, and trajectories of functioning are due to changes in the individual or the environments they inhabit. It is also necessary in order to

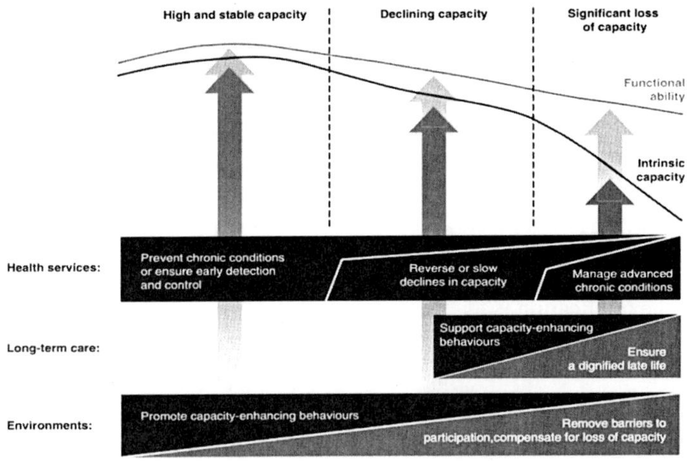

Fig. 8.2: Public Health Framework for Healthy Ageing: Opportunities for Action Across the Life Course, Reproduced from WHO 2015.

document what can be done to improve IC and FA for individuals, groups or populations, involving different policies, sectors, and interventions. The WHO Global Strategy and Action Plan and other recent publications outlines several strategic areas to transform the health services delivery systems from disease-centred practice to a more integrated conception of care from birth to very old age, coordinated across providers, favouring the highest intrinsic capacity and indeed functional ability, by placing functioning evaluation and maintenance as the first priority (Kuruvilla, Sadana, Villar Montesinos *et al.*, 2018). Two major questions emerge from this concept: the first is, what public health approach can be used to achieve the appropriate system of health and social care (see the WHO Report) (World Health Organization, 2015). This includes how best to design and evaluate interventions to facilitate healthy ageing and decrease/delay if not reverse the declines in capacity or ability, which are the two sides of the same coin. Numerous intervention studies have been performed, but have all focused on specific aspects of ageing (Michel, Dreux & Vacheron, 2016) and not on the whole integrated process, which would be more in line with the new concept of healthy ageing (Chen, 2016; Sadana, 2016). The second is how can we measure the life trajectories of intrinsic capacity and functional ability, discussed next.

The Old Age Pension Scheme, implemented by the Department of Social Welfare of Uttarakhand, provides monthly pension to those above

60 years of age living below the poverty line. This financial assistance helps the elderly meet their basic needs and improve their quality of life. The scheme ensures social security for the most vulnerable senior citizens in the state.

Indigenous Healthcare Practices for Old Aged People

Many cultures view health as an act of God or spirits rather than something that can be attributed to human activity. In order to support behaviours that are believed to improve health, cultural adaptation, modifications to conventions and traditions, and genetic adaptation are reinforced. In the past, it was typical for couples in India to produce large families in order to provide for the old and assure their survival. Family size was impacted by cultural norms that were supported by economic realities. Regardless of their cultural origin, many elders seem to struggle with unwanted seclusion. Elderly people's health and functioning are not adversely affected by traditional cultural practices (Alberta Multicultural Commission, 1986).

Uttarakhand has a rich history of indigenous health practices, incorporating herbal medicine and traditional Ayurvedic treatments, which are accessible and affordable for the elderly.

(a) **Use of Medicinal Plants:** Local plants, such as *ashwagandha*, *shilajit*, and *giloy*, are used for managing common age-related conditions like arthritis, diabetes, and fatigue. These natural remedies have anti-inflammatory and rejuvenating properties.
(b) **Home Remedies and Rituals:** Traditional healing methods, such as hot water fomentation, oil massages, and herbal teas, are common in Uttarakhand. These remedies help alleviate chronic pain and promote relaxation.
(c) **Ayurvedic and Spiritual Practices:** Practices such as meditation, *yoga*, and breathing exercises (*pranayama*) are integral to Uttarakhand's culture. These practices are beneficial for stress reduction and mental clarity, aiding in cognitive health and emotional stability.
(d) **Psychological Resilience and Spirituality:** Spirituality plays a key role in promoting resilience and mental health among the elderly in Uttarakhand.
(e) **Pilgrimage and Religious Practices**: Engaging in pilgrimages to holy sites like Kedarnath and Badrinath offers not only physical

exercise but also a sense of spiritual fulfilment, contributing to mental well-being.

(f) **Yoga and Meditation:** Many elderly individuals practice *yoga* and meditation regularly, which improves flexibility, balance, and mental focus. These practices are linked with lower stress levels and improved psychological resilience.

(g) **Belief Systems:** Faith and spiritual beliefs provide emotional support, helping individuals cope with the challenges of ageing. Such practices promote inner peace and life satisfaction.

It Appearing this

The cultural practices in Uttarakhand offer a holistic approach to healthy ageing by integrating physical activity, community support, nutrition, and spiritual well-being. These practices emphasize balance and harmony, which are essential components of a healthy lifestyle. The relevance of these traditional practices lies in their simplicity, accessibility, and alignment with natural processes, which are often missing in modern, urban lifestyles. Given the rising health issues among ageing populations globally, there is significant value in understanding and preserving these cultural practices.

The cultural practices in Uttarakhand represent a unique approach to healthy ageing, rooted in centuries-old traditions that emphasize harmony between physical, mental, and spiritual well-being. These practices include a natural, nutrient-rich diet, regular physical activity, strong social bonds, and deeply embedded spiritual practices. Each element plays a role in contributing to the overall health and resilience of elderly individuals in this region, illustrating that traditional lifestyles can be a valuable framework for modern public health initiatives.

The environment and geography of Uttarakhand naturally foster a physically active lifestyle, and the local diet—rich in whole grains, herbs, and seasonal foods—supports healthy ageing by providing essential nutrients and maintaining metabolic health. Social structures like joint families and community festivals provide emotional security, reinforce intergenerational bonds, and counteract the isolation that many elderly individuals experience. The practice of indigenous healthcare, relying on medicinal plants and *Ayurvedic* principles, underscores the importance of preventive health in this region, suggesting that traditional healthcare methods can supplement formal medical systems.

Notably, the high regard for elders within Uttarakhand's culture promotes their social standing and self-esteem, highlighting the role that cultural respect plays in mental well-being. Spiritual activities, such as *yoga*, meditation, and pilgrimage, further enhance psychological resilience, helping individuals cope with the challenges of ageing.

Conclusion

Uttarakhand's cultural practices provide a valuable model for promoting healthy ageing through a combination of physical, mental, and spiritual well-being. This review highlights the importance of traditional practices and their potential for supporting ageing populations. Integrating aspects of these practices into public health programmes could offer sustainable solutions for healthy ageing, especially in rural and mountainous regions worldwide.

The findings from Uttarakhand's elderly population reveal how cultural practices can create a supportive environment for healthy ageing. These traditions underscore the value of a lifestyle that includes balanced nutrition, regular physical activity, social support, and spiritual engagement. As the global population ages, the Uttarakhand model offers insights into holistic ageing that could inform broader public health policies aimed at promoting well-being among the elderly. By integrating aspects of traditional knowledge, diet, social structure, and mental health practices into public health strategies, other regions might enhance the quality of life for their older populations, fostering a society where ageing is not only prolonged but enriched in meaningful ways.

References

Alberta Multicultural Commission (1986). "Understanding Seniors and Culture. Multicultural Activities Guide 3", *Culture and Multiculturalism*, pp. 21-25.

Ali, M.A.Z. (2014). "A Study on Adjustmental Problems of Old Age Persons", *International Journal of Academic Research*, *1*(2): Retrieved from: http://ijar.org.in/stuff/issues/oct14/V-1-I-4(2)-oct14.pdf

Bhatt, A. (2023). "Indian culture: A study of Uttarakhand". *Research Gate. Bhava Prakasha*. Translator: Shri Kanta Murthy. Varanasi, India: Chaukhamba Orientalia, 1998.

Capistrant, B. & Ghosh, Subharati & Friedemann-Sánchez, Greta & Kowal, Paul & Mathur, Arvind (2015). "Culture and Caregiving for Older Adults in India: A Qualitative Study". *The Gerontologist. 55*. 10.1093/geront/gnv504.06.

Centres for Disease Control and Prevention. National Health and Nutrition Examination Survey 2017-March 2020 Prepandemic Data Files Development of Files and Prevalence Estimates for Selected Health Outcomes. *Found on the internet* at https://stacks.cdc.gov/view/cdc/106273

Centres for Disease Control and Prevention. *Overweight & Obesity. Why it Matters*. Found on the internet at https://www.cdc.gov/obesity/about-obesity/why-it-matters.html

Centres for Medicare & Medicaid Services. *Chronic Conditions. Chronic Conditions Prevalence.* State/County Table: Fee-for-Service Beneficiaries 65 Years and Over, 2018. Found on the internet at https://www.cms.gov/Research-Statistics-Data-and-Systems/Statistics-Trends-and-Reports/Chronic-Conditions/CC_Main

Charaka Samhita. Translator: P.V. Sharma. Varanasi, India: Chaukhamba Orientalia, 1981.

Chen, L.K. (2016). "Towards the Life Course Approach of Healthy Ageing". *Journal of European Geriatric Medicine* 7: 289-290.

Gahalawat, P., Lamba, N., Chaudhary, P. (2024). "Nutritional and Health Benefits of Millets: A Review Article". *Journal of Indian System of Medicine* 12(1): 4-11, January-March 2024. | DOI: 10.4103/jism.jism_71_23

Kalache, A. & Sen, K. (1998). "Ageing in Developing Countries". In *Principles and Practice of Geriatric Medicine*. Pathy (ed.). 3rd edn, Vol. II, New York: John Wiley & Sons, pp. 1561-1574.

Kumar, V. (1997). "Ageing in India—An Overview." *Indian Journal of Medical Research, 6*: 257-264.

Kuruvilla, S., Sadana, R., Villar Montesinos, E. *et al.* (2018). "A life-course Approach to Health: Synergy with Sustainable Development Goals". *Bulletin World Health Organization. 96*: 42-50.

Kusumastutia, S., Derksb, M.G.L., Tellier, S., Di Nucci, E., Lund, R., Mortensen E.L., Westendorp, R.G.J. (2016). "Successful Ageing: A Study of the Literature Using Citation Network Analysis". *Maturitas, 93*: 4-12.

Lohumi, P. (2023). *Festivals of Uttarakhand: A Journey into Cultural Riches*. https://www.youruttarakhand.com/post/festivals-of-uttarakhand

Michel, J.P., Dreux, C., Vachcron, A. (2016). "Healthy Ageing: Evidence That Improvement is Possible at Every Age". *European Geriatric Medical, 7*(4): 298-305.

National Council on Ageing. Chronic Inequities: Measuring Disease Cost Burden among Older Adults in the U.S. A Health and Retirement Study Analysis. Page 5, Figure 2. April 2022. Found on the internet at https://ncoa.org/article/the-inequities-in-the-cost-of-chronic-disease-why-it-matters-for-older-adults

Sadana, R. (2016). Commentary on "Healthy Ageing: Evidence That Improvement is Possible at Every Age". *European Geriatric Medical, 7*: 291-292.

Shankarananda Swami (1999). *An Introduction to Gerontology*. Central Chinmaya Mission Trust, Kanpur.

Sharngadhara Samhita (1984). Translator: Shri Kanta Murthy. Varanasi, India: Chaukhamba Orientalia.

Singh, R. (2015): "Social Conditions of Elderly and Problems". *Journal of Research in Humanities and Social Science, 3*(3). Retrieved from http://www.questjournals.org/jrhss/papers/vol3-issue3/I335254.pdf

Srivastava, M., Kapil, U., Kumar V., Dey, A.B., Nagarkar, K.M., Sekaran, G. (1996). "Knowledge, Attitude and Practices Regarding Nutrition in Patients Attending Geriatric Clinic at the AIIMS". In *Ageing : Indian Perspective and Global Scenario.* Kumar, V. (ed.). New Delhi: All India Institute of Medical Sciences, pp. 407-409.

Sushruta Samhita (1991). Translator: K.L. Bhishagratna. Varanasi, India: Chaukhamba Orientalia.

Thakur, M.K and Verma, D. (2022). "A Critical Review on Buransh (Rhododendron Arboreum)—An Unexplained Ayurvedic Gem in the Lap of Himalayas". *Journal of Research in Indian Medicine: An Official Publication of Bureau for Health & Education Status Upliftment.*

Üstün, T.B., Kostanjsek, N. Chatterji S., Rehm, J. (2010). "Measuring Health and Disability Manual for WHO Disability Assessment Schedule", *WHODAS 2.0.* WHO, Geneva.

World Health Organization, *Ageing and Health* (2024). https://www.who.int/news-room/fact-sheets/detail/ageing-and-health

World Health Organization (2015). *World Report on Ageing and Health.* WHO, Geneva.

World Health Organization (2016). *WHO global strategy and action plan on ageing and health* (*2016-2020*): WHO, Geneva.

World Health Organisation (2001). *The international classification of functioning, disability and health* (*ICF*)*:* WHO, Geneva.

9

The Role of Spirituality in Assuaging Death Anxiety Among Older Adults

A Comprehensive Overview

Himanshi Nigam, Shilpa Kumari and *Shobhna Joshi*

Introduction

The ageing process is a universal and natural occurrence. Development reaches a standstill at this final stage of human growth. Actually, it is meant to be a time of decline and degeneration. Traditionally, old age is considered to begin at the age of retirement (Budhiraja & Midha, 2017). Now that life expectancy has gone up, the technical growth on population forecasts estimates that by 2050, there would likely be 323 million elderly persons in India (Census of India, 2011). It also reveals that approximately 8.6 per cent of India's population is elderly. In general, elderly persons are overwhelmed by unpleasant emotions. Death anxiety is the most common fear among the elderly. The worry and apprehension about one's own death is known as death anxiety. It is a neurotic fear of losing oneself that is strongly accompanied by depression and learned helplessness (Budhiraja & Midha, 2017).

The North American Nursing Diagnosis (2007) defines death anxiety as a "vague uneasy feeling of discomfort or dread generated by perceptions of a real or imagined threat to one's existence." It is also among the most important aspects of mental health, and it can be influenced by a person's values, life purpose, and meaning. A person's thoughts, feelings, and attitudes towards their last experience of life under more typical circumstances are all included in death anxiety (Jong *et al.*, 2019). Death anxiety comprises a wide range of emotions, from a few fleeting seconds of terror to a full-blown panic attack (Sebea *et al.*, 2021).

Freud asserted that death anxiety was the first sign of neurosis in 1925, although he gave castration anxiety a greater significance in 1936. Nonetheless, he agreed that both concepts are linked to "a sense of loss". Accordingly, a large body of studies revealed a strong correlation between death anxiety, fear of separation, loss of meaning and control, and emotions of insecurity (Caras, 1995; Maxfield *et al.*, 2014; Menzies & Menzies, 2020; Noyes *et al.*, 2002).

Death anxiety is to some degree acceptable, and many resilient people manage even when they are reminded of death on a daily basis. As terror management theory (TMT) (Greenberg *et al.*, 1986, 1990) proposes that people in all cultures use their cultural worldviews as a buffer against death anxiety because they avoid thinking about or being reminded of death. Hence, cultural norms, customs, or beliefs become symbolic frameworks that offer some solace and security. Further research revealed that certain resilience factors or stress-buffer personality traits lessen or attenuate the impact of mortality inductions, particularly in cultural defenses (Greenberg *et al.*, 1993; Iverach *et al.*, 2014), and to offer positive adaptation in the face of adversity, anxiety, trauma, and threats (Bonanno, 2004; Dolcos *et al.*, 2016; Herrman *et al.*, 2011).

Additionally, various efforts have been made by the earlier researchers to identify the different dimensions of death anxiety. For instance, Swenson (1959) differentiated between "positive or forward looking", "evasive", and "fearful orientations towards death." Prior to this, Faunce and Fulton (1957) classified death attitudes according to temporal and spiritual frames of reference. Kalish (1963) also presented 20 factors taken from a set of 75 death attitude items. Later, Collett and Lester (1969) distinguished between four types of death fear: fear of death of self, fear of death of others, fear of dying of self, and fear of dying of others. Also, Nelson & Nelson (1975) identified four dimensions of death anxiety: death avoidance, death fear, death denial and reluctance to interact with the dying. Further, Conte and colleagues (1982) have also suggested 4 independent dimensions of death anxiety: Fear of the Unknown, Fear of Suffering, Fear of Loneliness, and Fear of Personal Extinction. However, Templer (1970) considered death anxiety as a unidimensional concept and developed his Death Anxiety Scale to capture a wider variety of death-related attitudes than death fear. Thus, in order to assess the presence and severity of death anxiety, a variety of self-report questionnaires have been created. A few of the most often used measures are the Collett-Lester Fear of Death Scale (Collett & Lester, 1969; Lester, 1990), the Death Anxiety Inventory (Tomas-Sabado & Gomez-Benito, 2005), the Death Anxiety

Scale (Royal & Elahi, 2011; Templer, 1970) and Thakur Death Anxiety Scale (Thakur & Thakur, 1984).

Everybody experiences death anxiety, which has varying effects on each individual. Nevertheless, an increased awareness of mortality is common in older persons, and this can result in death anxiety. According to Erikson's theory of psychosocial development (1950), older adults' average level of death anxiety may be explained by their wisdom from life experiences and their apparent development of "ego integrity", which enabled them to accept life as it is. The reason for its higher prevalence in older persons is that they experience or are more likely to experience various medical issues, chronic diseases, less mobility, physical disabilities, increased reliance on others (Nayak *et al.*, 2019), major losses (spouse, friends, and peers) (Nayak *et al.*, 2019; Aghajani *et al.*, 2011), and loneliness. Death anxiety can also be aggravated by retirement and the loneliness it brings (Aghajani *et al.*, 2011).

Although most of the studies on death anxiety were undertaken in nursing homes and residential settings, researchers have also tried to assess the predictors of death anxiety during and after the hospitalization among older adults. Hospitalization-related stressors, including being away from family, being in unfamiliar hospital settings, receiving diagnostic and therapeutic interventions, healthcare providers' poor communication with patients (Musavi *et al.*, 2016; Nasirizade *et al.*, 2018), fear of surviving serious health issues, pain and discomfort, lack of sleep, loss of independence in performing most daily living activities, loss of control over the environment, invasion of personal privacy, sensory overload, decreased social contribution, loss of respect and dignity, boredom during brief visits, and witnessing another patient's death (Ahmadi, 2014), may be responsible for the notable exacerbation of death anxiety during hospital stays. Consequently, the removal of these stressors, being placed in a familiar family setting, having familiar caregivers, receiving care, and having better health status may all contribute to the reduction of death anxiety following hospital discharge.

Additionally, Zahedi Bidgol and colleagues (2020) have indicated that death anxiety on the first day of hospitalization is significantly predicted by the age and the number of hospitalizations. Previous research has also suggested the significant correlation between age and death anxiety (John *et al.*, 2016; Harrawood *et al.*, 2009). The reason why death anxiety decreases with age could be that older persons view death as the end of their troubles, suffering, impairments, and low self-esteem; as a result, they experience less anxiety about dying. Similarly, an earlier study on

Iranian older individuals with diabetes found a strong association between hospitalizations and death anxiety (Azadi *et al.*, 2016). More hospital stays appear to not only exhaust patients but also give them the impression that they are suffering from serious illnesses, which lowers their hope of recovery and increases their fear of dying. Zahedi Bidgol and colleagues (2020) also found satisfaction with the work of hospital staff as a significant predictor of death anxiety among hospitalized older adults. The conduct and communication style of staff members, particularly nurses, have a major impact on patients' psychological security (Newell & Jordan, 2015) and their level of satisfaction with their performance (Jacelon, 2004).

Literature suggests that one significant aspect influencing death anxiety is gender. For instance, De Paola *et al.* (2003) found that older women experience higher levels of death anxiety than older men. Madnawat and Kachhawa (2007) and Saini *et al.* (2016) have also revealed similar findings about the elderly population of the Indian Subcontinent. This is in contrast to Fortner and Neimeyer's (1999) assessment of 49 studies on older individuals' death anxiety, which found that gender did not appear to predict death anxiety in this population. Other researchers, like Assari and Lankarani (2016) and Suhail and Akram (2002), also reported similar patterns of results. Hence, there is no consensus among the researchers on gender differences in death anxiety.

Since death is an unavoidable stressor, most older people attempt to emotionally ignore it or increasingly turn to philosophical and spiritual beliefs to cope with this uncontrolled condition (Taghiabadi *et al.*, 2018). Anxiety brought on by man's awareness of his own death can only be managed by acknowledging one's individuality. It is the spirituality which serves as an inner strength and allows one to move beyond self-interest and make sense of both lived experiences and transcendent (Staton *et al.*, 2001). According to World Health Organization, spirituality is a vital aspect of human health, alongside physical, psychological, and social health (Altimus *et al.*, 2017). Although there are many different definitions of spirituality, it is generally understood to be a source of the utmost concern for people, reflecting a sense of connectedness to the transcendental and the highest levels of moral, emotional, cognitive, and inter personal growth (Vaughan, 2002). Spirituality is the pursuit and expression of meaning and purpose in life, as well as a sense of connection to the present, to oneself, to others, to nature, and to the sacred or significant (Puchalski *et al.*, 2009).

According to Shaton *et al.* (2001), spirituality is the human tendency to explore life's concepts while feeling a need to grow oneself or connect with something greater than oneself. Thus, spirituality gives older adults another tool for finding meaning during the emotional and physical struggles that frequently accompany ageing and dying. Spirituality can function as a self-transcendent resource that allows an individual to develop, find meaning, and feel a sense of completion during the difficult existential experiences of ageing, loss, disability, and dying that can cause an ageing adult to become isolated from resources of support (Wong, 2008). Spirituality can also offer a sense of belonging, social support, and connection to the elderly (Koenig, 2012).

One aspect of spirituality is spiritual intelligence (SI). It is defined as heightened insight of one's inner mind and capacity to reflect on existential questions, evolving consciousness, and deepening awareness of the meanings of life (Gardner, 2000; Vaughan, 2002; Zohar *et al.*, 2000). King (2008) defines spiritual intelligence as the ability to recognise, integrate, and apply non-material and transcendent aspects of one's existence, resulting in deep existential reflection, enhanced meaning, self-awareness, and mastery of spiritual states. Based on an extensive review of literature, King and DeCicco (2009) developed a viable model of spiritual intelligence, which supported 4 main dimensions of spiritual intelligence: (1) critical existential thinking, (2) personal meaning production, (3) transcendental awareness, and (4) conscious state expansion. According to Emmons (2000), having spiritual intelligence helps people find significance in life's experiences and see each moment as a part of a greater journey; this in turn can lessen death anxiety. Not only this, researchers have suggested that spiritual intelligence: (SI) may be of great importance to human well-being because it reflects a developed capacity to reflect from numerous perspectives and to integrate relationships among perception, beliefs, and behaviours (Anandrajah & Hight, 2001; Daaleman *et al.*, 2004; Kennedy *et al.*, 2002; Van Ness & Kasl, 2003).

Spiritual well-being is another aspect of spirituality. Tumanggor (2019) asserts that spiritual well-being is a measure of spiritual health or the quality of life in the spiritual dimension. The inner life and its connection to the outside world are fundamental to spiritual well-being. Positive interactions with others and one's surroundings are indicators of spiritual well-being. Thus, it is essential to one's physical, mental, and emotional well-being, and is regarded as the main coping mechanism used during the healing and recovery process. It can or cannot be linked to a particular religion and is simply a person's personal quest to understand the meaning of life and where they fit in. Positive manifestations of spirituality are a sign of spiritual well-being (Shukla & Rishi, 2014). By decreasing feelings of sadness, anger and anxiety as well as raising feelings of optimism, spiritual well-being can enhance people's quality of life, thus making them more optimistic and regret-free (Al-Natour *et al.*, 2017). This can also promote acceptance of life's uncertainties (Cicirelli, 2002) and hence, help in the management of death anxiety.

The implications of death anxiety are not always negative as Hoelterhoff and Chung (2020) consider death anxiety as a motivating factor that encourages older adults to live life to the fullest and accept death as a normal process. However, a key aspect of successful ageing is accepting death and facing it peacefully. Since death is a natural part of life, having a low level of death anxiety throughout one's life is essential for engaging in constructive activities. Spirituality can help people in living a life of meaning and developing acceptance towards death.

Rationale

Elderly people frequently deal with certain existential issues, especially those pertaining to mortality, which can increase their death anxiety. Spirituality, on the other hand, has been demonstrated to provide possible protective advantages against a range of psychological distress, such as anxiety and death-related fear. Given the growing number of elderly people worldwide and the demand for interventions that support well-being in later life, it is particularly important to investigate the connection between spirituality and death anxiety in the elderly. To the best of my knowledge, no literature review has yet comprehensively described the relationship between spirituality and death anxiety among older adults. Thus, this narrative review helps in the consolidation of results, making connections and the identification of recurring patterns as well as current research needs in this area.

Review of Literature

Various studies have reported prevalence of different degree of death anxiety among older adults. Research conducted in Israel (2010) and Turkey (2019) found that most older persons experienced high levels of death anxiety (Azaiza *et al.*, 2010; Bakan *et al.*, 2019). Furthermore, a study conducted in India found that 60 per cent of older persons had moderate death anxiety, whereas 40 per cent had severe death anxiety (John *et al.*, 2016). However, some studies have also found low level of death anxiety in older adults (Moreno *et al.*, 2008; Almostadi, 2018; Sebea *et al.*, 2021). Negative health effects, such as a decline in bodily functions, psychological stress, impaired ego integrity, a deterioration in religious beliefs, life dissatisfaction, and low resilience, have been linked to death anxiety (Semenova & Stadtlander, 2016).

Previous research has shown the impact of spirituality on death anxiety and fear. Nonetheless, the importance of spirituality is manifold as research has demonstrated that spirituality is associated with improved mental, psychological, and physical health (Chibnall *et al.*, 2002; Meisnhelder & Chandler, 2002); subjective well-being (Micozzi, 2006; Fry, 2000); generativity and wisdom (Wink, 2008); life satisfaction (Wills, 2009); and a lower incidence of depression (Han & Richardson, 2010; Rykkje *et al.*, 2013). Furthermore, spiritual experiences have been shown to improve people's health, understanding of life's purpose, happiness, and cheer (Krishna Mohan, 1999); effective well-being, full participation in daily activities (Wink & Dillon, 2008); and infrequently experiencing sadness or depression (Baetz *et al.*, 2004).

As people age, spirituality plays an adaptive function in enhancing their quality of life and extending their lifespan. Thus, spirituality offers a framework for people to find solace and meaning, which may help in alleviating death anxiety. On this line, Budhiraja and Midha (2017) conducted a study on 200 elderly people from Rohtak city (Haryana). Their findings indicated the presence of high level of spirituality and average level of death anxiety among these elderly people. Also, a negative correlation was found between spirituality and death anxiety which indicates the healing power of spirituality among elderly. In an attempt to examine the relationship between death anxiety and different aspects of spiritual experiences, Taghiabadi and colleagues (2018) found a significant negative association between contact with God and fear of suffering after death. They concluded that contact with God demonstrates reliance on a higher power and thus, it may reduce death anxiety in the elderly whether through specific religious ceremonies or a personal experience.

Further, spirituality was found to be a significant predictor in a study conducted to assess the relationship between spirituality and death anxiety among 160 elderly people (Sharma *et al.*, 2019). In a contemporary study, Radhakrishnan (2019) examined the association between spirituality and attitudes towards death among 100 senior citizens in residential houses and in old age homes. It was found that that higher the level of spirituality (spiritual openness), lower the level of fear of death. This study also discovered a negative correlation between spirituality and positive dimension of attitude towards death (Escape acceptance).

Prior to this, Taghiabadi *et al.* (2017) concluded that using spiritual experiences and promoting life satisfaction can help reduce stressors in the elderly, including death anxiety. Recently, Soriano and Calong (2022) found significant negative relationship between spirituality and death anxiety among Filipino older adults. In another study, Waheed Elzohairy and colleagues (2022) undertook a study to determine the association between death anxiety, spiritual well-being, and successful ageing among community dwelling older adults of Egypt. Their results highlighted that there was significant positive relationship between spirituality and successful ageing which were also statistically significant negative predictors of death anxiety in older adults.

A study by Naderi and Roushani (2011) discovered a significant correlation between Ahwaz elderly women's spiritual intelligence and their death anxiety. Similarly, Taghipour *et al.* (2017) examined death anxiety and spiritual intelligence among 123 Iranian hemodialysis patients. They discovered a strong negative correlation between the two, suggesting that as spiritual intelligence increased, death anxiety could be reduced. However, a positive association was found between spiritual intelligence and death anxiety among 211 Iranian veterans (Pahlevan Sharif *et al.*, 2021). Another study on cancer patients found that one of the key factors lowering death anxiety and raising life satisfaction was spiritual intelligence (Shirkavand *et al.*, 2018). Moreover, Majidi and Moradi (2018) found that educating the elderly with the spiritual intelligence component reduced their death anxiety.

One of the most important and complex factors that plays a key role in the phenomenon of the death anxiety is spiritual well-being. Previous research has examined the relationship between death anxiety and spiritual well-being in individuals with chronic diseases. However, their findings show contradictory results. Various studies reveal a negative relationship between death anxiety and spiritual well-being in individuals with chronic diseases (Aderyani *et al.*, 2021; Mansori *et al.*, 2017; Shirkavand *et al.*, 2018). A recent meta-analysis on "Spiritual Well-being and Death Anxiety in Chronic Diseases" discovered a negative relationship between spiritual well-being and death anxiety in chronic diseases people with a low effect size. This implies that for those suffering from chronic illnesses, spiritual well-being may be a factor in lowering death anxiety (Putri & Anganthi, 2023).

Similarly, Shukla & Rishi (2014) conducted a study on 80 advance stage cancer patients, from six exclusive cancer hospitals of western and central zones of India. Their results revealed negative association between spiritual well-being and death anxiety, which indicated that enhancing the spiritual well-being of cancer patients can reduce their death anxiety and promote better quality of life. Another study aimed to examine the association of death anxiety with spiritual well-being among 248 community-dwelling Arabic older adults during the COVID-19 pandemic and spiritual well-being emerged as a significant predictor of death anxiety in older adults (Rababa *et al.*, 2021). Having clarity of thought regarding the order of things can improve spiritual well-being and even lessen death anxiety. According to Ebadi *et al.* (2009) and Gupta *et al.* (2016), the inner serenity that results from realizing one's own purpose in life fosters self-worth, adaptability, and responsibility in addition to lowering anxiety regarding death.

On the other hand, Soleimani and colleagues (2018) discovered no significant association between death anxiety and spiritual well-being in those with chronic diseases. Nevertheless, a positive relationship between death anxiety and spiritual well-being has also been found in those with chronic diseases (Taghipour *et al.*, 2017). Similarly, Zahedi Bidgol and colleagues (2020) examined hospitalized patients over 60 years of age and discovered that those with higher levels of spiritual well-being experienced lower death anxiety. This can be explained by the fact that the way people cope with the concept of death is greatly influenced by their spiritual well-being since it affects how they see their current situation (Soleimani *et al.*, 2016; Yaghoobzadeh *et al.*, 2017). Further, it was suggested that positive emotions regarding their current difficult circumstances and a powerful inner healing force are experienced by older persons who are spiritually well (Soleimani *et al.*, 2018). Hence, individuals with high levels of spiritual well-being are better able to manage their overwhelming anxiety related to the actual and anticipated death of themselves or their loved ones than those with low levels of spiritual well-being (MacLeod *et al.*, 2019).

Implications

Understanding the relationship between spirituality and death anxiety holds significance especially for elderly care. Examining the factors that affect death anxiety can enable healthcare providers to create strategies for reduce and/or controlling death anxiety. Additionally, by incorporating spiritual care into therapeutic practices, caregivers and mental health professionals can offer older persons more thorough assistance by helping them find peace, composure and resilience in the face of death. Moreover, it is believed that by identifying the vulnerability and upholding the dignity of elderly patients, spirituality assessments of this age group assist nurses in providing high-quality nursing care. By acknowledging that particular beliefs or concerns may cause people to have increased worry about dying, practitioners can be ready to address specific causes of spiritual anguish and create a nurturing environment that encourages acceptance and tranquility. As indicated by Lau & Cheng (2011), this can positively impact the quality of life, end-of-life decisions, life satisfaction, and improve the readiness and acceptance of death of older persons. These findings also highlight the significance of developing inclusive, culturally sensitive elder-care programmes that attend to the spiritual as well as physical and psychological needs of senior citizens. Therefore, quality of life and general wellness of older persons who are suffering death anxiety could thus be greatly enhanced by programmes that provide spiritual support services and spiritual sensitivity training for caregivers.

Future Suggestions

As previous studies have demonstrated contradictory results with respect to gender differences in death anxiety among the elderly, further studies are required to clarify this relationship. Nonetheless, future research needs to consider the wide variety of cultural, religious, and individual differences in spirituality, which can shape the experience and management of death anxiety. The major focus of prior research has been on specific religious populations, thus there is a need for further studies to understand how non-religious forms of spirituality or secular sources of meaning and purpose impact death anxiety in elderly individuals from diverse backgrounds impacts death anxiety. Also, future research with a standardized approach is required to accurately assess specific dimensions of spirituality—such as spiritual coping, existential well-being, and beliefs about the afterlife—that may play distinct roles in moderating death anxiety among older adults. There is also a need of longitudinal research to explore how the relationship between spirituality and death anxiety may evolve over time, particularly as individuals approach end-of-life stages. This will enable us to assess whether spirituality's impact on death anxiety remains stable, increases, or decreases as death becomes more imminent. Furthermore, only few studies have examined potential mediating or moderating variables that could explain or influence the connection between spirituality and death anxiety. This can help a number of initiatives and interventions in India which use spirituality to help manage death anxiety among the elderly. For instance, organizations like Indian Association of Palliative Care

(IAPC) work with healthcare providers to provide spiritual care training and bereavement counselling to staff members. Moreover, initiatives like Sanjeevani India provide spiritual and emotional support, assisting individuals in managing their death anxiety in a manner consistent with their spiritual beliefs. The National Programme for Health Care of the Elderly (NPHCE) urges healthcare professionals to respect and take into account the spiritual needs of the elderly while providing elderly with holistic care for their mental health and general well-being. Hence, there is a need for more studies in this regard which will not only help in strengthening the existing programmes and interventions but also develop new interventions tailored to the specific needs.

Conclusion

This review has examined the association between spirituality and death anxiety among the older adults. The findings of various research indicate that spirituality provides older persons with a feeling of purpose, connection, and serenity in the face of mortality, hence acting as a protective factor against death anxiety. However, spirituality's impact on death anxiety is inconsistent because it differs by culture, religion, and individual. Nevertheless, the knowledge of the relationship between spirituality and death anxiety can help us develop a person-centred, compassionate approach to eldercare that takes into account both spiritual, and psychological aspects of ageing.

References

Aghajani, M., Valiee, S. & Tol, A. (2011). "Death Anxiety Amongst Nurses in Critical Care and General Wards". *Iran J Nurs, 23*(67): 59-68.

Ahmadi, M.H. (2014). *Pathology of Stress and Control Methods: How to Be Calm*. Nazar Abad: Siyadat.

Almostadi, D. (2018). *The Moderating Effect of Religion on Death Distress and Quality of Life between Christian Cancer Patients in the United States with Muslim Cancer Patients in Saudi Arabia* (Ph.D. Thesis). University of South Florida.

Al-Natour, A., Al Momani, S.M. & Qandil, A.M.A. (2017). "The Relationship Between Spirituality and Quality of Life of Jordanian Women Diagnosed with Breast Cancer". *Journal of Religion and Health, 56*(6): 2096-2108.

Altimus, C., Ford, W., Chapman, B. & Tillery, C. (2017). "The Importance of a Holistic Safety, Health, and Wellness Research Programme". *Nat Inst J, 278.*

Anandrajah, G. & Hight, E. (2001). "Spirituality and Medical Practice: Using the Hope Questions as a Practical Tool for Spiritual Assessment in Office Practice". *American Family Physician, 63*(2): 81-88.

Assari, S. & Lankarani, M.M. (2016). "Race and Gender Differences in Correlates of Death Anxiety among Elderly in the United States". *Iranian Journal of Psychiatry and Behavioural Sciences, 10*(2).

Azadi, A., Taghinezhad, H., Bastami, M. & Bastami, A.R. (2016). "The Study Amount of Anxiety and Depression among Elderly Diabetic Patients Referred to Shahid Mostafa Khomeini in Ilam and Shohada Ashayer Hospitals in Khoramabad 2015". *Iranian Journal of Nursing Research, 11*(3): 1-9.

Azaiza, F., Ron, P., Shohamb, M. & Giginia, I. (2010). "Death and Dying Anxiety among Elderly Arab Muslims in Israel". *Death Studies, 34*, 351-364.

Baetz, M., Griffin, R., Bowen, R., Koenig, H.G. & Marcoux, E. (2004). "The Association Between Spiritual and Religious Involvement and Depressive Symptoms in a Canadian Population". *The Journal of Nervous and Mental Disease, 192*(12): 818-822.

Bakan, A.B., Arli, S.K. & Yildiz, M. (2019). "Relationship Between Religious Orientation and Death Anxiety in Elderly Individuals". *Journal of Religion and Health, 58*(6): 2241-2250.

Bonanno, G.A. (2004). "Loss, Trauma, and Human Resilience: Have We Underestimated the Human Capacity to Thrive After Extremely Aversive Events?". *American Psychologist, 59*(1): 20.

Budhiraja, A. & Midha, P. (2017). "Buffering Power of Spirituality Against Death Anxiety". *The International Journal of Indian Psychology, 4*, 59-65.

Caras, G.W. (1995). *The Relationships among Psychological Separation, the Quality of Attachment, Separation Anxiety and Death Anxiety* (Doctoral Dissertation, ProQuest Information & Learning).

Cheng, F.K. (2017). "Buddhist Insights into Life and Death: Overcoming Death Anxiety." *Athens Journal of Social Sciences, 4*(1): 67-87.

Chibnall, J.T., Videen, S.D., Duckro, P.N. & Miller, D.K. (2002). "Psychosocial-Spiritual Correlates of Death Distress in Patients with Life-Threatening Medical Conditions". *Palliative Medicine, 16*(4): 331-338.

Cicirelli, V.G. (2002). "Fear of Death in Older Adults: Predictions from Terror Management Theory". *The Journals of Gerontology Series B: Psychological Sciences and Social Sciences, 57*(4): P358-P366.

Collett, L.J. & Lester, D. (1969). "The Fear of Death and the Fear of Dying". *The Journal of Psychology, 72*(2): 179-181.

Conte, H.R., Weiner, M.B. & Plutchik, R. (1982). "Measuring Death Anxiety: Conceptual, Psychometric, and Factor-Analytic Aspects". *Journal of Personality and Social Psychology, 43*(4): 775-785.

Conte, H.R., Weiner, M.B. & Plutchik, R. (1982). "Measuring Death Anxiety: Conceptual, Psychometric, and Factor-Analytic Aspects". *Journal of Personality and Social Psychology, 43*(4): 775.

Daaleman, T.P., Perera, S. & Studenski, S.A. (2004). "Religion, Spirituality, and Health Status in Geriatric Outpatients". *The Annals of Family Medicine, 2*(1): 49-53.

Delhi, N. (2011). *Census of India*, 2011.

Depaola, S.J., Griffin, M., Young, J.R. & Neimeyer, R.A. (2003). "Death Anxiety and Attitudes Toward the Elderly among Older Adults: The Role of Gender and Ethnicity". *Death Studies*, *27*(4): 335-354.

Dolcos, S., Hu, Y., Iordan, A.D., Moore, M. & Dolcos, F. (2016). "Optimism and the Brain: Trait Optimism Mediates the Protective Role of the Orbitofrontal Cortex Gray Matter Volume Against Anxiety". *Social Cognitive and Affective Neuroscience*, *11*(2): 263-271.

Ebadi, A., Ahmadi, F., Ghanei, M. & Kazemnejad, A. (2009). "Spirituality: A Key Factor in Coping among Iranians Chronically Affected by Mustard Gas in the Disaster of War". *Nursing & Health Sciences*, *11*(4): 344-350.

Emmons, R.A. (2000). "Is Spirituality An Intelligence? Motivation, Cognition, and the Psychology of Ultimate Concern". *The International Journal for the Psychology of Religion*, *10*(1): 3-26.

Erikson, E.H. (1950). *Childhood and Society*. New York: Norton.

Faunce, W.A. & Fulton, R.L. (1957). "The Sociology of Death: A Neglected Area of Research". *Soc. F.*, *36*, 205.

Fortner, B.V., and Neimeyer, R.A. (1999): "Death Anxiety in Older Adults: A Quantitative Review". *Death Studies, 23*, 387-411.

Freud, S. (1925). *Thoughts for the Times on War and Death*. Hogart Press.

_____ (1936). *The Problem of Anxiety*. Norton Publishing.

Fry, P.S. Psychological Well-being in Community-Residing and Institutional Care Elders. *Ageing and Mental Health, 4*, 375-387.

Gardner, H.E. (2000). *Intelligence Reframed: Multiple Intelligences for the 21st Century*. Hachette UK.

Greenberg, J., Pyszczynski, T. & Solomon, S. (1986). "The Causes and Consequences of a Need for Self-Esteem: A Terror Management Theory". In *Public Self and Private Self* (pp. 189-212). New York: Springer.

Greenberg, J., Pyszczynski, T., Solomon, S., Pinel, E., Simon, L. & Jordan, K. (1993). "Effects of Self-Esteem on Vulnerability-Denying Defensive Distortions: Further Evidence of An Anxiety-Buffering Function of Self-Esteem". *Journal of Experimental Social Psychology*, *29*(3): 229-251.

Greenberg, J., Pyszczynski, T., Solomon, S., Rosenblatt, A., Veeder, M., Kirkland, S. & Lyon, D. (1990). "Evidence for Terror Management Theory II: The Effects of Mortality Salience on Reactions to Those Who Threaten Or Bolster the Cultural Worldview". *Journal of Personality and Social Psychology*, *58*(2): 308.

Gupta, S., Girls, G.D.H. & Khanna, P. (2016). "Pattern of Life Satisfaction and Death Anxiety in Civil Police and Provincial Armed Constabulary (PAC) Police: A Gender Based Study. *Journal Global Values*, *7*: 1-6.

Han, J. & Richardson, V.E. (2010). "The Relationship Between Depression and Loneliness among Homebound Older Persons: Does Spirituality Moderate This Relationship?" *Journal of Religion & Spirituality in Social Work: Social Thought, 29*(3): 218-236.

Harrawood, L.K., White, L.J. & Benshoff, J.J. (2009). "Death Anxiety in a National Sample of United States Funeral Directors and Its Relationship with Death Exposure, Age, and Sex". *OMEGA—Journal of Death and Dying*, *58*(2): 129-146.

Herrman, H., Stewart, D.E., Diaz-Granados, N., Berger, E.L., Jackson, B. & Yuen, T. (2011). "What is resilience?" *The Canadian Journal of Psychiatry*, *56*(5): 258-265.

Hoelterhoff, M. & Chung, M.C. (2020). "Self-Efficacy as an Agentic Protective Factor against Death Anxiety in PTSD and Psychiatric Co-Morbidity". *Psychiatr Q, 91*(1): 165-181.

Iverach, L., Menzies, R.G. & Menzies, R.E. (2014). "Death Anxiety and Its Role in Psychopathology: Reviewing the Status of a Transdiagnostic Construct". *Clinical Psychology Review*, *34*(7): 580-593.

Jacelon, C.S. (2004). "Managing Personal Integrity: The Process of Hospitalization for Elders". *Journal of Advanced Nursing*, *46*(5): 549-557.

John, M., Binoy, S., Reddy, V., Passyavula, S.K. & Reddy, P. (2016). "A Study to Assess the Level of Death Anxiety among Elderly People at Selected Area at Bhopal." *International Journal of Medical and Health Research, 2*(5): 23-24.

Jong, J., Halberstadt, J., Bluemke, M., Kavanagh, C. & Jackson, C. (2019). "Death Anxiety, Exposure to Death, Mortuary Preferences, and Religiosity in Five Countries". *Scientific Data, 6*, 154.

Kalish, R.A. (1963). "An Approach to the Study of Death Attitudes". *American Behavioural Scientist*, *6*(9): 68-70.

Kennedy, J.E., Abbott, R.A. & Rosenberg, B.S. (2002). "Changes in Spirituality and Well-being in a Retreat Programme for Cardiac Patients". *Alternative Therapies in Health and Medicine, 8*(4): 64-73.

King, D.B. & DeCicco, T.L. (2009). "A Viable Model and Self-Report Measure of Spiritual Intelligence". *International Journal of Trans Personal Studies, 28*, 68-85.

King, D.B. (2008). "Rethinking Claims of Spiritual Intelligence: A Definition, Model, and Measure". *Unpublished Master's Thesis,* Trent University, Peterborough, Ontario, Canada.

Koenig, H.G. (2012). "Religion, spirituality, and health: The research and clinical implications". *International Scholarly Research Notices*, (1): 278730.

Krishna Mohan, K. (1999). *Spirituality and Well-being: Effects of Spiritual Experiences and Spiritually Based Life Style Change Programme on Psychological Well-being*. [Unpublished Ph.D. thesis, Andhra University].

Lau, R.W. & Cheng, S. (2011). "Gratitude Lessens Death Anxiety". *European Journal of Ageing, 8*(3): 168-169.

Lester, D. (1990). "The Collett-Lester Fear of Death Scale: The Original Version and a Revision". *Death Studies*, *14*(5): 451-468.

MacLeod, R., Wilson, D.M., Crandall, J. & Austin, P. (2019). "Death Anxiety among New Zealanders: The Predictive Roles of Religion, Spirituality, and Family Connection". *OMEGA—Journal of Death and Dying, 80*(1): 3-19.

Madnawat, A.S. & Kachhawa, P.S. (2007). "Age, Gender, and Living Circumstances: Discriminating Older Adults on Death Anxiety". *Death Studies, 31*(8): 763-769.

Majidi, A. & Moradi, O. (2018). "Effect of Teaching the Components of Spiritual Intelligence on Death Anxiety in the Elderly". *Iranian Journal of Ageing, 13*(1): 110-123.

Maxfield, M., John, S. & Pyszczynski, T. (2014). "A Terror Management Perspective on the Role of Death-Related Anxiety in Psychological Dysfunction". *The Humanistic Psychologist, 42*(1): 35-53.

Meisenhelder, J.B. & Chandler, E.N. (2002). "Spirituality and Health Outcomes in the Elderly". *Journal of Religion and Health, 41*, 243-252.

Menzies, R.E. & Menzies, R.G. (2020). "Death Anxiety in the Time of Covid-19: Theoretical Explanations and Clinical Implications". *The Cognitive Behaviour Therapist, 13*, 1-19.

Micozzi, M.S. (2006). *Fundamentals of complementary and integrative medicine* (3rd ed.). St. Louis, MO: Saunders Elsevier.

Moreno, R., Solana, E., Aleixandre Rico, M. & Lozano, L. (2008). "Death Anxiety in Institutionalized and Non-Institutionalized Elderly People in Spain". *Omega, 58*, 61-76.

Musavi, Z., Alavi, M., Alimohammadi, N. & Hosseini, H. (2016). "Development and Initial Psychometric Evaluation of the Hospitalization-Related Stressors Questionnaire for Elderly Patients". *Iranian Journal of Nursing and Midwifery Research, 21*(5): 516-520.

Naderi, F. & Roushani, K.H. (2011). "The Relations Between Spiritual Intelligence, Social Intelligence and Death Anxiety in Ahwaz Women Senile". *Women and Culture, 2*(6): 55-67.

Nasirizade, M., Biabani, F. & Geraminejad, N. (2018). "Assessment of Nurses' Performance Regarding Patient Education from Patients' Standpoint". *Education Strategies in Medical Sciences, 11*(4): 123-128.

Nayak, S., Mohapatra, M.K. & Panda, B. (2019). "Prevalence of and Factors Contributing to Anxiety, Depression and Cognitive Disorders among Urban Elderly in Odisha—A Study Through the Health Systems' Lens". *Archives of Gerontology and Geriatrics, 80*, 38-45.

Nelson, L.D. & Nelson, C.C. (1975). "A Factor Analytic Inquiry into the Multidimensionality of Death Anxiety." *OMEGA—Journal of Death and Dying, 6*(2): 171-178.

Newell, S. & Jordan, Z. (2015). "The Patient Experience of Patient-Centred Communication with Nurses in the Hospital Setting: A Qualitative Systematic Review Protocol". *JBI Evidence Synthesis, 13*(1): 76-87.

North American Nursing Diagnosis Association. (2007). *NANDA-I Nursing Diagnoses: Definitions & Classification 2007-08*. NANDA International.

Noyes, J.R., Stuart, S., Longley, S.L., Langbehn, D.R. & Happel, R.L. (2002). "Hypochondriasis and Fear of Death". *The Journal of Nervous and Mental Disease, 190*(8): 503-509.

Pahlevan Sharif, S., Sharif Nia, H., Lehto, R.H., Moradbeigi, M., Naghavi, N., Goudarzian, A.H., Yaghoobzadeh, A. & Nazari, R. (2021). "The Relationship Between Spirituality Dimensions and Death Anxiety among Iranian Veterans: Partial Least Squares Structural Equation Modelling Approach". *Journal of Religion and Health, 60*, 999-1014.

Puchalski, C., Ferrell, B., Virani, R., Otis-Green, S., Baird, P., Bull, J., Chochinov H., Handzo, G., Nelson-Becker, H., Prince-Paul, M. (2009). "Improving the Quality of Spiritual Care as a Dimension of Palliative Care: The Report of the Consensus Conference". *Journal of Palliative Medicine, 12*(10): 885-904.

Putri, H.O. & Anganthi, N.R.N. (2023). "Spiritual Well-being and Death Anxiety in Chronic Diseases: A Meta-Analysis Study". *Indigenous: Journal Ilmiah Psikologi, 8*(2). 123-139.

Rababa, M., Hayajneh, A.A. & Bani-Iss, W. (2021). "Association of Death Anxiety with Spiritual Well-being and Religious Coping in Older Adults During the Covid-19 Pandemic". *Journal of Religion and Health, 60*(1): 50-63.

Radhakrishnan, R. (2019). "Spirituality and Attitude towards Death among Senior Citizens with Special Reference to Bengaluru, India". *International Journal for Research in Applied Sciences and Biotechnology, 6*(2): 1-8.

Royal, K.D. & Elahi, F. (2011). "Psychometric Properties of the Death Anxiety Scale (Das) among Terminally Ill Cancer Patients". *Journal of Psychosocial Oncology, 29*(4): 359-371.

Rykkje, L.L., Eriksson, K. & Raholm, M.B. (2013). "Spirituality and Caring in Old Age and the Significance of Religion—A Hermeneutical Study from Norway". *Scandinavian Journal of Caring Sciences, 27*(2): 275-284.

Saini, P., Patidar, A.B., Kaur, R., Kaur, M. & Kaur, J. (2016). "Death Anxiety and Its Associated Factors among Elderly Population of Ludhiana City, Punjab". *Indian Journal of Gerontology, 30*(1): 101-110.

Sebea, D.E., El-Geneidy, M.M., Abd-Elsalam, R.M. & Dawood, S.S. (2021). "Factors Associated with Death Anxiety among Community Dwelling Older Adults". *Alexandria Scientific Nursing Journal, 23*(1): 1-17.

Semenova, V. & Stadtlander, L. (2016). "Death Anxiety, Depression, and Coping in Family Caregivers". *Journal of Social, Behavioural, and Health Sciences, 10*(1): 34-48.

Sharma, P., Asthana, H.S., Gambhir, I.S. & Ranjan, J.K. (2019). "Death Anxiety among Elderly People: Role of Gender, Spirituality and Mental Health". *Indian Journal of Gerontology, 33*(3).

Shukla, P. & Rishi, P. (2014). "A Correlational Study of Psychosocial & Spiritual Well-being and Death Anxiety among Advanced Stage Cancer Patients". *American Journal of Applied Psychology, 2*(3): 59-65.

Soleimani, M.A., Lehto, R.H., Negarandeh, R., Bahrami, N. & Chan, Y.H. (2016). "Death Anxiety and Quality of Life in Iranian Caregivers of Patients with Cancer". *Cancer Nursing, 40*(1): 1-10.

Soleimani, M.A., Sharif, S.P., Yaghoobzadeh, A., Yeoh, K.K. & Panarello, B. (2018). "Exploring the Relationship Between Spiritual Well-being and Death Anxiety in Survivors of Acute Myocardial Infarction: Moderating Role of Sex, Marital Status and Social Support". *Journal of Religion and Health, 57*(2): 683-703.

Soriano, G.P. & Calong, K.A.C. (2022). "Religiosity, Spirituality, and Death Anxiety among Filipino Older Adults: A Correlational Study". *OMEGA—Journal of Death and Dying*, *85*(2): 445-454.

Staton, J., Shuy, R.W. & Byock, I. (2001). *A Few Months to Live: Different Paths to Life's End*. Georgetown University Press.

Suhail, K. & Akram, S. (2002). "Correlates of Death Anxiety in Pakistan". *Death Studies*, *26*(1): 39-50.

Swenson, W.M. (1959). "Attitudes Toward Death among the Aged; Their Significance in the Practice of Geriatric Medicine". *Minnesota Medicine, 42*(4): 399-402.

Taghiabadi, M., Babaie, K., Mehrabi, T., Shaermoghadam, S. & Mirhafez, S.R. (2018). "Association Between Death Anxiety and Various Aspects of Spiritual Experiences among Elderly People in Iran". *Medical Science, 22*(93): 478-483.

Taghiabadi, M., Kavosi, A., Mirhafez, S.R., Keshvari, M. & Mehrabi, T. (2017). "The Association Between Death Anxiety with Spiritual Experiences and Life Satisfaction in Elderly People". *Electronic Physician*, *9*(3): 3980.

Taghipour, B., Mehravar, F., Nia, H.S., Shahidifar, S., Hasani, S.A. & Alahyari, Z. (2017). "Association between Death Anxiety and Spiritual Intelligence with the Spiritual Health and Quality of Life in Hemodialysis Patients. *Journal of Nursing and Midwifery Sciences*, *4*(2): 26-32.

Templer, D.I. (1970). "The Construction and Validation of a Death Anxiety Scale". *The Journal of General Psychology*, *82*(2): 165-177.

Thakur, G.P. & Thakur, M. (1984). "Development of An Improved Measure of Death Anxiety Suitable to Indian Conditions". *Indian Journal of Clinical Psychology, 11*(1): 87-91.

Tomas-Sabado, J. & Gomez-Benito, J. (2005). "Construction and Validation of the Death Anxiety Inventory (DAI)". *European Journal of Psychological Assessment*, *21*(2): 108.

Tumanggor, R.O. (2019). "Analisa Konseptual Model Spiritual Well-being Menurut Ellison Dan Fisher". *Jurnal Muara Ilmu Sosial, Humaniora, Dan Seni*, *3*(1): 43.

Van Ness, P.H. & Kasl, S.V. (2003). "Religion and Cognitive Dysfunction in An Elderly Cohort". *The Journals of Gerontology Series B: Psychological Sciences and Social Sciences*, *58*(1): S21-S29.

Vaughan, F. (2002). "What Is Spiritual Intelligence?" *Journal of Humanistic Psychology, 42*(2): 16-33.

Waheed Elzohairy, N., Alsaied Alfayomy, N. & I. Hassan, N. (2022). "The Relationship between Death Anxiety, Spiritual Well-being, and Successful Ageing among Community Dwelling Older Adults". *International Egyptian Journal of Nursing Sciences and Research, 3*(1): 272-285.

Wills, E. (2009). "Spirituality and Subjective Well-being: Evidences for a New Domain in the Personal Well-being Index". *Journal of Happiness Studies, 10*(1): 49-69.

Wink, P. & Dillon, M. (2003). "Religiousness, Spirituality, and Psychosocial Functioning in Late Adulthood: Findings from a Longitudinal Study". *Psychology and Ageing, 18*(4): 916-924.

Wong, P.T. (2008). "Transformation of Grief Through Meaning: Meaning-Centred Counselling for Bereavement". *Existential and Spiritual Issues in Death Attitudes*, 375-396.

Yaghoobzadeh, A., Soleimani, M.A., Allen, K.A., Chan, Y.H. & Herth, K.A. (2017). "Relationship between Spiritual Well-being and Hope in Patients with Cardiovascular Disease". *Journal of Religion and Health, 57*(3): 938-950.

Zahedi Bidgol, Z., Tagharrobi, Z., Sooki, Z. & Sharifi, K. (2020). "Death Anxiety and Its Predictors among Older Adults". *Journal of Holistic Nursing and Midwifery, 30*(2): 101-110.

Zohar, D., Marshall, I. & Marshall, I. (2000). *SQ: Connecting with Our Spiritual Intelligence*. New York: Bloomsbury Publishing.

10

Journeying through Mental Landscapes

Overcoming Loneliness, Easing Distress, and Managing Anxiety for Optimal Wellness

Shakshi Priya Giri and *Anubhuti Dubey*

Introduction

In today's fast-paced world, the importance of mental health has taken centralize stage, it soliciting our attention and urging us to re-evaluate how we perceive and prioritize our well-being (Prince *et al.*, 2007). This shift is not just a passing trend but a profound recognition of the vital role that mental health plays in our overall quality of life (Fond *et al.*, 2021; Li *et al.*, 2021). The spotlight on mental health is getting brighter by an evolving understanding of the complex links between our minds, bodies, and the world around us. Scientific advancements in psychology and neuroscience have unravelled the complexity of mental processes, shedding light on the profound impact of mental health on our cognitive functions, emotional resilience, and even physical health (Kolappa *et al.*, 2013). As we delve deeper into the fields of neurobiology and psychology, it becomes increasingly evident that neglecting mental health is akin to overlooking a crucial component of our holistic health (Katon & Unützer, 2013).

Mental health is the bedrock of our overall well-being, encompassing not just the absence of mental illnesses but a positive state that empowers individuals to face life's challenges, recognize their potential, and contribute meaningfully to their communities (Prince *et al.*, 2007). The interconnectedness of mental health with emotions like loneliness, anxiety, and distress underscores the complex relationship between our psychological state and our general well-being (Katon & Unützer, 2013; Prince *et al.*, 2007). This holistic understanding is essential for addressing mental health comprehensively and fostering a positive and resilient approach to life's complexities.

In alignment with this perspective, this chapter extends its exploration into the intricate facets of loneliness as a precursor to mental health challenges. Loneliness, often underestimated, is recognized here as a significant factor contributing to mental health issues (Richardson *et al.*, 2017; Beutel *et al.*, 2017). By offering valuable insights into the pivotal role of social connections and support networks, we unveil the protective layers that such connections provide against the challenges posed by loneliness. Furthermore, the chapter delves further into the detrimental impacts of distress and anxiety on mental wellness. It carefully elucidates an array of preventive measures spanning cognitive, behavioural, and lifestyle interventions. Through this detailed examination, readers will gain a comprehensive understanding of how these preventive measures act as tools to fortify mental resilience and mitigate the adverse effects of distress and anxiety.

This chapter, in essence, is not only an exploration but a guide, empowering readers to actively engage in nurturing their mental health. By addressing critical aspects such as loneliness, distress, and anxiety, it aims to provide actionable insights and pragmatic strategies, emphasizing the paramount importance of adopting a holistic approach to health. The intrinsic link between mental well-being and the quest for a fulfilling and balanced life serves as the guiding principle, brings together science, compassion, and practicality for a comprehensive understanding and enhancement of mental health (Thieme *et al.*, 2015).

Before we embark on strategies to nurture mental well-being, let's establish a foundational understanding of what mental health truly encompasses.

Mental Health: Beyond Absence of Illness

As per the World Health Organization (2022), mental health is defined as "a state of mental well-being that enables people to cope with the stresses of life, realize their abilities, learn well and work well, and contribute to their community." This articulation underscores that mental health is not merely the absence of mental illnesses but a fundamental component of overall health, pivotal for effective functioning and individual flourishing (Thieme *et al.*, 2015). Embracing mental well-being, the prevention of mental disorders, and various approaches to treatment and rehabilitation, it stands as an integral element of holistic health (Beutel *et al.*, 2017).

Imagine mental health not as a fixed state but as a dynamic continuum. At one end lies optimal mental health, characterized by a sense of fulfilment, resilience, and effective coping mechanisms. At the other end, challenges such as stressors, loneliness, or distress may tip the balance (Rosenfield & Mouzon, 2013). Acknowledging this continuum is vital, as it reinforces the idea that everyone, regardless of their current mental state, has the potential for growth, improvement, and the pursuit of well-being (World Health Organization, 2005).

In the year 2019, a staggering 970 million individuals globally, equivalent to one in eight people, contended with a mental disorder, with loneliness, distress, anxiety, and depressive disorders prevailing as the most pervasive (Institute of Health Metrics and Evaluation, 2019). Moving into 2020, the seismic impact of the COVID-19 pandemic precipitated a significant upswing in the prevalence of anxiety and depressive disorders. Preliminary assessments reveal a remarkable 26 per cent surge in anxiety disorders and a notable 28 per cent increase in major depressive disorders within the span of a single year (World Health Organization, 2022).

This data underscores the critical nature of mental health on a global scale and highlights the escalating challenges posed by mental disorders, particularly exacerbated by the unprecedented circumstances of the COVID-19 pandemic (World Health Organization, 2022). It emphasizes the urgent need for a comprehensive understanding of mental health and the implementation of effective strategies to address the burgeoning impact on individuals and communities worldwide (Pathirathna *et al.*, 2022; Rogers *et al.*, 2020).

Having explored the foundational aspects of mental health, our journey now leads us to a critical component that often acts as a silent precursor to mental health challenges: loneliness. In the intricate tapestry of mental well-being, loneliness weaves a narrative that goes beyond mere solitude (Richardson *et al.*, 2017). As we delve into this chapter, we aim to unravel the threads connecting loneliness to mental health, understanding its nuances, impacts, and the pivotal role it plays in shaping our emotional landscapes.

Loneliness as a Precursor to Mental Health Challenges

Loneliness, often perceived as a transient emotional state, unveils a more profound impact on mental health than meets the eye. Loneliness transcends the mere absence of physical company (Hawkley & Cacioppo, 2010). It embodies a profound emotional state ch haracterized by a pervasive sense of disconnection and unmet social needs. Beyond the surface level of solitude, loneliness delves into the intricate realms of one's emotional landscape, where the yearning for meaningful connection and belonging takes precedence (Moustakas, 2016). This emotion is not a fleeting experience; it is a persistent and intense feeling that can evolve into a complex state with profound implications (Russell, 1982). When loneliness becomes prolonged or reaches heightened intensity, it ceases to be a passing sentiment and transforms into a significant precursor to mental health challenges (Cacioppo *et al.*, 2014).

Loneliness is not solely about being physically alone; it is a subjective experience influenced by the quality of social interactions and the perceived level of social support. One can feel lonely in a crowded room, emphasizing that loneliness is more about the quality and depth of connections rather than sheer physical proximity (Hawkley & Cacioppo, 2010). It is the unmet yearning for social connection, companionship, and understanding. This feeling signifies a gap between one's desired level of social interaction and the actual experiences of connection. This unfulfilled need for meaningful relationships can lead to a sense of isolation, further intensifying the emotional complexities associated with loneliness. Numerous studies (Victor & Yang, 2012; Heinrich & Gullone, 2006) have established a significant association between loneliness and adverse mental health outcomes. These encompass a spectrum of issues such as depression, suicidality, diminished positive emotions, compromised sleep quality, and overall health decline. Loneliness not only manifests in psychological realms but extends its reach to physiological changes, including an increased cortisol awakening response and pro-inflammatory gene expression (Victor & Yang, 2012).

Moreover, loneliness is not just a psychological concern; it intertwines with various facets of well-being. Research, particularly in men, indicates correlations with depression, low life satisfaction, and reduced resilience (Zebhauser *et al.*, 2014). Loneliness emerges as a considerable source of psychological stress (Friedler *et al.*, 2015), with its impact magnified when coupled with depression (Cacioppo *et al.*, 2006). Notably, researchers like Cacioppo and colleagues (e.g. Cacioppo *et al.*, 2006) emphasize the importance of distinguishing loneliness from depressive symptoms, highlighting a reciprocal relationship where both are intricately connected yet distinct in nature.

Beyond its influence on mental health, loneliness extends its grip on physical well-being, exacerbating the morbidity and mortality of cardiovascular, cerebrovascular, and chronic diseases (Friedler *et al.*, 2015). In the context of ageing, loneliness has been associated with cognitive decline and an increased risk of Alzheimer's disease, underscoring its pervasive impact on both mental and physical aspects of health. The intricate interplay between loneliness and diverse health outcomes reinforces the urgent need for comprehensive strategies that address the multifaceted nature of this pervasive emotional state (Zebhauser *et al.*, 2014).

As loneliness deepens, it intertwines with the individual's mental and emotional state, creating a feedback loop that exacerbates existing vulnerabilities or triggers the onset of mental health issues (Victor & Yang, 2012). The complex interplay between loneliness and mental health underscores the significance of addressing loneliness not only for emotional well-being but also as a proactive measure to safeguard mental health (Friedler *et al.*, 2015).

In essence, loneliness is a nuanced emotional experience that extends far beyond its surface appearance. Recognizing it as a complex state involving a yearning for connection and its potential to influence mental health underscores the importance of comprehensive strategies to address loneliness and its impact on individual well-being (e.g. Friedler *et al.*, 2015).

Distress and Anxiety's Detrimental Impacts

Distress and anxiety, prevalent emotional states, can exert a profound influence on mental wellness when left unmanaged (Keles *et al.*, 2020). *Distress* refers to a state of emotional suffering or discomfort that arises in response to challenging life circumstances. It often involves feelings of unease, sorrow, or a sense of being overwhelmed. Distress can be a natural response to stressors, but when prolonged or intense, it can evolve into a significant factor contributing to mental health issues (Dyrbye *et al.*, 2006). *Anxiety*, on the other hand, is characterized by excessive worry, apprehension, or fear about future events (Hope & Henderson, 2014). While it is a normal and adaptive response to certain situations, chronic anxiety becomes problematic. It may manifest as generalized anxiety disorder, panic disorder, social anxiety disorder, or specific phobias, each presenting unique challenges to mental well-being (e.g. Wang *et al.*, 2020; Dyrbye *et al.*, 2006).

Both distress and anxiety play pivotal roles in the development and exacerbation of mental health issues. When experienced persistently or intensely, they can contribute to conditions such as depression, panic disorders, and other anxiety-related disorders (Fu *et al.*, 2023; Wang *et al.*, 2017). The chronic activation of the stress response system associated with distress and anxiety may disrupt neural circuits, impacting mood regulation, cognitive function, and overall mental wellness (Wang *et al.*, 2020).

Consequences of Unmanaged Distress and Anxiety on Mental Wellness: A Closer Look

- *Depression:* Persistent distress and anxiety can be precursors to major depressive disorders. The constant emotional strain may lead to a pervasive sense of hopelessness and despair (Fu *et al.*, 2023).
- *Impaired Cognitive Function:* Chronic distress and anxiety can impair concentration, memory, and decision-making, hindering daily functioning and exacerbating mental health challenges (Wang *et al.*, 2020).
- *Physical Health Impact:* Unmanaged distress and anxiety are linked to physical health issues, including cardiovascular problems, gastrointestinal disorders, and weakened immune responses (Kolappa *et al.*, 2013; De Hert *et al.*, 2011).
- *Inter-personal Challenges:* Both distress and anxiety can strain relationships, leading to social isolation and further exacerbating emotional distress (Wang *et al.*, 2020).
- *Sleep Disturbances:* Persistent anxiety often contributes to sleep disorders, impacting the quality and duration of sleep, which is essential for mental well-being (Baglioni *et al.*, 2016).

A case study conducted by Johnson *et al.* in 2020 delves into the intricate dynamics of chronic stress and anxiety, shedding light on their negative effects on the brain and overall mental wellness. Employing a mixed-methods approach, the study explored the intricate interplay between persistent emotional states and their effects on neurobiological, cognitive, and psychological aspects. The findings highlighted neurobiological changes, particularly in regions associated with emotion regulation, such as the amygdala and prefrontal cortex. Participants with prolonged exposure to distress and anxiety exhibited cognitive impairments, affecting attention, memory, and executive functions. Psychological distress, including heightened levels of depression and decreased life satisfaction, was notably linked to chronic stress and anxiety. Beyond individual well-being, the study illuminated the impact on social functioning, with participants reporting strained relationships and increased social withdrawal. The research emphasized the existence of a vicious cycle, wherein chronic distress and anxiety contribute to neurobiological changes, perpetuating emotional and cognitive challenges.

Another cohort study conducted by Smith and colleagues in 2019 aimed to investigate the longitudinal effects of anxiety and depression on various mental health outcomes over an extended period. Key findings revealed a strong correlation between baseline anxiety and depression scores and the subsequent development of clinically significant mental health disorders. Participants with higher initial scores were more likely to experience conditions such as major depressive disorder and generalized anxiety disorder. The study highlighted a substantial decline in overall quality of life among individuals with persistent or escalating symptoms of anxiety and depression. Additionally, it showcased an increased risk of comorbid mental health conditions, including substance use disorders and somatic complaints, associated with chronic anxiety and depression. Longitudinal assessments indicated a negative impact on cognitive functioning over time, with declines observed in attention, memory, and executive functions. In conclusion, Smith *et al.*'s study underscores the enduring and far-reaching consequences of anxiety and depression on mental health outcomes.

These findings emphasize the importance of early intervention and comprehensive mental health strategies to address not only the symptoms of anxiety and depression but also their potential long-term implications for overall mental well-being.

Preventive Measures for Mental Well-being

Mental well-being is a dynamic state influenced by a combination of cognitive, behavioural, and lifestyle factors. Implementing preventive measures is crucial for promoting mental health and mitigating the risk of mental health disorders (Li *et al.*, 2023). Adopting a holistic approach, we'll explore cognitive strategies, behavioural interventions, and lifestyle changes, offering practical tips backed by evidence-based research.

1. Cognitive Strategies

(a) Mindfulness Meditation. *Description:* Mindfulness meditation involves cultivating awareness of the present moment without judgment. It has been associated with reduced symptoms of anxiety and depression.

Practical Tips: Start with short sessions and gradually extend the duration. Use guided meditation applications or videos for support.

Evidence-based Research: Numerous studies indicate that mindfulness-based interventions reduce symptoms of anxiety and depression (Hofmann *et al.*, 2010; Kabat-Zinn *et al.,* 2003).

(b) Cognitive Restructuring. *Description:* This involves identifying and challenging negative thought patterns. It aims to reframe distorted thinking and promote more balanced and positive perspectives (Wilson, 1999).

Practical Tips: Keep a thought journal to track and analyse negative thoughts. Question the validity of negative thoughts and replace them with more realistic ones.

Evidence-based Research: Cognitive restructuring is a central component of Cognitive Behavioural Therapy (CBT), which has demonstrated effectiveness in treating various mental health disorders. Extensive research, such as the work of Beck *et al.* (1979), supports the effectiveness of CBT in treating various mental health conditions.

2. Behavioural Interventions

(a) Social Connections. *Description:* Building and maintaining meaningful social connections is crucial for mental well-being. Social support acts as a buffer against stress and can alleviate symptoms of depression and anxiety.

Practical Tips: Actively engage in social activities and cultivate new friendships. Prioritize quality over quantity in relationships.

Evidence-based Research: Research by Holt-Lunstad *et al.* (2010) emphasizes the impact of social connections on mental health, longevity, and the protective role of social support against the development of mental health disorders.

(b) Behavioural Activation. *Description:* This involves increasing engagement in positive and fulfilling activities to counteract the effects of depression. It aims to disrupt the cycle of withdrawal and isolation (Dimidjian *et al.*, 2006).

Practical Tips: Identify enjoyable activities and schedule them regularly. Gradually increase the complexity of activities to maintain interest.

Evidence-based Research: Behavioural activation is a cornerstone of therapies like Behavioural Activation Treatment for Depression, with studies demonstrating its efficacy. Studies like Dimidjian *et al.* (2006) demonstrate the effectiveness of behavioural activation in treating depression.

3. Lifestyle Changes

(a) Physical Exercise. *Description:* Regular physical activity has been linked to improved mood, reduced anxiety, and enhanced cognitive function.

Practical Tips: Choose activities that you enjoy to make exercise more sustainable. Incorporate physical activity into daily routines, such as walking or cycling.

Evidence-based Research: Regular exercise is linked to reduced symptoms of anxiety and depression (Schuch *et al.*, 2018) because exercise has a large and significant antidepressant effect.

(b) Sleep Hygiene. *Description:* Prioritizing good sleep habits is crucial for mental health. Poor sleep can contribute to mood disturbances and cognitive impairments (Baglioni *et al.*, 2016).

Practical Tips: Establish a consistent sleep schedule. Create a relaxing bedtime routine to signal the body that it is time to wind down.

Evidence-based Research: Poor sleep is associated with increased risk of mental health disorders (Baglioni *et al.*, 2016), indicating the importance of sleep hygiene.

(c) Nutrition. *Description:* A balanced diet with essential nutrients contributes to overall well-being, impacting mood and cognitive function.

Practical Tips: Include a variety of fruits, vegetables, whole grains, omega-3 fatty acids and lean proteins in your diet. Limit the intake of processed foods and sugary drinks.

Evidence-based Research: Nutrient-rich diets are linked to a lower risk of depression and anxiety (Opie *et al.*, 2015).

Implementation Tips

- *Gradual Integration*: Start with small changes and gradually incorporate more preventive measures into your routine.
- *Consistency is Key*: Regularity enhances the effectiveness of these strategies. Consistent practice fosters lasting benefits.

- *Seek Professional Guidance*: If struggling to implement these measures independently, consider seeking guidance from mental health professionals or support groups.
- *Personalization:* Tailor these strategies to your unique preferences and needs. What works for one person may vary for another.

By incorporating these preventive measures, individuals can take an active role in fortifying their mental well-being. The robust support from evidence-based research underscores the efficacy of these strategies, laying a solid foundation for a life that is not only satisfying but also harmonious (Arango *et al.*, 2018).

Conclusion: Empowering Mental Well-being

In the dynamic exploration of mental health promotion and prevention, this chapter has unfolded a tapestry of strategies encompassing cognitive, behavioural, and lifestyle interventions. The essential understanding that has emerged is that proactive measures are pivotal in mitigating the challenges posed by mental health issues (Walsh, 2011). By addressing critical aspects such as loneliness, distress, and anxiety, a comprehensive exploration unfolded, encompassing multifaceted tactics necessary for averting mental health disorders and sustaining well-being.

The overarching objective of this chapter has been to furnish readers with actionable insights and pragmatic strategies, empowering them to actively elevate their mental health. The intrinsic link between mental well-being and the pursuit of a gratifying and harmonious life has served as the guiding principle, weaving together science, compassion, and practicality for a comprehensive understanding and enhancement of mental health (Arango *et al.*, 2018).

From cognitive strategies like mindfulness meditation and cognitive-behavioural therapy to behavioural interventions such as fostering social connections and behaviour activation, and lifestyle changes including regular exercise and balanced nutrition, the array of preventive measures presented in this chapter offers a holistic approach (e.g. Hofmann *et al.*, 2010). These strategies, supported by evidence-based research, provide not just a theoretical foundation but a practical roadmap for readers to navigate the complexities of mental well-being.

In adopting these measures, individuals can actively engage in the promotion of their mental health, creating a resilience that withstands the challenges of life (De Sio *et al.*, 2020). The chapter emphasizes the importance of consistency, gradual implementation, and seeking professional guidance when needed. By doing so, individuals not only enhance their mental health but also contribute to the cultivation of a community that prioritizes and supports collective well-being.

As we conclude this chapter, the profound message remains clear: mental health is an integral aspect of a fulfilling life, and by embracing preventive measures with dedication and mindfulness, individuals can pave the way towards a harmonious existence enriched by robust mental wellness.

References

Arango, C., Díaz-Caneja, C.M., McGorry, P.D., Rapoport, J., Sommer, I.E., Vorstman, J.A., & Carpenter, W. (2018). "Preventive Strategies for Mental Health". *The Lancet Psychiatry*, *5*(7): 591-604.

Baglioni, C., Nanovska, S., Regen, W., Spiegelhalder, K., Feige, B., Nissen, C., .. & Riemann, D. (2016). "Sleep and Mental Disorders: A Meta-Analysis of Polysomnographic Research". *Psychological Bulletin*, *142*(9): 969.

Beck, A.T. (Ed.). (1979). *Cognitive Therapy of Depression*. Guilford Press.

Beutel, M.E., Klein, E.M., Brähler, E., Reiner, I., Jünger, C., Michal, M., & Tibubos, A.N. (2017). "Loneliness in the General Population: Prevalence, Determinants and Relations to Mental Health". *BMC Psychiatry*, *17*(1): 1-7.

Cacioppo, S., Capitanio, J.P. & Cacioppo, J.T. (2014). "Toward a Neurology of Loneliness". *Psychological Bulletin*, *140*(6): 1464.

Cacioppo, J.T., Hughes, M.E., Waite, L.J., Hawkley, L.C. & Thisted, R.A. (2006). "Loneliness as a Specific Risk Factor for Depressive Symptoms: Cross-Sectional and Longitudinal Analyses". *Psychology and Ageing*, *21*(1): 140.

De Hert, M., Correll, C.U., Bobes, J., Cetkovich-Bakmas, M., Cohen, D.A.N., Asai, I., & Leucht, S. (2011). "Physical Illness in Patients with Severe Mental Disorders. I. Prevalence, Impact of Medications and Disparities in Health Care". *World Psychiatry*, *10*(1): 52.

De Sio, S., Buomprisco, G., Perri, R., Bruno, G., Mucci, N., Nieto, H.A., & Cedrone, F. (2020). "Work-Related Stress Risk and Preventive Measures of Mental Disorders in the Medical Environment: An Umbrella Review". *European Review for Medical & Pharmacological Sciences*, *24*(2).

Dimidjian, S., Hollon, S.D., Dobson, K.S., Schmaling, K.B., Kohlenberg, R.J., Addis, M.E., & Jacobson, N.S. (2006). "Randomized Trial of Behavioural Activation, Cognitive Therapy, and Antidepressant Medication in the Acute Treatment of Adults with Major Depression". *Journal of Consulting and Clinical Psychology*, *74*(4): 658.

Dyrbye, L.N., Thomas, M.R. & Shanafelt, T.D. (2006). "Systematic Review of Depression, Anxiety, and Other Indicators of Psychological Distress among US and Canadian Medical Students". *Academic Medicine, 81*(4): 354-373.

Fond, G., Nemani, K., Etchecopar-Etchart, D., Loundou, A., Goff, D.C., Lee, S.W., & Boyer, L. (2021). "Association Between Mental Health Disorders and Mortality among Patients with COVID-19 in 7 Countries: A Systematic Review and Meta-Analysis". *JAMA Psychiatry*, *78*(11): 1208-1217.

Friedler, B., Crapser, J. & McCullough, L. (2015). "One is the Deadliest Number: The Detrimental Effects of Social Isolation on Cerebrovascular Diseases and Cognition". *Acta Neuropathologica*, *129*, 493-509.

Fu, X.L., Qian, Y., Jin, X.H., Yu, H.R., Wu, H., Du, L., & Shi, Y.Q. (2023). "Suicide Rates among People with Serious Mental Illness: A Systematic Review and Meta-Analysis". *Psychological Medicine*, *53*(2): 351-361.

Hawkley, L.C. & Cacioppo, J.T. (2010). "Loneliness Matters: A Theoretical and Empirical Review of Consequences and Mechanisms". *Annals of Behavioural Medicine*, *40*(2): 218-227.

Heinrich, L.M. & Gullone, E. (2006). "The Clinical Significance of Loneliness: A Literature Review". *Clinical Psychology Review*, *26*(6): 695-718.

Hofmann, S.G., Sawyer, A.T., Witt, A.A. & Oh, D. (2010). "The Effect of Mindfulness-based Therapy on Anxiety and Depression: A Meta-Analytic Review". *Journal of Consulting and Clinical Psychology*, *78*(2): 169.

Holt-Lunstad, J., Smith, T.B. & Layton, J.B. (2010). "Social Relationships and Mortality Risk: A Meta-Analytic Review". *PLoS Medicine*, *7*(7): e1000316.

Hope, V. & Henderson, M. (2014). "Medical Student Depression, Anxiety and Distress Outside North America: A Systematic Review". *Medical Education*, *48*(10): 963-979.

Institute of Health Metrics and Evaluation (2019). *Global Health Data Exchange.* https://vizhub.healthdata.org/gbd-results/

Johnson, K., Jones, E. & Smith, S. (2020). "The Intricate Dynamics of Chronic Stress and Anxiety: A Case Study". *Journal of Clinical Psychology*, *76*(12): 2237-2245.

Kabat-Zinn, J. (2003). *Mindfulness-based Interventions in Context: Past, Present, and Future.*

Katon, W.J. & Unützer, J. (2013). "Health Reform and the Affordable Care Act: The Importance of Mental Health Treatment to Achieving the Triple Aim". *Journal of Psychosomatic Research*, *74*(6).

Keles, B., McCrae, N. & Grealish, A. (2020). "A Systematic Review: The Influence of Social Media on Depression, Anxiety and Psychological Distress in Adolescents". *International Journal of Adolescence and Youth*, *25*(1): 79-93.

Kolappa, K., Henderson, D.C. & Kishore, S.P. (2013). "No Physical Health without Mental Health: Lessons Unlearned?" *Bulletin of the World Health Organization*, *91*, 3-3a.

Li, C., Wu, M., Qiao, G., Gao, X., Hu, T., Zhao, X., & Yang, F. (2023). "Effectiveness of Continuity of Care in Reducing Depression Symptoms in

Elderly: A Systematic Review and Meta-Analysis". *International Journal of Geriatric Psychiatry*, *38*(3): e5894.

Li, Y., Scherer, N., Felix, L. & Ku per, H. (2021). "Prevalence of Depression, Anxiety and Post-Traumatic Stress Disorder in Health Care Workers During the Covid-19 Pandemic: A Systematic Review and Meta-Analysis". *PloS one*, *16*(3): e0246454.

Moustakas, C.E. (2016). *Loneliness*. Pickle Partners Publishing.

Opie, R.S., O'Neil, A., Itsiopoulos, C. & Jacka, F.N. (2015). "The Impact of Whole-of-Diet Interventions on Depression and Anxiety: A Systematic Review of Randomised Controlled Trials". *Public Health Nutrition*, *18*(11): 2074-2093.

Pathirathna, M.L., Nandasena, H.M.R.K.G., Atapattu, A.M.M.P. & Weerasekara, I. (2022). "Impact of the COVID-19 Pandemic on Suicidal Attempts and Death Rates: A Systematic Review". *BMC Psychiatry*, *22*(1): 1-15.

Prince, M., Patel, V., Saxena, S., Maj, M., Maselko, J., Phillips, M.R. & Rahman, A. (2007). "No Health without Mental Health". *The Lancet*, *370*(9590): 859-877.

Richardson, T., Elliott, P. & Roberts, R. (2017). "Relationship between Loneliness and Mental Health in Students". *Journal of Public Mental Health*, *16*(2): 48-54.

Rogers, J.P., Chesney, E., Oliver, D., Pollak, T.A., McGuire, P., Fusar-Poli, P., & David, A.S. (2020). "Psychiatric and Neuropsychiatric Presentations Associated with Severe Coronavirus Infections: A Systematic Review and Meta-Analysis with Comparison to the COVID-19 Pandemic". *The Lancet Psychiatry*, *7*(7): 611-627.

Rosenfield, S. & Mouzon, D. (2013). "Gender and Mental Health". *Handbook of the Sociology of Mental Health*, 277-296.

Russell, D. (1982). "The Measurement of Loneliness". *Loneliness: A Sourcebook of Current Theory, Research and Therapy*, 81-104.

Schuch, F.B., Vancampfort, D., Firth, J., Rosenbaum, S., Ward, P.B., Silva, E.S., & Stubbs, B. (2018). "Physical Activity and Incident Depression: A Meta-Analysis of Prospective Cohort Studies". *American Journal of Psychiatry*, *175*(7): 631-648.

Smith, J.A., Alloysius, A.L., Kautz, T.J. & Unutzer, J. (2019). "The Longitudinal Effects of Anxiety and Depression on Mental Health Outcomes: A 10-Year Follow-Up Study". *Journal of Affective Disorders*, *252*: 385-393.

Thieme, A., Wallace, J., Meyer, T.D. & Olivier, P. (2015, July). "Designing for Mental Well-being: Towards a More Holistic Approach in the Treatment and Prevention of Mental Illness". In *Proceedings of the 2015 British HCI Conference* (pp. 1-10).

Walsh, R. (2011). "Lifestyle and Mental Health". *American Psychologist*, *66*(7): 579.

Wang, J., Wu, X., Lai, W., Long, E., Zhang, X., Li, W., & Lin, H. (2017). "Prevalence of Depression and Depressive Symptoms among Outpatients: A Systematic Review and Meta-Analysis". *BMJ open*, *7*(8): e017173.

Wang, Y., Kala, M.P. & Jafar, T.H. (2020). "Factors Associated with Psychological Distress during the Coronavirus Disease 2019 (COVID-19) Pandemic on the Predominantly General Population: A Systematic Review and Meta-Analysis". *PloS One*, *15*(12): e0244630.

World Health Organization. Department of Mental Health, Substance Abuse, World Health Organization. Mental Health Evidence & Research Team (2005). *Mental Health Atlas 2005*. World Health Organization.

Victor, C.R. & Yang, K. (2012). "The Prevalence of Loneliness among Adults: A Case Study of the United Kingdom". *The Journal of Psychology*, *146* (1-2): 85-104.

Wilson, G.T. (1999). *Rapid Response to Cognitive Behaviour Therapy*.

World Health Organization. (2022). *Mental Health and COVID-19: Early Evidence of the Pandemic's Impact: Scientific Brief, 2 March 2022* (No. WHO/2019-nCoV/Sci_Brief/Mental_health/2022.1)

World Health Organization. (2022). *Mental Disorders*. https://www.who.int/news-room/fact-sheets/detail/mental-health-strengthening-our-response

World Health Organization. (2022). *Mental Health*. https://www.who.int/news-room/fact-sheets/detail/mental-health-strengthening-our-response

Zebhauser, A., Hofmann Xu, L., Baumert, J., Haefner, S., Lacruz, M.E., Emeny, R.T., & Ladwig, K.H. (2014). "How Much Does it Hurt to be Lonely? Mental and Physical Differences Between Older Men and Women in the KORA-Age Study". *International Journal of Geriatric Psychiatry*, *29*(3): 245-252.

11

Depression and Quality of Life among Indian Older Adults

A Correlational Study

Akanksha Bharti and *Das Ambika Bharti*

Introduction

There is a rapid rise in the population of older adults aged 60 and above worldwide, particularly in India. The second-most populous country in the world is India. Here, 104 million older people are of age 60 years or older, making up more than 8.6 per cent of the overall Indian population. Vardhan, H. (October 27, 2023). The population's rapid ageing has also raised several social, economic, and health-related challenges (Prudham & Evans, 1981).

Due to the physical changes associated with ageing, such as diminished muscle endurance, problems with balancing the body, and issues with quality of life, ageing has become the centre of attention and worry. Age-related illnesses are widespread, and many senior citizens list poor health as one of their main concerns. Furthermore, the condition of the elderly in old age homes is significantly worse. The majority of healthy older adults in industrialized nations participate actively in their communities; therefore, it is important to prioritize functional abilities and health over risk, disease, and vulnerability (Mishra & Mishra, 2016). Falling at this age can have several negative impacts, such as decreased physical health and joint restrictions, weak muscles, difficulty with everyday activities, social isolation, an increased reliance on others, and fear of falling (Mishra, Mishra & Bidija, 2017).

Depression is considered the most prevalent mental health issue among older adults. Even though evaluating the impact of depression on QOL is a viable and useful approach to assessing the suffering resulting from depression, assessing levels of suffering is complex (Chan *et al.*, 2006). Recent research has not revealed much about the relationship between depression in elderly Indians and QOL. To have a deeper understanding of QOL and depression in older people, research is necessary.

Quality of Life

Reduced physical and rational capabilities are a natural part of getting older (Heydarnejad & Dehkordi, 2010; Hassanpour-Dehkordi & Jalali, 2016; Southham, Agras Taylor, & Kraemer, 2001). These physical and psychological changes brought on by ageing in older adults make their QOL important and of great concern. The World Health Organization (WHO) defines QOL as a person's assessment of his or her place in the social milieu and value system to which they belong. An individual's life objectives, expectations, standards, and worries also correlate with QOL (WHOQOL Group, 1995). Furthermore, research suggests that older people's QOL scores differ from those of the common population. Although there has been discussion about QOL for more than 10 years, there are not many recent statistics on the QOL of older adults. Moreover, research has shown that mental health is one of the most crucial aspects of QOL (Mishra, Mishra & Bidija, 2017).

Depression

One of the prevalent psychiatric conditions affecting the elderly population is depression (Kaya, 1999; Ghaderi *et al.*, 2012). Depression is a common and incapacitating illness that affects QOL and raises the likelihood that older people will die (>60 years). In their earlier research, Mishra, Mishra & Bidija (2017) found that 27 per cent of urban elderly individuals (aged 60) and of rural elderly persons 65 years of age or older, 30.8 per cent, reported having depressive symptoms. For more than half of elderly people with depression, this is the first time they have ever experienced it. The signs of depression slightly differ in older adults and younger adults. Female gender, physical health problems, neurotic personality traits, living in nursing homes, inadequate life experiences, and a lack of social support are major predictors of the onset of depression in people over 60 (Erdoğan & Depresyon, 2007)

For a variety of reasons, mental health problems are more common among older people. 15 per cent to 25 per cent of older persons have reported major mental health problems; consequently, the prevalence of depressive disorders increases with each decade of age (Alipour *et al.*, 2009). The most common signs of depression in older adults include sleepiness, exhaustion, difficulty concentrating, impatience, frequent awakenings from sleep, loss of appetite, and physical discomfort (Sohrabi *et al.*, 2008). The elderly suffer loneliness for a variety of reasons, including physical impairments, the loss of family members, and decreased communication (Sheibani *et al.,* 2010). It has been determined that loneliness is a sign of depression and a separate risk factor for the psychological harm that comes with ageing (Henderson, 2005; Sheibani *et al.*, 2010). These individuals may experience low self-esteem, agitation, loneliness, frustration, despair, and most likely forgetfulness (Hosienabadi, Goorabi & Shareh, 2007).

The Need for the Study

There has been research on the relationship between indices of depression and QOL in older people in many different countries. However, no recent research could be found on Indian older adults, their mental health, or their QOL after the global pandemic COVID-19. The relationship between depression and QOL in older individuals remains unanswered. As a result, the current study was carried out with the objectives that are as follows:

Objectives

1. To assess the level of depression among older Indian individuals in the phase post-COVID-19.
2. To study gender differences in depression and QOL among the older adults.
3. To investigate any potential relationships between depression and QOL in this population.

Methods

Hypotheses

H_1 Majority of older adults would report depressive symptoms of mild to moderate level.

H_2 There would be significant gender difference in depression and overall QOL along with its dimensions among older adults

H_3 There would be significant association between depression of Indian older adults and their QOL.

H_4 Depression among Indian older adults would have a significant impact on their QOL.

Sample: The study used stratified random sampling to identify a sample of 136 older adults (N = 136) from Patna, Bihar. For this study, older adults staying at home who had no prior records of any recognized psychological impairments and were in a communicable state were selected. The criterion age of the sample was 60 years and older (mean age = 72.37, SD = ±7.46).

Study Design: *Cross-sectional correlational research design.*

Tools and Measures

Clinical and Socio-demographic data sheet: The researchers designed this semi-structured schedule for the present study to get relevant clinical and socio-demographic information from the participants. The researchers may gather data on age, gender, residence location, educational attainment, health status, chronic disease, duration of chronic illness, marital status, and family structure. We also included information on past clinical history.

Depression (DASS-21 Lovibond, 1995): It is a self-reported 4-point Likert questionnaire consisting of 21 questions in total and 7 items on each scale of depression, anxiety, and stress. In this study, depression is the sole scale that is employed. The depression scale evaluates dysphoria, hopelessness, life devaluation, and self-deprecation. It also measures a lack of interest and involvement. The assessment of disturbance can be assisted by a scale such as the DASS; for example, individuals who may not fit the clinical criteria for a certain disease can nonetheless be correctly classified as having severe symptoms and a high risk of acquiring new problems.

World Health Organisation Quality of Life, Brief Version (WHOQOL-BREF) (WHOQOL Group, 1998)—This scale consists of 26 items expressing the four categories of physical, psychological, social, and environmental quality of life. It is a cross-culturally valid QOL evaluation measure (Skevington, Lotfy & O'Connell, 2004). The WHOQOL-BREF's psychometric qualities have been examined in India, and results show that it has good validity and reliability for older individuals (Xia, Li, Hau, Liu & Lu, 2012). The questionnaire has 24 questions divided into four primary categories (physical health, psychological health, social interactions, and environment), plus two additional items measuring general health status and overall quality of life.

Domain 1 (physical health) measures physical pain, dependence on medical care, exhaustion, mobility, ability to do everyday tasks, and capacity for employment. Enjoyment of life, meaning in life, focus, acceptance of one's physical appearance, self-esteem, and unpleasant emotions are all aspects of domain 2 (psychological health). Personal relationships, sexual activity, and social support are the key topics of domain 3 (social interactions). Environment domain 4 evaluates security, the physical environment, available resources, information access, leisure activities, the home environment, access to healthcare, and transportation. A 5-point scale is used to grade each item, with higher scores indicating a higher quality of life (QOL).

Procedure

With a stratified random sampling technique, the sample of older adults over 60 was drawn from the state of Bihar. An overview of the study's objectives, associated potential costs and advantages, the length of the questionnaire, and any privacy concerns were then communicated to the participants. Informed consent in verbal and written form was obtained from each participant before collecting their data on relevant socio-demographic and clinical indexes, depression, and QOL.

The American Psychological Association's (APA 2010) ethical criteria were adhered to while gathering data. Next, we handled and analyzed the quantitative data obtained in this manner using SPSS-25, the Statistical Package for Social Sciences.

Ethical Approval

The Departmental Research Degree Committee (DRDC) at the authors' university granted ethical approval for the present study.

Table 11.1: Socio-demographic information of the sample of Indian older adults (N=136)

Sl. No.	Demographic variable	Total number	Category	Fre-quency	Percentage (%)
1.	Gender	136	Male	63	39.9
			Female	73	46.2
2.	Residential area	136	Rural	89	56.3
			Semi-urban	21	13.3
			Urban	26	16.5
3.	Health condition	136	Healthy	69	43.7
			Chronically-ill	67	42.4
4.	Marital status	136	Married	102	64.6
			Widow	30	19.0
			Widower	3	1.9

Results

Descriptive statistics and *Pearson's Product Moment Correlation* Method were used to statistically analyze the responses that had been collected. For assessing the gender differences in the QOL and depression level among the older adults, an independent sample t-test was then carried out. Further regression analysis was then run to explore the extent to which depression can predict quality of life, including its dimensions.

The prevalence was checked to determine the levels of depression among older adults (Table 11.2). An independent sample t-test was performed (Table 11.3) to determine if there are gender differences in depression and QOL in this population. The strength of the association between depression, QOL, and its dimensions were calculated using *Pearson's product-moment correlation coefficient* (Table 11.4). Regression analysis using depression as the predictor and QOL and its dimensions as the criterion was done to find the possible impact of depression on the QOL of the older adults in India (Table 11.5).

Table 11.2: Frequency distribution of the older adults reporting different levels of depression (N=136)

Values	Label	Frequency (f)	Percentage (%)
0-4	Normal	44	32.35
5-6	Mild	26	19.12
7-10	Moderate	47	34.56
11-13	Severe	16	11.76
14 and above	Extremely severe	3	2.21

Table 11.2 shows the levels of depression among older adults. It was found that the maximum number of older adults, i.e. 47 (34.56%) out of 136, fell into the moderate level of depressive symptoms category. 44 (32.35%) out of 136 had normal depressive symptoms. 26 (19.12%) out of 136 had mild depressive symptoms. 16 (11.76%) older adults had severe symptoms of depression, whereas 3 (2.21%) out of 136 fell into the category of extremely severe depressive symptoms. Hence, hypothesis 2, stating "the majority *of older adults would report depressive symptoms of a mild to moderate level*", was accepted.

Table 11.3: Mean, SD and t-value of males and females on the measures of depression, Quality of life and its dimensions among older adults (N=136)

Variables	*Category*	*N*	*Mean (SD)*	*T*
Depression	Male	63	5.76 (2.81)	3.27**
	Female	73	7.53 (3.42)	
Physical	Male	63	21.24 (3.76)	5.52**
	Female	73	17.81 (3.49)	
Psychological	Male	63	18.10 (3.46)	4.95**
	Female	73	15.29 (3.16)	
Social	Male	63	9.38 (2.26)	4.67**
	Female	73	7.88 (1.46)	
Environment	Male	63	23.35 (5.55)	5.09**
	Female	73	19.18 (3.97)	
Overall QOL	Male	63	3.35 (.95)	3.46**
	Female	73	2.82 (.82)	
General Health	Male	63	3.21 (.92)	2.94*
	Female	73	2.74 (.93)	

*p < .05, **p < .01.

Table 11.3 displays gender-specific mean scores on depression and quality of life, along with their dimensions. Results of the independent sample t-test indicated that women's depression scores were considerably greater (7.53) than men's (5.76). Men scored much higher (3.35) than women (2.82) in terms of overall QOL. Further, men also scored significantly higher on the dimensions of QOL, such as an individual's judgment of overall general health, physical health, psychological health, social relations, and environmental aspects. The mean difference is also statistically significant ($p \leq 0.01$). Hence, the data validates hypothesis 3, which states, "*There would be significant gender differences in depression and overall QOL along with its dimensions among the older adults*", and hence stands accepted.

Table 11.4: Correlational analysis of depression, quality of life, and its dimensions (N=136)

Measure	Dep-ression	Physical	Psycho-logical	Social relation	Environ-ment	Overall QOL	General Health
Depression	1	-.372**	-.509**	-.271**	-.465**	-.423**	-.401**
Physical		1	.815**	.556**	.716**	.592**	.624**
Psychological			1	.511**	.716**	.602**	.634**
Social relation				1	.692**	.495**	.383**
Environment					1	.613**	.562**
Overall QOL						1	.647**
General health							1

**p < .01.

Table 11.4 reveals that depression was significantly negatively correlated to overall QOL (r = -.423, p<0.01). It suggests that older adults who have depressive symptoms experience low QOL. Dimensions of QOL such as physical (r = -.372, p<0.01), psychological (r = -.509, p<0.01), social relations (r =-.271, p<0.01), environment (r =-.465, p<0.01), and an individual's perception of overall general health (r=-.401, p<0.01) were significantly negatively correlated to depression. Results imply that an increase in levels of depression in older adults is associated with low physical health, psychological health, their social relations, environmental aspects, and overall general health. Hence, it can be concluded that hypothesis 4: "*There would be a significant association between depression and QOL in Indian older adults*" was supported and accepted by the result.

Table 11.5: Summary of linear regression analysis for depression as predictor variable and Quality of Life and its dimensions as criterion variable (N = 136)

Predictors	R	R Square	R Square Change	Adjusted R Square	F Change	Sig. of F change	Beta	Sig.
Criterion: Physical Health (QOL)								
Depression	.372	.138	.138	.132	21.509	.01	-.372	.01
Criterion: Psychological Health (QOL)								
Depression	.509	.259	.259	.253	46.786	.01	-.509	.01
Criterion: Social Relation (QOL)								
Depression	.271	.074	.074	.067	10.660	.01	-.271	.01

(Contd.)

Predictors	R	R Square	R Square Change	Adjusted R Square	F Change	Sig. of F change	Beta	Sig.
Criterion: Environment (QOL)								
Depression	.465	.216	.216	.210	36.923	.01	-.465	.01
Criterion: Overall QOL								
Depression	.423	.179	.179	.173	29.193	.01	-.423	.01
Criterion: General health (QOL)								
Depression	.401	.161	.161	.155	25.702	.01	-.401	.01

Table 11.5 evidences that depression significantly predicted 17.3 per cent (adj. R2 =.173), 13.2 (adj. R2 =.132), 25.3 (adj. R2 =.253), 6.7 per cent (adj. R2 =.067), 21 per cent (adj. R2 =.210), and 15.5 per cent (adj. R2 =.155) of variance in the overall QOL, physical, psychological, social relationship, environment aspect, and individuals' perception of overall general health, respectively. Hence, it can be concluded that hypothesis 5, which states "*Depression among Indian older adults would have a significant impact upon their QOL*", stands accepted.

Discussion

The present study examines and explains its findings, drawing on prior research findings. A mild to moderate level of depression was seen among older adults. A significant gender difference was noticed in depression and QOL. Depression and QOL were found to be significantly correlated among Indian older adults. Furthermore, we found that depression significantly impacts QOL among older adults.

It has been observed that depression among older people is a widespread occurrence in several nations. According to various research studies, depression became more common as people aged. Research undertaken by Feng, Yap & Ng (2013); Garcia-Pena *et al.* (2013); Ho, Feng, Fam, Mahendran, Kua & Ng (2014); Hsu (2009); Lue, Chen, & Wu (2010); Shrira (2012); and Wolinsky *et al.* (2006) has found that depression in older people (60 years of age and older) is common in communal living settings. Causes of psychological distress in older adults are found to be related to a decrease in sleep quality and mortality (Atkins, Naismith, Luscombe & Hickie, 2013). Severe depression was prevalent among senior people at a rate of 19 per cent, moderate depression at 33 per cent, and mild depression at 38 per cent (Mortazavi *et al.,* 2011). According to another study, serious depression affected 14.7 per cent and mild depression

16.8 per cent of elderly people (Mahdizadeh, 2007). Findings indicated that the incidence of moderate depression was 10 per cent and severe depression was prevalent among 3 per cent of older adults (Gharanjik *et al.,* 2011), and our study's findings are supported by these outcomes. The findings of a study conducted in Greece revealed a prevalence of 12 per cent for moderate to severe depression and 27 per cent for mild to major depression (Papadopoulos *et al.,* 2005). In a different study, among older people living in rural China, 26.5 per cent had mild depression and 4.3 per cent had severe depression (Gao *et al.,* 2009). According to William (1980), moderate depression has a prevalence of 5 per cent to 44 per cent among Americans over 65 and a prevalence of 2 per cent to 4 per cent for major depression (Blazer & Williams, 1980). It is understood that risky behaviours, excessive behaviour, stressful life events, and unpleasant emotions all contribute to the symptoms of depression. The events of one's life have a major effect on when these symptoms start to appear in old age (Hu, Xiao, Peng, Kuang & He, 2018). Additionally, even though depression is common in older adults, reports indicate that it is less severe, more persistent, and can endure for years, having a significant impact on the emotional, psychological, functional, and cognitive elements of this population (Wannmacher, 2016). Physical and mental healthcare are necessary due to the prevalence and complexity of depression in the older population, which is frequently at risk from the process of human ageing itself since they are dealing with loss and illness (Wannmacher, 2016). The elderly are vulnerable to a variety of depression risk factors due to their age. It is thought that senior people with robust resources and traits, such as emotional regulation, optimism, maintenance of social relationships, and autonomy, are better equipped to manage circumstances before the onset of depressive symptoms (Huisman, Klokgieters & Beekman, 2017).

Women were found to be more depressive than men in this study, which was consistent with earlier research by the WHO (2008), WHO (2017), and Cole and Dendukuri (2003). Physical health and limitations on mobility experienced by older men significantly influence the prevalence of depression within this demographic. Additionally, because they receive less social and familial support whereas, older women exhibit increased signs of depression and anxiety (Alizadeh-Khoei, Khosbin & Khavarpour, 2010). Numerous studies have shown that women are more likely than men to experience depression (Mobasheri & Moezy, 2010). According to a study by Mortazavi (2010), the prevalence of depression was estimated at 31.8 per cent for older men and 52.8 per cent for older women (Mortazavi *et al.,* 2011). A different study on older Chinese people in Hong Kong found that 11 per cent of men and 14 per cent of women had depression (Chi *et al.,* 2005).

Our results demonstrate the association between older adults' quality of life and depression. Every WHOQOL-BREF domain showed a negative correlation with depression, which is in line with other researchs (Luo, Zhang & Liu, 2020). In each of the four WHOQOL-BREF domains, the mean scores of the depressed people were lower. A prior study that looked at the relationship between QOL and depression among older Chinese people in Hong Kong found a significant relationship between depression and scores on all four WHOQOL-BREF domains (Luo, Zhang & Liu, 2020).

The health-related quality of life (HQOL) is negatively correlated with depressive symptoms, as found by Akyol, Durmuş, Doan, Bek & Cantürk (2010), Gallegos-Carrillo *et al.* (2009), Dragomirecká *et al.* (2008), Helvik, Engedal & Selbaek (2010), McCurren, Hall & Rowles (1993), and Street, O'Connor & Robinson (2007).

According to Brown and Roose's (2011) study, a higher score for depressive symptoms was inversely related to physical quality of life. Similar findings were reported by Galhardo *et al.* (2010), Deslandes *et al.* (2008), Margis, Donis, Schönwald & Rieder (2010), in which they found a negative relationship between a higher score for depressive symptoms and the HQOL, general health, mental health, and vitality categories. According to Coleman, Philp & Mullee's (1995) study, people with depression had a poorer QOL than people without depression. Diefenbach, Tolin & Gilliam (2012) reported similar findings, demonstrating a relationship between the depressive symptom score and impairments in physical, emotional, mental health, and bodily pain.

In individuals who had depression, the HQOL aspects that influenced physical health, mental health, and physical functioning were inversely correlated with a higher depressive score. Older people without depression performed better to older people with depression in 5 out of 8 domains (*overall health, mental health index, role emotional, social function, and vitality*) (Doraiswamy, Khan, Donahue & Richard, 2002; Galhardo *et al.,* 2010), According to Gonzalez-Celis and Gómez-Benito (2013), depression was adversely correlated with the HQOL areas of physical health, psychological health, independence, social relationships, and environment. According to Park *et al.* (2010), groups of depressed people showed lower mental and physical HQOL than groups of non-depressed people. Poorer QOL and the prevalence of depressive symptoms were shown to be related in other study findings too (Chang *et al.,* 2016; Silveira & Portuguez, 2017).

The research that is now available implies that depression may in fact occur before a decrease in quality of life (Bruce, Davis & Davis, 2005). However, reversed causality cannot be discounted, for example, by the fact that depressive symptoms first appear in people with chronic illnesses who have a lower quality of life. Elderly people typically have at least one chronic ailment due to age-related health concerns. Because of this, a higher prevalence of mental and physical illnesses is associated with older age (Cassidy *et al.,* 2004; Yan, 2009). Movement disorders, osteoporosis (Todd & Robinson, 2003), cancer (Friedenreich & Orenstein, 2002), diabetes (Kriska, 2003), cardiovascular conditions (Thomson *et al.,* 2003), depression, anxiety, and dementia are all observed to be common in later years of life (Hall, Ekkekakis & Petruzzello, 2002). Mental illness is the second most common cause of death (Almeida, Norman, Hankey, Jamrozik & Flicker 2006).

Age, sex, marital status, level of education, and income are among the many variables known to affect both depressive symptoms and quality of life. The relationship between depressive symptoms and quality of life may be complicated by several factors. In about half of the reviewed studies, these characteristics were not adjusted for in statistical analyses. The studies that did take these factors into account, however (Kriegsman *et al.,* 1996; Gregg *et al.,* 2002; Bruce, Davis & Davis, 2005; Jacobson, De Groot & Samson, 1997; Zhang and Sullivan, 2007; Pawaskar, Anderson, Balkrishnan, 2007; Egede, 2004), did not show significant effects on the association between depressive symptoms and quality of life. This may imply that these factors will not significantly confound the associations discussed here. Confounding, however, is a significant problem in epidemiology. The finding that roughly half of studies did not account for confounding factors in their analyses shows that further thorough research on this topic is necessary. The quality-of-life scores for both physical and mental health were associated with depressive symptoms.

The findings of this study demonstrated the association between depression and elderly people's quality of life. According to this result, older adults who were depressed had a poor quality of life. Poor and decreased quality of life in elderly individuals may be subject to ageing. It has also been reported in the study of Carta *et al.* (2012) that in the general population, quality of life (QOL) gradually declines with age. Research has demonstrated that the elderly perceive their Quality of Life (QOL) to be significantly lower than that of younger people. Also, chronic diseases (Mura *et al.,* 2012), endocrine disorders (de Ornelas Maia, 2013), degenerative illnesses (Carta *et al.,* 2012), and mood disorders (Lino *et al.,* 2019) are also associated with poor quality of life in older adults.

Therefore, to determine the impact of depression on QOL, this study also evaluated the level of depression in older individuals.

According to this study, depression negatively affects the QOL of older adults, which is in line with findings from other studies by Victor, Scambler, Bowling & Bond (2005), Wilkinson & Izmeth (2016), Mottram, Wilson, Scally & Vassilas (2000). According to another study (Halvorsrud, Kirkevold, Diseth & Kalfoss, 2010), depressive symptoms had a detrimental indirect impact on HQOL *via* physical functioning and health satisfaction.

Conclusion

As per the findings of the study, older adults are going through mild to severe depression. This depression may be the cause of ageing effects, chronic illnesses, and other ageing-related issues. The study also suggested that women are suffering more from depressive symptoms as compared to men. In the study, depression and QOL, along with their dimensions (physical, psychological, social relations, and environment), were found to be negatively correlated. Further, the study also examined whether depression predicted poor quality of life in elderly individuals. Therefore, we observe QOL deficits in depressed individuals. Given the high incidence of depression in the elderly and the high prevalence of depression in older women, the application of interventions, such as education about depression symptoms for early diagnosis and timely referral of older adults, is extremely important. Additionally, because a moderate level of depression is so common, careful planning is required for prompt identification, attention, and cure. This association has profound implications for the design of intervention programmes and rehabilitation services aimed at enhancing QOL and reducing depression in Indian older adults. Studies are also required to improve depression screening, establish strategies for high-risk groups, and fine-tune therapies. Future studies need to emphasize enhancing our knowledge of the association between depression and QOL in various samples of elderly people, including those with chronic illnesses, those who are hospitalized, those who live in old age homes etc.

References

Akyol, Y., Durmuþ, D., Doğan, C., Bek, Y. & Cantürk, F. (2010). "Quality of Life and Level of Depressive Symptoms in the Geriatric Population". *Archives of Rheumatology*, *25*(4): 165-173.

Alipour, F., Sajadi, H., Forouzan, A., Nabavi, H. & Khedmati, E. (2009). "The Role of Social Support in the Anxiety and Depression of Elderly". *Iranian Journal of Ageing*, *4*(1): 0-0.

Alizadeh-Khoei, M., Khosbin, S. & Khavarpour, F. (2010). "Assessing Quality of Life, Well-being and Depression among Iranian Ederly in Australia". *Iranian Journal of Ageing*, *4*(4): 0-0.

Almeida, O.P., Norman, P., Hankey, G., Jamrozik, K. & Flicker, L. (2006). "Successful Mental Health Ageing: Results from a Longitudinal Study of Older Australian Men". *The American Journal of Geriatric Psychiatry*, *14*(1): 27-35.

American Psychological Association. (2010). *Publication Manual of the American Psychological Association*. American Psychological Association.

Atkins, J., Naismith, S.L., Luscombe, G.M. & Hickie, I.B. (2013). "Psychological Distress and Quality of Life in Older Persons: Relative Contributions of Fixed and Modifiable Risk Factors". *BMC Psychiatry*, *13*, 1-10.

Blazer, D. & Williams, C.D. (1980). "Epidemiology of Dysphoria and Depression in An Elderly Population". *The American Journal of Psychiatry*.

Brown, P. J. & Roose, S.P. (2011). "Age and Anxiety and Depressive Symptoms: The Effect on Domains of Quality of Life". *International Journal of Geriatric Psychiatry*, *26*(12): 1260-1266.

Bruce, D.G., Davis, W.A. & Davis, T.M. (2005). "Longitudinal Predictors of Reduced Mobility and Physical Disability in Patients with Type 2 Diabetes: The Fremantle Diabetes Study". *Diabetes Care*, *28*(10): 2441-2447.

Carta, M.G., Aguglia, E., Caraci, F., Dell'Osso, L., Di Sciascio, G., Drago, F.,. .. & Balestrieri, M. (2012). "Quality of Life and Urban/Rural Living: Preliminary Results of a Community Survey in Italy". *Clinical Practice and Epidemiology in Mental Health: CP & EMH*, *8*, 169.

Carta, M.G., Mura, G., Sorbello, O., Farina, G. & Demelia, L. (2012). "Quality of Life and Psychiatric Symptoms in Wilson's Disease: The Relevance of Bipolar Disorders". *Clinical Practice and Epidemiology in Mental Health: CP & EMH*, *8*, 102.

Cassidy, K., Kotynia-English, R., Acres, J., Flicker, L., Lautenschlager, N.T., Almeida, O.P.,. .. & Almeida, O.P. (2004). "Association Between Lifestyle Factors and Mental Health Measures among Community-Dwelling Older Women". *Australian and New Zealand Journal of Psychiatry*, *38*(11-12): 940-947.

Chan, S.W., Chiu, H.F., Chien, W.T., Thompson, D.R. & Lam, L. (2006). "Quality of Life in Chinese Elderly People with Depression". *International Journal of Geriatric Psychiatry*, *21*(4): 312-318.

Chang, Y.C., Ouyang, W.C., Lu, M.C., Wang, J.D. & Hu, S.C. (2016). "Levels of Depressive Symptoms may Modify the Relationship between the WHOQOL-BREF and Its Determining Factors in Community-Dwelling Older Adults". *International Psychogeriatrics*, *28*(4): 591-601.

Chi, I., Yip, P.S., Chiu, H.F., Chou, K.L., Chan, K.S., Kwan, C.W.,. .. & Caine, E. (2005). "Prevalence of Depression and Its Correlates in Hong Kong's Chinese Older Adults". *The American Journal of Geriatric Psychiatry*, *13*(5): 409-416.

Cole, M.G. & Dendukuri, N. (2003). "Risk Factors for Depression among Elderly Community Subjects: A Systematic Review and Meta-Analysis". *American Journal of Psychiatry*, *160*(6): 1147-1156.

Coleman, P.G., Philp, I. & Mullee, M.A. (1995). "Does the Use of the Geriatric Depression Scale Make Redundant the Need for Separate Measures of Well-being on Geriatrics Wards?" *Age and Ageing*, *24*(5): 416-420.

de Ornelas Maia, A.C.C., de Azevedo Braga, A., Paes, F., Machado, S., Carta, M.G., Nardi, A.E. & Silva, A.C. (2013). "Comorbidity of Depression and Anxiety: Association with Poor Quality of Life in Type 1 and 2 Diabetic Patients". *Clinical Practice and Epidemiology in Mental Health: CP & EMH*, *9*, 136.

Deslandes, A.C., De Moraes, H., Pompeu, F.A., Ribeiro, P., Cagy, M., Capitão, C.,. .. & Laks, J. (2008). "Electroencephalographic Frontal Asymmetry and Depressive Symptoms in the Elderly". *Biological Psychology*, *79*(3): 317-322.

Diefenbach, G.J., Tolin, D.F. & Gilliam, C.M. (2012). "Impairments in Life Quality among Clients in Geriatric Home Care: Associations with Depressive and Anxiety Symptoms". *International Journal of Geriatric Psychiatry*, *27*(8): 828-835.

Doraiswamy, P.M., Khan, Z.M., Donahue, R.M. & Richard, N.E. (2002). "The Spectrum of Quality-of-Life Impairments in Recurrent Geriatric Depression". *The Journals of Gerontology Series A: Biological Sciences and Medical Sciences*, *57*(2): M134-M137.

Dragomirecká, E., Bartoňová, J., Eisemann, M., Kalfoss, M., Kilian, R., Martiny, K.,. .. & Schmidt, S. (2008). "Demographic and Psychosocial Correlates of Quality of Life in the Elderly from a Cross-Cultural Perspective". *Clinical Psychology & Psychotherapy*, *15*(3): 193-204.

Egede, L.E. (2004). "Diabetes, Major Depression, and Functional Disability among US Adults". *Diabetes Care*, *27*(2): 421-428.

Erdoğan, S. & Depresyon, C.S. (2007). "Anksiyete ve Yeme Bozukluklari". Kutsal, Y.G.(ed.) *Temel Geriatri. Ankara, Güneş Tip Kitabevleri*, 1203-17.

Feng, L., Yap, K.B. & Ng, T.P. (2013). "Depressive Symptoms in Older Adults with Chronic Kidney Disease: Mortality, Quality of Life Outcomes, and Correlates". *The American Journal of Geriatric Psychiatry*, *21*(6): 570-579.

Friedenreich, C.M. & Orenstein, M.R. (2002). "Physical Activity and Cancer Prevention: Etiologic Evidence and Biological Mechanisms". *The Journal of Nutrition*, *132*(11): 3456S-3464S.

Galhardo, V.A., Magalhaes, M.G., Blanes, L., Juliano, Y. & Ferreira, L.M. (2010). "Health-Related Quality of Life and Depression in Older Patients with Pressure Ulcers". *Wounds*, *22*(1): 20-26.

Gallegos-Carrillo, K., García-Peña, C., Mudgal, J., Romero, X., Durán-Arenas, L. & Salmerón, J. (2009). "Role of Depressive Symptoms and Comorbid Chronic Disease on Health-Related Quality of Life among Community-Dwelling Older Adults." *Journal of Psychosomatic Research*, *66*(2): 127-135.

Gao, S., Jin, Y., Unverzagt, F.W., Liang, C., Hall, K.S., Ma, F.,. .. & Hendrie, H.C. (2009). "Correlates of Depressive Symptoms in Rural Elderly Chinese". *International Journal of Geriatric Psychiatry*, *24*(12): 1358-1366.

García-Peña, C., Wagner, F.A., Sánchez-García, S., Espinel-Bermúdez, C., Juárez-Cedillo, T., Pérez-Zepeda, M.,. .. & Gallo, J.J. (2013). "Late-Life Depressive Symptoms: Prediction Models of Change". *Journal of Affective Disorders*, *150*(3): 886-894.

Ghaderi, S., Sahaf, R., Mohammadi Shahbalaghi, F., Ansari, G., Gharanjic, A., Ashrafi, K., & Najafi, F. (2012). "Prevalence of Depression in Elderly Kurdish Community Residing in Boukan, Iran". *Iranian Journal of Ageing*, *7*(1): 57-66.

Gharanjik, A., Mohammadi Shahbolaghi, F., Ansari, G., Najafi, F., Ghaderi, S., Ashrafi, K., & Sahaf, R. (2011). "The Prevalence of Depression in Older Turkmen Adults in 1389". *Iranian Journal of Ageing*, *6*(3): 34-39.

González-Celis, A.L. & Gómez-Benito, J. (2013). "Spirituality and Quality of Life and Its Effect on Depression in Older Adults in Mexico". *Psychology*, *4*(3): 178.

Gregg, E.W., Mangione, C.M., Cauley, J.A., Thompson, T.J., Schwartz, A.V., Ensrud, K.E., & Study of Osteoporotic Fractures Research Group. (2002). "Diabetes and Incidence of Functional Disability in Older Women". *Diabetes Care*, *25*(1): 61-67.

Group, T.W. (1998). "The World Health Organization Quality of Life Assessment (WHOQOL): Development and General Psychometric Pro perties". *Social Science & Medicine*, *46*(12): 1569-1585.

Hall, E.E., Ekkekakis, P. & Petruzzello, S.J. (2002). "The Affective Beneficence of Vigorous Exercise Revisited". *British Journal of Health Psychology*, *7*(1): 47-66.

Halvorsrud, L., Kirkevold, M., Diseth, Å. & Kalfoss, M. (2010). "Quality of Life Model: Predictors of Quality of Life among Sick Older Adults". *Research and Theory for Nursing Practice*, *24*(4): 241-259.

Hassanpour-Dehkordi, A. & Jalali, A. (2016). "Effect of Progressive Muscle Relaxation on the Fatigue and Quality of Life among Iranian Ageing Persons". *Acta Medica Iranica*, 430-436.

Helvik, A.S., Engedal, K. & Selbæk, G. (2010). "The Quality of Life and Factors Associated with It in the Medically Hospitalised Elderly". *Ageing & Mental Health*, *14*(7): 861-869.

Henderson, M.J. (2005). *In-Home Preventive Health Assessment and Telephone Case Management for Over 75S Living Alone in Independent Living Units: A Cluster Randomised Controlled Trial* (Doctoral dissertation, Queensland University of Technology).

Heydarnejad, S. & Dehkordi, A.H. (2010). "The effect of an exercise programme on the health-quality of life in older adults." *Dan Med Bull*, *57*(4): 113-117.

Ho, C.S., Feng, L., Fam, J., Mahendran, R., Kua, E.H. & Ng, T.P. (2014). "Coexisting Medical Comorbidity and Depression: Multiplicative Effects on Health Outcomes in Older Adults". *International Psychogeriatrics*, *26*(7): 1221-1229.

Hosienabadi, R., Goorabi, K. & Shareh, H. (2007). "Hearing Aid Effect on Elderly's Depression in Tehran's Nursing Homes". *Iranian Journal of Ageing*, *2*(1): 205-209.

Hsu, H.C. (2009). "Physical Function Trajectories, Depressive Symptoms, and Life Satisfaction among the Elderly in Taiwan". *Ageing and Mental Health*, *13*(2): 202-212.

Hu, T., Xiao, J., Peng, J., Kuang, X. & He, B. (2018). "Relationship Between Resilience, Social Support as Well as Anxiety/Depression of Lung Cancer Patients: A Cross-Sectional Observation Study". *Journal of Cancer Research and Therapeutics*, *14*(1): 72-77.

Huisman, M., Klokgieters, S.S. & Beekman, A.T.F. (2017). "Successful Ageing, Depression and Resilience Research: A Call for *a priori* Approaches to Investigations of Resilience". *Epidemiology and Psychiatric Sciences*, *26*(6): 574-578.

Jacobson, A.M., De Groot, M. & Samson, J.A. (1997). "The Effects of Psychiatric Disorders and Symptoms on Quality of Life in Patients with Type I and Type II Diabetes Mellitus". *Quality of Life Research, 6.*

Kaya, B. (1999). "Yashhk ve depresyon-I tam ve değerlendirme". *Turkish Journal of Geriatrics*, *2*(2): 72-82.

Kriegsman, D.M., Penninx, B.W., Van Eijk, J.T.M., Boeke, A.J.P. & Deeg, D.J. (1996). "Self-Reports and General Practitioner Information on the Presence of Chronic Diseases in Community Dwelling Elderly: A Study on the Accuracy of Patients' Self-Reports and on Determinants of Inaccuracy". *Journal of Clinical Epidemiology*, *49*(12): 1407-1417.

Kriska, A. (2003). "Can a Physically Active Lifestyle Prevent Type 2 Diabetes?". *Exercise and Sport Sciences Reviews*, *31*(3): 132-137.

Lino, V.T.S., Rodrigues, N.C.P., Andrade, M.K.D.N., Reis, I.N.D.C., Lopes, L.A.E. & Atie, S. (2019). "Association between Visual Problems, Insufficient Emotional Support and Urinary Incontinence with Disability in Elderly People Living in a Poor District in Rio de Janeiro, Brazil: A six-year follow-up study". *PloS one*, *14*(5): e0217456.

Lovibond, S.H. (1995). "Manual for the Depression Anxiety Stress Scales". *Sydney Psychology Foundation*.

Lue, B.H., Chen, L.J. & Wu, S.C. (2010). "Health, Financial Stresses, and Life Satisfaction Affecting Late-Life Depression among Older Adults: A

Nationwide, Longitudinal Survey in Taiwan". *Archives of Gerontology and Geriatrics*, *50*, S34-S38.

Luo, R., Zhang, C. & Liu, Y. (2020). "Health Risk Assessment Indicators for the Left-behind Elderly in Rural China: A Delphi Study". *International Journal of Environmental Research and Public Health*, *17*(1): 340.

Mahdizadeh, F. (2007). "Comparative Study of Cognitional Situation and Depression among Elderly of Nursing Homes of Shahrood and Elderly Living at Home in 2007". In *Book of Abstract of the Third Congress on Elderly in Iran and the World.*

Margis, R., Donis, K.C., Schönwald, S.V. & Rieder, C.R. (2010). "WHOQOL-OLD Assessment of Quality of Life in Elderly Patients with Parkinson's Disease: Influence of Sleep and Depressive Symptoms". *Brazilian Journal of Psychiatry*, *32*, 125-131.

McCurren, C.D., Hall, L.A. & Rowles, G.D. (1993). "Community Elders: Prevalence and Correlates of Depressive Symptoms". *Clinical Nursing Research*, *2*(2): 128-144.

Mishra, A.K. & Mishra, N. (2016). "Physical status of elderly people in old age homes in South Gujarat: an overview". *International Journal of Health Sciences & Research*, *6*(2).

Mishra, N., Mishra, A.K. & Bidija, M. (2017). "A Study on Correlation Between Depression, Fear of Fall and Quality of Life in Elderly Individuals". *Int J Res Med Sci*, *5*(4): 1456.

Mobasheri, M. & Moezy, M. (2010). "The prevalence of depression among the elderly population of Shaystegan and Jahandidegan nursing homes in Shahrekord". *Journal of Shahrekord University of Medical Sciences*, *12*(2): 89-94.

Mortazavi, S., Eftikhar Ardabili, H., Mohammad, K. & Dorali Bani, R. (2011). "The Mental Health of the Elderly in Shahrekord and Its Relationship with Demographic and Social Factors". *Payesh*, *10*(4): 485-92.

Mottram, P.G., Wilson, K., Scally, L. & Vassilas, C. (2000). "Psychotherapeutic Treatments for Older Depressed People". *Cochrane Database of Systematic Reviews*, (4).

Mura, G., Bhat, K.M., Pisano, A., Licci, G. & Carta, M.G. (2012). "Psychiatric Symptoms and Quality of Life in Systemic Sclerosis". *Clinical Practice and Epidemiology in Mental Health: CP & EMH*, *8*, 30.

Papadopoulos, F.C., Petridou, E., Argyropoulou, S., Kontaxakis, V., Dessypris, N., Anastasiou, A.,. .. & Lyketsos, C. (2005). "Prevalence and Correlates of Depression in Late Life: A Population Based Study from a Rural Greek Town". *International Journal of Geriatric Psychiatry: A Journal of the Psychiatry of Late Life and Allied Sciences*, *20*(4): 350-357.

Park, J.H., Lee, J.J., Lee, S.B., Huh, Y., Choi, E.A., Youn, J.C.,. .. & Kim, K.W. (2010). "Prevalence of Major Depressive Disorder and Minor Depressive Disorder in an Elderly Korean Population: Results from the Korean Longitudinal Study on Health and Ageing (KLoSHA)". *Journal of Affective Disorders*, *125*(1-3): 234-240.

Pawaskar, M.D., Anderson, R.T. & Balkrishnan, R. (2007). "Self-Reported Predictors of Depressive Symptomatology in an Elderly Population with Type 2 Diabetes Mellitus: A Prospective Cohort Study". *Health and Quality of Life Outcomes*, *5*: 1-6.

Prudham, D. & Evans, J.G. (1981). "Factors Associated with Falls in the Elderly: A Community Study". *Age and Ageing*, *10*(3): 141-146.

Sheibani Tazraji, F., Pakdaman, S., Dadkhah, A. & Hasanzadeh Tavakoli, M.R. (2010). "The Effect of Music Therapy on Depression and Loneliness in Old People". *Iranian Journal of Ageing*, *5*(2): 0-0.

Shrira, A. (2012). "The Effect of Lifetime Cumulative Adversity on Change and Chronicity in Depressive Symptoms and Quality of Life in Older Adults". *International Psychogeriatrics*, *24*(12): 1988-1997.

Silveira, M.M.D. & Portuguez, M.W. (2017). "Analysis of Life Quality and Prevalence of Cognitive Impairment, Anxiety, and Depressive Symptoms in Older Adults". *Estudos de Psicologia* (*Campinas*): *34*, 261-268.

Skevington, S.M., Lotfy, M. & O'Connell, K.A. (2004). "The World Health Organization's WHOQOL-BREF Quality of Life Assessment: Psychometric Properties and Results of the International Field Trial". A Report from the WHOQOL Group." *Quality of Life Research*, *13*: 299-310.

Sohrabi, M.B., Zolfaghari, P., Mahdizade, F., Aghayan, S.M., Ghasemian-Aghmashhadi, M., Shariati, Z. & Khosravi, A. (2008). "Evaluation and Comparison of Cognitive State and Depression in Elderly Admitted in Sanitarium with Elderly Sited in Personal Home". *Knowledge & Health*, *3*(2): 27-31.

Southham, M., Agras, W.S., Taylor, B. & Kraemer, H. (2001). "Stress Management at the Work for Elderly People Compliance, Cost Benefits, Health Care and Hy pertension-Related Variable". *Psychosom Med*, *46*(52): 387-97.

Street, H., O'Connor, M. & Robinson, H. (2007). "Depression in Older Adults: Exploring the Relationship Between Goal Setting and Physical Health". *International Journal of Geriatric Psychiatry: A Journal of the Psychiatry of Late Life and Allied Sciences*, *22*(11): 1115-1119.

Thompson, P.D., Buchner, D., Piña, I.L., Balady, G.J., Williams, M.A., Marcus, B.H.,. .. & Wenger, N.K. (2003). "Exercise and Physical Activity in the Prevention and Treatment of Atherosclerotic Cardiovascular Disease: A Statement from the Council on Clinical Cardiology (Subcommittee on Exercise, Rehabilitation, and Prevention) and the Council on Nutrition, Physical Activity, and Metabolism (Subcommittee on Physical Activity)". *Circulation*, *107*(24): 3109-3116.

Todd, J.A. & Robinson, R.J. (2003). "Osteoporosis and Exercise". *Postgraduate Medical Journal*, *79*(932): 320-323.

Vardhan H. (October 27, 2023). *Ageing and Health India*. World Health Organization https://www.who.int/india/health-topics/ageing

Victor, C.R., Scambler, S.J., Bowling, A.N.N. & Bond, J. (2005). "The Prevalence of, and Risk Factors for, Loneliness in Later Life: A Survey of Older People in Great Britain". *Ageing & Society*, *25*(6): 357-375.

Wannmacher, L. (2016). "Abordagem da depressão maior em idosos: medidas não medicamentosas e medicamentosas". *OPAS/OMS. Representação Brasil, 1*(1).

Whoqol Group. (1995). "The World Health Organization Quality of Life Assessment (WHOQOL): Position Paper from the World Health Organization". *Social Science & Medicine, 41*(10): 1403-1409.

Wilkinson, P. & Izmeth, Z. (2016). "Continuation and Maintenance Treatments for Depression in Older People". *Cochrane Database of Systematic Reviews*, (9).

Williams, C. D. (1980). "Epidemiology of Dysphoria and Depression in an Elderly Population". *The American Journal of Psychiatry*.

Wolinsky, F.D., Unverzagt, F.W., Smith, D.M., Jones, R., Wright, E. & Tennstedt, S.L. (2006). "The Effects of the ACTIVE Cognitive Training Trial on Clinically Relevant Declines in Health-Related Quality of Life". *The Journals of Gerontology Series B: Psychological Sciences and Social Sciences, 61*(5): S281-S287.

World Health Organization. (2008). *World Health Statistics 2008*. World Health Organization.

World Health Organization. (2017). *Depression and Other Common Mental Disorders: Global Health Estimates* (No. WHO/MSD/MER/2017.2). World Health Organization.

Xia, P., Li, N., Hau, K.T., Liu, C. & Lu, Y. (2012). "Quality of Life of Chinese Urban Community Residents: A Psychometric Study of the Mainland Chinese Version of the WHOQOL-BREF". *BMC Medical Research Methodology, 12*(1): 1-11.

Yan, T. (2009). *Translating Two Physical Activity Programmes for Older Adults Into Home-and Community-Based Settings: "Active Start" and "Healthy Moves for Ageing Well"* (Doctoral dissertation, University of Southern California).

Zhang, W. & Sullivan, P.W. (2007). "Minor Depression and Health Status among US Adults with Diabetes Mellitus". *Am J Manag Care, 13*: 65-72.

12

Promoting Wellness among Elderly

Touching New Horizons

Shilpa Singh and *Archana Shukla*

Life is a beautiful journey spanning across various stages. Out of all the stages, childhood and old age are considered to be the most crucial ones. And the reason is quite obvious; in both these periods, a human being is vulnerable and needs care and support from others to sustain himself; both physically and emotionally. An individual who in his youthful days, acts as a financial and emotional supporter of his family, becomes a responsibility for the family himself in his old age. During later years of life, it becomes the duty of the whole family to look after an elderly's physical as well as psychological requirements, without being overtly productive in the eyes of the family and society at large.

Universally and since ages old age has been considered to be the evening phase of life. This last quarter of life has been associated with deteriorating physical and mental health, social neglect and isolation, loneliness, depression and many other issues. However, that is just one face of the coin. Very few can understand the beauty of this quiet and soothing evening. There are innumerable joys which only an elderly can enjoy. The utmost satisfaction from one's life, a relaxed and self-oriented routine, joy of being a grandparent, knowledge and experience which only passing years can give and last but not the least, a wiser mind and peaceful solitude—these are the advantages only elderly can enjoy. In past few decades, researches have started focusing on the positive aspects of ageing rather than lamenting on the negative aspects. Therefore, today not only youth, even elderly themselves pay more attention to maintaining health, engaging in productive activities and hobbies and focusing on their mental health, happiness, and overall wellness.

Across the world, declining fertility and increased longevity have jointly resulted in higher numbers and proportions of older persons 60 years and above. This trend will continue as the estimated 737 million older persons in 2009 (United Nations, 2009) is likely to increase to two billion by 2050 at which time the population aged 60 and above will outnumber children 0-14 years of age. In fact, WHO has indicated that the global population of the people above 60 years old will approximately double from 12 per cent to 22 per cent by the year 2050 (WHO, 2022). The oldest-old age segment (80 years and above) is the fastest-growing segment and by 2050, about 20 per cent of older persons will be of 80 years and above. The coming decades therefore are characterized by ageing of the aged (Subaiya and Bansod, 2011).

Not only around the globe, ageing population has led to the birth of grave concerns in India also, where it is one of the fastest growing sections of the population. In India, the proportion of the population aged 60 years and above was 10.5 per cent in 2023 and is projected to increase to 20.8 per cent by 2050 (UNFPA India, 2023). In absolute numbers, the elderly population in 2009 was approximately 88 million and is expected to sharply increase to more than 315 million by 2050 (Subaiya and Bansod, 2011). At present, India is home to one-fourth of the global geriatric population (UN, 2019).

The above statistics not only indicates increasing physical deterioration with increasing age, it also gives alarming signal about attached psycho-social issues during the later years of life. For instance, a study by Kumar *et al.* (2022) reports the level of social isolation at almost 34 per cent among Indian elderly population and will continue to rise in future due to urbanization and vanishing joint family structure in the society. In fact, loneliness has been a major challenge which nearly 55.4 per cent of Indian elderly are facing (Grover *et al.*, 2019).

Thus, an overview of the demographic status depicts the necessity of the government, policy makers and the society in general to make sure that the geriatric population receives the care and support required for a healthy, fulfilling and dignified life (UNFPA India, 2023). For the same, the Government of India is trying to cater to the needs and upcoming challenges of this population through set up of National Policy for Older Persons (NPOP, 1999) and providing facilities like geriatric wards and pension schemes etc. However, still a lot remains to be done for enhancing physical and psychological health, happiness, positivity and quality of life of this rapidly growing elderly population and thus promoting Overall Wellness.

The term Wellness is used by various people and organizations since the sharp rise in healthcare costs, diabetes and obesity during the past decade. Wellness has traditionally been viewed as freedom from disease. However, this perspective is changing. Wellness is not the mere absence of disease, but it is a proactive, preventive approach designed to achieve optimum levels of health, social and emotional functioning. It indeed is a positive approach to living—an approach that emphasizes the whole person.

Wellness is described as "*a higher order construct integrating these domains (physical, psychological, social and environmental) drawing on individual self-perception* (Schuster *et al.*, 2004). The notion that Wellness is more a psychological than a physical state has been a focus of several researchers. Jonas (2005) explains Wellness as a way of life and living in which one is always exploring and searching, finding new questions and discovering new answers along the three primary dimensions of living—the physical, the mental and the social; a way of life designed to enable each of us to achieve, in each of the dimensions our maximum potential that is realistically and rationally feasible for us at any given time in our lives.

Wellness has a very important work to do. It integrates mind, body and spirit of an individual to produce a balanced lifestyle (Pufal, 2001). It is a lifelong process of moving towards enhancing one's physical, intellectual, emotional, social, spiritual and environmental well-being, which requires patience and persistence. Each person has a responsibility to provide for such health essentials as good nutrition, proper weight control, exercise and controlling of risk factors such as smoking, alcohol and drug abuse. All these factors play a vital role in Wellness.

As is evident, Wellness is not a simple and unidimensional concept. Rather, it is apt to term it as an 'Umbrella Concept', i.e. it includes various dimensions and aspects under one broad concept. A need, therefore, emerges to understand these various aspects of Wellness and their importance in various stages of life, especially during old age.

A wide range of Models of Wellness have been propounded by psychologists on the basis of researches conducted over decades. For instance, Stoewen (2017) has emphasized on the following dimensions of Wellness.

Physical Wellness

The Physical dimension of Wellness encourages cardiovascular flexibility, regular physical activity, knowledge about food and nutrition and discourages drug abuse. People experiencing Wellness in the physical dimension work towards investing time each week in the pursuit of

endurance, flexibility and strength. Physical Wellness involves taking responsibility and care for minor illness and also knowing when professional medical attention is necessary. Physical Wellness includes being able to monitor one's own vital signs whether perceived or measured. It entails an understanding of the relationship between sound nutrition and the functioning of the body. Included in Physical Wellness is an awareness of the body's true identity, depth of feelings, tension patterns, reactions, balance and harmony. The body is recognized as a formal expression of physiological development and personal evolution.

As age increases, muscles weaken and aerobic capacity and flexibility and balance are reduced. However, through exercise one may help slow down or even reverse many of the effects of ageing (Fries, 2002). A study reported that older women who lifted weights regularly were able to carry bags of groceries with 36 per cent less effort and to get up from their chairs with 40 per cent less stress on their leg muscles (Mayo Health, 2001).

The gradual reduction in physical activity is also accompanied by a diminution in appetite which leads to a remarkable amount of disease and disability. Nutrition is an important yet often overlooked aspect of a healthy lifestyle for older people. Good nutrition can help control blood triglycerides and cholesterol levels, both of which tend to increase with age, potentially accelerating the development of cardiovascular diseases, cancer and other chronic illnesses (Sacco *et al.*, 2001). It, therefore, becomes essential to follow a good nutritional plan and an exercise regimen for improving Physical Wellness during later years.

Social Wellness

The Social dimension of Wellness encourages contributing to one's human and physical environment to the common welfare of one's community. It emphasizes the interdependence with others and nature and includes harmony in one's family, neighbourhood and society. Social Wellness follows these tenets:

- It is better to contribute to the common welfare of our community than to think only of ourselves.
- It is better to live in harmony with others and our environment than to live in conflict with them.

Social Wellness is very important to our overall health. A person who is socially healthy has the skills to socialize, be confident and function in all situations that involve other people. A person lacking Social Wellness tends to lack the ability to adjust to social situations.

Components of Social Wellness include:

- The caring and healthy relationships you have in your life.
- Your social network, such as what clubs and/or organizations you belong to.
- Your level of safety.
- Your housing situation.
- Your level of interdependence, and if you are willing to accept and give help to other people.
- Positive interactions with your community (i.e. volunteer work).
- Your acceptance of diversity. This means accepting people regardless of their ethnicity, gender, sexual orientation, ability or religion.

(Thompson Rivers University, 2013)

Ryff and Singer (2006) indicate that quality ties to others are central to optimal living and are connected to psychological factors. They cited epidemiological studies stating that mortality is significantly lower among persons who are more socially integrated. During later years, as loneliness and social isolation start playing their part, it becomes essential for the elderly to try to become more socially active and involved especially males, as most of the females being housewives, they already maintain their social relations due to ample opportunities they get to socialize. A study shows that men with few social contacts had a higher risk of death than others, while women who belonged to social clubs had a better chance for living longer (Bowling, Grundy and Farquhar, 1997).

Spiritual Wellness

The Spiritual Wellness involves seeking meaning and purpose in human existence. It includes the development of a deep appreciation for the depth and expanse of life and natural force that exists in the universe. It is possibly the most developed and discussed topic in the Wellness literature (Banks, 1980; Hatch, Burg, Naberhaus and Hellmich, 1998; Ingersoll, 1994; Pargament, 1999).

An individual's journey to attain and maintain Spiritual Wellness is highly personal and unique. Evidence indicates that the spiritual dimension of our holistic nature becomes more important in our lives as we grow older. In old age, spiritual practices and meditation can help elderly to deal with inner pressures and worries, improving their overall sense of well-being.

There may be a tendency for some people to perceive religion and spirituality as one in the same because there may be shared rituals that are part of each, such as prayer and meditation. Religion involves specific, agreed upon beliefs and practices by a group of people whereas spirituality involves exploring sources of power and meaning in a person's life that may occur outside of a religious base. Gerontology professionals agree that spirituality is important to older adults towards effective psychosocial function and successful ageing (Miller, 2004).

Spiritual Wellness involves personal growth at every age:

- Enhancing body, mind, spirit connection.
- Sensing purpose and meaning to life.
- Learning how to experience love, joy and fulfilment.
- Embracing our personal ethics, values, and code of living (may or may not be part of formal religion) (Canadian government website, November 2008).

Emotional Wellness

Emotional Wellness includes the ability to experience, manage, and express appropriately one's emotional life. It also involves a recognition and acceptance of the physical and emotional selves, including strengths and limitations.

The Emotional Wellness emphasizes the awareness and acceptance of one's feelings and related behaviours including the realistic assessment of one's limitations, development of autonomy and ability to cope effectively with stress. According to McGrath, Health and Wellness Centre (2013), Emotional Wellness is:

- important to our physical, intellectual, spiritual and social lives.
- self-awareness, self-acceptance and self-confidence.
- having the ability to share our feelings with others.
- recognizing our problems and finding solutions.

Increasing age brings with itself various emotional changes which an elderly has to deal with. Suicide and depression are often seen in old people (Camacho *et al.*, 1993). The need is to deal with emotional pressures and cope with them effectively.

An emotionally well person is both aware of and accepts a wide range of feelings in him/her and others. He/she is able to freely express feelings and to manage feelings effectively to arrive at personal choices/decisions based upon the integration of feelings, cognition and behaviour. He/she is self-aware and self-accepting while remaining flexible and continually open to personal development.

The emotionally well person can function autonomously but is aware of personal limitations and the value of seeking inter personal support and assistance. He/she also forms interdependent relationships based upon mutual commitment, trust and respect. The emotionally well person is willing to accept challenges, take risks, and acknowledge conflict as being potentially healthy. The emotionally well person maintains a generally positive approach to life that is rooted in his/her sense of personal responsibility for, and ability to manage, his/her life in personally fulfilling ways. Emotional Wellness is thus not an end stage but a continual process of change and growth.

To sum up, achieving Emotional Wellness is an ongoing process of making choices towards a healthy and fulfilling life. The choices one makes in terms of managing emotional issues can contribute to overall wellness or illness.

Intellectual Wellness

Intellectual Wellness may be defined as engaging the individual in creative and stimulating mental activities to expand their knowledge and skills and help them discover the potential for sharing their gifts with others.

The dimension of Intellectual Wellness encourages creative, stimulating mental activities. In addition to attending cultural events, Leafgren (1990) cites that stimulation can come from reading, studying, travelling and exposure to media. An intellectually well person uses the resources available to expand his knowledge and improve skills along with expanding potential for sharing with others. Intellectual Wellness, according to Thompson River University (2013) is based on some of the following factors—Critical thinking, problem solving, creativity, education and learning goals, ability to adapt to change, ability to access resources, mental status and abilities or challenges. In other words, an intellectually well person:

- Cherishes mental growth and stimulation.
- Is involved in intellectual and cultural activities.
- Is engaged in the exploration of new ideas and understandings.

Intellectual Wellness involves utilizing learning resources to expand knowledge, improve skills and experience life more fully. Intellectual Wellness refers to active participation in scholastic, cultural, and community activities. It also involves assimilating what is learned in the classroom with life experience. Valuing and nurturing creativity, curiosity and lifelong learning are part of Intellectual Wellness. Intellectually well people are open to new ideas, think critically and seek out new challenges. People who develop Intellectual Wellness are more likely to maintain good cognitive function as they age.

An elderly can improve his intellectual capacities by playing brain games (puzzles, Sudoku etc.), reading and engaging in other mentally stimulating activities. In a study, it was found that a cognitively active person in old age was 2.6 times less likely to develop dementia and Alzheimer's disease than a cognitively inactive person in old age (Wilson, Scherr, Schneider, Tang and Bennett, 2007).

Environmental Wellness

The Environmental Wellness includes respecting nature and species living in it. Environmental Wellness involves limited exposure or satisfactory management of aspects of the environment that can affect health and well-being, including, toxic chemicals, radiation, biological agents, electromagnetic radiation, noise, air and water pollution, tobacco smoke, climate change, food safety, waste disposal, hazardous materials and vector control.

Environmental Wellness can affect emotional, physical and mental wellness. For example, people can have the following adverse health effects from noise pollution: hearing loss, sleep disturbances and cardiovascular problems as well as mental and psychological problems resulting in performance reduction and behaviour problems.

An elderly can help in increasing Environmental Wellness by simply leading an environmentally conscious life. Ryan and Deci (2001) found cultural differences when looking at Environmental Wellness across 61 nations, suggesting that the cultural environment is an important factor.

It is evident from the above discussion that Wellness is an attribute which is commonly used in day-to-day life and easily defined but is difficult to be achieved. However, recent researches have suggested numerous strategies and techniques which can help an individual to reach a level of Overall Wellness which will ultimately result in healthier, happier, energetic and satisfying later years of life.

Promoting Wellness among Elderly

1. Maintain healthy eating habits, take adequate sleep and keep the body properly hydrated. This collectively results in supporting physical fitness and overall health (Sleep Foundation, 2023).
2. Exercise, in any form always carries physical benefits. Try to find out an enjoyable activity such as stretching, walking, and balance exercise etc. and continue till it becomes a routine and ritual (CCDPHP, 2023).
3. Monitor the calorie intake as with age the metabolism of the body slows down (Manini, 2010).
4. Maintain an active social life. Try to meet people and attend nearby social gatherings. Social connections help in improving cognitive outcomes and lower the likelihood of developing debilitating neurodegenerative conditions (Sommerlad *et al.*, 2023).
5. An initiative should be taken for a co-interaction between elderly and younger generation through social events and day-to-day interactions. During such meetings, the older generation can provide wisdom, values, skills, attention, and affection for the young who in return can provide more up-to-date skills and knowledge as well as attention and affection to the old (Annear *et al.*, 2017). Generally termed as intergenerational programme this approach enhances the

social connection between the younger and older generations by facilitating partnerships in the search for well-being (Butts, 2007, WHO, 2021).

6. Try to be actively involved with your community, make new friends, and be surrounded with peers (Chiang *et al.,* 2008).
7. For elderly with physical restrictions connecting with technology has been found to improve some dimensions of social connectedness by providing virtual social support and networks (Morris *et al.*, 2014).
8. Try to find deeper meanings in your life and analyse frequently occurring patterns. This will help in visualizing your self-control over the destiny. Being aware of this can help you achieve a happy and healthy life (Prajapati, 2020).
9. Practice some form of *yoga* daily as it can help improve the spiritual wellness by reducing emotional and physical strains both physically and mentally. Numerous researches have found *yoga* helpful in reducing stress, fatigue, anxiety and depression, lowering the blood pressure, boosting the immune system and curing insomnia. It has also been found to be effective in developing coping skills and reaching a more positive outlook on life (Prajapati, 2020).
10. Start viewing things in your life in a positive manner. This will help your mind refocus itself to a healthier and happier place. Eliminating negativity and reframing your thought process will help you to be more relaxed (Prajapati, 2020).
11. Practice meditation for at least 5-10 minutes daily as it helps you connect with yourself. This will free your mind and foster a stronger relationship with your spiritual wellness (Prajapati, 2020).
12. Always set and maintain boundaries among your various roles in life to maintain your emotional wellness. Know and accept your limits. Understand that it's okay to say no sometimes even to your loved ones (USDHHS, 2016).
13. Listen to soothing music to shift your mood (USDHHS, 2016).
14. Utilize available supports: Family, friends, neighbours, counsellors, specialists and support groups during emotional upheavals (USDHHS, 2016).
15. Practice an attitude of gratitude towards people around you (USDHHS, 2016).
16. Make it a point to laugh throughout each day (USDHHS, 2016).
17. Read something positive each day, such as a quote, mantra or article (USDHHS, 2016).

18. Journaling, i.e. expressing in writing what is in your mind also enhances healthy processing of emotions; self-discovery, creativity, and expression; stress reduction; as well as problem-solving and conflict resolution. Try to record your thoughts and ideas in a journal. This may lead to positive intellectual wellness benefits (Purcell, 2018).
19. Art therapy, i.e. drawing painting or any other art used to express self-thoughts can enhance intellectual wellness by supporting self-discovery, expression, and growth. Art therapy has been shown to decrease symptoms of depression, anxiety, and trauma; and may help reduce stress (Bitonte, 2014).
20. Ensure that you spend some time in the lap of nature outside (e.g. at parks, beaches, forests, farms, lakes, rivers, gardens). This can actively help in lowering stress, improving mood, and enhancing overall well-being (Crane, 2016).
21. Try to keep the environment clean—organized spaces can "help ease stress and anxiety, as well as promote stronger decision-making skills (CDCP, 2018).
22. Make sure the environment is safe—identify and address occupational hazards and create supportive environments that are inclusive for all abilities (Kellar-Guenther, 2016).

All these strategies and techniques will help elderly to enhance their Wellness in different aspects of life which will help them to lead a healthier and meaningful life. However, as the elderly face various challenges like deteriorating physical and mental health, social isolation and neglect and being away from their loved ones, it becomes the responsibility of the family, relatives, neighbourhood, peers and society in general to take initiative in making collaborative efforts to help them understand their value for the family and society, to make them realize that despite them feeling physically unproductive they are still regarded for their immense knowledge, wisdom and worldly experience and they are loved, listened, and regarded during their sunset years of life.

References

Annear, M.J., Elliott, K.J., Tierney, L.T., Lea, E.J., Robinson, A. (2017). *Bringing the Outside World in: Enriching Social Connection Through Health Student Placements in a Teaching Aged Care Facility Health Expect*, *20*(5): pp. 1154-1162 https://onlinclibrary.wilcy.com/doi/full/10.1111/hcx.12561

Banks, R. (1980). "Health and the Spiritual Dimension: Relationships and Implications for Professional Preparation Programmes". *The Journal of School Health, 50,* 195-202.

Bitonte, R.A. & De Santo, M. (2014). "Art Therapy: An Underutilized, Yet Effective Tool". *Mental Illness, 6*(1). https://doi. org/10.4081/mi.2014.5354

Bowling, A., Grundy, E. & Farquhar, M. (1997). *Living Well Into Old Age: Three Studies of Health and Well-being among Older People in East London and Essex.* Age Concern England. Funded by the Joseph Rowntree Foundation.

Butts, D. (2007). *Intergenerational Solidarity: Strengthening Economic and Social Ties Expert Group Meeting October 2007*, United Nations Headquarters, New York.

Canadian Government Website (2008) focused on Six Dimensions of Wellness, Available. November 2008.

Camacho, T.C., Strawbridge, W.J., Kaplan, G.A., and Cohen, R.D, (1993) "Functional Ability in the Oldest Old: Cumulative impact of risk factors from the preceding two decades". *Journal of Ageing and Health, 5*, 439-454

CDCP (2018). Centres for Disease Control and Prevention. Organizational-level assessment: Environmental assessment. Retrieved from https://www.cdc.gov/workplacehealthpromotion/model/assessment/environmental.html

CCDPHP (2023). *Centre for Chronic Disease Prevention and Health Promotion: Adults 50 and Older Need More Physical Activity; 2023.* Available from: https://www.cdc.gov/physicalactivity/inactivity-among-adults-50 plus/index.html. Accessed January 29, 2023.

Chiang, K., Seman, L., Belza, B., Tsai, J.H. (2008). "It Is Our Exercise Family: Experiences of Ethnic Older Adults in a Groups-Based Exercise Programme". *Prev Chronic Dis, 5*(1): pp. 1-12.

Crane, K. (2016). "Why Decluttering is Good for Your Health". *U.S. News and World Report.* Retrieved from https://health. usnews.com/wellness/mind/articles/2016-11-08/why-decluttering-is-good-for-your-health

Fries, James J. (December 25, 2002). "Reducing Disability in Older Age". *The Journal of the American Medical Association. 288*(24): 3164-66

Grover, S., Verma, M., Singh, T., Dahiya, N., Nehra, R. (June 2019). "Loneliness and Its Correlates amongst Elderly Attending Non-Communicable Disease Rural Clinic Attached to a Tertiary Care Centre of North India". *Asian J Psychiatr. 43*:189-196. doi: 10.1016/j.ajp.2019.06.001. Epub 2019 Jun 10. PMID: 31229701.

Hatch, R.L., Burg, M.A., Naberhaus, D.S. & Hellmich, L.K. (1998). "The Spiritual Involvement and Beliefs Scale: Development and Testing of a New Instrument". *The Journal of Family Practice, 46*(6): 476-484.

Ingersoll, R.E. (1994). "Spirituality, Religion, and Counselling: Dimensions and Relationships". *Counselling and Values, 38:* 98-111.

Jonas, S. (2005). "The Wellness Process for Healthy Living: A Mental Tool for Facilitating Progress Through the Stages of Change". *AMAA Journal, Health Care Industry,* Winter.

Kellar-Guenther, Y. (2016). "Workplace Wellness Programmes and Accessibility for All". *The AMA Journal of Ethics*, *18*(4): 393-398. https://doi.org/10.1001/journalofethics.2016.18.4.nlit1-1604

Kumar, M., Ruikar, M., Surya, V.L. (September 2022). "Prevalence and Determinants of Social Isolation among Elderly in an Urban Slum of Raipur City—A Community Based Cross-Sectional Study". *Int J Geriatr Psychiatry*. *37*(9). doi: 10.1002/gps.5797. PMID: 35962476.

Leafgren, F. (1990). "Being a Man Can Be Hazardous to Your Health: Life-Styles Issues". In D. Moore & F. Leafgren (Eds.): *Problem Solving Strategies and Interventions for Men in Conflict* (pp. 265-311). Alexandria: American Association for Counselling and Development.

Manini, T.M. (2010). "Energy Expenditure and Ageing". *Ageing Res Rev.*, *9*(1):1-11. PMID: 19698803; PMCID: PMC2818133. doi: 10.1016/j.arr.2009.08.002

Mayo Health (2001). *Mayo Clinic Proc.*, *76*: 923-929.

McGrath Health and Wellness Centre (2013). *Emotional Wellness* http://www.xavier,edu/health-wellness/prevention/emotional-wellness.cfm

Miller, C. (2004). *Nursing for Wellness in Older Adults: Theory and Practice* (4th edn.). Philadelphia: Williams, Lippincott Williams & Wilcott.

Morris, M.E., Adair, B., Ozanne, E., Kurowski, W., Miller, K.J., Pearce, A.J., *et al.* (2014). "Smart Technologies to Enhance Social Connectedness in Older People Who Live at Home", *Australas J Ageing*, *33*(3): 142-152, 10.1111/ajag.12154

NPOP (1999). *National Policy for Older Persons*. Ministry of Social Justice and Empowerment, Shastri Bhawan, New Delhi.

Pargament, K.I. (1999). "The Psychology of Religion and Spirituality? Yes, and No". *The International Journal for the Psychology of Religion, 9*(1): 3-16.

Prajapati, Hemlata. (2020). "7 Ways to Improve Your Spiritual Health". *Human Studies*. 1. 2.

Pufal, Sandra L. (2001). "Enhancing the Wellness of Reserve Forces : A Strategic Challenge". *Strategy Research Project*, USAWC.

Purcell, M. (2018). "The health benefits of journaling". *Psych Central*. Retrieved from https://psychcentral.com/lib/the-healthbenefits-of-journaling/

Ryan, R.M. & Deci, E.L. (2001). "On Happiness and Human Potentials: A Review of Research on Hedonic and Eudemonic Well-being". *Annual Review of Psychology, 52,* 141-166.

Ryff, C.D. & Singer, B.H. (2006). "Best News Yet on the Six-Factor Model of Well-being". *Social Science Research*, 35: 1103-1119.

Sacco, R.L., Adams, R., Albers, G. *et al.* (2006). "Guidelines for Prevention of Stroke in Patients with Ischemic Stroke or Transient Ischemic Attack". *Stroke* 37577-617.617.

Schuster, T.A., Dobson, M., Jauregui, M. & Blanks, R.H. (2004). "Wellness Lifestyles I: A Theoretical Framework Linking Wellness, Health Lifestyles, and Complementary and Alternative Medicine". *Journal of Alternative and Complementary Medicine*, (10):2, 349-356.

Sleep Foundation (2023). *Diet, Exercise, and Sleep.* Available from: https://www.sleepfoundation.org/physical-health/diet-exercise-sleep. Accessed January 27, 2023.

Sommerlad, A., Kivimäki, M., Larson, E.B., Röhr, S., Shirai, K., Singh-Manoux, A. & Livingston, G. (2023). "Social Participation and Risk of Developing Dementia". *Nature Ageing, 3*(5): 532-545. https://doi.org/10.1038/s43587-023-00387-0

Stoewen, Debbie L. (2017). "Dimensions of Wellness: Change Your Habits, Change Your Life". *The Canadian Veterinary Journal. 58*(8): 861-862. ISSN 0008-5286. PMC 5508938. PMID 28761196

Subaiya, Lekha and Dhananjay W. Bansod. (2011). "Demographics of Population Ageing in India: Trends and Differentials", *BKPAI Working Paper No. 1,* United Nations Population Fund (UNFPA): New Delhi.

Thompson River University (2013). *Social Wellness.* Retrieved from http://www.tru.ca/wellness/social.html

United Nations (2009). *World Population Prospects: The 2008 Revision.* New York: United Nations.

United Nations (2019). Department of Economic and Social Affairs, Population Division. World Population Prospects 2019: Data Booklet (ST/ESA/SER.A/424). New York, United Nations.

UNFPA India. (26 September 2023). *Caring for our Elders Institutional Responses. India Ageing Report* 2023. UNFPA India. https://india.unfpa.org/en/publications/caring-our-elders-institutional-responses-india-ageing-report-2023 [Google Scholar

USDHHS (2016). *Creating a Healthier Life: A Step-By-Step Guide to Wellness 2016*, U.S. Department of Health and Human Services, Substance Abuse and Mental Health Services Administration. https://store.samhsa.gov/sites/default/files/d7/priv/sma16-4958.pdf

Wilson, R.S., Scherr, P.A., Schneider, J.A., Tang, Y., Bennett, D.A. (2007). "Relation of Cognitive Activity to Risk of Developing Alzheimer Disease". *Neurology. 69*: 1911-1920.

WHO (2021). *World Health Organization Active Ageing: A Policy Framework.* https://www.who.int/ageing/publications/active_ageing/en/ [accessed on 18 April 2021].

WHO (2022). World Health Organization (1 October 2022). *Ageing and Health.* www.who.int. https://www.who.int/news-room/fact-sheets/detail/ageing-and-health#:~:text=By%202030%2C%201%20in%206

13

Loneliness Unveiled

Mindset Matters in Geriatric Wellness

Prerna Arora and *Ritu Singh*

Introduction

People move through a continuum characterized by a wide range of physiological and psychological changes as they go through the phases of life. But nowhere are these changes more obvious than in the older population, where ageing brings with it a whole new set of difficulties and adaptations? The most notable of these difficulties are degeneration on both a physical and emotional level, which has a big impact on how older persons experience life.

The physical effects of ageing cause the human body to gradually deteriorate in many physiological areas. The loss of bone density and muscle mass, which lowers strength and mobility, is one of the most obvious signs of this decline. Once-easy tasks may become difficult undertakings when muscles weaken and joints stiffen. Elderly people are also more vulnerable to a wide range of chronic illnesses, such as diabetes, osteoporosis, and cardiovascular disorders.

In the journey of ageing, older persons experience significant changes in their physical and mental well-being. Physically, they suffer from a decline in bone density, muscular mass and sensory abilities, which results in a decrease in energy, a reduction in movement, and an increased vulnerability to long-term illnesses. These physical changes are accompanied by an emotional decline characterised by mood swings, heightened susceptibility to mental health issues, cognitive degradation, and existential difficulties. Emotional anguish is exacerbated by social isolation and a loss of purpose in life, which negatively affects mental health and quality of life. To tackle these obstacles, all-encompassing strategies involving medical services, social support systems, and mental health therapies customised to older individuals' specific requirements are needed.

In the twilight years of life, where wisdom meets the whispers of memories, there exists a silent companion that walks hand-in-hand with many elders: loneliness. Loneliness in old age transcends simple isolation and is a deep emotional state that reverberates through life, powerfully influencing experiences and perceptions. The focus on this frequently disregarded aspect of elderly health has shifted in recent years, revealing its profound effects on general health and quality of life. Being alone is not just the lack of company; loneliness is a complicated fabric made of several strands, including existential longing, emotional detachment, and social exclusion. The transition into old age can be difficult for many seniors, who may experience a loss of friends and partners who have been in their lives as well as a shrinking social circle due to declining mobility and health. Even while these changes are unavoidable, they might shade what ought to be a period of introspection and satisfaction by opening the door for the sneaky arrival of loneliness.

In the context of geriatric health, addressing loneliness is not just a practical concern; it is an essential component of providing compassionate care. The substantial effects of loneliness on one's physical and mental health have been brought to light by recent research, which has also linked loneliness to a number of unfavourable health outcomes, such as cardiovascular disease, cognitive decline, and even early mortality. Furthermore, loneliness can worsen pre-existing medical disorders, adding to the stress on carers and the healthcare system (Holt-Lunstad *et al.*, 2015).

When loneliness is understood, it is clear that it is more than just emotional misery; rather, loneliness can be considered a sickness of the mind-set, an ingrained cognitive framework that distorts one's view of the world and of oneself. This conceptual change has important ramifications for the way we approach elderly citizens who are experiencing loneliness in terms of therapies and support networks. Understanding loneliness as a result of both external events and internal stories allows us to explore comprehensive strategies that address social isolation as well as the psychological underpinnings that keep people apart. The neurological foundation of loneliness has provided insight into the complex interactions between social cues and brain architecture. Furthermore, a variety of interventions have surfaced, spanning from digital platforms to community-based programmes, which present promising means of mitigating loneliness and promoting deep connections among older persons (Masi *et al.,* 2011).

A rising public health issue, loneliness affects people of all ages, but it particularly affects the elderly. To learn more about older persons' lived experiences of loneliness and how it affects the ageing population, qualitative research has been done (Centres for Disease Control and Prevention, 2020). Manchana (2024) studied thirty adults between the ages of 60 and 78 and stated loneliness in older people is linked to feelings of not belonging in life and not having someone to confide in when necessary. Decreased social engagement and mental health problems in later life are linked to the lack of deep social interactions and inadequate familial support.

Objectives

The purpose of this research is to investigate loneliness as a mind-set disease among the elderly. It looks at attitudes and thought processes in an effort to determine how mentality influences loneliness in later life. It provides insights to support social connection and emotional well-being by highlighting implications for intervention techniques and holistic approaches to managing loneliness in older individuals through a review of the research and empirical data.

Methodology

The entire study is based on secondary data, wherein data have been collected from various secondary sources, like journals, books, websites and other online sources. Descriptive research design has been adopted for explaining the observation.

Discussion

Understanding Loneliness in Elderly

Among elderly persons, loneliness encompasses a wide range of intricate emotional and psychological experiences. Loneliness is defined as the subjective impression of social isolation or discontent with social connections (Victor *et al.,* 2005). This multifaceted concept encompasses social loneliness, which is defined by a lack of social integration or companionship, as well as emotional loneliness, which is defined by a lack of close relationships or emotional support (Luo *et al.,* 2012). As society ages, understanding and addressing the nuances of loneliness in the elderly becomes increasingly critical for enhancing their quality of life and well-being.

Psychological Effects of Loneliness

Older persons who experience loneliness suffer from severe and complex psychological effects. Loneliness has been linked in studies to higher risks of death, cognitive decline, anxiety, and depression (Perissinotto *et al.,* 2012; Gerst-Emerson & Jayawardhana, 2015). Loneliness can also worsen pre-existing medical issues, suppress the immune system, and interfere with coping strategies, which can result in a downward spiral of deteriorating mental and physical health (Leigh-Hunt *et al.,* 2017; Hawkley & Cacioppo, 2010). Loneliness is a predictor of increased mortality, independent of other risk factors such as depression (Steptoe, Shankar, Demakakos, and Wardle, 2013).

Additionally, loneliness has been shown to be a risk factor for cognitive decline and dementia. Feelings of loneliness are associated with an increased risk of developing dementia in older adults (Holwerda *et al.,* 2014). The emotional and psychological burden of loneliness can also lead to significant stress, which in turn can affect cardiovascular health (Cacioppo *et al.,* 2002).

Characteristics of Elderly

Physical Changes Associated with Ageing

People experience a variety of physical changes that have a substantial influence on their health and well-being as they get older. A decrease in bone density, muscle mass and sensory abilities are some of these alterations (Guralnik *et al.,* 1993). Older persons may have less energy, decreased mobility, and an increased risk of developing chronic illnesses like arthritis and cardiovascular disease. These bodily alterations exacerbate emotions of vulnerability and reliance in addition to impairing an individual's capacity to carry out daily chores (Fried *et al.,* 2001). Furthermore, reduced sensory abilities such as impaired vision and hearing loss can lead to decreased social interactions, contributing to feelings of isolation (Heine & Browning, 2014).

Chronic conditions prevalent in older age, such as diabetes, hy pertension, and osteoporosis, often require long-term management and frequent medical visits. These conditions can limit the ability to engage in social activities, thus heightening the risk of loneliness. Additionally, mobility impairments can reduce the likelihood of participating in community events, exacerbating the sense of social isolation (Rosso *et al.,* 2013).

Emotional Challenges in Later Life

As older persons traverse later life, they encounter a variety of emotional difficulties in addition to physical changes. These difficulties could include existential questions about meaning and purpose, identity changes brought on by retirement, and sadness and loss brought on by the loss of a loved one (Pinquart & Schindler, 2007). Older persons may struggle with feelings of social isolation, loneliness, and a lack of deep social ties. Because of the potential consequences, these emotional difficulties may have on mental health and general well-being, it is critical to address psychosocial needs in older adults.

The transition to retirement can particularly affect one's identity and sense of purpose, as work often provides a significant source of social interaction and personal fulfilment.

Retirement can lead to decreased social engagement and increased loneliness, particularly for those who have not cultivated social networks outside of their workplace (Wang, Henkens, and van Solinge, 2011).

Bereavement and the loss of close companions also significantly impact the emotional well-being of older adults. The death of a spouse or close friend can lead to profound grief and a sense of emptiness (Jiao *et al.,* 2023).

Factors Contributing to Loneliness

The causes of loneliness in the elderly are numerous and intricate. A significant sensation of emptiness and loneliness can result after losing a spouse, especially for elderly persons who might not have as much social support (Jiao *et al.,* 2023). Retirement can exacerbate loneliness in older persons since they may no longer have a feeling of purpose or social ties (National Academies of Sciences, 2020). Seniors with low incomes may find it difficult to maintain social relationships or participate in social events, which can also result in social isolation. In addition, elderly adults may feel lonely as a result of their children moving out and their loss of social support and companionship (Manchana, 2024).

Geographical isolation is another significant factor contributing to loneliness. Older adults living in rural areas often have less access to social and recreational activities, which can intensify feelings of isolation. Rural seniors report higher levels of loneliness compared to their urban counterparts, largely due to reduced access to social services and transportation (Smith *et al.,* 2009).

Health-related factors such as chronic illness, disability, and sensory impairments can also contribute to loneliness. For instance, older adults with mobility issues may find it difficult to leave their homes, limiting their social interactions (Goll *et al.,* 2015). Sensory impairments such as hearing loss can hinder communication, making social interactions more challenging and less enjoyable (Heine & Browning, 2014).

Intervention Strategies and Holistic Approach

Psychosocial therapies are essential in alleviating loneliness in the senior population. Such interventions are meant to strengthen social support, develop effective coping mechanisms, and cultivate significant social ties (Masi *et al.,* 2011). Support groups, social clubs, and cognitive-behavioural therapy are a few types of psychosocial therapies (Verlinde *et al.,* 2019). These programmes lessen feelings of loneliness and isolation in older individuals by giving them chances for social interaction, emotional expression, and skill development. Support groups provide a structured environment where individuals can share their experiences and receive emotional support from others facing similar challenges. These groups can be particularly beneficial for those dealing with grief or chronic illness, offering a sense of community and understanding (McAuley *et al.,* 2000). Cognitive-behavioural therapy (CBT) helps older adults challenge negative thought patterns and develop more adaptive coping strategies, thereby reducing feelings of loneliness and enhancing overall well-being (Cacioppo *et al.,* 2015).

Social clubs and community-based programmes facilitate social engagement and recreational activities, fostering a sense of social connectedness and belonging. For instance, initiatives such as the Men's Sheds programme in Australia provide communal spaces where older men can engage in activities and socialize, significantly reducing loneliness and improving mental health (Golding, 2011).

Encouraging Emotional Health and Social Connectivity

Fighting loneliness in older individuals requires fostering social interaction and mental health. Loneliness can be lessened by interventions that emphasize strengthening social support networks, encouraging meaningful social contacts, and offering chances to participate in community activities (Hagan *et al.,* 2020). The goal of these treatments, which could include peer support efforts, volunteer programmes, and intergenerational activities, is to establish supportive environments that encourage social interaction and mental health.

Peer support initiatives involve matching older adults with peers who can provide companionship and support. These programmes can help reduce feelings of isolation and improve mental health outcomes. For example, the Befriending Networks in the UK match volunteers with older adults to provide regular social interaction and emotional support (Cattan *et al.,* 2005).

Volunteer programmes offer older adults opportunities to engage in meaningful activities and contribute to their communities. Volunteering can enhance social connections and provide a sense of purpose, thereby reducing feelings of loneliness. Volunteering is associated with better mental health and reduced loneliness among older adults (Windsor, Anstey, and Rodgers, 2008).

Intergenerational activities involve bringing together individuals from different age groups to engage in shared activities. These programmes can help bridge the generational gap and foster mutual understanding and respect. Studies have shown that intergenerational programmes can significantly reduce loneliness and improve well-being in older adults (Martinez *et al.,* 2020).

Mind-set Approaches in Loneliness Therapies

Mind-set interventions emphasize resilience, self-efficacy, and constructive coping methods in order to change people's attitudes and beliefs regarding loneliness. Mind-set therapies encompass several techniques such as mindfulness-based interventions, cognitive restructuring techniques, and narrative therapy approaches. The objective of these approaches is to enable older persons to confront negative thought patterns and cultivate flexible coping strategies to overcome feelings of loneliness (Cacioppo *et al.,* 2011). Mindfulness-based interventions help individuals develop present-moment awareness and self-compassion, which can reduce rumination and enhance emotional well-being. Studies have shown that mindfulness practices can significantly reduce symptoms of anxiety and depression, contributing to improved mental health and reduced loneliness (Creswell *et al.*, 2012). Cognitive restructuring techniques support a more realistic and optimistic outlook by helping older adults identify and challenge irrational beliefs about themselves and their relationships. This approach can foster a healthier mind-set and improve social interactions (Segal *et al.*, 2018). Narrative therapy encourages individuals to reframe their life stories, emphasizing strengths, resilience, and growth potential. This can lead to a more positive self-perception and greater social engagement (White & Epston, 1990).

Leverageing Technology to Combat Loneliness

In recent years, technology has emerged as a valuable tool in combating loneliness among the elderly. Digital platforms can facilitate social connections, provide access to information and services, and offer opportunities for learning and entertainment. For instance, social networking sites like Facebook and video communication tools like Skype and Zoom can help older adults stay connected with family and friends, reducing feelings of isolation (Tsai *et al.,* 2016). Programmes that provide digital literacy training for older adults can empower them to use technology effectively and confidently. Initiatives such as the Digital Inclusion for seniors programme in Australia offer training sessions that help seniors navigate the internet use social media, and access online resources, thereby enhancing their social connectivity and reducing loneliness (O'Rourke *et al.,* 2018). Moreover, Tele-health services can provide remote access to healthcare and mental health support, ensuring that older adults receive the care they need without the barriers of distance and mobility. Tele-health interventions can significantly improve mental health outcomes and reduce loneliness in older adults (Czaja *et al.,* 2015).

Community-based Initiatives and Policies

Community-based initiatives play a crucial role in addressing loneliness among the elderly. Advanced community centres tailored specifically for older people can offer a range of services and activities aimed at promoting social interaction, physical activity, and mental stimulation. These centres can provide access to resources such as support groups, counselling services, and educational programmes, serving as vital hubs for older adults seeking connection and support (Kaur, 2019). Policies that prioritize the needs of older adults and promote social inclusion are essential in addressing loneliness among older populations. For example, age-friendly city initiatives, as promoted by the World Health Organization, encourage the development of environments that are inclusive and accessible to older adults. These initiatives focus on improving public transportation, enhancing outdoor spaces, and promoting social participation, thereby reducing social isolation (Plouffe & Kalache, 2010). Government policies that support affordable housing, healthcare, and social services for older adults can also mitigate the risk of loneliness. Providing accessible and affordable housing options can help older adults remain in their communities and maintain social connections. Access to comprehensive healthcare services, including mental health support, is crucial for addressing the physical and emotional aspects of loneliness (National Academies of Sciences, 2020).

Cultural Considerations and Tailored Interventions

Addressing loneliness among the elderly requires considering cultural contexts and tailoring interventions to meet the specific needs of different populations. Cultural norms and values influence how loneliness is experienced and addressed. For instance, in collectivist cultures, family and community play a central role in providing social support, and interventions that strengthen family ties and community engagement may be particularly effective (Choudhury, 2019). In India, where family structures and community bonds are traditionally strong, initiatives that involve family members and community leaders in support programmes can enhance their effectiveness. Programmes that encourage intergenerational living arrangements, where older adults live with younger family members, can help reduce loneliness and foster social connections (Sharma *et al.,* 2020). Culturally tailored interventions that respect and incorporate traditional practices and beliefs can also enhance their acceptability and effectiveness. For example, incorporating traditional arts, crafts, and cultural activities into community programmes can provide meaningful engagement for older adults and strengthen their sense of identity and belonging (Mohan *et al.,* 2018).

Case Studies and Successful Programmes

Several successful programmes worldwide have demonstrated the effectiveness of various interventions in combating loneliness among older adults. For example, the Elderly Resource Centres in Kerala, India, offer a comprehensive range of services, including health check-ups, recreational activities, and educational programmes, aimed at promoting social interaction and well-being among older adults. These centres have significantly improved the quality of life for many seniors, reducing feelings of loneliness and enhancing their overall health (Mohan *et al.,* 2018).

In the UK, the Campaign to End Loneliness has been instrumental in raising awareness about the issue and promoting evidence-based interventions. The campaign collaborates with local authorities, healthcare providers, and community organizations to implement programmes that foster social connections and support older adults. Initiatives such as the "Men's Sheds" and "Silver Line" helpline have been particularly successful in providing companionship and reducing loneliness (Campaign to End Loneliness, 2017).

Conclusion

Loneliness among older adults is a multifaceted issue that necessitates a comprehensive and holistic approach to address effectively. Understanding the psychological, physical, and emotional dimensions of loneliness is crucial for developing targeted interventions that can significantly improve the well-being and quality of life for the elderly. By integrating psychosocial therapies, mind-set approaches, community-based initiatives, and leverageing technology, we can create a robust framework to combat loneliness. Psychosocial therapies, including support groups, social clubs, and cognitive-behavioural therapy, are instrumental in addressing the emotional and psychological aspects of loneliness. These interventions provide opportunities for older adults to engage in meaningful social interactions, express their emotions, and develop coping skills. For instance, cognitive-behavioural therapy helps individuals challenge negative thought patterns and develop more constructive coping strategies, thereby reducing feelings of isolation and enhancing emotional well-being. Mind-set approaches focus on changing individuals' attitudes and beliefs about loneliness, emphasizing resilience, self-efficacy, and positive coping mechanisms. Techniques such as mindfulness-based interventions, cognitive restructuring, and narrative therapy empower older adults to confront negative thoughts and cultivate adaptive coping strategies. Mindfulness-based interventions, for example, promote present-moment awareness and self-compassion, reducing rumination and improving emotional health. Community-based initiatives are crucial for fostering social connectivity and promoting mental health among older adults. These initiatives, including intergenerational programmes, volunteer opportunities, and peer support groups, create supportive environments that encourage social interaction and engagement. Successful programmes from around the world offer valuable insights and models that can be adapted to different cultural contexts. For example, intergenerational programmes in various countries have demonstrated effectiveness in bridging generational gaps and fostering mutual understanding and support. Technology also plays a vital role in combating loneliness by enhancing social connectivity and providing access to resources and support. Digital platforms and social networking sites can facilitate communication and interaction, reducing social isolation among older adults. Programmes that teach older adults to use technology effectively can help them stay connected with family, friends, and community resources, thereby reducing feelings of loneliness. Culturally tailored interventions are essential for addressing loneliness among older adults in diverse communities. Understanding cultural, social, and health-related factors is crucial for developing effective interventions that resonate with the target population. Culturally sensitive programmes that consider the unique needs and preferences of older adults can significantly enhance the effectiveness of interventions and promote social inclusion. Supportive policies and initiatives are also critical for creating an age-friendly and inclusive environment. Advocating for policies that prioritize the needs of older adults and promote social inclusion can help mitigate loneliness and improve the overall quality of life for the elderly. For example, policies that support the development of community centres, accessible healthcare, and social support services can create a supportive infrastructure that addresses the diverse needs of older adults. Addressing loneliness in the elderly not only enhances their quality of life but also contributes to healthier, more connected, and resilient communities. The serious problem of loneliness has taken centre stage in the lives of senior citizens, casting a pall over their well-being. The results serve as a sobering reminder that loneliness is a real, widespread reality that affects older people's daily lives and is not just a remote or isolated phenomenon. The disclosure supports an all-encompassing strategy that includes creating targeted interventions, improving access to community support services, and fostering deep social ties for senior citizens. In addition, future investigations should explore the complex mechanisms that underlie loneliness as a mental illness, taking into account cultural, social, and health-related elements. By adopting a comprehensive outlook and executing research-backed tactics, we can endeavour to mitigate isolation and cultivate a more empathetic, inclusive community that advances the welfare and respect of senior citizens. Ultimately, addressing loneliness among older adults is not just about enhancing their individual well-being but also about building stronger, more supportive communities. By fostering social connectivity, promoting mental health, and providing accessible resources and support, we can create an environment where older adults feel valued, connected, and empowered. Through collaborative efforts and a commitment to understanding and addressing the complexities of loneliness, we can ensure that older adults lead fulfilling, connected lives, contributing to the overall health and resilience of our communities.

Future Suggestions

The problem of loneliness in older persons is becoming better acknowledged; it is characterised by feelings of alienation, loneliness, and a lack of social support. Not only is social isolation an emotional state, but it also poses serious risks to one's physical and mental well-being. Loneliness has negative impacts on one's ability to grow personally, one's sense of self-worth, and it can exacerbate mental health conditions like despair and anxiety. It is imperative to address loneliness in older adults in order to create a welcoming and inclusive environment that improves their quality of life and overall well-being. The physical and emotional well-being of elderly individuals can be significantly impacted by loneliness. According to research, loneliness raises the risk of heart disease, high blood pressure, and a reduced immune system reaction (Hawkley & Cacioppo, 2010). In addition, loneliness raises the risk of dementia and can cause cognitive deterioration (Holwerda *et al.,* 2014). Elderly people's overall quality of life is further diminished by the emotional toll that loneliness takes, which frequently takes the form of persistent depression, anxiety, and decreased life satisfaction (Cacioppo, Hawkley & Thisted, 2010).

Community Centres: A Possible Remedy

Establishing state-of-the-art community centres with a focus on serving the needs of older folks is a potential strategy to prevent loneliness. These facilities can offer a range of programmes and services intended to encourage mental, physical, and social stimulation.

Activities and Services Provided

A vast array of services and activities catered to the needs and interests of senior citizens can be found at community centres. Among them are:

1. Social Engagement

Movie evenings, board games, and cultural events are examples of social activities that might support the development and maintenance of social bonds among older persons. Frequent social connection with peers can promote a sense of belonging and reduce feelings of loneliness (Victor *et al.,* 2005).

2. Exercises

Exercise regimens designed specifically for senior citizens, such as *yoga, tai chi,* and mild aerobics, can enhance their physical well-being and mobility. Additionally, exercise is associated with better mental health by lowering anxiety and depressive symptoms (Fox, 1999).

3. Psych Stimulus

Puzzles, memory games, and educational workshops are examples of cognitive exercises that can help preserve cognitive function and postpone the onset of dementia. Opportunities for lifelong learning, such book clubs or computer lessons, help keep the mind sharp and interested (Wilson *et al.,* 2002).

4. Counselling and Support Group Services

Having access to counselling and support groups can assist older persons deal with life events like retirement or the death of a spouse and offer them emotional support.

In addition to providing techniques for stress and anxiety management, professional counselling can address mental health difficulties (Andersson, 1985).

5. Obtaining Resources

Giving older persons access to tools and knowledge about them, such as financial planning, legal counsel, and healthcare services, can help them stay independent and make wise decisions. Community centres can act as hubs for the distribution of crucial information and the connection of senior citizens with essential services (Cattan *et al.*, 2005).

In order to effectively combat loneliness among older individuals, it is critical to support laws and initiatives that put their needs first and encourage social inclusion.

Encouragement of Community Centres: Governments must to set aside money for the creation and upkeep of community centres designed with senior citizens' needs in mind. To accommodate a range of interests and requirements, these centres ought to be easily accessible and provide a wide range of services and activities (Victor, Scambler & Bond, 2009).

Campaigns for Public Awareness: Public campaigns to raise awareness of loneliness among older individuals can lessen stigma and foster support from the community. Public awareness of the value of social relationships and the resources available can motivate senior citizens to ask for assistance and take part in neighbourhood activities (Campaign to End Loneliness, 2017).

Non-Governmental Organisations (NGOs) and Collaboration: Governments and non-governmental organisations working together can improve the success of programmes meant to lessen loneliness. NGOs can be extremely helpful in connecting with lonely older persons since they frequently possess the knowledge and resources necessary to carry out community-based projects (Age UK, 2018).

Education for Social Workers and Health Professionals: It is im perative that health and social care personnel receive training on identifying and addressing loneliness in older individuals. When it comes to spotting people who are at risk and directing them towards the right resources, these experts can be quite helpful (NHS England, 2018).

Technology: Reducing isolation among older persons can be achieved by using technology to connect them with friends, family, and community resources. Programmes that teach senior citizens how to use digital resources, such social media and video calling, can help them connect with others and get information (Tsai *et al.,* 2016).

References

Age, U.K. (2018). *No One Should Have No One: Working to End Loneliness Amongst Older People.*

Andersson, L. (1985). "Intervention against Loneliness in a Group of Elderly Women: An Impact Evaluation". *Social Science & Medicine, 20*(4): 355-364.

Cacioppo, J.T., Grippo, A.J., London, S., Goossens, L. & Cacioppo, S. (2015). "Loneliness: Clinical Import and Interventions". *Perspectives on Psychological Science, 10*(2): 238-249.

Cacioppo, J.T., Hawkley, L.C. & Thisted, R.A. (2010). "Perceived Social Isolation makes me Sad: 5-Year Cross-Legged Analyses of Loneliness and Depressive Symptomatology in the Chicago Health, Ageing, and Social Relations Study. *Psychology and Ageing, 25*(2): 453-463.

Cacioppo, J.T., Hawkley, L.C., Crawford, L.E., Ernst, J.M., Burleson, M.H., Kowalewski, R.B. & Berntson, G.G. (2002). "Loneliness and Health: Potential Mechanisms". *Psychosomatic Medicine, 64*(3): 407-417.

Cacioppo, J.T., Hawkley, L.C., Ernst, J.M., Burleson, M., Berntson, G.G., Nouriani, B. & Spiegel, D. (2006). "Loneliness within a Nomological Net: An Evolutionary Perspective". *Journal of Research in Personality, 40*(6): 1054-1085.

Cacioppo, J.T., Reis, H.T. & Zautra, A.J. (2011). "Social Resilience: The Value of Social Fitness with An Application to the Military". *American Psychologist, 66*(1): 43-51.

Campaign to End Loneliness. (2017). *The Facts on Loneliness*. Retrieved from https://www.campaigntoendloneliness.org

Cattan, M., White, M., Bond, J. & Learmouth, A. (2005). "Preventing Social Isolation and Loneliness among Older People: A Systematic Review of Health Promotion Interventions". *Ageing and Society, 25*(1): 41-67.

Centres for Disease Control and Prevention. *Loneliness and Social Isolation Linked to Serious Health Conditions*. Published May 26, 2020.

Choudhury, M. (2019). "Addressing Elder Loneliness in Indian Communities: The Role of Cultural Sensitivity". *Journal of Cross-cultural Gerontology, 34*(3): 297-314.

Creswell, J.D., Irwin, M.R., Burklund, L.J., Lieberman, M.D., Arevalo, J.M.G., Ma, J.,. ..& Cole, S.W. (2012). "Mindfulness-Based Stress Reduction Training Reduces Loneliness and Pro-Inflammatory Gene Expression in Older Adults: A Small Randomized Controlled Trial. *Brain, Behaviour, and Immunity, 26*(7): 1095-1101.

Czaja, S.J., Boot, W.R., Charness, N., Rogers, W.A. & Sharit, J. (2015). "Improving Social Support for Older Adults through Technology: Findings from the PRISM Randomized Controlled Trial". *The Gerontologist, 55*(5): 753-766.

Fox, K.R. (1999). "The Influence of Physical Activity on Mental Well-being". *Public Health Nutrition, 2*(3a): 411-418.

Fried, L.P., Tangen, C.M., Walston, J., Newman, A.B., Hirsch, C., Gottdiener, J.,. .. & McBurnie, M.A. (2001). "Frailty in Older Adults: Evidence for a

Phenotype". *The Journals of Gerontology Series A: Biological Sciences and Medical Sciences*, *56*(3): M146-M156.

Gerst-Emerson, K. & Jayawardhana, J. (2015). "Loneliness as a Public Health Issue: The Impact of Loneliness on Health Care Utilization among Older Adults". *American Journal of Public Health*, *105*(5): 1013-1019.

Golding, B. (2011). "Older Men's Well-being through Community Participation in Australia". *International Journal of Men's Health*, *10*(1): 26-44.

Goll, J.C., Charlesworth, G., Scior, K. & Stott, J. (2015). "Barriers to Social Participation among Lonely Older Adults: The Influence of Social Fears and Identity". *PLoS ONE*, *10*(2): e0116664.

Guralnik, J.M., Ferrucci, L., Simonsick, E.M., Salive, M.E. & Wallace, R.B. (1993). "Lower-Extremity Function in Persons over the age of 70 years as a Predictor of Subsequent Disability". *New England Journal of Medicine*, *329*(9): 556-561.

Hagan, R., Manktelow, R., Taylor, B.J. & Mallett, J. (2014). "Reducing Loneliness amongst Older People: A Systematic Search and Narrative Review". *Ageing & Mental Health*, *18*(6): 683-693.

Hawkley, L.C. & Cacioppo, J.T. (2010). "Loneliness Matters: A Theoretical and Empirical Review of Consequences and Mechanisms". *Annals of Behavioural Medicine*, *40*(2): 218-227.

Heine, C. & Browning, C.J. (2014). "Communication and Psychosocial Consequences of Sensory Loss in Older Adults: Overview and Rehabilitation Directions". *Frontiers in Ageing Neuroscience*, *6*: 83.

Holt-Lunstad, J., Smith, T.B., Baker, M., Harris, T. & Stephenson, D. (2015). "Loneliness and Social Isolation as Risk Factors for Mortality: A Meta-Analytic Review". *Perspectives on Psychological Science*, *10*(2): 227-237.

Holwerda, T.J., *et al.* (2014). "Feelings of Loneliness, but not Social Isolation, Predict Dementia Onset: Results from the Amsterdam Study of the Elderly (AMSTEL)". *Journal of Neurology, Neurosurgery & Psychiatry*, *85*(2): 135-142.

Jiao, K., Zhang, J., Liu, M. & Xu, M. (2023). "Interaction of Widowhood, Gender, and Age in Predicting Loneliness among Older Adults in China". *Journal of Women & Ageing*, 1-14.

Kaur, H. (2019). "Senior Citizen Community Centre: A Case Study". *Journal of Ageing & Society*, *45*(3): 112-129.

Leigh-Hunt, N., Bagguley, D., Bash, K., Turner, V., Turnbull, S., Valtorta, N. & Caan, W. (2017). "An Overview of Systematic Reviews on the Public Health Consequences of Social Isolation and Loneliness". *Public Health*, *152*, 157-171.

Luo, Y., Hawkley, L.C., Waite, L.J. & Cacioppo, J.T. (2012). "Loneliness, Health, and Mortality in Old Age: A National Longitudinal Study". *Social Science & Medicine*, *74*(6): 907-914.

Manchana, V. (2024). "Loneliness and Social Connections: Lived Experiences on Predictors and Coping with Loneliness among Indian Older Adults:

A Phenomenological Study". *Journal of Human Behaviour in the Social Environment*, 1-16.

Martinez, A., Richard, L., Prévost, V. & Gauvin, L. (2020). "Intergenerational Programmes and Social Inclusion of the Elderly: A Critical Review and Research Agenda". *Journal of Ageing Studies*, *55*: 100879.

Masi, C.M., Chen, H.Y., Hawkley, L.C. & Cacioppo, J.T. (2011). "A Meta-Analysis of Interventions to Reduce Loneliness". *Personality and Social Psychology Review*, *15*(3): 219-266.

McAuley, E., Blissmer, B., Marquez, D.X., Jerome, G.J., Kramer, A.F. & Katula, J. (2000). "Social Relations, Physical Activity, and Well-being in Older Adults". *Preventive Medicine*, *31*(5): 608-617.

Mohan, S., Joseph, B. & Varghese, M. (2018). "Elderly Resource Centres in Kerala: An Initiative for Successful Ageing". *Indian Journal of Gerontology*, *32*(2): 192-203.

National Academies of Sciences, Division of Behavioural, Medicine Division, Board on Behavioural, Sensory Sciences, Board on Health Sciences Policy,. .. & Loneliness in Older Adults (2020). *Social Isolation and Loneliness in Older Adults: Opportunities for the Health Care System*. National Academies Press.

NHS England. (2018). *Loneliness in Older People: A National Perspective*. Retrieved from https://www.england.nhs.uk

O'Rourke, H.M., Collins, L. & Sidani, S. (2018). "Interventions to Address Social Connectedness and Loneliness for Older Adults: A Scoping Review". *BMC Geriatrics*, *18*(1): 214.

Perissinotto, C.M., Cenzer, I.S. & Covinsky, K.E. (2012). "Loneliness in Older Persons: A Predictor of Functional Decline and Death". *Archives of Internal Medicine*, *172*(14): 1078-1084.

Pinquart, M. & Schindler, I. (2007). "Changes of Life Satisfaction in the Transition to Retirement: A Latent-Class Approach". *Psychology and Ageing*, *22*(3): 442.

Plouffe, L. & Kalache, A. (2010). "Towards Global Age-friendly Cities: Determining Urban Features that Promote Active Ageing". *Journal of Urban Health*, *87*(5): 733-739.

Segal, Z.V., Williams, J.M.G. & Teasdale, J.D. (2018). *Mindfulness-based Cognitive Therapy for Depression*. Guilford Publications.

Sharma, A., Verma, V.K. & Kumari, S. (2020). "Family Dynamics and Social Support in Old Age: An Empirical Study". *Journal of Geriatric Care and Research*, *7*(2): 47-53.

Smith, A.E., Sim, J., Scharf, T. & Phillipson, C. (2009). "Determinants of Quality of Life amongst Older People in Deprived Neighbourhoods". *Ageing and Society*, *29*(4): 561-589.

Steptoe, A., Shankar, A., Demakakos, P. & Wardle, J. (2013). "Social Isolation, Loneliness, and All-Cause Mortality in Older Men and Women". *Proceedings of the National Academy of Sciences*, *110*(15): 5797-5801.

Tsai, H.S. *et al.* (2016). "The Role of Social Support in the Relationship Between Loneliness and Social Networking Site Use among Older Adults". *Geriatric Nursing*, *37*(6): 423-428.

Victor, C.R., *et al.* (2005). "Loneliness in Later Life: Social and Emotional Patterns of Loneliness among Older Adults in the UK". *Research on Ageing*, *27*(2): 178-200.

Victor, C.R., Scambler, S.J., Bowling, A.N.N. & Bond, J. (2005). "The Prevalence of and Risk Factors for, Loneliness in Later Life: A Survey of Older People in Great Britain". *Ageing & Society*, *25*(6): 357-375.

Victor, C.R., Scambler, S. & Bond, J. (2009). *The Social World of Older People: Understanding Loneliness and Social Isolation in Later Life*. McGraw-Hill Education.

Wang, M., Henkens, K. & van Solinge, H. (2011). "Retirement Adjustment: A Review of Theoretical and Empirical Advancements". *American Psychologist*, *66*(3): 204-213.

White, M. & Epston, D. (1990). *Narrative Means to Therapeutic Ends*. Norton & Company.

Wilson, R.S., *et al.* (2002). "Participation in Cognitively Stimulating Activities and Risk of Incident Alzheimer Disease". *JAMA*, *287*(6): 742-748.

Windsor, T.D., Anstey, K.J. & Rodgers, B. (2008). "Volunteering and Psychological Well-being among Young-Old Adults: How Much Is Too Much?" *The Gerontologist*, *48*(1): 59-70.

14
Role of Spirituality in Positive Ageing for Older Adults

Priyanka Shukla

Introduction

Ageing is an inevitable stage of life that all of us face, sooner or later. Some people define ageing as joining a group that has members who live longer than normal. Others link getting older to specific changes in their lives or social responsibilities (such as becoming grandparents), the range and depth of social support networks they have access to, and their ability to access financial resources (Buch, 2015).

There is *vanaprastha*, a period of time when people give up their active lives, pass on their obligations to the next generation, and become advisers. The word *vanaprastha* comes from the words *vana*, which means "forest", and *prastha*, which means "going to". This means that it could be translated as "retiring to the forest". In Hinduism, this is one of the most important ideas because it shows the third of the four *ashramas*, or stages of life. As people age, they move from taking care of their home and family to a more reflective and contemplative state of mind. In the beginning, one will act as a wise teacher, helping people who need it. Over time, he or she will slowly pull away from everyone to live a more spiritual and alone life.

A report has warned about the rising population of senior citizens in India. According to the 'India Ageing Report 2023', the United Nations Population Fund (UNFPA) in collaboration with the International Institute for Population Sciences (IIPS), India's one-fifth of the population will comprise people over 60 by 2050.

The general perception of ageing on an individual level varied, but *most cultures viewed ageing through a negative lens*. Negative stereotypes about ageing typically include physical decline, mental disease, financial hardship, and dependency. The negative ideas of emptiness or a loss of purpose in life that person encounters add to all this negativity. Every person has a life goal that they have worked towards for a long time. Making one's own parents or guardians proud is the initial goal, although a theoretical one. The individual then strives for financial stability as their goal. Marriage gradually brings the goal of social security to fruition. The process of reproduction then begins in order to fulfil the obligations of society. Eventually, a person experiences emptiness after fulfilling all of their obligations. Their existence loses meaning and purpose. It's at this point that students ought to understand the value of self-worth. This is the only time that the person can focus all his or her attention on themselves. The purpose of living can be re-focused on oneself. This is the time when spirituality comes into play.

Spirituality contributes to a healthy and positive outlook towards one's own life. Many questions remain unanswered, despite the availability of scientific data and information. Hope, therefore, emerges when a person lives with a higher being. A person's attitude can be positively influenced by this hope. Thus, contemplating ageing in a good light is made easier by the positive mindset that spirituality fosters. One of the most significant sources of support and guidance in a person's life is their spirituality. It's a human phenomenon that practically everyone experiences. While avoiding connotations of restrictive, dogmatic ideas and required religious observances, the term "spirituality" is typically used to refer to certain good internal attributes and perceptions (Wulff, 1996). A cohesive quality of the mind, heart, and soul is called spirituality. It deals with personal, subjective experiences that are occasionally shared with others. In Indian society, spirituality is significant for people of all ages. As one ages, faith plays an increasingly important role.

The idea of "positive ageing", which takes into account a variety of aspects of older individuals' lives, is becoming more and more popular in the literature as a strategy for health and well-being. These elements go beyond the goal of promoting solely physical and mental health, which is occasionally unachievable at a later age, and instead support an awareness of older folks as complete people rather than a collection of health difficulties. One factor that has received little attention in the literature on positive ageing is the role of religion, spirituality, and/or belief. Many individuals still place a high value on religion, spirituality, and/or belief because they give their daily lives structure, meaning, and comprehension, as well as assistance when they face difficulties (Manning, 2013).

Conceptual Understandings of "Spirituality and Positive Ageing"

Spirituality is a broader concept, generally associated with searching for the meaning and existence of life (Chattopadhyay, 2007). Spirituality has been defined as "self-awareness; connectedness with self, others, and a larger reality." Spirituality is the process of reflecting on one's meaningful life and engaging in introspection. It improves self-actualization and lessens stress by fostering optimism, understanding, happiness, and coping skills. Spirituality is viewed as being cheerful, happily involved in the day-to-day activities of life, enjoying the art, music, and beautiful nature, and having an urge to contribute to making life on earth better (Chaves *et al.*, 2015).

Although people often use spirituality and religion interchangeably, they are not the same. Some authors contend that spirituality involves a personal quest for meaning in life, while religion involves an organized entity with rituals and practices focusing on a higher power, or God.

People frequently perceive or define spirituality as:

- A broad, subjective, and unifying concept.
- Informal and non-denominational.
- Highly personal and not dogmatic.
- Feeling-oriented.
- An inward experience.

A common perception or description of religion is:

- Well-defined and highly structured.
- Formal and denominational.
- Focused on community, rituals, and specific doctrines.
- Behaviour-oriented.
- An outward experience with inward benefits.

Spirituality, an important attribute of a sound body, is gaining importance, and much research is now focusing on spiritual health. The World Health Organization and its member countries are exploring spirituality as the fourth dimension of health (Chaves, Gil & Gil, 2015). Religiousness is not a prerequisite for being spiritual. Spirituality can be attained through religion. Spirituality offers solutions and self-assurance to overcome a circumstance or issue in one's life. People, therefore, have a tendency to become more spiritual as concerns about ageing develop.

Positive ageing is a term used to describe the process of maintaining a positive attitude, feeling good about yourself, keeping fit and healthy, and engaging fully in life as you age (Australian Psychological Society). The concept of positive ageing is gaining attention in the literature as an approach to health and well-being that incorporates a range of factors in the lives of older adults.

A number of studies have been conducted and a number of papers have been written that explore positive ageing. The meaning of positive ageing is not clear-cut, but a definition from the Centre for Positive Ageing states:

> "'Positive Ageing' denotes the aspirations of individuals and communities to plan for, approach and live life's changes and challenges as they age and approach the end of their lives, in a productive, active and fulfilling manner. The focus embraces the idea of making the most of opportunities, innovations and research which promote a person's sense of independence, dignity, well-being, good health and enable their participation in society" (Stock *et al.*, 2017).

A person's positive attitude towards their age is known as positive ageing. A few conclusions about positive ageing can be drawn from a review of the current literature. These factors can be categorized into broader categories of relationship resources, physical well-being, positive mental states, engaging activity, financial security, and spirituality.

Following are the explanations of the factors:

1. *Relational Resource:* Supportive Family and Friend.
2. *Physical Well-being:* Optimal functioning of mind and body.
3. *Positive Mental States:* Well-being, happiness, and satisfaction with life.
4. *Engaging Activity:* Active participation in mental and physical activity.
5. *Spirituality and Financial Stability:* Spirituality is harmony with oneself and with the natural and social environment. Financial stability is the equilibrium of one's future needs with their finances.

Among all the above factors, spirituality has been found to gain a little more advantage in India. Researchers from all around the world are working to find a workable way for people to embrace their own ageing. Recent studies have demonstrated that spirituality is a useful strategy for developing a positive outlook on life.

Theoretical Basis for Research on Spirituality and Ageing

Interest in spirituality and ageing has increased recently, primarily owing to empirical research overwhelmingly demonstrating the various health benefits of spirituality and religious participation (Koenig *et al.*, 2001). Studies have also shown that spirituality tends to increase during later adulthood (Moberg, 2005). Despite the major secularization of society over the past 50 years, the tendency of older individuals to engage in more religious activities and spiritual development persists in modern society. Spirituality moderate positive associations with different life satisfaction metrics, psychosocial wellness, physical and mental health, and the search for life's meaning and purpose.

Increasing longevity in modern society puts the spiritual needs of older adults at the forefront of societal priorities in providing care for the elderly. However, anti-ageing sentiments persist in Western society, ignoring the abilities and inventive contributions of senior citizens, as seen by the dearth of possibilities for community service or occupational retraining and employment. Furthermore, retirement homes tend to prioritize activities over the spirituality of creativity. Historically, the elders of society functioned as transmitters of sacred knowledge and rituals. They established an awareness of the culture and roots that are necessary for the health and growth of the community (Moberg, 2006). The function of an elder in society should be expanded in light of the growing number of older persons in order to improve and provide purpose to the lives of the country's ageing population.

Research into ageing and spirituality is based on the assumption that ageing is a journey, a search for meaning, balance, integration, and reconciliation (Mowat, 2004). There are a number of key theorists who have influenced those looking for a theory of ageing and spirituality. Although others have built a foundation for specific understandings of spirituality using the work of these theorists, they do not immediately equate spirituality with the search for meaning.

Victor Frankl (1984) posits man's search for meaning as a dominant conscious and unconscious driver. His incarceration in the Auschwitz concentration camp during the Second World War offered him the opportunity to develop his theories as part of his own survival strategy. His very powerful ideas of the capacity of man to be stripped of all the 'trappings' of life and to still find ultimate meaning underpin much of the work subsequently produced on ageing and spirituality (Kimble, 2000; Mackinlay, 2001).

Erik and Joan Erikson (1997) theorized stages of life. In each stage, the individual tries to achieve balance between two 'states' with associated virtues. Later in life, one must strike a balance between integration and despair, with wisdom as the associated virtue (Capps, 2008). This philosophy is based on the concepts of advancement and a journey.

Carl Jung (1970) was particularly interested in the second half of life and the importance of a life review to find meaning. He wrote:

> "One cannot live the afternoon of life according to the programme of life's morning, for what was great in the morning will be of little importance in the evening, and what was true in the morning will in the evening have become a lie" (Jung, 1970, p. 399).

Antonovsky (1987) was interested in what psychological processes allow people to maintain themselves in a state of good health. His research on coherence creates a paradigm and an empirically verified questionnaire that give physicians a means of evaluating coherence. Strong internal coherence is beneficial to maintaining healthy health. The multidisciplinary study of spirituality and ageing offers opinions based on facts, research based on actual data, theory development, and philosophical insights.

Practicing Spirituality in Daily Life

Spirituality is a vital component of physical and mental health. Meditation can be a potential tool for general well-being. It comes from the word "medere", which means "whole", the same source from which "healing" takes its origin. The very concept of "meditation" is taken in a very esoteric sense. However, it has been referred to as a "*disciplined way of reflecting on one's self, one's relationship with the world, the present and future paths of life, and the meaning or greater purpose of life.*" The techniques range from practices of concentration, awareness, or altered states of consciousness based on any directional or non-directional stimulus (Goleman, 1976).

Meditation is similar but not akin to mindfulness, which is defined as "awareness that arises when paying attention to the present moment non-judgmentally" (Kabat Zinn, 2003). Additionally, it is linked to positive ageing and a sense of acceptance. It has been suggested that resilience, acceptance, and a sense of purpose can "rejuvenate" metabolic degradation, cellular senescence, and inflammatory processes, therefore, mitigating the fragility of ageing. Based on data from the Health and Retirement Study, one of the classical longitudinal studies of ageing, sense of purpose in life was associated with significantly better objective (physical) measures of frailty in older adults (Kim *et al.*, 2017).

Compassion and empathy in day-to-day activities are other doable attributes of spirituality. **Trzeciak and his colleagues** talk about "compassionomics" and the benefits that it has for a variety of health conditions. Even if empathy and compassion are im personal qualities that are difficult to quantify, it is nonetheless possible to incorporate them into regular interactions and acts. Studies have demonstrated that empathy enhances adaptability, mitigates burnout, and reverses the healthcare expense crisis.

Lastly, we must practice the discipline of leisure and forgiveness. In later life, forgiveness is strongly associated with health and a state of "wholeness" and is characterized by dedication, empathy, acceptance, and compassion. Research has indicated a noteworthy affirmative relationship between psychosocial well-being and self-forgiveness, as well as forgiveness inspired by spirituality. It has been shown to be a moderator for reducing inward anger and suicidal behaviour (Long *et al.*, 2020). On the other hand, leisure practices have been studied as activities with anti-depressant effects that improve emotional well-being (Fullagar, 2008). A recent narrative review by **Fancourt and his colleagues** (2021) conceptualizes the bio-psycho-socio-cultural impact of leisure activities on health through a multilevelled theoretical framework. It has been demonstrated that leisure and self-acceptance have positive impacts on anxiety, depression, and overall psychological well-being (Nimrod *et al.*, 2012). Research has demonstrated that other characteristics of spirituality, such as social support, social involvement, and wisdom, can mitigate loneliness and fatigue in later life.

Hence, in many ways, the *Vanaprastha Ashram* is that time of life where loneliness strikes the most and a spiritual journey may help with a gradual withdrawal from routine materialistic pathways. This can manifest in daily life in a number of ways and to different degrees, including: a real and strong desire to change over time; being in the company of like-minded individuals; reflecting on one's inner stories; and engaging in spiritual discourse. All of these, in turn, help form a *"larger sense of purpose"* and help one stay connected, which is vital to counteracting the challenges of old age.

Conclusion

Either it be the life of an elderly or an ageing person, it has been seen that spirituality is a key to a positive outlook. The present chapter focuses on the importance of spirituality as a key factor in attaining positive ageing. Spirituality has been in practice for ages, but it is degrading somehow in the fast pace of the world, where people are becoming thankless day by day. This might have been due to the world running on just facts and figures. Spirituality is more of a person's energy in the form of faith, diverted to an unseen authority power in the hope that hurdles can be taken care of with a little bit of personal effort and optimism.

As discussed in this chapter, positive ageing can be described as the positive attitude of a person towards his or her ageing. This field has come to light due to the constant deterioration of life expectancy and standard of living of the 'Grey Population'. A positive attitude towards ageing can be fostered by a variety of variables, including engaging activities, financial security, physical fitness, a happy mental state, and support from family. People around the world teach and practice spirituality in a variety of ways. Making it simpler for a larger population to follow, many regard it as a religion, while others see it as *karma*, cosmic force, or some other combination of the three. Thus, spirituality is one of the useful strategies for achieving positive ageing among all the variables, fostering a positive outlook on life and ageing in the process.

References

abat-Zinn, J. (2003). "Mindfulness-based Stress Reduction (MBSR)". *Constructivism in the Human Sciences*, *8*(2): 73.

Buch, E.D. (2015). "Anthropology of Ageing and Care". *Annual Review of Anthropology*, *44*, 277-293.

Capps, D. (2008). *The Decades of Life: A Guide to Human Development*, London: Westminster John Knox Press.

Chattopadhyay, S. (2007). "Religion, Spirituality, Health and Medicine: Why Should Indian Physicians Care?" *Journal of Postgraduate Medicine*, *53*(4): 262.

Chaves, L.J., & Gil, C.A. (2015). "Older People's Concepts of Spirituality, Related to Ageing and Quality of Life". *Ciência Amp Saúde Coletiva*, *20*(12): 3641-3652.

Erikson, E. and Erikson, J. (1997). *The Life Cycle Completed: Extended Version*, New York: Norton and Co.

Fancourt, D., Aughterson, H., Finn, S., Walker, E. & Steptoe, A. (2021). "How Leisure Activities Affect Health: A Narrative Review and Multi-level Theoretical Framework of Mechanisms of Action" (Vol. 8, p. 329). *Lancet Psychiatry*, *8*(4): E12-E13.

Frankl, V. (1984). *Man's Search for Meaning*, New York: Washington Square Press.

Fullagar, S. (2008). "Leisure Practices as Counter-Depressants: Emotion-work and Emotion-play within Women's Recovery from Depression". *Leisure Sciences*, *30*(1): 35-52.

Goleman, D. (1976). "Meditation and Consciousness: An Asian Approach to Mental Health". *American Journal of Psychotherapy*, *30*(1): 41-54.

Jung, C.G. (1970). *Collected Works* (*Volume 8*), New Jersey: Princeton University Press.

Kim, E.S., Kawachi, I., Chen, Y. & Kubzansky, L.D. (2017). "Association Between Purpose in Life and Objective Measures of Physical Function in Older Adults". *JAMA Psychiatry*, *74*(10): 1039-1045.

Kimble, M. (2000) *Victor Frankl's Contribution to Spirituality and Ageing*, New York: Haworth Press.

Koenig, H.G., McCullough, M.E. & Larson, D.B. (2001). *Handbook of Religion and Health*. New York: Oxford University Press, USA.

Long, K.N., Chen, Y. & Potts, M. (2020). "Spiritually Motivated Self-forgiveness and Divine Forgiveness, and Subsequent Health and Well-being among Middle-aged Female Nurses: An Outcome-wide Longitudinal Approach". *Frontiers in Psychology*, *11*: 523673.

Mackinlay, E. & Trevitt, C. (2010). "Living in Aged Care: Using Spiritual Reminiscence to Enhance Meaning in Life for those with Dementia". *International Journal of Mental Health Nursing*, *19*: 394-401.

Manning, L.K. (2013). "Navigating Hardships in Old Age: Exploring the Relationship Between Spirituality and Resilience in Later Life". *Qualitative Health Research*, *23*(4): 568-575.

Moberg, D.O. (2005). "Research in Spirituality, Religion, and Ageing". *Journal of Gerontological Social Work*, *45*(1-2): 11-40.

_______ (2012). *Ageing and Spirituality: Spiritual Dimensions of Ageing Theory, Research, Practice, and Policy*. Routledge.

Mowat, H. (2004). "Successful Ageing and the Spiritual Journey", In A. Jewell (Ed.) *Ageing Spirituality and Well-being*, London: Jessica Kingsley.

Nimrod, G., Kleiber, D.A. & Berdychevsky, L. (2012). "Leisure in Coping with Depression". *Journal of Leisure Research*, *44*(4): 419-449.

Stock, J., Schofield, P. & Docking, R.E. (2017). "What Is Positive Ageing?" In *International Handbook of Positive Ageing* (pp. 5-13). Routledge.

Wulff, D.M. (1996). "The Psychology of Religion: An Overview". In E.P. Shafranske (Ed.): *Religion and the Clinical Practice of Psychology* (pp. 43-70). American Psychological Association. https://doi.org/10.1037/10199-002

15

Mental Health for Geriatric Population: Creating a Positive Environment for the Elderly

Approaches, Models, and Intervention Strategies

Hemanthakumara V.

Introduction

The geriatric population, comprised individuals, aged 65 and older, is a rapidly growing demographic worldwide. The World Health Organization (WHO) predicts that the global population of individuals aged 60 and over will reach 2.1 billion by 2050, nearly double the number in 2015. With this demographic shift comes an increased need for attention to the mental health and well-being of the elderly. Creating a positive environment for the elderly is a critical aspect of geriatric care, and it involves a multifaceted approach that encompasses physical, social, and psychological elements.

The geriatric population often faces a unique set of challenges that can impact their mental health. These challenges include chronic health conditions, the loss of loved ones, social isolation, reduced mobility, cognitive decline, and financial constraints, among others. As a result, the promotion of mental well-being in older adults has become an urgent public health priority. A positive environment can play a crucial role in addressing these challenges and enhancing the overall quality of life for the elderly.

Approaches to creating a positive environment for the elderly are diverse, and they draw from a variety of models and intervention strategies. These approaches, which encompass both healthcare and community settings, aim to promote physical and emotional well-being and social engagement. This introduction will provide an overview of these approaches, models, and intervention strategies that contribute to the mental health of the geriatric population.

One of the key elements in creating a positive environment for the elderly is recognizing the importance of social connections. Loneliness and social isolation are prevalent among older adults and can have detrimental effects on their mental health. The socio-emotional selectivity theory posits that as individuals age, they become more selective in their choice of social partners, prioritizing relationships that provide emotional support and fulfilment. Interventions such as social support groups, community centres, and senior living facilities that facilitate these meaningful social connections can significantly enhance the mental well-being of the elderly.

In addition, cognitive stimulation is another critical aspect of maintaining mental health in the elderly. Cognitive decline is a common concern with advancing age, and interventions that challenge and engage older adults cognitively are vital. The Cognitive Reserve Theory suggests that a lifetime of cognitive engagement and learning can help build resilience against age-related cognitive decline. Older adults can incorporate activities like puzzles, brain-training exercises, and creative hobbies into their daily lives to promote cognitive health and maintain a positive environment.

Physical health is inseparable from mental well-being. Promoting a positive environment for the elderly involves addressing their physical health through nutrition, exercise, and healthcare access. Studies have shown that regular physical activity can improve mood, reduce the risk of depression, and enhance cognitive functioning in older adults. Nutritional support ensures that elderly individuals receive the necessary nutrients to maintain both their physical and mental health.

Additionally, creating a positive environment for the elderly requires recognizing and addressing the unique mental health needs of this population. Geriatric mental health often involves coping with grief and loss, managing chronic conditions, and addressing issues like anxiety and depression. Evidence-based therapeutic interventions such as cognitive-behavioural therapy, reminiscence therapy, and mindfulness-based approaches can help older adults navigate these challenges and promote psychological well-being.

In this context, it is essential to acknowledge the role of healthcare professionals and caregivers. They play a crucial role in assessing the mental health of the elderly and providing appropriate care and support. Training and education for healthcare providers and caregivers on geriatric mental health issues and effective intervention strategies are essential components of creating a positive environment for the elderly.

In conclusion, the mental health of the geriatric population is a pressing concern as the world's elderly population continues to grow. Creating a positive environment for the elderly is an intricate process that encompasses physical, social, and psychological dimensions. Approaches, models, and intervention strategies that emphasize social connections, cognitive stimulation, physical health, and tailored mental healthcare are integral to promoting the well-being of older adults. This overview sets the stage for exploring these elements in greater depth, and it underscores the importance of prioritizing geriatric mental health as a global public health im perative. By understanding and implementing these approaches, we can contribute to a better quality of life for the elderly and ensure that they age with dignity and happiness.

Approaches to Geriatric Mental Health

1. Holistic Care in Geriatric Mental Health: An Integrated Approach

Geriatric mental health is a critical aspect of healthcare as the world's population continues to age. The World Health Organization estimates that by 2050, the number of individuals over 60 years old will nearly double. This demographic shift necessitates a comprehensive approach to address the mental health needs of older adults. Holistic care is one such approach that recognizes the interconnectedness of physical, emotional, and social well-being. This chapter explores the concept of holistic care in geriatric mental health, delving into its components and benefits, and providing relevant references to support its effectiveness.

Understanding Holistic Care

Holistic care is an approach to healthcare that acknowledges the interdependence of physical, emotional, social, and spiritual well-being. It recognizes that health is not just the absence of illness but a state of overall well-being. In geriatric mental health, this approach takes into account not only the specific mental health issues older adults may face but also their physical health, emotional needs, social interactions, and spiritual or existential concerns.

Physical Well-being: The physical aspect of holistic care involves addressing chronic illnesses, managing medications, promoting healthy lifestyles, and ensuring regular health check-ups. Physical health is closely linked to mental health in older adults, as the presence of chronic illnesses and physical discomfort can contribute to depressive symptoms and anxiety.

Emotional Well-being: The emotional well-being of older adults is vital to geriatric mental health. This component focuses on identifying and addressing emotional issues, such as anxiety, depression, grief, and loneliness. Therapies, like cognitive-behavioural therapy (CBT) and mindfulness-based approaches can help manage these emotional concerns.

Social Well-being: Social well-being emphasizes the importance of social connections and a support system. It includes family, friends, and community engagement. Isolation and loneliness are common concerns among older adults, and social well-being plays a crucial role in mitigating these issues.

Spiritual and Existential Well-being: For many older adults, existential and spiritual concerns become more prominent as they age. These concerns may include questions about the meaning of life, end-of-life decisions, and the search for purpose. Addressing these existential and spiritual aspects is essential for holistic care.

Benefits of Holistic Care in Geriatric Mental Health

Holistic care in geriatric mental health offers numerous benefits for both patients and healthcare systems.

Enhanced Quality of Life: By addressing not only mental health issues but also physical, emotional, and social needs, holistic care can significantly enhance the overall quality of life for older adults. This approach helps individuals maintain their independence, engage with their communities, and experience a higher level of life satisfaction.

A Comprehensive Approach to Care: Geriatric mental health often involves complex and interconnected issues. Holistic care provides a comprehensive framework for addressing these issues. This reduces fragmented care and ensures that all aspects of an older adult's well-being are considered.

Early Detection and Prevention: Holistic care encourages regular check-ups and screenings, which can help detect and address mental health issues at an earlier stage. Early intervention is often more effective and can prevent the escalation of mental health problems.

Improved Medication Management: Many older adults are on multiple medications, which can have side effects or interact with one another.

Holistic care involves close monitoring of medication and can help prevent adverse effects, improving overall well-being.

Reduced Healthcare Costs: While holistic care may require initial investments in multidisciplinary teams and care coordination, it can ultimately reduce healthcare costs. By addressing physical, emotional, social, and spiritual needs comprehensively, older adults are less likely to experience costly health crises.

Holistic Care Approaches in Geriatric Mental Health

The field of geriatric mental health commonly uses several approaches to implement holistic care effectively.

Interdisciplinary Teams: Holistic care often relies on interdisciplinary teams composed of physicians, nurses, psychologists, social workers, and spiritual care providers. These teams collaborate to address the various dimensions of an older adult's well-being.

Person-Centred Care: Person-centred care is a cornerstone of holistic care. It involves tailoring treatment plans to meet an individual's specific needs and preferences, fostering a sense of autonomy and dignity.

Geriatric Assessment: Comprehensive geriatric assessments evaluate an older adult's physical, mental, and social health. These assessments help identify areas of concern and inform treatment planning.

Integrated Care Models: Integrated care models connect various healthcare settings, such as primary care, speciality mental health services, and long-term care facilities. This coordination ensures that older adults receive consistent and comprehensive care.

Evidence Supporting Holistic Care

A growing body of research supports the effectiveness of holistic care in geriatric mental health. Numerous studies have highlighted the benefits of this approach.

In 2018, the *Journal of the American Geriatrics Society* published a study that revealed improved emotional well-being, physical health, and social engagement among older adults receiving integrated, holistic care. This approach reduced the risk of depression and anxiety among participants.

Research in the *International Journal of Geriatric Psychiatry* has shown that person-centred care in geriatric mental health improves treatment adherence and satisfaction, leading to better mental health outcomes.

A systematic review in the *Journal of Ageing Research and Clinical Practice* demonstrated the positive impact of interdisciplinary teams in geriatric mental health. Researchers found these teams effective in addressing complex needs and enhancing overall well-being.

A report from the World Health Organization emphasizes the importance of a holistic approach to mental health in older adults, stressing the need to address physical, emotional, social, and spiritual well-being to achieve better mental health outcomes.

2. The Biopsychosocial Approach

Mental health issues among the elderly population are a growing concern worldwide. The geriatric population faces unique challenges, including cognitive decline, depression, anxiety, and other mental health disorders. Addressing these challenges necessitates a comprehensive approach that considers biological, psychological, and social factors. The biopsychosocial approach to geriatric mental health integrates these elements to provide a holistic understanding and effective interventions for the elderly. This chapter explores the biopsychosocial approach, its key components, and its significance in geriatric mental healthcare.

Biological Aspects

The biological aspect of the biopsychosocial approach emphasizes the impact of physical health on mental well-being in the elderly. Age-related changes in the brain, such as neurodegenerative disorders like Alzheimer's disease, can significantly affect mental health. Additionally, chronic illnesses and medication side effects often play a role in the development or exacerbation of mental health disorders among the elderly. Understanding these biological factors is crucial for accurate diagnosis and tailored treatment strategies.

Psychological Aspects

The psychological component of the biopsychosocial approach recognizes the importance of individual experiences, emotions, and thought patterns in geriatric mental health. Elderly individuals often face grief due to the loss of loved ones, retirement, or declining physical abilities, leading to conditions like depression and anxiety. Furthermore, cognitive impairments, such as dementia, pose unique challenges in managing mental health issues. We can tailor psychosocial interventions, such as cognitive-behavioural therapy and reminiscence therapy, to address these psychological aspects and promote mental well-being among the elderly.

Social Aspects

The social dimension of the biopsychosocial approach highlights the influence of social interactions, relationships, and support systems on geriatric mental health. Loneliness and social isolation are prevalent issues among the elderly, contributing to feelings of depression and anxiety. Social engagement, community involvement, and strong social support networks are essential in promoting mental health and preventing social withdrawal. Interventions focusing on enhancing social connections, such as support groups and social activities, are integral components of the biopsychosocial approach.

Significance of the Biopsychosocial Approach

Holistic Understanding: The biopsychosocial approach offers a holistic understanding of geriatric mental health by considering the interplay of biological, psychological, and social factors. This comprehensive perspective enables healthcare professionals to develop personalized and effective interventions for elderly individuals.

Tailored Interventions: By addressing biological, psychological, and social aspects, the biopsychosocial approach allows for the development of tailored interventions. Customized treatment plans that consider the unique needs and challenges of each elderly individual can significantly improve treatment outcomes.

Prevention and Early Intervention: Understanding the various factors contributing to geriatric mental health issues facilitates prevention and early intervention efforts. Identifying risk factors and implementing appropriate measures can prevent the onset or progression of mental health disorders among the elderly.

Enhanced Quality of Life: By addressing the biological, psychological, and social aspects of mental health, the biopsychosocial approach contributes to enhancing the overall quality of life for elderly individuals. It promotes not only the absence of mental illness but also a positive state of mental well-being and life satisfaction.

3. Positive Ageing

The field of geriatric mental health has evolved significantly over the years, shifting from a primarily problem-focused perspective to one that emphasizes positive ageing. As the global population continues to age, there is a growing need for a more holistic and optimistic approach to the mental well-being of older adults. This chapter explores the concept of positive ageing as an approach to geriatric mental health, highlighting its key principles, benefits, and the impact it can have on the mental well-being of older adults.

Positive Ageing: An Overview

Positive ageing is a comprehensive approach that focuses on promoting mental and emotional well-being among older adults. Unlike traditional models that primarily address deficits and illnesses, positive ageing seeks to enhance the quality of life by emphasizing the strengths, resources, and opportunities that come with ageing. Positive ageing acknowledges ageing as a natural and continuous process, managing its associated challenges with a positive mindset, appropriate interventions, and community support.

Key Principles of Positive Ageing

Resilience: Positive ageing recognizes the inherent resilience of older adults. It emphasizes their ability to adapt to life's challenges, recover from setbacks, and grow from their experiences. This principle encourages older individuals to view adversity as an opportunity for personal growth.

Personal Growth: Positive ageing encourages older adults to continue pursuing personal growth and development. It highlights the importance of setting and achieving goals, learning new skills, and embracing new experiences, which can contribute to a sense of purpose and life satisfaction.

Social Engagement: Social connections are vital for mental well-being. Positive ageing emphasizes the importance of maintaining and nurturing social relationships. Activities such as volunteering, participating in community groups, or spending time with family and friends can achieve this.

Health and Wellness: Taking care of physical and mental health is a key aspect of positive ageing. This includes regular exercise, a balanced diet, adequate sleep, and practices that promote mental well-being, such as mindfulness and stress management techniques.

Optimism and Positivity: A positive attitude can significantly impact mental health. Positive ageing encourages older adults to focus on the positive aspects of life, maintain a hopeful outlook, and practice gratitude.

Benefits of the Positive Ageing Approach

Improved Mental Health: The positive ageing approach can lead to improved mental health outcomes among older adults. Research has shown that older individuals who adopt a positive attitude towards ageing experience lower rates of depression and anxiety, higher life satisfaction, and better overall well-being.

Enhanced Quality of Life: By focusing on strengths and opportunities, positive ageing contributes to an enhanced quality of life in later years. Older adults who embrace this approach tend to have a greater sense of purpose and satisfaction with their lives.

Increased Resilience: Positive ageing fosters resilience, enabling older adults to better cope with life's challenges. They are more likely to bounce back from setbacks, adapt to changing circumstances, and maintain a sense of control over their lives.

Social Connections: Engaging in social activities and maintaining strong relationships can reduce feelings of isolation and loneliness, which are common issues among older adults. Positive ageing encourages social engagement, leading to increased social support and well-being.

Longevity and Health Benefits: Research has suggested that a positive outlook on ageing can lead to increased longevity. Additionally, adopting a healthier lifestyle as part of positive ageing practices can lead to better physical health, reducing the risk of chronic diseases.

Impact on Geriatric Mental Health Services

The positive ageing approach has shaped the delivery and customization of geriatric mental health services to meet the needs of older adults. Professionals in the field have recognized the importance of integrating positive ageing principles into their practices to support mental well-being. Here are a few ways in which the approach has impacted geriatric mental health services:

Strength-Based Interventions: Mental health professionals are increasingly using strength-based interventions that focus on an older individual's existing resources and capacities rather than solely addressing deficits or problems. This approach encourages older adults to take an active role in their well-being and empowers them to use their strengths to overcome challenges.

Holistic Assessment: When assessing the mental health of older adults, geriatric mental health services now take a more holistic approach. They consider physical health, social support systems, and an individual's overall quality of life. This approach allows for a more comprehensive understanding of an older person's mental well-being.

Preventative Measures: Positive ageing encourages the adoption of preventive mental health measures to maintain well-being and reduce the risk of developing mental health issues. The focus of mental health services is increasingly on promoting resilience, reducing stigma, and providing education on the benefits of a positive outlook on ageing.

Community-Based Support: Community organizations and support networks play a crucial role in positive ageing. Geriatric mental health services are increasingly collaborating with community resources to provide older adults with opportunities for social engagement, skill-building, and mental health support.

Tailored Treatment Plans: Recognizing that every older adult is unique, geriatric mental health services are developing more personalized treatment plans that align with the principles of positive ageing. These plans consider an individual's strengths, preferences, and goals, ensuring a client-centred approach.

Models for Enhancing Geriatric Mental Health

1. The Ecological Model for Creating a Positive Environment for the Elderly

As the global population continues to age, creating a positive and supportive environment for the elderly has become a pressing concern. The Ecological Model offers a comprehensive framework for understanding and addressing the complex interplay of factors that influence the well-being of elderly individuals. This model takes into account the intricate web of physical, social, and psychological aspects of an individual's life and the environment they inhabit. In this chapter, we will delve into the ecological model, exploring its core principles and components and discussing its practical application in designing environments that promote the well-being of the elderly.

Understanding the Ecological Model

Urie Bronfenbrenner initially developed the Ecological Model, also known as the Ecological Systems Theory, in the late 20th century. Urie Bronfenbrenner developed the Ecological Model in the late 20th century, emphasizing the deep influence of various systems on individuals. These systems, grouped into different levels, or "ecological systems", interconnect and influence each other. The model consists of several nested levels, each of which plays a significant role in an individual's life.

Microsystem: The innermost level of the ecological model comprises the immediate environments that directly impact an individual. For the elderly, this may include their family, friends, and caregivers. These primary relationships have a profound impact on their emotional and physical well-being.

Mesosystem: The mesosystem is composed of the interconnections between various microsystems. For elderly individuals, this could include the interaction between family members and healthcare professionals or between different caregivers. Effective communication and cooperation among these microsystems are crucial for the elderly's well-being.

Exosystem: The exosystem encompasses broader social settings that indirectly influence the elderly. This might involve government policies, healthcare systems, or community support structures. These external factors can significantly impact the quality of life for the elderly population.

Macrosystem: The macrosystem is the broader cultural and societal context that shapes the values, norms, and beliefs related to ageing. It encompasses how a society perceives and treats its elderly population, including issues like ageism and discrimination.

Chronosystem: The chronosystem recognizes that life events and experiences change over time. This includes historical events, cultural shifts, and personal life events such as retirement, the loss of loved ones, or health changes. Understanding the temporal dimension is essential for creating a positive environment for the elderly.

Practical Application of the Ecological Model

Housing and Living Arrangements: The ecological model can inform the design and development of elderly-friendly housing and living arrangements. Microsystem factors like family support and caregiver accessibility are essential. A well-designed mesosystem, ensuring that healthcare professionals and community services are readily available, can enhance the elderly's well-being. On the exosystem level, policies that promote age-friendly housing and financial support for the elderly are vital. A supportive macrosystem can challenge ageist stereotypes and foster positive attitudes towards ageing. Finally, a responsive chronosystem would account for changing needs as individuals age.

Healthcare and Support Services: Elderly individuals often require extensive healthcare and support services. The ecological model suggests that a holistic approach, involving collaboration among microsystems (family, healthcare providers, and social services), is crucial. The exosystem must provide accessible and affordable healthcare services, and the macrosystem should promote research, funding, and advocacy for the elderly. The chronosystem recognizes the evolving healthcare needs of the elderly as they age.

Social Engagement and Inclusion: Social isolation is a significant concern for the elderly. The ecological model underscores the importance of microsystem interactions with family and friends to provide emotional support. On the mesosystem level, senior centres, community programmes, and volunteer organizations can facilitate social engagement. The exosystem should promote policies that combat social isolation and provide resources for elderly-friendly activities. The macrosystem should challenge ageist stereotypes and promote a culture of inclusion. A dynamic chronosystem acknowledges that the social needs of the elderly change as they transition through different life stages.

Mental Health and Well-being: The mental health of the elderly is intricately connected to the ecological model. Microsystem support from family and caregivers is essential. The mesosystem should ensure collaboration between healthcare professionals and mental health services. The exosystem must offer access to mental health resources, including therapy and counselling. The macrosystem can contribute to reducing stigma around mental health issues among the elderly. A responsive chronosystem should adapt mental health services to the changing needs of the elderly population as they age.

2. The Social Convoy Model for Creating a Positive Environment for the Elderly

As the global population ages, creating a positive environment for the elderly has become an im perative. The well-being of older adults is not only crucial for their individual quality of life but also for society as a whole. In this context, the Social Convoy Model has emerged as a valuable framework for understanding and promoting a positive environment for the elderly. Developed by Kahn and Antonucci in the late 1970s, this model provides insights into the social dynamics and relationships that shape the lives of older individuals. This chapter delves into the Social Convoy Model, its fundamental principles, and its potential applications in fostering a positive environment for the elderly. To support our discussion, we draw upon relevant research and evidence.

Understanding the Social Convoy Model

The Social Convoy Model, initially proposed by Toni Antonucci and Laura L. Carstensen, posits that social relationships and interactions form a dynamic and ever-changing support network around an individual. This network, referred to as a "convoy", plays a significant role in an individual's well-being. Family members, friends, and acquaintances make up the convoy, which undergoes evolution throughout an individual's lifespan. It adapts to changing needs, preferences, and circumstances, which can vary as one ages.

The Central Components of the Social Convoy Model Include

Social Relationships: The model recognizes the importance of social relationships as key components of an individual's life. These relationships provide emotional support, companionship, and opportunities for social engagement. The model emphasizes that the nature and composition of these relationships may change with age.

Dynamics of Change: The convoy is not static; it evolves over time. Friends and family members may come and go, and the nature of interactions may change. The model acknowledges that these changes can have both positive and negative implications for an individual's well-being.

Selective Optimization with Compensation: The Social Convoy Model closely links to the theory of selective optimization with compensation (SOC). This concept highlights that as individuals age, they often adapt by selectively choosing certain goals and optimizing their resources to achieve those goals. At the same time, they may compensate for losses or limitations in other areas. In this context, the convoy may provide essential support in helping older adults navigate these changes.

The Social Convoy Model has Applications for Creating a Positive Environment for the Elderly

Creating a positive environment for the elderly involves various aspects, including physical, social, and emotional well-being. You can effectively address these aspects by applying the Social Convoy Model.

Emotional Well-being: The emotional well-being of older adults is closely tied to their social circle. To promote emotional well-being, it is essential to facilitate the maintenance and development of supportive relationships. Creating spaces for older individuals to connect with peers, fostering intergenerational connections, and addressing potential barriers to social engagement, such as transportation or mobility issues, can achieve this.

Social Engagement: The model suggests that active social engagement is critical for a positive elderly environment. Community organizations, retirement homes, and senior centres can implement programmes that encourage social activities, providing older adults with opportunities to build and maintain their communities. Activities like group outings, classes, and volunteering can facilitate these interactions.

Physical Health: The physical health of older adults is not only influenced by their own behaviours but also by the support they receive from their family. Healthcare professionals, family members, and friends play a crucial role in advocating for and providing access to healthcare services. Promoting a positive environment for the elderly should include mechanisms for ensuring that these support systems are in place.

Adaptation to Change: The Social Convoy Model acknowledges that as individuals age, they may face various life changes, including health issues and losses. To create a positive environment, it is essential to help older adults adapt to and cope with these changes. Counselling services, support groups, and education on strategies like selective optimization with compensation can achieve this.

Intervention Strategies for the Elderly

1. Cognitive and Emotional Support as an Intervention Strategy for the Elderly

As the global population ages, there is an increasing need for effective strategies to support the well-being and quality of life of the elderly.

Cognitive and emotional support has emerged as a promising intervention strategy that addresses the unique needs of this population. This approach acknowledges that ageing can bring cognitive and emotional challenges and aims to provide tailored support to enhance mental and emotional health. In this chapter, we will explore the importance of cognitive and emotional support for the elderly, discuss the various components of this intervention model, and highlight the impact of such support on the well-being of elderly individuals.

Cognitive and Emotional Challenges in the Elderly

Cognitive and emotional changes often accompany the ageing process, impacting an individual's daily life and overall well-being. Cognitive decline, such as memory problems and reduced processing speed, is a common experience among the elderly. Additionally, emotional challenges, including loneliness, depression, and anxiety, can significantly impact their mental health.

Cognitive and emotional challenges in the elderly are not solely a result of ageing itself but can also be exacerbated by factors like social isolation, physical health issues, and the loss of loved ones. These challenges can hinder an individual's ability to engage in daily activities, maintain social connections, and enjoy life. Therefore, addressing these issues is crucial for maintaining a high quality of life in old age.

Components of Cognitive and Emotional Support

Cognitive Training and Enhancement: Cognitive support involves activities and programmes designed to enhance cognitive functions. These programmes often include exercises that target memory, problem-solving, and other cognitive skills. Various methods such as computer-based programmes, group activities, and one-on-one sessions can provide cognitive training. For instance, programmes like brain training games and puzzles have gained popularity in recent years for their potential to improve cognitive function in the elderly.

Emotional and Social Support: Emotional and social support are fundamental aspects of caring for the elderly. Loneliness and social isolation can lead to depression and other emotional issues. Therefore, maintaining social connections is crucial for emotional well-being. Group activities, senior centres, or simply spending time with loved ones can achieve this. Emotional support also involves providing a safe and open environment for the elderly to express their feelings and concerns.

Mental Health Services: For individuals struggling with more severe emotional challenges, mental health services such as counselling or therapy can be a vital component of cognitive and emotional support. These services can help elderly individuals address issues like depression, anxiety, and grief. Trained professionals can provide the necessary tools and strategies for coping with emotional distress and improving mental health.

Caregiver Training and Education: Caring for the elderly often falls on family members or professional caregivers. Educating these individuals on the unique needs of elderly individuals, including cognitive and emotional support, is essential. Caregiver training programmes can teach effective communication, stress management, and strategies for providing emotional support to the elderly.

Assistive Technologies: Advancements in technology have led to the development of various assistive technologies that can aid the elderly in their daily lives. These technologies can include reminder apps, medical alert systems, and communication tools that help combat social isolation. They offer practical support for managing cognitive and emotional challenges.

The Impact of Cognitive and Emotional Support is Significant

Enhanced Cognitive Function: Cognitive support can improve memory, problem-solving skills, and cognitive resilience in the elderly. Studies have shown that cognitive training programmes can lead to significant cognitive improvements, particularly in the domains of memory and processing speed. This enhanced cognitive function can enable the elderly to continue living independently and engaging in various activities.

Improved Emotional Well-being: Emotional and social support can reduce feelings of loneliness and depression in the elderly. Regular social interactions and emotional support from family, friends, or caregivers have been associated with higher levels of emotional well-being and a reduced risk of mental health issues. Moreover, mental health services can provide necessary intervention for those struggling with severe emotional challenges.

Enhanced Quality of Life: Cognitive and emotional support contribute to an improved quality of life for the elderly. When individuals are better equipped to cope with cognitive and emotional challenges, they can continue to lead fulfilling lives, pursue hobbies, and enjoy their golden years. This not only benefits the elderly but also their families and communities.

Delayed Cognitive Decline: While cognitive decline is a natural part of ageing, cognitive support can help delay the onset and progression of cognitive impairment. Engaging in cognitive training and staying mentally active can promote brain health and slow down cognitive decline, allowing elderly individuals to maintain their independence and autonomy for longer.

Reduced Healthcare Costs: Investing in cognitive and emotional support for the elderly can lead to cost savings in the healthcare system. Proactively addressing emotional and cognitive challenges may reduce the need for more intensive medical and psychiatric care. This not only benefits the elderly but also eases the burden on healthcare resources.

2. Social Engagement as an Intervention Strategy for the Elderly

As the global population ages, addressing the well-being of the elderly has become a critical concern. Ageing is associated with various physical, cognitive, and emotional challenges, often leading to social isolation and loneliness. Social engagement, which encompasses a wide range of activities and interactions with others, has gained recognition as a valuable intervention strategy to enhance the overall quality of life for the elderly. This chapter explores the significance of social engagement as an intervention model for the elderly, its benefits, and evidence-based approaches, with reference to relevant research studies and literature.

The Importance of Social Engagement for the Elderly

Social engagement is a multifaceted concept that encompasses social interactions, participation in community activities, and maintaining relationships with family and friends. For the elderly, social engagement is crucial for several reasons:

Mental and Emotional Well-being: Social engagement promotes mental stimulation, reduces the risk of depression and anxiety, and enhances emotional well-being. Regular social interactions can provide a sense of purpose and belonging, mitigating feelings of loneliness and isolation (Cacioppo *et al.*, 2011).

Cognitive Health: Engaging in conversations, playing games, or participating in group activities can help maintain cognitive function and delay cognitive decline. The challenges and novelty of social interactions can stimulate the brain and enhance memory and problem-solving skills (Holt-Lunstad *et al.*, 2010).

Physical Health: Socially engaged individuals are more likely to engage in physical activities and maintain healthier lifestyles. A strong social network can provide support for managing chronic conditions and adhering to medical recommendations (Berkman *et al.*, 2000).

Quality of Life: Maintaining social connections and engaging in social activities can contribute to an improved overall quality of life. It provides a sense of purpose and satisfaction in one's later years, promoting happiness and life satisfaction (Pinquart & Sörensen, 2001).

Benefits of Social Engagement for the Elderly

Research has consistently demonstrated the numerous benefits of social engagement for the elderly population. Several key advantages include:

Emotional Support: Social engagement offers emotional support, reducing the risk of depression and loneliness. Engaging with peers and friends can provide a sense of security and comfort, promoting a positive emotional state (Hawkley & Cacioppo, 2010).

Cognitive Enhancement: Regular social interactions challenge the brain and can lead to improved cognitive function. Engaging in conversations, games, and puzzles can help maintain memory and problem-solving abilities (Fratiglioni *et al.*, 2004).

Physical Well-being: Socially active individuals are more likely to engage in physical activities, leading to better physical health and a decreased risk of chronic illnesses. Additionally, the social support system can assist with managing health conditions (Uchino *et al.*, 1996).

Extended Lifespan: Studies have suggested that strong social ties are associated with a longer life expectancy. Socially engaged individuals tend to adopt healthier behaviours and adhere to medical recommendations (House *et al.*, 1988).

Challenges and Considerations

While social engagement is a promising intervention strategy for the elderly, we must address the following challenges and considerations:

Individual Differences: The needs and preferences of the elderly vary widely. Some may prefer group activities, while others may feel more comfortable with one-on-one interactions. Tailoring interventions to individual preferences is crucial.

Physical and Cognitive Limitations: Some elderly individuals may have physical or cognitive limitations that affect their ability to engage in certain activities. It is important to provide adaptive options and accessibility support.

Transportation: Access to social engagement opportunities can be challenging for those with limited mobility. Providing transportation options or bringing social activities into the home can help overcome this barrier.

Sustainability: To guarantee ongoing benefits, it is crucial to establish long-term social engagement programmes that can endure over time.

3. Physical Health and Nutrition as an Intervention Strategy for the Elderly

The ageing population is growing rapidly, and with it, the prevalence of age-related health issues and chronic diseases. As people age, maintaining physical health and proper nutrition becomes crucial for maintaining a high quality of life and overall well-being. This chapter explores the significance of physical health and nutrition as an intervention strategy for the elderly, emphasizing the importance of a holistic approach to ageing well.

The Ageing Population: A Global Challenge

The world's population is ageing at an unprecedented rate. The World Population Prospects 2019 predicts that by 2050, the number of individuals aged 60 and older will double, posing significant implications for healthcare and social support systems. This demographic shift poses a considerable challenge in terms of healthcare and demands effective intervention strategies to ensure the elderly population's health and well-being.

The importance of physical health in ageing is significant

Physical Activity and Functional Independence: Physical activity is a cornerstone of healthy ageing. Regular exercise promotes muscle strength, flexibility, and cardiovascular health, reducing the risk of falls and enhancing functional independence. Engaging in activities like walking, swimming, or strength training can help elderly individuals maintain their mobility and vitality.

Chronic Disease Management: Ageing often brings an increased risk of chronic diseases such as hy pertension, diabetes, and osteoporosis. Physical activity can play a vital role in managing and preventing these conditions. For instance, regular exercise helps control blood sugar levels in diabetics and maintain bone density in osteoporosis.

Cognitive Benefits: There is a strong correlation between physical health and cognitive health. Exercise has been associated with improved cognitive function, including memory, attention, and executive function. The maintenance of cognitive abilities is crucial for independent living in old age.

The Role of Nutrition in Ageing

Nutrient Requirements: As people age, their nutritional needs change. The elderly require fewer calories but more essential nutrients. Adequate intake of vitamins, minerals, and macronutrients is essential to support overall health and well-being.

Bone Health: Osteoporosis, a common concern among the elderly, can lead to fractures and decreased mobility. Adequate calcium and vitamin D intake is crucial to maintaining bone health and reducing the risk of fractures.

Weight Management: Maintaining a healthy weight is important for reducing the risk of obesity-related conditions, such as heart disease and diabetes. A balanced diet can help the elderly manage their weight effectively.

The Synergy of Physical Health and Nutrition

Comorbidity and Frailty: Comorbidity, the presence of multiple chronic conditions, is common in the elderly. Frailty, a state of increased vulnerability to adverse health outcomes, often accompanies comorbidity. Poor nutrition can exacerbate frailty and contribute to the progression of chronic diseases, thereby interlinking physical health and nutrition.

Preventing Malnutrition: Malnutrition is a significant concern among the elderly, affecting both undernutrition and overnutrition. An appropriate balance of physical activity and good nutrition can help prevent malnutrition and its associated complications.

Lifestyle Interventions: Research has shown that combining physical activity and proper nutrition can improve overall health outcomes in the elderly. These interventions may include personalized exercise programmes and dietary counselling.

A Holistic Approach to Ageing Well

Emotional and Social Well-being: A holistic approach to ageing well also addresses emotional and social aspects. Loneliness and depression are common among the elderly, which can negatively impact physical health and nutrition. Encouraging social interaction, engagement, and emotional well-being is essential.

Healthcare Access: Access to healthcare is crucial for the timely diagnosis and management of age-related health issues. Regular check-ups and preventive healthcare can help maintain physical health and address nutritional concerns.

Home and Environment: Creating a safe and supportive home environment is vital for the elderly. This includes modifications to prevent falls, promote independence, and ensure access to nutritious food.

Barriers and Challenges

While the importance of physical health and nutrition in ageing is well documented, there are several barriers and challenges that must be considered:

Economic Constraints: Economic limitations can restrict access to nutritious food and healthcare services, making it difficult for some elderly individuals to maintain their physical health and nutrition adequately.

Cognitive Decline: Cognitive decline may affect an individual's ability to plan and prepare balanced meals, adhere to exercise routines, and seek appropriate healthcare.

Socio-economic Disparities: Socio-economic disparities can result in unequal access to resources that promote physical health and nutrition, leading to health inequalities among the elderly.

4. Family and Caregiver Support as an Intervention Strategy for the Elderly

The world's population is ageing at an unprecedented rate, leading to an increased prevalence of elderly individuals. As people age, they may face a myriad of physical, emotional, and cognitive challenges. To address these challenges, it is im perative to explore and implement effective intervention strategies. One such strategy is the provision of family and caregiver support, which has been shown to be a vital component in ensuring the well-being and quality of life of the elderly population. In this chapter, we will delve into the importance of family and caregiver support as an intervention strategy for the elderly, highlighting its benefits and providing evidence-based insights on its effectiveness.

The Ageing Population: A Global Phenomenon

The demographic transition, characterized by decreasing birth rates and increasing life expectancy, has led to an ageing population worldwide. The United Nations predicts that by 2050, the global population aged 60 and over will be more than double, reaching 2.1 billion. This demographic shift brings about a multitude of challenges, including increased healthcare costs, a greater burden on healthcare systems, and the need for comprehensive support systems to ensure the elderly can maintain their quality of life.

Family and Caregiver Support

Family and caregiver support involves a range of services and assistance provided by family members, friends, or professional caregivers to meet the needs of the elderly. It encompasses various aspects, such as emotional support, daily living assistance, healthcare management, and social engagement. This support system plays a crucial role in improving the lives of elderly individuals, offering them a sense of security, companionship, and access to necessary resources.

The Importance of Family Support

Emotional Well-being: Ageing often comes with a heightened risk of loneliness and depression. Family members can provide emotional support, companionship, and a sense of belonging, which are vital for the mental well-being of the elderly. *The Journal of Gerontology and Geriatric Research* (2015) published a study that linked strong family bonds to a decreased risk of depression in elderly individuals.

Physical Assistance: As people age, they may encounter physical limitations that impede daily activities. Family support can help with mobility, transportation, meal preparation, and housekeeping, allowing the elderly to maintain their independence and quality of life.

Healthcare Management: Many elderly individuals require healthcare management due to chronic conditions or age-related ailments. Family members can assist in medication management, scheduling doctor's appointments, and ensuring adherence to treatment plans. This support is critical to preventing complications and improving overall health.

The Role of Professional Caregivers

While family support is invaluable, not all elderly individuals have immediate family members available to provide care. In such cases, professional caregivers play a vital role in ensuring the well-being of the elderly. You can hire these caregivers from home care agencies, nursing homes, or assisted living facilities. They receive training to offer a diverse range of services such as personal care, medical assistance, and companionship.

Benefits of Family and Caregiver Support

Enhanced Quality of Life: Family and caregiver support contribute significantly to improving the overall quality of life for the elderly. This support meets their physical, emotional, and healthcare needs, resulting in a more fulfilling and satisfying life.

Delayed Institutionalization: Many elderly individuals can continue living in their own homes with adequate support, avoiding placement in nursing homes or other institutions. Ageing in place allows individuals to remain in familiar surroundings, promoting a sense of comfort and security.

Reduced Healthcare Costs: By actively participating in healthcare management, family members and caregivers can help prevent hospital admissions and complications. This not only enhances the elderly person's health but also reduces the financial burden on the healthcare system.

Emotional Well-being: Having consistent companionship and emotional support helps combat feelings of isolation and depression in the elderly. This, in turn, leads to better mental health and a more positive outlook on life.

Evidence-based Effectiveness

Numerous studies support the effectiveness of family and caregiver support as an intervention strategy for the elderly.

A study published in *JAMA Internal Medicine* in 2019 found that informal caregiving provided by family members reduced the risk of mortality for the care recipient. This study demonstrated that the provision of support not only improved the elderly individual's quality of life but also had a tangible impact on their lifespan.

Research published in the *Journal of the American Medical Directors Association* (2018) found that family and caregiver support were associated with better management of chronic conditions in the elderly. This led to reduced hospitalizations and healthcare costs.

A study in the journal *Gerontology & Geriatrics Education* (2017) indicated that professional caregivers can significantly improve the cognitive function of elderly individuals through structured activities and cognitive stimulation.

A report by the AARP Public Policy Institute highlights the economic value of family caregiving, estimating that family caregivers provide approximately $470 billion worth of unpaid care to elderly individuals annually in the United States.

In summary, promoting mental health in the elderly population is a critical issue that requires careful and thorough methods. The book "*Creating a Positive Environment for the Elderly: Approaches, Models, and Intervention Strategies*" explores a number of topics related to enhancing senior citizens' well-being. As this investigation has shown, a multifaceted approach that takes into account psychological, social, and environmental factors is crucial.

One cannot stress the need for customized intervention tactics. Success depends on putting models into practice that acknowledge the special requirements and difficulties that the senior population faces. The establishment of a pleasant atmosphere necessitates the combination of technology, community participation, and person-centred care. Elderly people's mental health and general sense of well-being can be improved by creating surroundings that prioritize empowerment, social interaction, and the inclusion of therapeutic activities.

Collaboration between caregivers, community organizations, and healthcare professionals is also essential. A comprehensive strategy that combines medical attention with social assistance can have a positive synergistic effect on older people's mental resilience. The mental health of the senior population will be crucially dependent on ongoing research, policy lobbying, and the use of evidence-based practices as society navigates an ageing demographic environment. In the end, we can help create a society in which ageing is linked to both lifespan and continued mental and emotional health for our senior folks by adopting these all-encompassing techniques.

References

Adams, K.B., Leibbrandt, S. & Moon, H. (2011). "A Critical Review of the Literature on Social and Leisure Activity and Well-being in Later Life". *Ageing & Society*, *31*(4): 683-712.

Alexopoulos, G.S. (2005). "Depression in the Elderly". *The Lancet Neurology*, *4*(12): 879-888.

Alexopoulos, G.S., Raue, P.J., Kanellopoulos, D., Mackin, R.S., Kallner, K.E. & Sirey, J.A. (2014). "Problem-Solving Therapy and Supportive Therapy in Older Adults with Major Depression and Executive Dysfunction: Effect on Disability". *Archives of General Psychiatry*, *71*(12): 1289-1297.

Antonucci, T.C. & Akiyama, H. (1987). "Social Networks in Adult Life and a Preliminary Examination of the Convoy Model". *Journal of Gerontology*, *42*(5): 519-527.

Berkman, L.F., Glass, T., Brissette, I. & Seeman, T.E. (2000). "From Social Integration to Health: Durkheim in the New Millennium". *Social Science & Medicine*, *51*(6): 843-857.

Black, D.S. & Slavich, G.M. (2016). "Mindfulness Meditation and the Immune System: A Systematic Review of Randomized Controlled Trials". *Annals of the New York Academy of Sciences*, *1373*(1): 13-24. doi:10.1111/nyas.12998

Blazer, D.G. (2003). "Depression in Late Life: Review and Commentary". *The Journals of Gerontology Series A: Biological Sciences and Medical Sciences*, *58*(3): 249-265.

Ball, K., Berch, D.B., Helmers, K.F., Jobe, J.B., Leveck, M.D., Marsiske, M., ... & Willis, S.L. (2002). "Effects of Cognitive Training Interventions with Older Adults: A Randomized Controlled Trial". *JAMA*, *288*(18): 2271-2281.

Beaudart, C., Reginster, J.Y., Slomian, J., Buckinx, F., Dardenne, N., Quabron, A., ... & Bruyère, O. (2017). "Estimation of Sarcopenia Prevalence Using Various Assessment Tools". *Experimental Gerontology*, *92*, 48-53.

Brodaty, H., Donkin, M. (2009). "Family caregivers of people with dementia". *Dialogues Clin Neurosci.*, *11*(2): 217-228.

Bronfenbrenner, U. (1979). *The Ecology of Human Development: Experiments by Nature and Design*. Harvard University Press.

Byers, A.L. & Yaffe, K. (2011). "Depression and Risk of Developing Dementia". *Nature Reviews Neurology*, *7*(6): 323-331.

Cacioppo, J.T., Hawkley, L.C. & Thisted, R.A. (2010). "Perceived Social Isolation Makes Me Sad: Five-Year Cross-Legged Analyses of Loneliness and Depressive Symptomatology in the Chicago Health, Ageing, and Social Relations Study". *Psychology and Ageing*, *25*(2): 453-463.

Cao, L., Morley, J.E. & Duthie Jr, E.H. (2010). "Sarcopenia is Recognized as an Independent Condition by an International Classification of Disease, Tenth Revision, Clinical Modification (ICD-10-CM) Code". *The Journal of the Frailty & Ageing*, *1*(1): 22-24.

Carstensen, L.L. (1992). "Social and Emotional Patterns in Adulthood: Support for Socio-emotional Selectivity Theory". *Psychology and Ageing*, *7*(3): 331-338.

Cesari, M., Pahor, M., Lauretani, F., Zamboni, V., Bandinelli, S., Bernabei, R. & Guralnik, J.M. (2009). "Skeletal Muscle and Mortality Results from the InCHIANTI Study". *The Journals of Gerontology Series A: Biological Sciences and Medical Sciences*, *64*(3): 377-384.

Chida, Y., Steptoe, A. (2008). "Positive Psychological Well-being and Mortality: A Quantitative Review of Prospective Observational Studies". *Psychosomatic Medicine*, *70*(7): 741-756.

Chiesa, A. & Serretti, A. (2010). "A Systematic Review of Neurobiological and Clinical Features of Mindfulness Meditations". *Psychological Medicine*, *40*(8): 1239-1252. doi:10.1017/S0033291709991747

Coe, N.B., Van Houtven, C.H. (2009). "Caring for Mom and Neglecting Yourself? The Health Effects of Caring for an Elderly Parent". *Health Econ.*, *18*(9): 991-1010.

Craft, S. (2009). "The Role of Metabolic Disorders in Alzheimer Disease and Vascular Dementia: Two Roads Converged". *Archives of Neurology*, *66*(3): 300-305.

Dening, T., Greenish, W., Jones, L. & Mandal, U. (2018). "Person-centred Care for People with Dementia: A Quality Improvement Programme". *International Journal of Geriatric Psychiatry*, *33*(1): 94-102.

Findlay, R.A. (2003). "Interventions to Reduce Social Isolation Amongst Older People: Where is the Evidence?" *Ageing & Society*, *23*(5): 647-658.

Fratiglioni, L., Paillard-Borg, S. & Winblad, B. (2004). "An Active and Socially Integrated Lifestyle in Late Life Might Protect Against Dementia". *The Lancet Neurology*, *3*(6): 343-353.

Gaugler, J.E., Kane, R.L., Kane, R.A., Newcomer, R. (2005). "The Effects of Duration of Caregiving on Institutionalization". *The Gerontologist*. *45*(1): 78-89.

Gitlin, L.N., Hodgson, N., Jutkowitz, E., Pizzi, L. (2010). "The Cost-effectiveness of a Non-pharmacologic Intervention for Individuals with Dementia and Family Caregivers: The Tailored Activity Program". *Am J Geriatr Psychiatry* *18*(6): 510-519.

Gitlin, L.N. & Hodgson, N.A. (2015). "Caregivers as Therapeutic Agents in Dementia Care: The Context of Caregiver Interventions for Persons with Dementia". *The New England Journal of Medicine*, *373*(8): 744-751.

Hales, C.M., Carroll, M.D., Fryar, C.D. & Ogden, C.L. (2020). "Prevalence of Obesity and Severe Obesity among Adults: United States, 2017-2018". *NCHS Data Brief*, *360*: 1-8.

Hawkley, L.C. & Cacioppo, J.T. (2010). "Loneliness Matters: A Theoretical and Empirical Review of Consequences and Mechanisms". *Annals of Behavioural Medicine*, *40*(2): 218-227.

Hill, A.M., Hoffmann, T., Hill, K. & Oliver, D.S., Beer, C., McPhail, S. & Brauer, (2010). "The Effect of a Specialized Falls Prevention Programme on Falls in Residential Aged Care". *Age and Ageing*, *39*(2): 306-312.

Hilliard, R.E. (2019). "The Role of Spirituality in the Lives of Older Adults". *Journal of Gerontological Social Work*, *62*(8): 841-855. doi:10.1080/01634372.2019.1633313

Holt-Lunstad, J., Smith, T.B. & Layton, J.B. (2010). "Social Relationships and Mortality Risk: A Meta-Analytic Review". *PLOS Medicine*, *7*(7): e1000316.

Kanis, J.A., Johnell, O., Oden, A., Johansson, H., De Laet, C. & Eisman, J.A. (2005). "Smoking and Fracture Risk: A Meta-analysis". *Osteoporosis International*, *16*(2): 155-162.

Keyes, C.L. (2002). "The Mental Health Continuum: From Languishing to Flourishing in Life". *Journal of Health and Social Behaviour*, *43*(2): 207-222.

Koenig, H.G. (2012). "Religion, Spirituality, and Health: The Research and Clinical Implications". *ISRN Psychiatry*, 278730. doi:10.5402/2012/278730

Lawton, M.P. & Nahemow, L. (1973). "Ecology and the Ageing Process". In C. Eisdorfer & M.P. Lawton (eds.): *The Psychology of Adult Development and Ageing* (pp. 619-674). American Psychological Association.

Lloyd-Sherlock, P., Ebrahim, S., McKee, M. & Prince, M.J. (2012). "Institutional ageism in global health policy". *BMJ*, 345, e7205.

Mat, S., Tan, M.P. (2013). "Medications in frail older adults". In Onder, G., Sinclair A. (eds.) *Evidence-based Geriatric Medicine*. Springer, London.

Ministry of Health and Family Welfare, Government of India (2013). *Clinical Practice Guidelines for Assessment and Management of Geriatric Syndromes*. Retrieved from https://www.ignou.ac.in/userfiles/3.%20-%20MoHFW%20Clinical%20Guidelines.pdf

Morley, J.E., Vellas, B., van Kan, G.A., Anker, S.D., Bauer, J.M., Bernabei, R., ...& Fried, L.P. (2013). "Frailty Consensus: A Call to Action". *Journal of the American Medical Directors Association*, *14*(6): 392-397.

National Academies of Sciences (2016). "Engineering, and Medicine". *Families Caring for an Ageing America*. Washington, DC: The National Academies Press.

National Council on Ageing (2020). *Ageism in America*. https://www.ncoa.org/article/ageism-in-america/

Nelson, M.E., Rejeski, W.J., Blair, S.N., Duncan, P.W., Judge, J.O., King, A.C., ...& Castaneda-Sceppa, C. (2007). "Physical activity and public health in older adults: recommendation from the American College of Sports Medicine and the American Heart Association". *Medicine and Science in Sports and Exercise*, *39*(8): 1435-1445.

Pickett, Y.R. & Thielke, S.M. (2019). "Patient-centred Care for Older Adults with Depression and Anxiety: A Concise Review". *The Primary Care Companion for CNS Disorders*, *21*(1).

Pinquart, M. & Sörensen, S. (2001). "Influences on Loneliness in Older Adults: A Meta-Analysis". *Basic and Applied Social Psychology*, *23*(4): 245-266.

_______(2003). "Associations of Stressors and Uplifts of Caregiving with Caregiver Burden and Depressive Mood: A Meta-analysis". *The Journals of Gerontology Series B: Psychological Sciences and Social Sciences*, *58*(2): P112-P128.

_______(2007). "Correlates of Physical Health of Informal Caregivers: A Meta-analysis". *J Gerontol B Psychol Sci Soc Sci.*, *62*(2): P126-137.

Reichstadt, J., Sengupta, G., Depp, C.A., Palinkas, L.A. & Jeste, D.V. (2010). "Older Adults' Perspectives on Successful Ageing: Qualitative Interviews". *The American Journal of Geriatric Psychiatry*, *18*(7): 567-575.

Reilly, S. & Walsh, C.D. (2018). "Integrated Care in Geriatric Psychiatry: A Review". *Journal of the American Geriatrics Society*, *66*(9): 1753-1760.

Reiner, K., Tibi, L. & Lipsitz, J.D. (2013). "Do Brain-Training Games Work? A Review of the Evidence". *Journal of Cognitive Enhancement*, *1*(1): 63-68.

Rowe, J.W. & Kahn, R.L. (1997). "Successful Ageing". *The Gerontologist*, *37*(4): 433-440.

Sahyoun, N.R., Jacques, P.F., Zhang, X.L., Juan, W. & McKeown, N.M. (2006). "Whole-grain Intake Is Inversely Associated with the Metabolic Syndrome and Mortality in Older Adults". *The American Journal of Clinical Nutrition*, *83*(1): 124-131.

Schulz, R., Martire, L.M. (2004). "Family caregiving of persons with dementia: prevalence, health effects, and support strategies". *Am J Geriatr Psychiatry.* *12*(3):240-249.

Schwarzbach, M. & Luppa, M. (2013). "Social Relationships and the Maintenance of Emotional Well-being in Old Age: Results from the Longitudinal Ageing Study in Amsterdam". *International Psychogeriatrics*, *25*(12): 1893-1903.

Sindi, S., Hagman, G., Håkansson, K., Kulmala, J., Nilsen, C., Kåreholt, I.,... & Kivipelto, M. (2018). "Midlife Work-related Stress Is Associated with Late-Life Cognition". *Journal of Alzheimer's Disease*, *63*(4): 1589-1596.

Steptoe, A., Deaton, A. & Stone, A.A. (2015). "Subjective Well-being, Health, and Ageing". *The Lancet*, *385*(9968): 640-648.

Stern, Y. (2002). "What Is Cognitive Reserve? Theory and Research Application of the Reserve Concept". *Journal of the International Neuropsychological Society*, *8*(3): 448-460.

United Nations (2019). Department of Economic and Social Affairs, Population Division." *World Population Prospects 2019: Highlights.* Retrieved from https://population.un.org/wpp/Publications/Files/WPP2019_Highlights.pdf

Visser, M., Goodpaster, B.H., Kritchevsky, S.B., Newman, A.B., Nevitt, M., Rubin, S.M.,... & Harris, T.B. (2005). "Muscle Mass, Muscle Strength, and Muscle Fat Infiltration as Predictors of Incident Mobility Limitations in

Well-Functioning Older Persons". *The Journals of Gerontology Series A: Biological Sciences and Medical Sciences*, *60*(3): 324-333.

White, H., McConnell, E., Clipp, E., Bynum, L., Teague, C., Navas, L.,... & Steadman, L. (2003). "Surfing the Net in Later Life: A Review of the Literature and Pilot Study of Computer Use and Quality of Life". *Journal of Applied Gerontology*, *22*(3): 342-362.

Wilcox, V.L., Kasl, S.V., & Berkman, L.F. (1994). "Social Support and Physical Disability in Older People after Hospitalization: A Prospective Study". *Health Psychol. 13*(2):170-179.

World Health Organization. (2007). *Global Age-Friendly Cities: A Guide*. Retrieved from https://www.who.int/ageing/publications/Global_age_friendly_cities_Guide_English.pdf

World Health Organization (2015). *World Report on Ageing and Health*. Retrieved from https://www.who.int/ageing/events/world-report-2015-launch/en/

World Health Organization. (2018). *Mental Health of Older Adults*. [https://www.who.int/news-room/fact-sheets/detail/mental-health-of-older-adults]

Zizza, C.A., Herring, A.H. & Stevens, J., Popkin, B.M. (2007). "Length of time in the United States is associated with rapid weight gain in Mexican-American women". *The Journal of Nutrition*, *137*(8): 1987-1993.

16

Prevalence and Associated Factor of Depression Among Elderly Population in Rasuwa, Nepal

Narendra Singh Thagunna, Renu Khayamali, Binu Koirala and *Jyotshna Dangi*

Introduction

Mental health and emotional well-being are important part of healthy ageing. Over 20 per cent of geriatric population suffer from a mental or neurological disorder globally (WHO, 2017). Out of the psychiatric disorders among the elderly, depression is one of the most frequent and debilitating mental disorders, with a world-wide prevalence of about 10-15 per cent (National Alliance on Mental health, 2009). Depression occupied first place in the rank of major diseases that cause most non-fatal disabilities and third place in the global burden of disability, and it is estimated that by 2030 the condition will have the highest global burden among diseases (WHO, 2004). It emphasizes that depression can lead to multidimensional health problems. The prevalence of depression among geriatric population varies globally and range between 10-55 per cent (WHO, 2016). Depression is an important public health concern associated with increased health burden, morbidity and mortality. It increases the risk of suicide, increased self-neglect and reduced physical, mental, and social functioning (Blazer, 2003).

Most of the symptoms of depression in old age are misjudged as physiological process due to increased age such as reduced motivation, sleep disturbances, obsessive worry and others (Mental Health and Suicide Prevention, 2013). Symptoms of depression are often overlooked and untreated when they coincide with other medical illnesses or life events that commonly occur as people age, e.g. loss of loved ones, death of the spouse, retirement and inter personal difficulties with family members, poverty and loneliness. These situations greatly impact the psychological statuses of the elderly, making them prone to depression (National Institute of Mental Health, 2017).

Depression in old age can complicate the physical conditions resulting in poor outcomes. Moreover, depression in older adults may be disregarded as frailty or it may be regarded as inevitable physiological chances, chronic illness and disability. The symptoms may be neglected as their natural response to illness or life changes. Older adults themselves also accept the belief and has low help-seeking behaviour and lack knowledge about the care and treatment needed (National Centre for Chronic Disease Prevention and Health Promotion, 2017). Recognizing the sign and symptoms and seeking healthcare can make real difference to well-being and enhance quality of life (National Alliance on Mental Illness, 2009).

Ageing is an emerging public health issue for Nepal due to increasing life expectancy and reduced fertility rate (Nepal Population Report, 2016). The population census in Nepal shows increasing trend of geriatric population. The ageing population of Nepal was only 6.5 per cent (1.5 million) of total population in 2001 which increased to 8.14 per cent in 2011 (CBS and UNFPA, 2002).

Studies have shown that the older adults are vulnerable to mental health problems due to many social factors. The established culture and tradition of respecting older adults are decreasing day by day and the increased brain-drain among the younger generations for better opportunity has increased the mental health problems like depression, loneliness, stress, anxiety and other physical diseases (Dahal, 2007). Similarly, study conducted in Nepal among elderly population showed the prevalence of mental health 29.7 per cent (Chalise Homnath, 2013).

Depression is predominant public health concern (WHO, 2011) which can occur at any age and the prevalence may increase in old age due to multiple social, physical, emotional and cognitive factor which is associated with morbidity and disability as well as mortality among the elderly (Cole and Dendukuri, 2003).

A cross-sectional study carried out among 165 elderly by Chalise and Sailaxmi (2013) among the Rai older living in Kathmandu valley using Geriatric Depression Scale (GDS) showed the prevalence of depression 29.7 per cent. The study showed significant relation between the feeling of depression and gender, age, marital status, family size, instrumental activities of daily living, loneliness and participation in household activities. The findings suggest that many Nepalese older adult experiences some form of depression despite living in joint family.

Choulagai, P.S., Sharma, C.K., Choulagai, B.P. (2010) conducted cross-sectional descriptive study among 78 elderly on prevalence and associated factor of depression among elderly population living in geriatric homes in Kathmandu valley using semi-structured interview where geriatric depression scale was considered the major tool. The study revealed that the prevalence of depression was 51.3 per cent and severe and mild depression was 15.4 per cent and 35.9 per cent respectively. Majority of severely depressed respondents were widow/widower (75%), illiterate (85.7%), no children (75%) and most of the depressed respondents (90.9%) had difficulty to carry out daily living activities due to health problems. The study showed more than half of the respondents to be depressive and the associated factors with depression were age, gender (more in female) and situational and developmental crisis (Choulagai, 2013).

Chalise (2014) conducted a cross-sectional study on depression living in Devghat area of Nepal in 2012. Total 185 subject were interviewed by face-to-face interview using Geriatric Depression scale. Findings revealed that prevalence of depression was 57.8 per cent. Among them 46.7 per cent had mild and 8.9 per cent had moderate and 2.2 per cent had severe depression. Findings revealed that there is significant correlation between feeling of depression and age, sex, previous family type, ethnicity, feeling of loneliness and instrumental activities of daily living. The study suggests that there should be some interruption from the concerned authorities so that depression could be reduced and which will support to the well-being and quality of life of elderly (Chalise, 2014).

Bhattarai and Dutta (2013) conducted study on prevalence and depression among elderly people living in old age home in the capital city Kathmandu among 150 elderly people residing in social welfare centrely home, Pashupatinath, Gaushala, Kathmandu Nepal using Geriatric depression scale. The findings showed the prevalence of depression to be 47.3 per cent and mild and severe depression was 70.42 per cent and 29.58 per cent respectively. It was also found that the prevalence of depression is associated with physical illness (Ranjan, 2013).

Poudel (2005) stated that elderly people also have to face economic and social difficulties. Because of modernization, the traditional joint family is slowly being replaced by nuclear family in urban areas. Therefore, the caring of elderly population is a major problem. The older members of family are being isolated because of this trend of nuclear family. Old people long for love, proper nourishment, happiness and relaxing conversations from other family members. This system of nuclear family and busy lifestyle of people have secluded them from other family associates. Therefore, these issues can cause many psychosocial problems in elderly (Poudel, 2005).

Etemadi *et al.,* (2009) concluded that the most worrying issues for the elderly were economic status (55.8%), lack of social relations (55%), dissatisfaction with old age (45.8%), lack of favourite activities (45%), fear of future (30%), dissatisfaction with environment of the elderly home (24.2%) and dissatisfaction with the treatment were the factors associated with Elderly Anxiety and Depression of elderly home official (17%). Therefore, living at an elderly home means staying away from family support and that it is considered reproachable, attending to psychological and emotional needs of the elderly home residents is essential (Etemadi, 2009).

In a study it was observed that the prevalence of anxiety and depression were higher in older women which was found to be 70.4 per cent and 62.8 per cent respectively. It was higher in illiterate, married, housewives and those having no personal source of income. Further, the study showed that there was a significant difference in stress, anxiety, and depression for education, income, occupational status (Thagunna, 2020).

Over the last decade, depression is considered a growing concern at the national and international level. From the reviewed articles depression are more prevalent in elderly people. Various precipitating factors are associated to trigger the increase rate of depression. The proportion of elderly in Nepal is increasing rapidly and reaching 8.2 per cent of total population. But the Government of Nepal has not given priority to identify the problem of elderly and the resident living in rural areas are neglected more. Number of elder aged home studies has been conducted in Nepal which show high prevalence but very few studies have been done indicating level of depression and factor associated with depression. So this study was planned to assess level of depression among one of the rural area and to study prevalence of depression and factor associated with depression among elderly and to determine the association between socio-demographic factors and depression among elderly residing in Rasuwa.

Method

The study was a cross-sectional descriptive study using simple random sampling method. Data was collected by face-to-face interview with elderly, conducted within 6 wards of Naukunda Rural Municipal, province

3 of Rasuwa District in 2075 B.S. Elderly of 60 years or above male and female were included in the study and maximum of two persons of opposite sex are taken from one house as study subject and in case of persons between same sex group the elder person was given preference. Elderly people suffering from severe mental and physical illness like dementia, hearing impairment, dumbness, not giving consent were excluded.

Measurement

Geriatric Depression Scale (GDS) and a structured questionnaire was used to assess the data. For self-designed questionnaire a list of 16 items were used to collect information. GDS is a 30 item questionnaire especially developed as a screening instrument of depressive symptom in elderly. The GDS is a simple questionnaire and questions are answered "yes" or "no". One point is assigned to each answer and the cumulative score is rated on a scoring grid. The grid sets a range of 0-9 as "normal", 10-19 as "mildly depressed", and 20-30 as "severely depressed". GDS is an internationally validated questionnaire showing a sensitivity of 85 per cent and specificity of 74 per cent and has excellent reliability and validity (test retest reliability = 0.85 internal consistency = 0.04). This scale has also been found to be reliable and valid in Nepal.

Ethical Considerations

The verbal as well as written informed consent was taken from each participant before data collection and were explained about the study procedure, purpose, significance of the study in simple language, assured of full confidentially during and after the study period and can withdraw from the study at anytime without giving any reason.

Data Analysis

All data were primary and obtained from 210 respondents of old aged. After completion of data collection, data were checked for their accuracy and completeness and was transferred to Microsoft excel and double entry was done in SPSS software. It was used to enter, code, edit and analyze data. Descriptive statistics and inferential statistics were used to analyze the data. Under descriptive statistics percentage and frequency was used for describing variables, using the inferential statistics, chi-square test was done to find the association between the dependent and independent variable.

Result

The study shows that majority 85 (40.5%) respondents were between 60-64 years age group and minority, 7 (3.3%) respondents were between 80-84 years age group. Majority of the respondents, 115 (54.8%), were male, illiterate 115 (92.9%), and widow 125 (59.5%). The socio-demographic characteristics of the respondents on different components shows that the living arrangement nearly half of the respondents living with spouse, in majority the number of children 132 (62.9%) of the respondents had four and more children, majority ethnic group 141 (67.1%) respondents were *janajati*. Regarding the religion majority 89 (42.4%) respondents were Hindu and the occupation majority of the respondents had none 155 (73.8%). The result of socio-demographic variables and characteristics is given in Tables 16.1 and 16.2.

Table 16.1: Age, Sex, Education and Marital Status of Respondents

n = 210

	Frequency	Per cent
Age		
60-64	85	40.5
65-69	52	24.8
70-74	29	13.8
75-79	13	6.2
80-84	7	3.3
85-90	16	7.6
90 years and above	8	3.8
Sex		
Male	115	54.8
Female	95	45.2
Education		
Illiterate	195	92.9
Literate	15	7.1

(Contd.)

	Frequency	Per cent
Marital status		
Widow/widower	125	59.5
Married	85	40.5

Table 16.2: Living arrangement, Number of children, Ethnicity, Religion, Occupation of Respondents

n = 210

	Frequency	Per cent
Living arrangement		
Living alone	107	51
Living with spouse	102	48.6
Living with family	1	0.5
How many children do you have		
One	16	7.6
Two	29	13.8
Three	33	15.7
Four and above	132	62.9
Ethnicity		
Newar	22	10.5
Brahmin	18	8.6
Kshetri	12	5.7
Janajati	141	67.1
Dalit	17	8.1
Religion		
Hindu	89	42.4
Buddhism	84	40
Christian	29	13.8
Others	8	3.8
Occupation		
Farming	42	20
Business	13	6.2
None	155	73.8

Table 16.3 shows the health problems and types of difficulties of the respondents.

Table 16.3: Characteristics of the respondents on Health problem, types of difficulties

n = 210

	Frequency	Per cent
Any health problem		
Yes	187	89.0
No	23	11.0
Type of Difficulties Facing		
In performing daily activities	186	88.6
Trouble while sleeping	154	73.3
Could not go anywhere	58	27.6
Could not eat favourite food	22	10.5
Worries about		
Financial Security	176	83.8
Lack of Social Relation	36	17.1
Dissatisfaction with old age	73	34.8
Lack of favourite activities	35	16.7
Fear of future	133	63.3
Fear of death	185	88.1
Worries regarding going outside	46	21.9
Feel lonely		
Often	18	8.6
Sometime	139	66.2
Rarely	53	25.2
Usually feel stress		
Yes	77	36.7
No	133	63.3
Any caregivers constantly to look after you		
Yes	85	40.5
No	125	59.5

(Contd.)

	Frequency	Per cent
If Yes, n = 85		
Wife	32	38.0
Children	35	41.0
Relative	18	21.0
Engaged in any mind diversional activities		
Yes	184	87.6
No	26	12.4
If yes, n = 184		
Reading religious book	37	20.1
Going to Pravachan	28	15.2
Other	119	64.7

The response of respondents on each question of Depression Assessment tool are given in Table 16.4.

Table 16.4: Response of respondents on each question of Depression Assessment tool

n = 210

Sl. No.		Yes	Percentage
1	Satisfied with your life	196	93.3
2	Dropped many of your activities and interests	148	70.5
3	Feel life is empty	126	60.0
4	Get bored	148	70.5
5	Hopeful about the future	153	72.9
6	Bothered by thoughts can't get out of your head	43	20.5
7	In good spirits most of the time	82	39.0
8	Afraid that something bad is going to happen	143	68.1
9	Feel happy most of the time	93	44.3
10	Often feel helpless	43	20.5
11	Get restless and fidgety	29	13.8
12	Prefer to stay at home, rather than going out	128	61.0
13	Frequently worry about the future	113	53.8
14	More problems with memory than most	90	42.9

(Contd.)

Sl. No.		Yes	Percentage
15	Think it is wonderful to be alive now	176	83.8
16	Often feel downhearted and blue	38	18.1
17	Feel pretty worthless the way you are now	48	22.9
18	Worry a lot about the past	137	65.2
19	Find life very exciting	90	42.9
20	Hard for to get started on new projects	124	59.0
21	Feel full of energy	120	57.1
22	Feel that your situation is hopeless	99	47.1
23	Most people are better off than you are	71	33.8
24	Frequently get upset over little things	154	73.3
25	Frequently feel like crying	134	63.8
26	Trouble concentrating	115	54.8
27	Enjoy getting up in the morning	179	85.2
28	Prefer to avoid social gatherings	70	33.3
29	Easy for to make decisions	87	41.4
30	Mind as clear as it used to be	34	16.2

Prevalence of depression

The depression level shows 76 (36.2%) respondents were normal and 134 (63.8%) had depression. Out of theses 134 respondents, 113 (53.8%) and 21(10%) respondents had mild and severe depression respectively. The overall mean and standard deviation of depression was 13.37 ± 5.24. The minimum and maximum score was 2 and 22 respectively.

Regarding age, the score of depression was high, i.e. 14.6±4.8 and low, i.e. 13± 5.3 mean and S.D. in 76-90 years as well as 60-75 years age group respectively. Regarding sex of respondents, the score of depression was high, i.e. 13.5±5.4 and low, i.e. 13.2±5.1 mean and S.D. in female and male respectively. Regarding education, the score of depression was slightly high, i.e. 13.7±5.2 and slightly low, i.e. 9.3±3.3 mean and S.D. in illiterate and literate respectively. Regarding marital status, the depression score was high, i.e. 14.3±4.7 and low, i.e. 12.0±5.7 mean and S.D. in widow/widower and married respectively. Regarding number of children, the depression score was high, i.e. 15.1±4.2 and low, i.e. 13.0±5.5 mean and S.D. in one children and three children respectively. Regarding number of children, the depression score was high, i.e. 15.1±4.2 and low, i.e. 13.0±5.5 mean and S.D. in one children and three children respectively. Regarding ethnicity the depression score was high, i.e. 14.1±4.7 and low, i.e. 13.3±5.5 mean and S.D. in Brahmin and Kshetri respectively. Regarding Religion the depression score was high, i.e. 14.6±5.1 and low, i.e. 11.5±5.6 mean and S.D. in Buddhist and Christian respectively. Regarding occupation the depression score was high, i.e. 14.4±5.6 and low, i.e. 9.8±4.3 mean and S.D. in farming and business respectively.

The prevalence of depression are given in Table 16.5 and the descriptive statistics of score regarding depression scale with socio-demographic factors are given in Table 16.6.

Table 16.5: Prevalence of depression among elderly residing in Naukunda rural Municipal

n = 210

Level of depression	Frequency	Per cent
Normal	76	36.2
Mild	113	53.8
Severe	21	10.0
Mean ± SD	13.37 ± 5.24	
Minimum	2.00	
Maximum	22.00	

Table 16.6: Descriptive Statistics of Score regarding Depression Scale with Socio-demographic Factors

n = 210

Characteristics	Mean	Standard deviation	p-value
Age			
60-75	13.0	5.3	.083
76-90	14.6	4.8	
Sex			
Male	13.2	5.1	.698
Female	13.5	5.4	
Education			
Illiterate	13.7	5.2	.002*
Literate	9.3	3.3	

(*Contd.*)

Characteristics	Mean	Standard deviation	p-value
Marital Status			
Widow/Widower	12.0	5.7	<0.001*
Married	14.3	4.7	
Living arrangement			
Living with spouse	12.0	5.4	.003*
Living alone/living with family	14.7	4.8	
Number of children			
One	15.1	4.2	.916
Two	13.8	5.5	
Three	13.0	5.5	
Four and above	13.2	5.2	
Ethnicity			
Newar	13.5	5.0	.005*
Brahmin	14.1	4.7	
Kshetri	13.3	5.5	
Janajati	13.4	5.4	
Dalit			
Religion			
Hindu	12.6	5.1	.006*
Buddhist	14.6	5.1	
Christian and others	11.5	5.6	
Occupation			
Farming	14.4	5.6	0.021*
Business	9.8	4.3	
None	13.4	5.1	

*Statistically significant at 5 per cent level of significance.

Association

The association between socio-demographic factor and depression among elderly are given in Tables 16.7 and 16.8. The statistically significant variables were education, marital status, living arrangement, health problem, difficulties in performing daily activities, difficulties in trouble while sleeping, worries about financial security, worries about lack of social relation, worries about dissatisfaction with old age, worries about lack of favourite activities, worries about fear of future, worries about fear of death, worries about going outside and caregivers constantly to look after.

Table 16.7: Association between socio-demographic factor and depression among elderly

n = 210

Characteristics	Depression		χ^2	p-value
	No	Yes		
Age				
60-75	64 (38.6)	102 (61.4)	1.91	0.166
76-90	12 (27.3)	32 (72.7)		
Sex				
Male	43 (37.4)	72 (62.6)	0.15	0.69
Female	33 (34.7)	62 (65.3)		
Education				
Illiterate	64 (32.8)	131 (67.2)	13.42	<0.001*
Literate	12 (80)	3 (20)		
Marital Status				
Widow/Widower	34 (27.2)	91 (72.8)	10.08	0.001*
Married	42 (49.4)	43 (50.6)		
Living arrangement				
Living alone/living with family	24 (22.4)	83 (77.6)	17.88	<0.001*
Living with spouse	52 (50.5)	51 (49.5)		
Number of children				
Less than two	13 (28.9)	32 (71.1)	1.32	0.25
More than two	63 (38.2)	102 (61.8)		
Ethnicity				
Newar	8 (36.4)	14 (63.6)	1.6	0.8
Brahmin	5 (27.8)	13 (72.2)		

(Contd.)

Characteristics	Depression		χ^2	p-value
	No	Yes		
Kshetri	5 (41.7)	7 (58.3)		
Janajati	50 (35.5)	91 (64.5)		
Dalit	8 (47.1)	9 (52.9)		
Religion				
Hindu	36 (40.4)	53 (59.6)	2.5	0.28
Buddhist	25 (29.8)	59 (70.2)		
Christian and others	15 (40.5)	22 (59.2)		
Occupation				
Farming/Business	23 (41.8)	32 (58.2)	1.02	0.31
None	53 (34.2)	102 (65.8)		

*Statistically significant at 5 per cent level of significance.

Table 16.8: Association between individual factor, contextual factor and other factors with depression among elderly

n = 210

Characteristics	Depression		χ^2	p-value
	No	Yes		
Any Health Problem				
Yes	61 (32.6)	126 (67.4)	9.24	0.002*
No	15 (65.2)	8 (34.8)		
Type of Difficulties Facing				
In Performing Daily Activities	61 (32.8)	125 (67.2)	8.12	0.004*
Trouble While Sleeping	48 (31.2)	106 (68.8)	6.3	0.012*
Could not Go Anywhere	17 (29.3)	41 (70.7)	1.64	0.2
Could not Eat Favourite Food	7 (31.8)	15 (68.2)	0.203	0.652
Worries About				
Financial Security	58 (33)	118 (67)	4.92	0.026*
Lack of Social Relation	11 (30.6)	25 (69.4)	0.597	0.44

(Contd.)

Characteristics	Depression		χ^2	p-value
	No	Yes		
Dissatisfaction with Old Age	33 (45.2)	40 (54.8)	3.93	0.047*
Lack of Favourite Activities	7 (20)	28 (80)	4.76	0.029*
Fear of Future	35 (26.3)	98 (73.7)	15.31	<0.001*
Fear of Death	60 (32.4)	125 (67.6)	9.5	0.002*
Worries Regarding Going Outside	11 (23.9)	35 (76.1)	3.84	0.047*
Feel Lonely				
Often	7 (38.9)	11 (61.6)	7.18	0.066
Sometimes	56 (40.6)	82 (59.4)		
Rarely	13 (22.6)	41 (77.4)		
Usually Feel Stress				
Yes	25 (32.5)	52 (67.5)	0.73	0.39
No	51 (38.6)	82 (61.7)		
Any Caregivers Constantly to Look After You				
Yes	71 (35.3)	130 (64.7)	1.52	0.21
No	5 (55.6)	4 (44.4)		
If Yes, N = 85				
Wife/Children	75 (39.1)	117 (60.9)	8	0.005*
Relative	1 (5.6)	17 (94.4)		
Engaged in Any Mind Diversional Activities				
Yes	71 (38.6)	113 (61.4)	3.69	0.055
No	5 (19.2)	21 (80.8)		

*Statistically significant at 5 per cent level of significance.

Discussion

Over the last decade, depression has become a growing concern at the national and international level. So, this research design was planned in

Naukunda rural municipality on topic "Prevalence and Associated Factor of Depression among Elderly Residing in Naukunda Rural Municpality". Total 210 elderly aged people were included in the study.

The study showed that the prevalence of depression among elder people is 63.8 per cent which in accordance to the result reported by (Chalise Homnath, 2014) were 57.8 per cent. Among them 46.7 per cent has mild an 8.9 per cent has severe depression. Whereas this study concluded 53.8 per cent has mild and 10 per cent has moderate depression.

This study suggest that there is significant association between depression and socio-demographic variable such as education, marital status and living arrangement.. The present study reveals that female have more depression. This may be because Nepal is patriarchal society. In Nepalese society from early age women have to depend on someone else either to take decision or to live a life and have to go through lots of pain where they constantly suffer from loneliness, irritation, hopelessness.

Similarly, the mean score of depression was high, i.e. 14.6±4.8 and low, i.e. 13±5.3 mean and S.D. in 76-90 years as well as 60-75 years age group respectively. More than half of the respondents were aged between 60-69 years, however, the score of depression was high in 76-90 years, i.e 14.63±4.8 which slightly resemble the study conducted by (Petronell *et al.,* 2008). This study highlight the fact that older adult may also sense a loss of control over his or her life due to failing eyesight, hearing loss and other physical changes, as well as external pressures such as limited financial resources and these and other issues often give rise to negative emotions such as sadness, anxiety, loneliness and lowered self-esteem, which in turn lead to social withdrawal and apathy.

Level of education also define the depression in elderly people which will differ in coping strategies of the individual. In present study more than half of the respondents were illiterate (92.9%) where 67.2 per cent of illiterate respondents were having depression. The study shows score of depression was slightly high in illiterate compared to literate 13.±5.2.

Regarding marital status, the depression score was higher in widow/ widower than married, i.e. 14.3±4.7 in widower and 12.0±5.7 in married. The study shows most of the severely depressed respondents (75%) were widower and most of the mild depressed respondents (85.7%) were illiterate and concluded increasing age and being female is associated with depression.

Whereas risk of having depression in living arrangement who are living alone were 3.08 (with 95% CI +1.464 to 6.43) times as compared to those respondents who are living with family. Other factor associated with Nepalese older concluded there us significant correlation between feeling of depression with age, sex, marital status, family size.

Similarly, the study reveals that there is some association between worries specially worries about lack of favourable activities and worries about fear of death. It was found that risk of having depression to those respondents who worries about the lack of favourite activities were 4.167 (with 95% CI = 1.160 to 14.960) times as compared to those respondents who worries about lack of favourable activities. Similarly, the risk of having depression to those respondents who worries about the death were 6.66 (with 95% CI = 1.59 to 27.27) times as compared to those respondents who are not worried about death activities.

The study also concluded that the risk of having depression to those respondents whose caregivers constantly look after relative 8.42 (with 95% CI = 1.44 to 32.82) times as compared to those respondents whose look after wife/children which shows that elder people more confide with their wife and children rather than relatives.

Limitation

Data was collected by questionnaire method only. Observation and other methods were not used in the study. There may be sampling and respondent bias. As the sample size is smaller (210), the result could not be generalized.

Future Research Directions

Similar study can be conducted in a large population within the districts and also including other districts. And different method of data collection can also be incorporated and indepth qualitative study for the assessment can be more significant to collect quality and rich data.

Conclusion

Depression may be caused by chemical imbalance in the brain but the exact cause is unknown and it could be triggered by various factors. The main objective of the study was to find out the prevalence rate of elderly aged people residing in Naukunda rural municipality which was identified as out of 134 respondents 53.8 per cent has mild depression and 10 per cent has severe depression.

There, found to be significant association with the socio-demographic variables such as age, sex, marital status, education. Where the score of depression was high in increasing age. As it may be the fact that as age increases their dependency level to others increases as well. Similarly, depression was slightly higher in female rather than male and more widow/ widower are affected than married couple. Similary, there was significant association between worries of elderly people. In contextual factor significant variables were health problem, difficulties in performing daily activities, difficulties troubling while sleeping, difficulties in performing daily activities, worries about financial security, worries about lack of social relation, worries about dissatisfaction with old age, worries about fear of death. Similarly, in contextual factor there seems an association between depression and caregiver constantly look after. Hence, the study suggest that elder people should be given more care and moral support. As they should be continuously engaged in some of the extra-curricular activities which would reduce their loneliness.

The high rate of prevalence of depression (74.8%) in this study warrant heightened attention. As these informations very clearly suggest the depression in elderly community is very serious problem. It may be due to the fact that still in many parts of our country people are unaware of the psychosocial problems that they are facing everyday. Apart from this, the increase in rate of depression is due to lack of counselling service that could help the elder people ventilate their feelings. As depression in older age may be regarded as frailty or as inevitable result of the changes and healthcare provider may mistake older adult symptoms of depression as natural reaction of ageing which make them left untreated. Most importantly older age people do not seek for help as they believe in themselves if they seek help then they might face a problem or their children may suffer as they belongs from low economic profile. Consequently more people are staying along which make them vulnerable to mental problems. Even among those detected the intervention appears to be modest. Though many organizations and national policies have been working in aspect of mental health but our study highlights the wide gap between the reality and practice. So, prompt and appropriate intervention should be made for the proper diagnosis, treatment and rehabilitation of the elderly suffering from mental illness.

Conflict of interest: No

Acknowledgement

The authors like to express their humble gratitude to all the paticipants of the study.

References

Blazer, D.G. (2003). "Depression in Late Life: Review and Commentary". *National Library of Medicine.*

CBS (2001). *Population Monograph*. Kathmandu: Nepal Central Bureau of Statistics.

Chalise, H.N. (2014). "Depression among Elderly Living in Briddashram (Old Age Home)". *Research Gate.*

Chalise, H.N., Laxmi, Rai, S. (2013). "Prevalence and Correlates of Depression among Nepalese Rai Older Adults". *J Gerontol Geriat Res*; *2*: 130.

Choulagain, P.S. Sharma, Saillaxmi Rai, Choulagain, B.P. (2013). "Prevalence and Associated Factors of Depression among Elderly Population Living in Geriatric Homes in Kathmandu valley. Older Adults". *Journal of Institute of Medicine*; *35*: 1.

Cole, M.G. & Dendukuri, N. (2003). "Risk Factors for Depression among Elderly Community Subjects: A Systematic Review and Meta-analysis". *American Journal of Psychiatry*; *160.*

Etemadi (2009). "Factors associated with Anxiety and Depression among Elderly". *NHRC.*

Khattri, J.B. &, Nepal, M.K. (2006). "Study of Depression among Geriatric Population in Nepal". *Nepal Medical College Journal*; *8*(4): 220-23.

Mental Health and Suicide Prevention (2013). Retrieved from https://www.stevens.edu

Narendra Singh Thagunna, K.R. (October 2020). *Research Gate*. Retrieved from https://www.researchgate.net/publication/344895002: https://www.researchgate.net/publication/344895002_Demographic_factors_in_stress_anxiety_and_depression_of_older_women

National Alliance on Mental Health (2009). Retrieved from https://www.nami.org.

Poudel, N. (2005). "Problems of Elderly Population". *Global Action on Ageing.*

P.S. Choulagai, C.S. (2013). "Prevalence and associated Factors of Depression among Elderly Population Living in Geriatric Homes in Kathmandu Valley". *JIOM.*

S. Ranjan, A.B. (2013). "Prevalence of Depression among Elderly People Living in Old Age Home in the Capital City Kathmandu". *NEPJOL.*

Vyas, J.N. & Ahuja, N. (1999). *Textbook of Postgraduate Psychiatry*; 2nd edn; New Delhi, Jaypee Brothers Medical Publishers (P) Ltd.

Wikipedia, "The Free Encyclopedia". *Geriatric Depression Scale.* http://en.wikipedia.org/wiki/ Geriatric Depression Scale.

World Health Organization (WHO) (2005). *World Health Report.*

17

Scoping Review on the Predictors of Happiness and Life Satisfaction among the Older Adults

Richa Chaudhary

Introduction

Given the growing number of older adults and the growing concern about an ageing population, it is important to recognise the significance of their health. Ageing is a natural stage of life development for everyone, and seniors can successfully manage their ageing process by making positive changes to their health and quality of life.

Globally, people are living longer. Most people today aim to live well into their sixties and beyond. Both the percentage and absolute number of older people in the population are rising in many of the world's nations. Rowe and Kahn agreed that both extrinsic and intrinsic factors played a role in successful ageing. While extrinsic factors are more concerned with lifestyle factors, intrinsic factors also include genetic components. If one adopts the simplistic view that ageing is determined primarily by genetics, extrinsic factors such as personal habits, diet, exercise, and psychosocial aspects of ageing are often overlooked. Every person's life has stages, and if they can successfully navigate these stages in their own lives, they can balance their health.

According to the Rowe and Kahn Model (1997), successful ageing focuses include avoiding illness and disability, maintaining high levels of physical and cognitive function, and engaging in social and productive activities consistently. Ageing populations are a worldwide phenomenon. The improvement of the health and medical care system is correlated with an inevitable demographic reality. With declining fertility rates and longer lifespans, the population of older people (60 years of age and above) is growing faster than the global population overall. The last few decades have seen a significant shift in the population due to a large increase in the number of older people. India's senior population (those 60 and older) is expected to increase from 138 million in 2021 to roughly 194 million in 2031.

The affective and emotional state of happiness is defined by a sense of fulfilment and enjoyment. According to Miller (2004), ageing is frequently associated with positive attributes such as happiness, contentment, well-being, life satisfaction, successful ageing, quality of life, and leading a fulfilling life. One way to characterise happiness is as a critical evaluation of one's life. Sonja Lyubomirsky, a researcher in positive psychology, defined happiness as having a sense of good, meaningful, and worthwhile life along with feelings of joy, contentment, or positive well-being. The external standards of virtue and holiness are also the foundation of happiness. In addition to scientific knowledge, Aristotle listed other external measures like pride, friendliness, honesty, wittiness, intellectual virtue, and rationality in judgement.

Joy and contentment with a sense of significance are experiences that can be summed up as happiness. For older adults, cultivating meaningful living requires a great deal of inner happiness. Maintaining the physical health and mental well-being of older adults is crucial because ageing frequently brings with it disease, meaninglessness, energy loss, and a host of other external issues.

Life satisfaction is considered the best indicator of the quality of life. A broad and profound inner happiness that results from unique experiences in the outside world is known as life satisfaction. Stated differently, it conveys the person's optimistic outlook on life and conveys how they feel about their past, present, and future (Yeniaras, 2017). Higher life satisfaction in older adults appears to be associated with higher levels of health behaviour promotion (Vijaykumar, 2016). Global cognitive judgement of life quality is also measured by life satisfaction (Diener, 1985). According to Diener (1984), it is also regarded as a significant determinant of subjective well-being.

Given the significance of life satisfaction in an individual's life, it is pertinent to comprehend the correlates that contribute to life satisfaction. Elderly people are, as we all know, more vulnerable to a wide range of illnesses and other health-related issues. Taking this into account, a variety of reviews are gathered in order to identify the key elements influencing life satisfaction.

As such, it is im perative that we emphasise the benefits of ageing and turn this stage of life into a joyful one. A person's level of happiness is very important in their life. It can have a variety of positive effects on an older adult. Sustaining a high degree of happiness is regarded as the primary factor in positive ageing. An older adult who is happy is not only revitalised, but also has the resilience to handle challenges and hope for a better life. An older adult's ability to live a positive life is enhanced by happiness and an understanding of life's true purpose. Happy older adults are invaluable for their own and the community's overall social, familial, intellectual, and developmental needs.

Review of Literature

Nazri & Vanoh (2020) conducted a study entitled Malnutrition, Low Diet Quality, and its Risk Factors among Older Adults with Low Socio-economic Status: A Scoping Review. This chapter focuses on the available literature to find the prevalence of malnutrition, poor diet quality, and its associated risk factors among older adults with lower socio-economic status. Most of the studies (60%) included in this review used Body Mass Index as the tool to identify malnutrition, but none of the nutritional screening tools were considered to be the gold standard. Older adults with low socio-economic status show a poor nutritional status and lack of good quality diet. Hence, it is important to establish nutrition-related programmes and interventional studies among older adults to improve their health status as well as the quality of life.

In a study done in 2019, Harpreet Kaur Vilkhu & Sudarsan Behera aim to investigate elderly people's life satisfaction and happiness in relation to their self-esteem in New Delhi. Using the purposive sampling technique, 150 older people in New Delhi were selected for the sample, 87 of whom were male and the remaining 63 were female. Data was gathered. According to the results, there is a significant difference in the self-esteem, happiness, and life satisfaction of elderly people based on where they live, but there is no significant difference in these domains between male and female old age populations. Happiness, life satisfaction, and self-esteem were found to be positively correlated, with self-esteem serving as a major predictor of both of these outcomes.

In a study conducted by Lalitha Kumari *et al.* (2019), a descriptive research methodology was chosen to evaluate the life satisfaction and quality of life of 100 senior citizens in particular Tirupati neighbourhoods.

There was a strong correlation found between their level of education, occupation, health, access to healthcare, and government programmes and their quality of life. Life satisfaction is linked to a person's health, family income, education, access to government programmes and services, non-governmental organisations, and medical assistance. The study's findings indicated that among older adults, life satisfaction and quality of life were positively correlated.

Tan and Abdin (2019) conducted a study titled 'Happiness and Cognitive Impairment among Older Adults' to investigate the roles of Depression, Disability, and Loneliness. This study demonstrates that there has been a neglect of the notion that older persons with cognitive impairment have lower levels of happiness. The study reveals the degree of happiness among senior citizens in Singapore and examines the possible mediating effects of loneliness, social contact frequency, depression, and disability in separating happiness and cognitive scores. Approximately, 96.2 per cent of the participants expressed feeling either moderately or extremely happy. According to the regression analysis, people with higher levels of education, married or cohabiting status, or Malay ancestry were more likely to report being unhappy. Higher cognitive scores were linked to increased disability, depression, loneliness, and frequency of friend contact after socio-demographic variables were taken into account. While the majority of older adults reported being fairly or extremely happy, previous studies on the cognitively impaired showed limited reversibility. It may be possible to lessen the level of unhappiness experienced by older adults with cognitive impairment by implementing interventions that target the comorbid conditions of depression, disability, and social isolation.

Mamta Chaudhary (2017) used data from the Strategic Advisory Group of Experts to investigate socio-economic gradients in frailty among older adults in India. This study closes the knowledge gap on the relationship between adult health and global ageing by using participants who are 50 years of age or older. The study's goal was to look at the relationship between frailty and socio-economic status and how it differs by age group. The results show a negative correlation between the number of frail markers and socio-economic status, with a decrease in the overage group, both when background traits, health-risk factors, and biomarkers were controlled for. Out of the participants, roughly 26 per cent, 55 per cent, and 20 per cent, respectively, displayed 1-2 trail markers, 3-5 frailty markers, and no frailty marker. The total number of frailty markers was positively correlated with lower income and education levels in both the controlling and non-controlling groups.

Pallavi Banjare *et al.* (2015) conducted a study that examined the variables linked to life satisfaction in older rural residents of Odisha, India. The indicator of an individual's subjective well-being, life satisfaction has a direct correlation to an older adult's health and mortality. In total, 310 people responded. According to the findings, life satisfaction was most significantly influenced by cognitive health in both men and women. For both genders who live alone, have a disability, and score poorly on daily living activities, there was a significant decrease in perceived life satisfaction. Analysing and concentrating on the key elements that can raise older people's Life Satisfaction levels is crucial. Gaining more insight into these variables is beneficial. Gaining a deeper comprehension of these elements aids in dispelling the widespread fear of ageing in society.

Research on the Factor Structure of the Centre for Epidemiological Studies-Depression Scale among older adults in Chennai, India was conducted in 2013 by Srinivasan Chokkanathan and Jayashree Mohanty. This study examines the psychometric qualities of the 20-item, and the data was gathered from 200 elderly residents of Chennai, India who were 65 years of age or older and lived in the community. For both the confirmatory and exploratory factor analyses, the data were randomly divided. Two factors—positive and depressed—were found by exploratory factor analysis on a subsample (n = 200). The overall scale and its subscales were found to have a higher internal consistency. The Centre for Epidemiological Studies Depression Scale's measurement qualities were found to be appropriate based on the results. Studies and research pertaining to older adults in India are scarce.

Using data from a sample of older adults, Kamel Gana *et al.* (2013) conducted research to examine the simultaneous and cross-lagged effects between physical health (measured by self-reported diseases and self-perceived health) and life satisfaction (functioning as an enduring component of subjective well-being). There were about 899 participants in the study, ranging in age from 64 to 97. The structural equation model was used to focus and compute cross-lagged and simultaneous models. Life satisfaction did not predict the subsequent amount of health, but poor health significantly predicted the subsequent amount of life dissatisfaction, according to both cross-lagged and simultaneous coefficients.

Methodology

The original research studies and articles on determining the correlates of happiness and life satisfaction among older adults in India and other nations were taken into consideration for the literature review. Research Gate and Google Scholar were used to search for and examine the studies and articles. To find the studies that were available in the database, the search strategies were applied efficiently and in a sequential manner. Old age factors of life satisfaction were often employed as a successful search tactic. After reviewing more than five hundred research papers, we selected some for our investigation. The studies that met the inclusion criteria were chosen based on their examination of the relationships between various factors and life satisfaction in older adults. Excluded studies were those that did not meet the inclusive criteria. Full-text research and studies with an emphasis on India and other nations were extracted. The research design, inclusion-exclusion criteria, sample size, systematic definitions, and sampling strategies were used to evaluate the quality of the research studies.

Results

Following a review of the numerous research papers and articles, a noteworthy list of studies was created that was specifically focused on our investigation. The study sample, year of study, author, journal name, and title are all listed in Table 17.1. The key correlates of happiness and life satisfaction among older adults are revealed by the research studies.

Table 17.1: Various Review of Literature

Title	Author	Name of the Journal	Year of the Study	Study Sample
Malnutrition, Low Diet Quality, and its Risk Factors among Older Adults with Low Socio-economic Status: A Scoping Review	Nazri & Vanoh	Nutrition Research review	2020	Above 60 years
A Study on Happiness and Life-Satisfaction among Elderly in Relation with Self-Esteem	Harpreet Kaur Vilkhu & Sudarsan Behera	The International Journal of Indian Psychology	2019	60 and above
Assessment of Quality of Life and Life Satisfaction among Senior citizens in Selelected Areas of Triputi	T. Lalitha Kumari *et al.*	International Journal of Health Science and Research	2019	Above 60 years

(*Contd.*)

Title	Author	Name of the Journal	Year of the Study	Study Sample
Happiness and Cognitive Impairment among Older Adults: Investigating the Mediational Roles of Disability, Depression, Social Contact Frequency, and Loneliness	Tan and Abdin	International Journal of Environmental Research and Public Health	2019	60 and above
Age and socio-economic gradients in frailty among older adults in India	Mamta Chaudhary	Journal of Public Health	2017	Above 50 years
Factors associated with the life satisfaction amongst the rural elderly, Odisha, India	Pallavi Banjare *et al.*	Health and quality of life outcomes	2015	Above 60 years
Factor structure of the CES-D scale among older adults in Chennai, India	Srinivasan Chokkanathan and Jayashree Mohanty.	Ageing and Mental Health	2013	65 and above
Relationship between Life Satisfaction and Physical Health in Older Adults: A Longitudinal Test of Cross-Lagged and Simultaneous Effects	Kamel Gana *et al.*	Health Psychology	2013	60 and above

After reading through a number of research papers, we came to the conclusion that happiness and life satisfaction has a number of significant correlates and is important for everyone's life, but it is especially important for older adults. For happiness and life satisfaction, the reviews concluded that physical and psychological well-being, socio-demographic variables, education, financial resources, physical health, psychological health, social support, self-esteem, cognitive health, and quality of life are the significant factors responsible for it. Depending on the population and other demographic variables, there may be more variables. One can age successfully as an older adult if the various correlates are in balance.

Table 17.2: Various factors for the happiness and life satisfaction among old aged population

Correlates of Happiness and Life Satisfaction

Physical and Psychological Well-being	**Socio-Demographic Variables (Age)**
Education	Financial Resources
Physical Health	Psychological Health
Social Support	Self-esteem
Cognitive health	Quality of life

Discussion and Conclusion

Our present study focused on the correlates of happiness and life satisfaction among older adults. Numerous literature reviews show that various factors are responsible for the satisfaction in life and happiness among older adults. Reviews also reveal that several determinants are accountable for life satisfaction and happiness particularly in older adults. Among the various factors, physical and psychological health played a prominent role in an older adult's life. The various correlates of life satisfaction includes:

Physical and Psychological Well-being

The physical and mental health of older adults is a major factor in their life satisfaction. Maintaining physical well-being lowers the chance of internal health issues and preserves one's capacity for independent living. It also lowers the chance of developing diabetes, cancer, high Blood Pressure, and coronary heart disease.

Nutritious food, clean clothes, cosy housing, restful sleep, good health, improved sanitation, work adjustment, sufficient income, leisure, and reliable transportation are among the physiological needs.

Socio-Demographic Variables (Age)

Numerous socio-demographic factors are linked to older adults' life satisfaction. Age is a significant correlate because it offers a wealth of life experience and self-awareness. They support people's constructive growth. They also offer friendship and emotional support to all the other family members.

Education

Studies have shown that older adults with higher levels of education had fewer increases in signs of brain degeneration than older adults with lower levels of education. Even in old age, a quality education and lifelong learning are beneficial in many ways. Education helps older adults gain confidence in addition to imparting knowledge. Making the best decisions for oneself and fostering personal development are aided by it.

Finanacial Resources

For older adults, socio-economic status contributes to a high quality of life as well as other aspects of living that contribute to life satisfaction. Social and economic standing has an impact on the mental well-being of the elderly population. Age and socio-economic gradients in frailty among older adults in India is the title of a study conducted in 2019 by Mamta Chaudhary and Ravindra Chowdhary. Frail older adults from lower socio-economic backgrounds are more vulnerable to morbidity and early death. The study's goal was to determine the relationship—and how it differs among age groups—between frailty and socio-economic status. When confounders were controlled for and not, there was a positive correlation found between the fragility measure and lower income and education levels. The findings demonstrated that among older adults, socio-economic status plays a significant role.

Physical Health

Maintaining our health helps to reduce persistent pain from ailments like pinched nerves and arthritis. In terms of longevity, good health enhances our immune system, lowers blood pressure, increases metabolism, and keeps us from acquiring diseases like diabetes and obesity. Sakamoto and Okumiya's (2016) study, "Health and Happiness among community-dwelling older adults in Domkhar Valley, Ladakh, India", the survey included 117 individuals in Domkhar who were 60 years of age or older, and Japanese individuals based on their age and sex were also included. It was discovered that, despite experiencing more difficulty with everyday tasks, Domkhar residents had a higher subjective quality of life than Japanese controls.

Psychological Health

The ability to concentrate, recall, and filter out unpleasant memories is a function of cognitive health. Their thought processes and ways of looking at the world enable them to control their emotions and have a positive outlook on life. A study titled "Hypertension and Cognitive Health Among Older Adults in India" was carried out by Farron & Kabeto *et al.* (2020). This study assesses the prevalence of both diagnosed and undiagnosed hy pertension in older adults in India, as well as the relationship between it and cognitive function. Poor cognitive test performance was linked to older age, female sex, lower education, widowed status, low consumption, and underweight.

Social Support

Depression, anxiety, and stress can all be lessened with social support. It also fosters active awareness and the development of social skills in senior citizens. People who are happy with their lives also take better care of their health and share what they know about it with others. A higher quality of life is significantly promoted by social factors that are linked to life satisfaction.

Self-esteem

It is important to dispel negative stereotypes, and maintaining a healthy balance in life fosters the growth of self-esteem in older adults. The research paper, "Predictors of happiness among older Korean women living alone" (Kim & Song *et al.,* 2019), can be found here. The psychological and physical well-being of older adults determines their degree of happiness. Finding the factors that predict happiness is the main goal of this research. The demographic factors observed included health-related information, self-esteem perception, and depressive symptoms as independent variables predicting happiness.

Cognitive Health

Many of our mental and cognitive capacities begin to deteriorate as we age. These comprise deficits in processing speed, short-term working memory, memory retrieval, attention, and other problem-solving techniques. Normal ageing includes a gradual decline in both physical and psychological functioning. For this reason, an older adult's physical fitness is more crucial. Improving memory, cognitive function, and response time can have a significant impact on older adults' cognitive health.

Quality of Life

For older adults, especially those coping with significant life changes and other chronic illnesses, a high quality of life is crucial. For someone to be happy from the inside and out, they must feel needed or useful, and one way to achieve this is by engaging in creative mental activities. A study conducted in Kerala, India by Deshmukh & Dongre *et al.* (2015) was titled "Role of Social, Cultural, and Economic Capitals in Perceived Quality of Life Among Old Age People". The purpose of this study was to investigate the relationship between a population's collective social, economic, and cultural characteristics and the elderly population's perceived quality of life. All three capitals significantly viewed the environment and psychological health domains as troubled.

As one ages and experiences more losses, it is critical to maintain growth-related objectives to enhance life satisfaction rather than concentrating solely on setbacks. The aforementioned result demonstrates the variety of factors influencing older adults' life satisfaction. Physical and mental health, education, financial resources, social support, economic satisfaction, cognitive health, quality of life, self-esteem, and happiness are among the various factors. A person's level of life satisfaction may be influenced by a variety of factors.

After analysing the research and literature, it is clear that older people can benefit from appropriate positive interventions, which can improve their psychological well-being and help them age gracefully.

Being old is not just about how old you are; it is also about how much fun you have had and how well you've lived your life. People's opinions no longer easily flustering them. We learn to feel at ease in our own flesh. In one's life, having a purpose and maintaining relationships have different positive effects. Therefore, it is up to the individual to age well. Important happiness supplements that support older adults in leading positive lives include social relationships, self-esteem, well-being, quality of life, life satisfaction, health, work status, positive thinking, economical needs, and forgiveness. All it takes to make the elderly happy is a little respect and consideration.

References

Banjare, P., Dwivedi, R. & Pradhan, J. (2015). "Factors Associated with the Life Satisfaction amongst the Rural Elderly in Odisha, India". *Health and Quality of Life Outcomes. 13*(1).

Brasher, M., George, L., Shi, X., Yin, Z., Zeng, Y. (2017). "Incorporating Biomarkers into the Study of Socio-economic Status and Health among Older Adults in China". *SSM—Population Health.*

Chaudhary, M., Chowdhary, R. (2018). "Age and Socio-economic Gradients in Frailty among Older Adults in India". *J Public Health. 27*(5): 675-685.

Chokkanathan, S., Mohanty, J. (2013). "Factor Structure of the CES-D Scale among Older Adults in Chennai, India". *Ageing & Mental Health. 17*(4): 517-525.

Diener, E., Emmons, R.A., Larsen, R.J. & Griffin, S. (1985). "The Satisfaction with Life Scale". *Journal of Personality Assessment, 49*, 71-75.

Diener, E. (1984). "Subjective well-being". *Psychological Bulletin, 95*, 542-575.

Kim, J., Song, Y., Kim, T., Park, K. (2019). "Predictors of Happiness among Older Korean Women Living Alone". *Geriatr Gerontol Int.*

Farron, M.R., Kabeto, M., Dey, A.B., Banaerjee, J., Levine, D.A., Langa, K. (2020). "Hypertension and Cognitive Health among Adults in India". *J Am Geriatr Soc.*

Kumari, L.T., Hemalatha, S. & Bhagyalaxmi, M. (2019). "Assessment of Quality of Life and Life Satisfaction among Senior Citizens in Selected Areas of Triputi". *International Journal of Health Science and Research.*

Nazri, N.S., Vanoh, D., Leng, S.K. (2020). "Malnutrition, Low Diet Quality and its risk factor among Older Adults with low Socio-Economic Status: A Scoping Review". *Nutrition Research Review.*

Tan, J.H. (2019). "Happiness and Cognitive Impairment among Older Adults: Investiagating the Mediational roles of Disability, Depression, Social Contact Frequency and Loneliness". *Int. J. Environ. Res. Public Health. 16*(24).

World Health Organization (2015). *World Report on Ageing and Health* (W.H. Organization, Ed.): World Health Organization. Luxembourg: World Health Organization.

18

Preserving Health

Understanding Diabetes and Mental Well-being in the Elderly Persons of India

Eshita Chatterjee, Sanchita Ghosh and *Sristi Dutta*

The relationship between diabetes, mental well-being, and ageing in the context of the elderly population in India is a complex interplay of physical and psychological factors that requires a multidisciplinary approach, which includes psychology as a crucial component. Understanding what diabetes is and how it affects the body is crucial in order to appreciate the intricate connection between diabetes and mental health.

What is diabetes?: Diabetes, commonly known as diabetes mellitus, is a persistent medical condition impacting the body's control of blood sugar (glucose). Glucose serves as a vital energy source for cells and muscles, necessitating proper regulation to ensure the body's optimal functioning.

Prevalence in India

People frequently refer to India as the 'diabetes capital' of the world, with urban areas bearing a heavier burden. The Union Ministry of Family and Health Welfare conducted a study in January 2021 and found that 26.1 per cent of urban respondents aged 60 or older had high blood sugar levels, while only 9.3 per cent of senior citizens in rural areas had the same condition. Among Indians over 45, 11.5 per cent were diagnosed with diabetes, and senior citizens had a higher prevalence (14%) compared to those aged 45–59 (9%). Gender did not significantly affect diabetes cases among senior citizens (Mishra *et al.*, 2021).

Biological Interplay of Diabetes

Different types of diabetes are classified based on different causes and will vary depending on the underlying causes of their treatment. Understanding the specific type of diabetes is crucial, as its management may differ from that of other types. Diabetes has the potential to directly influence the brain and its functioning. Understanding these biological interactions is crucial to comprehending how diabetes can affect mental health.

Classification of Diabetes

Type 1 diabetes: It is a condition that develops when the immune system unintentionally targets and destroys the cells in the pancreas that make insulin. Insulin is a necessary hormone that facilitates the uptake of glucose into cells, aiding in blood sugar regulation. For the remainder of their lives, people with this type of diabetes need to inject insulin or use an insulin pump to manage their blood sugar levels.

Type 2 diabetes: This is a common kind of diabetes that is frequently associated with sedentary lifestyles, bad eating habits, and obesity. In this kind of situation, the pancreas may find it difficult to generate enough insulin to maintain an appropriate blood sugar balance, and the body becomes resistant to the effects of insulin. Initially, we can control it through dietary modifications, physical activity, and lifestyle adjustments, oral medicines or insulin injections.

Gestational diabetes: This type arises during pregnancy due to hormonal changes leading to insulin resistance. It typically resolves post-pregnancy, but women with a history of gestational diabetes face an elevated risk of developing Type 2 diabetes later in life.

Pre-diabetes: Blood sugar levels that are higher than usual but not quite to the point of Type 2 Diabetes is referred to as pre-diabetes. It acts as a warning indicator, suggesting a higher chance of Type 2 Diabetes later on. Elevated blood sugar levels fall short of the diabetic threshold ranges are found in people with prediabetes.

Geriatric Conditions and Diabetes

Geriatric Syndromes: The co-existence of diabetes and various geriatric syndromes, such as falls, cognitive decline, and dizziness, adds a layer of complexity to care for the elderly. Understanding the connections between these syndromes and diabetes is vital for a comprehensive approach.

Urinary Incontinence and Visual Impairment: Elderly individuals with diabetes are at a greater risk of experiencing urinary incontinence and visual impairment. We need to address these conditions, often linked to diabetes, from both a medical and psychological perspective. Coping with these challenges can affect mental well-being.

Diabetes and Mental Health Challenges in the Elderly

This topic delves into the intersection of diabetes and mental health in the elderly, emphasizing their distinct challenges and elaborating on comorbid conditions associated with diabetes, exploring the effects of depression, anxiety, eating disorders, and sleep disorders.

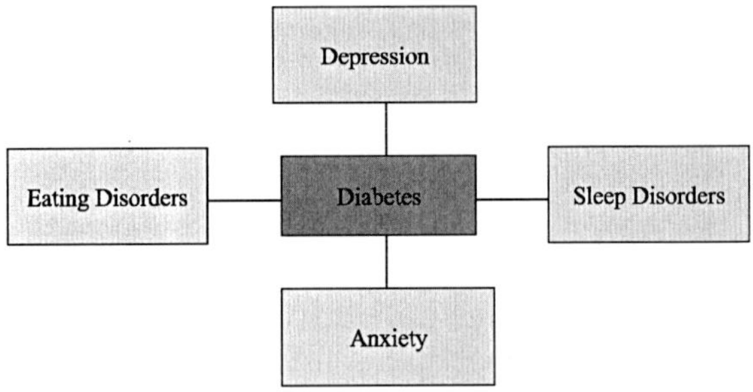

Fig. 18.1: Mental Illness Associated with Diabeties

Depression: It is a medical condition characterized by enduring feelings of sadness and a reduced interest in activities that were previously pleasurable. This emotional state can significantly impact your ability to function effectively both in your social, professional, and personal lives. The incidence of medically significant depressive symptoms among individuals with diabetes stands at approximately 30 per cent. Simultaneously, estimates place the occurrence of major depressive disorder (MDD) at around 10 per cent, which is twice as high as the general prevalence among individuals without chronic medical conditions. In the elderly, the coexistence of diabetes and depression poses a complex and interrelated set of challenges. This demographic is already more susceptible to both conditions due to age-related physiological changes and life circumstances. According to Varghese *et al.* (2017), elderly individuals (60+) with diabetes have a heightened risk of experiencing geriatric conditions. Notably, urinary incontinence and visual impairment are prevalent in this group. Research confirms links between diabetes and various geriatric syndromes—falls, cognitive decline, depression, dizziness, and hearing issues—across diverse racial and geographical contexts. The prevalence of depression is not only higher in elderly people with diabetes, but there is also a greater likelihood of developing anxiety.

Anxiety: Anxiety, characterized by feelings of apprehension, fear, or heightened alertness, is the response of your mind and body to Individuals with diabetes face a 20 per cent higher likelihood of ex periencing anxiety at certain stages of their lives compared to those without diabetes. Anxiety is a prevalent concern among the geriatric population dealing with diabetes. The unique challenges of ageing and managing diabetes can contribute to increased levels of anxiety in this group. Factors such as health complications, medication management, and lifestyle adjustments can all contribute to heightened anxiety levels among older adults with diabetes. The incidence of anxiety is not only elevated in elderly individuals with diabetes, but there is also an increased probability of developing eating disorders.

Eating Disorders: Compared to the general population, people with diabetes, both type 1 and type 2, have a higher prevalence of eating disorders, which include symptoms like binge eating, bulimia nervosa, and anorexia nervosa. The occurrence of eating disorders is not only heightened in elderly individuals with diabetes, but there is also an increased likelihood of developing sleep disorders.

Sleep Disorders: The incidence of sleep disorders is notably higher in individuals with diabetes when compared with those who do not have diabetes. People with diabetes often have trouble sleeping because of a number of factors, such as pain or discomfort from peripheral neuropathy, regular limb movements, sudden changes in blood glucose levels at night that can cause hypoglycemic and hyperglycemic episodes, having to go to the bathroom at night, and depression that is linked to these issues. Older individuals with diabetes often experience disruptions in their sleep patterns, which can exacerbate the challenges posed by their condition. These sleep disturbances might include difficulties in falling asleep, staying asleep throughout the night, or experiencing poor sleep quality. The interaction between diabetes and sleep disorders can create a complex cycle, as inadequate sleep can negatively impact blood glucose control, while elevated blood sugar levels can also interfere with sleep. According to Öztürk *et al.* (2015), the study indicates that depression and subpar sleep quality are prevalent within the elderly diabetic population. Alongside the duration of diabetes, the presence of microvascular complications, particularly retinopathy and neuropathy, emerges as a notable factor influencing both sleep quality and the individual's state of depression.

Relationship between Diabetes and Mental Health

Indeed, there are several connections between diabetes and mental health. Here is an elaboration on the relationship between diabetes and mental well-being. Diabetes is a persistent medical condition that affects the body's capacity to regulate blood glucose levels effectively.

Biological Factors: The brain relies on glucose as its primary energy. When blood glucose levels are consistently too high (as in uncontrolled diabetes), it can affect cognitive function. This may result in symptoms such as memory problems, difficulty in concentrating, and altered emotional states. In severe cases, excessively high or low blood sugar levels can even lead to confusion and altered consciousness. Reaven *et al.* (1990) provided evidence indicating that there was an inverse relationship between glycemic control and performance on cognitive tasks evaluating learning, reasoning, and complex psychomotor skills in a limited sample of elderly individuals with Type 2 diabetes.

Emotional and Psychological Impact: Coping with diabetes can indeed present emotional challenges. The constant need to monitor blood sugar, take medication, and make dietary and lifestyle adjustments can lead to stress, anxiety, and depression. The fear of complications associated with diabetes, such as vision problems, nerve damage, and wounds that heal slowly, can also contribute to mental health issues—Acceptance of diagnosis, denial, and uncertainty. Individuals recently diagnosed with diabetes may struggle with accepting the condition, leading to a range of emotional responses, from depression and grief to denial and avoidance. These emotional responses can hinder effective self-management and glycemic control. Diabetes management can be a significant source of psychological distress (Garrett & Doherty, 2014).

Behavioural Factors: Diabetes management requires individuals to make significant lifestyle changes, including dietary modifications and regular exercise. For some, adhering to these changes can be difficult, leading to feelings of guilt, frustration, and self-blame when blood sugar levels are not well controlled. This can negatively impact self-esteem and contribute to mental health challenges.

Self-efficacy, as proposed by Bandura (1977), suggests that the level of confidence individuals have in their ability to effectively carry out health-related behaviours plays a crucial role in determining which specific behaviours they are likely to adopt. Research has shown a positive correlation between high self-efficacy and diabetes self-management (Krichbaum, Aarestad & Buethe, 2003; Sarkar *et al.*, 2006). Therefore, individuals who have elevated self-efficacy and a positive attitude towards self-care are more likely to participate in diabetes self-management activities (Rose, Fliege, Hildebrandt, Schirop & Klapp, 2002). Therefore, a reduction in diabetes-related distress and an increased sense of competence in carrying out the necessary self-management tasks required for enhancing overall health outcomes may be associated with high self-efficacy.

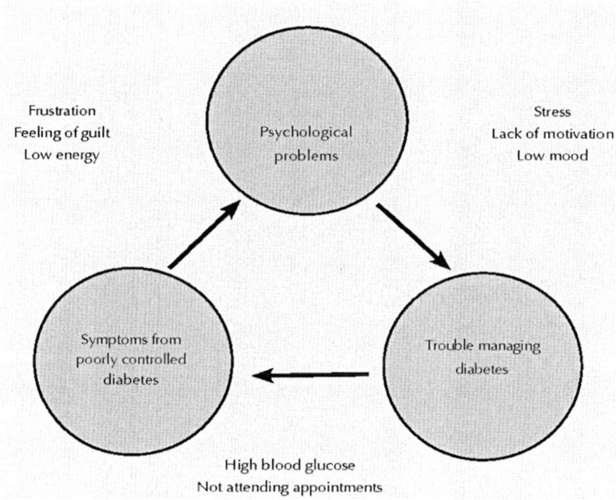

Fig. 18.2: Diagnosis of and screening for diabetes

Early diagnosis and screening for diabetes are critical to preventing complications and managing the condition effectively. This chapter explores the various methods and criteria used to diagnose and screen for diabetes.

Methods for Diagnosing Diabetes

Fasting Blood Glucose Test: This diagnostic evaluation involves examining blood glucose levels after an overnight fast. A fasting blood glucose measurement of 126 mg/dL or higher on two separate occasions is a dependable indication of diabetes.

Blood Sugar Charts: Doctors work with individuals to set appropriate blood sugar targets, which vary based on factors like age, to help them manage their diabetes effectively. Optimal blood sugar levels are as follows:

	Optimal blood sugar levels for non-diabetic individuals	**Optimal blood sugar levels for diabetic individuals**
Prior to meals	72-99 mg/dL	80-130 mg/dL
2 hours post-meal	Below 140 mg/dL	Below 180 mg/dL

Hemoglobin A1c Test

The A1c test assesses the average blood glucose levels over the preceding two to three months. An A1c level of 6.5 per cent or above is a sign of diabetes, as indicated in the chart below:

	A1C Percentage	**Estimated Average Glucose (EAG)**	
In-range	< 5.7%	< 117 mg/dL	6.5 mmol/L
Prediabetes	5.7-6.4%	117-137 mg/dL	6.5-7.6 mmol/L
Diabetes	> 6.4%	> 137 mg/dL	> 7.6 mmol/L
Increased risk of complications	6.5%	140 mg/dL	7.8 mmol/L
	7.0%	154 mg/dL	8.6 mmol/L
	7.5%	169 mg/dL	9.4 mmol/L
	8.0%	183 mg/dL	10.1 mmol/L
	8.5%	197 mg/dL	10.9 mmol/L
	9.0%	212 mg/dL	11.8 mmol/L
	9.5%	226 mg/dL	12.6 mmol/L
	10%	240 mg/dL	13.4 mmol/L

Screening for diabetes

Risk Assessment: Identifying individuals at risk of developing diabetes is crucial. Factors such as obesity, family history, and a sedentary lifestyle increase the likelihood of developing diabetes. This chapter outlines how healthcare providers assess risk and provide recommendations for regular check-ups and lifestyle modifications.

Screening in High-Risk Groups: Certain populations, such as those with a family history of diabetes or a history of gestational diabetes, require early and specific screening. This section also discusses the importance of culturally tailored approaches, particularly for high-risk ethnic groups.

Continuous Glucose Monitoring (CGM): An in-depth exploration of CGM devices and their role in diabetes management and diagnosis, particularly in cases of poorly controlled diabetes or hypoglycemia risk.

Screening for Mental Disorders

Screening for mental health disorders in individuals with diabetes is an important aspect of their overall care. It helps identify and address any psychological or emotional issues that may be impacting their well-being and diabetes management.

Regular Assessment: Healthcare providers should conduct regular assessments of mental health as part of the routine care for individuals with diabetes. Healthcare providers can conduct these assessments during diabetes check-ups or as part of a comprehensive annual examination.

Questionnaires and Interviews: Healthcare professionals may use standardized questionnaires and interviews to assess a patient's mental health. For example, the Global Mental Health Assessment Tool (GMHAT) app was used to screen for mental illness among type 2 diabetes mellitus people in Mysore (Majgi *et al.*, 2022).

Clinical Observation: Healthcare providers should also pay attention to clinical observations, such as changes in mood, behaviour, and psychosocial functioning during interactions with the patient.

Management and Treatment of Diabetes

Lifestyle Modifications: In the management of diabetes, lifestyle modifications play a central role. These changes encompass dietary adjustments, physical activity, and stress management.

Dietary Modifications: Macronutrient Balance: Understanding the balance of carbohydrates, fats, and proteins in one's diet is essential. This chapter delves into the science of macronutrients, explaining how different dietary choices can impact blood glucose levels.

Glycemic Index and Portion Control: Exploring the concept of glycemic index helps individuals make informed food choices. Portion control is also crucial to maintaining stable blood sugar levels.

Medications and Insulin: The management of diabetes often involves medications and, in some cases, insulin therapy. There are various classes of diabetes medications and their mechanisms of action.

This includes oral medications like metformin, sulfonylureas, and newer classes like SGLT-2 inhibitors and GLP-1 receptor agonists. But it is also important for individuals to understand the potential side effects and risks associated with different medications.

Various forms of insulin are available, encompassing rapid-acting, short-acting, intermediate-acting, and long-acting insulin varieties and their respective roles in blood glucose control, along with the methods of delivering insulin, from traditional injections to more advanced insulin pumps and continuous glucose monitoring (CGM) systems. We emphasize the importance of individualized insulin regimens, taking into account factors like meal timing and activity levels.

Psychotherapy for the Treatment of Diabetes and its Comorbid Conditions

Mental health conditions, similar to diabetes, are manageable, and the presence of both conditions does not diminish their treatability. Rather, it means that each condition necessitates distinct treatment approaches. Therapy is indeed a valuable and effective treatment option that can benefit individuals, whether they have mental health conditions or not. It provides a safe space to explore and address various challenges, understand one's mental health, and develop strategies to cope with life's stressors.

Skilled professionals assist individuals in navigating sources of stress, gaining insight into their mental health conditions, recognizing triggers that exacerbate their issues, and acquiring valuable coping skills. There are several common types of therapy:

Cognitive-Behavioural Therapy (CBT): Cognitive-Behavioural Therapy o perates on the premise that thoughts, feelings, and behaviours are interconnected. The time is ripe for healthcare organizations to emphasize the effectiveness of CBT for individuals with diabetes and comorbid depression and to make CBT readily accessible to patients within primary care settings (Li *et al.*, 2017). CBT has two main aspects. The cognitive aspect aims to cultivate constructive beliefs about one's life, while the behavioural side focuses on acquiring skills to engage in healthier actions. Through CBT, patients learn to recognize negative or unhelpful thoughts related to their diabetes, such as feelings of hopelessness or self-blame, and it also works on replacing negative thought patterns with more constructive ones, which can lead to a healthier emotional response. With the help of CBT, patients also learn to recognize warning signs and triggers for relapse into negative thought patterns or behaviours and employ strategies to prevent them. Cognitive behavioural therapy (CBT) stands out as a proven and well-supported intervention for alleviating diabetes distress, depressive symptoms, and health-related anxiety in individuals managing diabetes.

Extensive evidence attests to the effectiveness of CBT in enhancing treatment adherence and overall quality of life for diabetic patients. Targeted therapeutic techniques aid individuals in managing their daily routines, sustaining motivation for treatment, and cultivating a positive outlook on life. This comprehensive approach contributes significantly to the holistic well-being of patients grappling with diabetes (Abbas *et al.*, 2023).

Cutting-edge studies propose that cognitive behavioural therapy (CBT) can effectively tackle psychological insulin resistance by directly targeting the underlying beliefs contributing to this phenomenon.

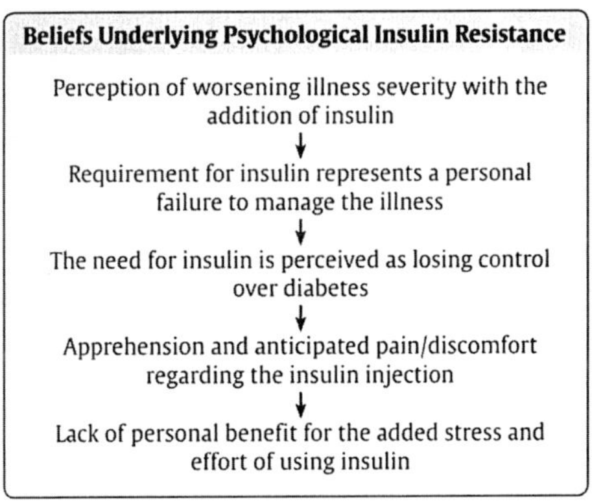

Features of Psychological Insulin Resistance

Since diabetes management relies significantly on the ongoing engagement of the individual, motivational and behaviour-change strategies can be potent tools. Healthcare professionals involved in diabetes care can bolster successful behaviour changes by utilizing motivational techniques, such as guiding individuals in weighing the pros and cons of change and boosting their self-confidence. Research has indicated that optimism and compassion can also be beneficial in this regard.

Family Therapy: The purpose of family therapy is to enhance communication, resolve conflicts, and improve problem-solving within a family unit. People frequently use this approach to address concerns like eating disorders. The process begins with an understanding of the dynamics within the family, exploring how family members' behaviours and communication patterns might be affecting the individual's diabetes management and mental health. It provides psycho-education about diabetes and mental health issues, helping family members gain a better understanding of the conditions, their symptoms, and the challenges faced by the individual.

Family therapy also aims to enhance the support system for the individual by encouraging family members to be more involved in the diabetic person's care and provide emotional and practical support. Therapists work with the family to improve communication skills since open and effective communication is vital for addressing the individual's needs and concerns regarding their health and mental well-being.

Furthermore, family therapy provides a safe space for family members to express their emotions, fears, and concerns related to the diabetic individual's condition, fostering empathy and support. If the individual's condition leads to conflicts within the family, family therapy can constructively address and resolve these conflicts. Additionally, it can be helpful in setting realistic and achievable goals for managing both diabetes and mental health issues, emphasizing the importance of teamwork.

Stress Management: A diabetes diagnosis often brings prolonged stress, which can potentially contribute to elevated blood sugar levels. Moreover, stress can make it more challenging to adhere to your diabetes management plan. It is advisable to monitor your stress levels along with your blood sugar readings and look for any patterns. By doing so, you can become more aware of your stress triggers and warning signs, allowing you to take proactive steps to prevent stress-related blood sugar spikes. This may involve seeking guidance from a professional to acquire relaxation and coping techniques. Stress management techniques can help individuals with diabetes better control their condition. Some effective stress management strategies include mindfulness meditation, deep breathing exercises, progressive muscle relaxation, regular physical activity, adequate sleep, and seeking support from friends, family, or support groups etc. A study provides evidence that outpatient stress management training can effectively enhance glycemic control in individuals with Type 2 diabetes. After a 1-year follow-up period, participants who underwent stress management skill training exhibited an approximate 0.5 per cent decrease in their Hb A1c levels compared to the control group (Surwit *et al.*, 2002).

Mindfulness-based Cognitive Therapy (MBCT): Sasikumar & Latheef (2017) conducted a study that highlights the potential benefits of mindfulness-based stress reduction and *yoga* in diabetes management for the elderly. A separate research investigation demonstrated the enduring efficacy of mindfulness-based cognitive therapy (MBCT) in diminishing emotional distress among individuals with diabetes and compromised emotional well-being. Given the correlation between emotional distress and unfavourable diabetic outcomes, incorporating MBCT into the treatment regimen could prove to be a significant supplementary strategy for effectively managing diabetes (van Son *et al.*, 2014). These approaches integrate psychological well-being with physical health. Psychologists can play a key role in teaching mindfulness techniques and helping elderly individuals with diabetes reduce stress and improve their emotional well-being.

Behavioural Interventions: Psychologists can provide behavioural interventions to promote lifestyle modifications, such as encouraging physical activity, dietary changes, and stress management techniques, which are integral to effective diabetes management.

Diabetes Care Teams

Diabetes management is a collaborative effort that involves the roles of various healthcare professionals.

Endocrinologists: We explain the roles and responsibilities of endocrinologists in diabetes care, including their ex pertise in hormone-related disorders.

Dietitians: The role of dietitians is to provide guidance on meal planning and nutrition. We highlight the role of Certified Diabetes Educators (CDEs) in educating and supporting individuals with diabetes.

Podiatrists: The role of podiatrists in foot care and the prevention of diabetes-related complications is also very significant.

Psychologists: Psychologists provide assistance for individuals with diabetes by offering emotional support to help them navigate the psychological and emotional difficulties associated with living with a chronic condition. This involves addressing issues such as stress, anxiety, depression, and other emotional challenges linked to managing diabetes.

Psychiatrists: Individuals with diabetes experience severe mental health issues, such as clinical depression or anxiety disorders. A psychiatrist prescribes and manages medications to address these conditions.

Conclusion

In conclusion, this chapter has explored the intricate relationship between diabetes and mental well-being in the elderly population of India. As we delved into the challenges and comorbid conditions, it became evident that managing diabetes transcends the physical realm and deeply impacts psychological health.

India's ageing population faces unique challenges in coping with diabetes and its emotional toll. The burden of chronic disease, coupled with cultural factors and limited access to mental health resources, necessitates a comprehensive approach. Understanding the interplay between these two health domains is a crucial step towards preserving the well-being of elderly individuals. This chapter underscores the vital importance of understanding and addressing the intricate relationship between diabetes and mental well-being among elderly people in India. Through this understanding and compassionate care, we can pave the way for healthier, happier, and more fulfilling lives for our elderly population.

References

Abbas, Q., Latif, S., Ayaz Habib, H., Shahzad, S., Sarwar, U., Shahzadi, M.,. .. & Washdev, W. (2023). "Cognitive Behaviour Therapy for Diabetes Distress, Depression, Health Anxiety, Quality of Life and Treatment Adherence among Patients with Type-II Diabetes Mellitus: A Randomized Control Trial". *BMC Psychiatry, 23*(1): 86. https://doi.org/10.1186/s12888-023-04546-w

Bandura, A. (1977). "Self-Efficacy: Toward a Unifying Theory of Behavioural Change". *Psychological Review, 84*(2): 191. https://psycnet.apa.org/doi/10.1037/0033-295X.84.2.191

Britneff, E. & Winkley, K. (2013). *The Role of Psychological Interventions for People with Diabetes and Mental Health Issues.*

Centres for Disease Control and Prevention. (2023, May 15). *Diabetes and mental health.* Centres for Disease Control and Prevention. https://www.cdc.gov/diabetes/managing/mental-health.html

Diabetes and mental health. Mental Health America (n.d.). https://www.mhanational.org/diabetes-and-mental-health

Garrett, C. & Doherty, A. (2014). "Diabetes and mental health". *Clinical Medicine, 14*(6): 669. https://doi.org/10.7861%2Fclinmedicine.14-6-669

Joseph, N., Unnikrishnan, B., Babu, Y.R., Kotian, M.S. & Nelliyanil, M. (2013). "Proportion of Depression and Its Determinants among Type 2 Diabetes Mellitus Patients in Various Tertiary Care Hospitals in Mangalore City of South India". *Indian Journal of Endocrinology and Metabolism, 17*(4): 681. https://doi.org/10.4103%2F2230-8210.113761

Khandelwal, D., Dutta, D., Chittawar, S. & Kalra, S. (2017). "Sleep Disorders in Type 2 Diabetes". *Indian Journal of Endocrinology and Metabolism, 21*(5): 758. https://doi.org/10.4103%2Fijem.IJEM_156_17

Krichbaum, K., Aarestad, V. & Buethe, M. (2003). "Exploring the Connection Between Self-Efficacy and Effective Diabetes Self-F Management". *The Diabetes Educator*, *29*(4): 653-662.

Latheef, F. (2017). *Effects of Mindfulness Based Stress Reduction (MBSR) on Stress, Depression and Mindfulness Among Type 2 Diabetics-A Randomized Pilot Study.*

Li, C., Xu, D., Hu, M., Tan, Y., Zhang, P., Li, G. & Chen, L. (2017). "A Systematic Review and Meta-Analysis of Randomized Controlled Trials of Cognitive Behaviour Therapy for Patients with Diabetes and Depression". *Journal of Psychosomatic Research*, *95*, 44-54.

Majgi, S.M., Mal, N.M., Krishna, M., Suresh, H., Ebuenyi, I.D. & Jones, S. (2022). "Screening for Mental Illness Using GMHAT App of Patients with Type 2 Diabetes Mellitus at a Teaching Institute Hospital in India—A Cross-sectional Study". *Journal of Family Medicine and Primary Care*, *11*(10): 5924. https://doi.org/10.4103%2Fjfmpc.jfmpc_277_22

Mishra, N.L., Gaikwad, R. & Bapat, S. (2021). "Diabetes among Senior Citizens more Prevalent in Urban India: LASI Report". *Health. Down To Earth.*

Öztürk, Z.A., Yesil, Y., Kuyumcu, M.E., Savas, E., Uygun, Ö., Sayýner, Z.A. & Kepekçi, Y. (2015). "Association of Depression and Sleep Quality with Complications of Type 2 Diabetes in Geriatric Patients". *Ageing Clinical and Experimental Research*, *27*, 533-538.

Professional, C.C. Medical. (n.d.). *A1C: What it is, Test, Levels & Chart. Cleveland Clinic.* https://my.clevelandclinic.org/health/diagnostics/9731-a1c

Reaven, G.M., Thompson, L.W., Nahum, D. & Haskins, E. (1990). "Relationship Between Hyperglycemia and Cognitive Function in Older NIDDM Patients". *Diabetes Care, 13*(1): 16-21. https://doi.org/10.2337/diacare.13.1.16

Robinson, D.J., Coons, M., Haensel, H., Vallis, M., Yale, J.F. and Diabetes Canada Clinical Practice Guidelines Expert Committee. (2018). "Diabetes and Mental Health". *Canadian Journal of Diabetes*, *42*: S130-S141. https://doi.org/10.1016/j.jcjd.2017.10.031

Robinson, D.J., Luthra, M., Vallis, M. and Canadian Diabetes Association Clinical Practice Guidelines Expert Committee. (2013). "Diabetes and Mental Health". *Canadian Journal of Diabetes*, *37*: S87-S92. https://doi.org/10.1016/j.jcjd.2013.01.026

Rose, M., Fliege, H., Hildebrandt, M., Schirop, T. & Klapp, B.F. (2002). "The Network of Psychological Variables in Patients with Diabetes and their Importance for Quality of Life and Metabolic Control". *Diabetes Care*, *25*(1): 35-42. https://doi.org/10.2337/diacare.25.1.35

Surwit, R.S., Van Tilburg, M.A., Zucker, N., McCaskill, C.C., Parekh, P., Feinglos, M.N.,. ...& Lane, J.D. (2002). "Stress management improves long-term glycemic control in type 2 diabetes". *Diabetes Care*, *25*(1): 30-34. https://doi.org/10.2337/diacare.25.1.30

Types of diabetes. Diabetes Education online (11 July 2012). "https://dtc.ucsf.edu/types-of-diabetes/

van Son, J., Nyklíček, I., Pop, V.J., Blonk, M.C., Erdtsieck, R.J. & Pouwer, F. (2014). "Mindfulness-Based Cognitive Therapy for People with Diabetes and Emotional Problems: Long-Term Follow-up Findings from the DiaMind Randomized Controlled Trial". *Journal of Psychosomatic Research*, *77*(1): 81-84. https://doi.org/10.1016/j.jpsychores.2014.03.013

19

Understanding the Complex Nexus of Mental Health and Ageing in India

Challenges, Initiatives and Pathways to Psychological Well-being

Arpita Kackar

Introduction

Health is a multidimensional concept that encompasses physical, mental and social well-being. As individuals age, the importance of health takes on a new dimension, with an emphasis on maintaining a good quality of life and independence. The World Health Organization (WHO) defines health as "A state of complete physical, mental and social well-being and not merely the absence of disease or infirmity".

From a biomedical perspective health is often seen as the absence of disease. This view focuses on diagnosing and treating specific-illnesses without necessarily considering the broader aspects of well-being. Many health professionals advocate for holistic approach to health, which takes into account physical, mental, emotional and social factors. This perspective recognizes that these aspects are interconnected and impart overall well-being.

Some emphasize health as the ability to perform daily activities and maintain independence. This becomes particularly relevant in old age when the ability to carry out routine tasks determines the quality of life.

Importance of Health in Old Age

- ***Maintaining independence:*** Health is crucial in old age as it directly influences an individual's ability to remain independent. Good health enables seniors to perform daily activities without assistance, preserving their autonomy and dignity.

- ***Quality of life:*** Health is a major determinant of quality of life in old age. Physical well-being allows seniors to engage in hobbies, social activities and spend time with loved ones, contributing to a fulfilling and joyful life (Bowling, 2007).
- ***Reducing dependency:*** Poor health can lead to increased dependency on others, causing emotional and psychological distress. Maintaining health minimizes the need for constant care giving, fostering a sense of self-reliance (Bloom, 2015).
- ***Preventing chronic conditions:*** As individuals age, the risk of chronic conditions such as diabetes, heart disease and arthritis increases. Prioritizing health through regular exercise a balanced diet and medical check-ups can help prevent or manage these conditions effectively (Centres for Disease Control, 2022).
- ***Mental health:*** Mental well-being is equally important in old age. Addressing mental health issues like depression and anxiety contributes to cognitive function, memory and overall emotional stability.
- ***Social engagement:*** Staying socially active promotes mental stimulation and emotional well-being. Good health enables seniors to participate in social activities, fostering a sense of belonging and reducing feeling of isolation.
- ***Coping with changes:*** Ageing comes with physical and emotional changes. Good health provides resilience to cope with these changes, making the transition into old age smoother and more positive.
- ***Longevity:*** While genetics play a role, leading a healthy lifestyle can significantly increases one's chances of a longer, more vibrant life. By avoiding risky behaviours and adopting healthy habits, seniors can enhance their longevity.

Health and Mental health are closely intertwined and significantly impact each other. A strong relationship exists between physical well-being and mental well-being, with both aspects influencing one another in various ways:

- ***Biological interconnection:*** The brain and body are interconnected through complex biological systems. Neurotransmitters and hormones that regulate physical health can also affect mood, emotions and cognitive function. For instance, imbalances in neurotransmitters like serotonin can contribute to both mental health disorders and physical conditions.

- ***Impact of physical health on mental health:*** Poor physical health, chronic illnesses and pain can lead to emotional distress, anxiety and depression. Individuals dealing with chronic pain or serious illnesses may experience feeling of hopelessness, frustration and a decline in their overall mental well-being.
- ***Impact of mental health on physical health:*** Mental health issues can contribute to physical health problems. Stress, anxiety and depression, for example, can weaken the immune system, increase inflammation and potentially lead to conditions like cardiovascular disease, gastrointestinal issues or autoimmune disorders.
- ***Lifestyle choices:*** Lifestyle factors play a role in both physical and mental health. Engaging in regular exercise, maintaining a balanced diet, getting enough sleep and avoiding harmful substances can positively impact both aspects. Conversely, unhealthy lifestyle choices can contribute to poor mental health and exacerbate physical health issues.
- ***Chronic conditions:*** Managing chronic physical health conditions can be emotionally taxing and impact mental well-being. The stress of managing a condition like diabetes or heart disease can lead to anxiety and depression.
- ***Ageing:*** As individuals age the relationship between health and mental health becomes more evident. Older adults may experience cognitive changes, chronic illnesses and social isolation, all of which can impact mental well-being.
- ***Coping and resilience:*** Good physical health can provide a foundation for coping with stressors and challenges, enhancing one's resilience to mental health issues. Similarly, strong mental health enables individuals to cope better with physical health challenges.
- ***Self-esteem and body image:*** A positive self-image and body image contribute to mental well-being conversely, struggling with body image or self-esteem issues due to physical appearance can lead to emotional distress.
- ***Mind body techniques:*** Practice such as meditation, mindfulness and *yoga* demonstrate the connection between mental and physical health. These techniques can reduce stress, improve mood and positively impact physical health markers like blood pressure and heart rate.

- ***Quality of life:*** Both physical and mental health are critical determinants of an individual's overall quality of life. When one aspect is compromised, it can affect an individual's ability to engage in daily activities, maintain relationships and find enjoyment in life.

Mental Health

Mental health refers to a person's emotional and psychological well-being encompassing their ability to handle stress, maintain healthy relationships, make sound decisions and cope with life challenges. It involves emotional resilience, self-esteem and the capacity to experience a wide range of emotions in a balanced manner.

Importance of Mental Health in Geriatric Population

- ***Coping with transitions:*** Old age often involves significant life transitions, such as retirement, loss of loved ones and changes in physical health. These transitions can lead to feelings of isolation, grief and anxiety. Good mental health equips seniors with tools to cope with these changes and maintain a positive outlook.
- ***Preventing cognitive decline:*** Mental health plays a pivotal role in preserving cognitive function. Engaging in mentally stimulating activities such as reading and social interactions can help to delay the onset of cognitive decline, such as dementia and Alzheimer's diseases.
- ***Enhancing quality of life:*** Seniors with good mental health experience higher quality of life. They are more likely to engage in activities they enjoy, maintain relationships and find joy in their daily routines.
- ***Fostering resilience:*** Resilience is the ability to bounce back from adversity; seniors with strong mental health are better equipped to handle setbacks, maintaining a positive attitude even in challenging situations.
- ***Promoting social connections:*** Mental well-being encourages social interactions. Seniors who feel mentally healthy are more likely to participate in social activities, fostering a sense of belonging and reducing feeling of loneliness.
- ***Reducing the stigma:*** Encouraging discussions around mental health in old age reduces the stigma associated with seeking help.

This enables geriatrics to reach out for support when needed, ensuring timely interventions.

- ***Managing chronic conditions:*** Many older adults grapple with chronic health conditions. Good mental health helps them manage these conditions more effectively, promoting adherence to treatment plans and reducing stress-related complications.
- ***Embracing positive ageing:*** Ageing is a natural process and mental health plays a significant role in embracing it positively. Seniors who prioritize their mental well-being are more likely to see ageing as an opportunity for growth, wisdom and now experiences.
- ***Family and community dynamics:*** Sound mental health enables seniors to maintain positive relationship with family members and their communities. This support network is invaluable for emotional well-being and sense of belonging.
- ***Reducing healthcare costs:*** Investing in mental health can lead to substantial savings in healthcare tools. Preventive measures, like managing stress and practicing mindfulness can contribute to better physical health and reduced medical expenses.

Mental health is an integral part of overall well-being, especially in old age. It influences how geriatrics navigate the challenges, transitions and joys that come with ageing. By promoting mental health through, engagement in stimulating activities, seeking social connections and addressing psychological well-being, older adults can lead richer, more fulfilling lives. Recognizing the significance of mental health in old age paves the way for a society that values the holistic well-being of its ageing population.

As individuals grow older, their mental health can become more vulnerable. While everyone's experience is unique, here are some of the common symptoms to watch for:

- ***Persistent sadness or depression:*** A prolonged feelings of sadness, hopelessness or loss of interest in previously enjoyed activities could be a sign of depression. Older adults might also experience physical symptoms like change in appetite or sleep patterns.
- ***Anxiety and excessive worry:*** Frequent and excessive worrying, restlessness, irritability and difficulty in concentrating could indicate an underlying anxiety disorder. Physical symptoms, such as muscle tension or rapid heart rate may also be present (Domenech-Abella, 2019).

- ***Social withdrawal:*** Avoiding social interactions, isolating one from friends and family and losing interest in social activities may point to poor mental health. Isolation can exacerbate feelings of loneliness and sadness.
- ***Changes in appetite and weight:*** Significant changes in eating habits resulting in either weight gain or weight loss may signal emotional distress. Poor mental health can impact one's relationship with food.
- ***Sleep disturbances:*** Insomnia trouble, falling asleep or staying asleep and restless sleep can be indicative of mental health issues conversely. Oversleeping or excessive fatigue can also be related to poor mental well-being.
- ***Lack of interest or motivation:*** Losing interest in hobbies, activities and responsibilities that were once enjoyable or important may suggest a decline in mental health. A lack of motivation can impact daily functioning.
- ***Feeling of worthlessness:*** Persistent feelings of low self-worth, guilt or feeling like a burden on others can be signs of poor mental health. Negative self-talk and sense of hopelessness are also concerning.
- ***Difficulty in concentrating or making decisions:*** Cognitive changes such as trouble in concentrating, making decisions or remembering things could indicate underlying mental health issues, such as depression or anxiety.
- ***Physical complaints:*** Unexplained physical symptoms, such as headaches, stomachaches or general aches and pains may have an underlying mental health component. Emotional distress can manifest as physical discomfort.
- ***Irritability or agitation:*** Frequent irritability, restlessness or angry outbursts that are out of character may be signs of underlying emotional struggles.
- ***Negative changes in hygiene or self-care:*** A decline in personal grooming, neglecting hygiene and a lack of interest in self-care could be indicative of poor mental health.
- ***Increased substance use:*** Turning to alcohol, prescription medications or other substances to cope with emotional distress can be a sign of poor mental health.
- ***Memory problems:*** While mild memory changes are normal with ageing, severe memory problems that impact daily functioning and relationships may indicate a more significant issue.

- ***Suicidal thoughts or self-harm:*** Any mention of suicide or self-harm should be taken seriously. If you or someone you know is experiencing these thoughts seeks help immediately while ageing is a natural part of life, certain factors can contribute in the potential symptoms to arise.

Some Common Causes of Poor Mental Health in Old Age

- ***Physical health issues:*** The presence of chronic illnesses, pain and physical limitation can lead to feeling of frustration conditions such as arthritis, heart disease and mobility issues can impact both physical and mental well-being (Blazer, 2003).
- ***Isolation and loneliness:*** Seniors may experience social isolation due to factors like the loss of friends and family members, retirement or limited mobility. Loneliness can lead to feelings of sadness, anxiety and a decline in mental health.
- ***Loss and grief:*** The loss of loved ones, whether through death or other circumstances, can trigger intense grief and mourning. Coping with multiple losses as one age can contribute to depression and sense of emptiness.
- ***Financial stress:*** Limited income, increased medical expenses, and the rising costs of living can create financial stress for seniors. Worrying about security can lead to anxiety and negatively impact well-being.
- ***Cognitive decline:*** Age related cognitive changes and potential development of conditions like dementia can lead to frustration, confusion and a sense of control. These challenges can impact mental health and emotional stability.
- ***Transitions and change:*** Life transitions such as retirement, moving to a new location, or adjusting to an empty nest can disrupt routines and a sense of purpose, potentially causing anxiety and depression.
- ***Stigma and lack of support:*** Older adults may come from generations that stigmatized mental health issues, leading them to avoid seeking help. Additionally, limited access to mental health resources and support can increase their challenges.
- ***Loss of independence:*** Reliance on others for daily activities can lead to a loss of independence, resulting in feelings of frustration, helplessness and a decline in self-esteem.
- ***Limited social connections:*** Reduced social opportunities due to physical limitations or the loss of friends can lead to feelings of isolation and further contribute to poor mental health.

- ***Negative attitudes towards ageing:*** Societal stereotypes and negative attitudes towards ageing can impact self-perception and contribute to feelings of worthlessness or a lack of purpose.
- ***Medication side effects:*** Many seniors take multiple medications for various health conditions. Some medications may have side effects that impact mental health, such as cognitive changes or mood disturbances (Pratt *et al.*, 2011).
- ***Lack of meaningful activities:*** A lack of engaging and fulfilling activities can lead to boredom and a sense of purposelessness, negatively affecting mental well-being.
- ***Unresolved past trauma:*** Past experiences, including trauma, can resurface and impact mental health as individual age. These experiences may not have been properly addressing earlier in life.

Geriatric mental health stands apart from other mental health domains due to the unique needs of the elderly population, presenting a multitude of hurdles. These difficulties permeate all aspects of care, from acknowledging mental health issues to seeking assistance and maintaining treatment adherence. The nation grapples with challenges such as an insufficient number of trained professionals, limited geriatric mental health infrastructure and inadequate financial resources (United Nations, 2002). Although early intervention can lead to accurate diagnosis and successful treatment of geriatric mental health problems, there is a mistaken belief that these issues are an inherent part of ageing. The rapidly increasing ageing demographic intensifies the significance of geriatric mental health as a substantial public health predicament in India (Agrawal & Arokiasamy, 2010). Here are some general and specific clinical challenges in Indian geriatric mental health, accompanied by potential solutions to address these obstacles.

Challenges in Geriatric Mental Health in India

1. ***Shifting demographics of ageing:*** With a population of 1.31 billion, India holds the first largest population globally (Rao & Shaji, 2007). Remarkable progress in medicine, public health, nutrition and sanitation has significantly prolonged life expectancy (Prince *et al.*, 2007). The ageing demographic currently exceeding 100 million is projected to reach 324 million by 2050 (Liebig & Rajan, 2003), accounting for 20 per cent of the total population. Notably,

elderly women, due to social vulnerability and health concerns, tend to experience more emotional and financial insecurities than men (Rajan, Mishra & Sarma, 2013; Nygren *et al.*, 2005; Patel *et al.*, 2006; Singh & Pradhan 2006). This disparity contributes to a higher prevalence of mental health issues among elderly women. Moreover, a substantial portion of the elderly resides in rural regions and often possesses limited education, resulting in a heightened correlation with dementia and related challenges.

2. ***Diverse clinical presentation in geriatric mental health:*** A significant challenge in geriatric mental health revolves around the wide-ranging diversity in clinical presentations, which complicates the process of diagnosing and treating these issues. Unlike the clear-cut clinical patterns often found in textbooks, there is usually an absence of such patients. Many patients tend to deny the existence of mental health problems and are hesitant to seek assistance (O'Sullivan & Chao, 2008; Liberman *et al.*, 2001). Frequently physical symptoms take precedence as the primary concern, masking the underlying psychological issues. Variability in mobility levels among patients necessitates a thorough understanding on the part of clinicians. Additionally, patients frequently take multiple medications and consult multiple doctors, necessitating a collaborative approach among healthcare providers for optimal outcomes (Katon, 2003).
3. ***Dementia care complexity in india:*** Dementia poses a prominent challenge in the realm of elderly care in India. Beyond depression, dementia stands as the most prevalent neuropsychiatric condition among individuals aged 60 and above. Extensive epidemiological studies have demonstrated that dementia's prevalence among those over 85 years ranges from 18 per cent to 38 per cent escalating to 28 per cent to 44 per cent among those exceeding 90 years (Kalaria *et al.*, 2008). Projections indicate a potential doubling of these figures by 2030. Notably, research underscores that up to 90 per cent of challenging or psychiatric behaviours in individuals with dementia, who lack the capacity to articulate their symptoms, may stem from environmental factors or caregiver interactions (Shaji, Jithu & Jyothi, 2010; Shaji, Bose & Kuriakose, 2009).
4. ***Societal influences on geriatric mental health:*** Numerous factors, encompassing social, psychological and biological dimensions, intricately shape an individual' mental well-being at any given juncture. Among the various life stressors, ageing individuals

grapple with loss of independent living capabilities, exposing them to heightened susceptibility for socio-economic decline during retirement (Mudey, Ambekar, Goyal, Agarekar & Wagh, 2011). In India, the elderly population faces distinct social challenges. This includes:

Eighty per cent of the entire population of elderly citizens lives in rural areas, making up the majority of the senior population. There will be challenges in providing services to them as a result of this (Kaushal, 2014).

Only 2.76 million of the 28 million senior people are covered by the government's pension programme, with the majority of those people living in urban areas (Chakrabati & Sarkar, 2011).

Thirty per cent of the older population is living below the poverty line, which is a significant share. There are a number of underlying social factors that have an impact, either directly or indirectly, on the mental well-being of the elderly population. These factors include transitions into retirement, housing concerns, financial insecurities, limited access to transportation, and separation from children as a result of parents living in India and children living abroad (Pal & Palacios, 2011).

5. ***Elderly rehabilitation and intervention in senior residences:*** Old age homes provide a crucial haven for elderly individuals grappling with solitude, health issues and depression (Kumar, Roy & Kar, 2012). Four resource categories contribute to addressing geriatric mental health concerns in India:

   (a) Psychiatric hospitals and state funded nursing homes.
   (b) Private psychiatric clinics, hospitals and nursing homes.
   (c) Non-governmental organizations.
   (d) Informal support *via* family caregivers (Murali & Tibrewala, 2008).

   Various early intervention approaches for health and social services are currently implemented and feasible for our country, including community-centred interventions:

   (a) Outpatient clinics.
   (b) Domiciliary visits.
   (c) Geriatric day care programmes.

Additional rehabilitation approaches encompass:

(a) Residential care and nursing support.
(b) Hospital based care.
(c) Respite care.
(d) Home-based solutions.

These services are essential in India for the following reasons:

(a) Due to decreasing family sizes and the patriarchal society, women often shoulder the responsibility of caring for the elderly, even when they willingly take it up. This prolonged caregiving can negatively impact their emotional and physical health, even in larger households (Shaji, Smitha, Lal & Prince, 2003).
(b) The growing burden of providing care for patients suffering from mental disorders, particularly those exhibiting severe symptoms, has resulted in an increase in the amount of stress experienced by caregivers (Agrawal, 2013).
(c) Caregivers often face blame and accusations of providing inadequate care (Emmatty *et al.*, 2006), with minimal community-based mental health services available to support the elderly suffering from chronic disorders and their caregivers (Shaji, Arun Kishore, Lal & Prince, 2002). The lack of such services poses challenges for geriatric mental healthcare and increases the risks for the elderly (Patel & Thara, 2003).

6. ***Limited awareness of geriatric mental health care in primary care settings:*** Primary healthcare providers who visit patients lack the necessary training to detect and address mental health issues like dementia and depression in the elderly which are prevalent in over 40 per cent-50 per cent of the population (Brijnath & Manderson, 2003). Despite increased sub-speciality geriatric training, there is still a lack of focus on recognizing and treating mental illness among the elderly (Mccabe, 2006). Consequently, it is important to provide training for peripheral health workers and community health volunteers to identify and refer elderly patients for timely and appropriate rehabilitation, addressing the needs of this vulnerable population.
7. ***Integrating religion and spirituality into geriatric mental health care:*** Religion and spirituality play significant roles as social and psychological factors in the lives of older adults, and there

is ongoing interest in understanding how they impact health (Thompson, 2013). Numerous studies have revealed that older individuals with stronger religiosity tend to report better health status (Agarwal *et al.*, 2011). The connection between organized religiosity and health status has been established as positive. It is crucial for psychologist to engage in open discussions about these aspects and to honour the religious beliefs of their clients during treatment (Tharayil, Thomas, Balan & Shaji, 2013).

8. ***Establishing geriatric mental health clinics in india:*** In India, the ratio of mental health professionals with approximately 5000 psychiatrists, to 21 million geriatric population in need of mental health services is inadequate (Shaji, George, Prince & Jacob, 2009). Geriatric clinics are often operated within hospitals through departments like neurology, psychiatry and geriatrics (Schölzel-Dorenbos, Meeuwsen & Olde Rikkert 2010). Given the Indians context, the following actions are urgently needed:

    (a) Implementation of cost free or subsidized memory clinics that not only diagnose dementia in the elderly but also provide education and support to families in need.
    (b) Careful consideration of clinic naming, positioning and promotion strategies.
    (c) Addressing the potential misconceptions that memory clinic's solely target memory problems.
    (d) Procurement or creation of suitable materials for the clinic's operation, considering the societal context and target audience.
    (e) Adaptation of assessment tools and procedures for cognitive evaluation including tests in local languages and those suitable for literate individuals.

9. ***Absence of appropriate diagnostic tools in India:*** The existing diagnostic criteria are not tailored to effectively evaluate the mental health of older individuals. This often results in either misdiagnosis or lack of diagnosis altogether, leaving the disorder untreated. It is crucial to develop Indian diagnostic criteria that take into account the cultural nuances of psychiatric assessment (Azermai *et al.*, 2012; Taylor, Aizenstein & Alexopoulos, 2015). Recent findings highlight that dementia in the elderly is influenced by a DLB phenotype distinct from that in younger adults. Overall, the absence of proper diagnostic criteria and clinical interventions exacerbates the challenges faced by geriatric mental health in India.

10. ***Misconceptions about ageing in India:*** Numerous misconceptions surround the concept of ageing. Worth-mentioning is that these misconceptions are embraced by practitioners, patients and policy makers alike. These include the following points:

    (a) Associating age with illness.
    (b) Assuming that disability is an unavoidable and escalating aspect of old age.
    (c) Believing that the loss of social connections results in older adults becoming lonely and isolated.
    (d) Incorrectly assuming that most elderly individuals are depressed, suffering from dementia, or reliant on others.
    (e) Mistakenly thinking that old age leads to both physiological and social uniformity.
    (f) Erroneously equating ageing with mortality.

11. ***Addressing clinical issues of geriatric depression:*** Depression often remains inadequately treated in elderly patients due to the presence of multiple concurrent medical and psychological concerns (Jain & Aras, 2010; Grover & Malhotra, 2015). Among older adults, there is a tendency to experience syndrome depression, a state not always meeting the complex criteria for a major depression diagnosis but capable of progressing to major depression if untreated or undiagnosed (Sengupta & Benjamin, 2015). According to World Health Organization (WHO, 2001) report, individuals aged 55 and above dealing with depression exhibit a death rate four times higher than those without depression, underscoring a notably elevated prevalence of geriatric depression in India, with a median rate of 21.9 per cent (Sharma *et al.*, 2016). Research has identified a demographic factor linked to symptoms of geriatric depression, which often go unnoticed by many seniors due to the perpetuation of a stereotype that associates depression with normal ageing (Fountoulakis *et al.*, 2003). Geriatric depression might manifest as a recurrence of prior depressive episodes experienced at younger age or as an initial episode arising in late life (Fiske *et al.*, 2003). Typically, depression in older adults is closely associated with physiological changes or brain abnormalities (Taylor, Aizenstein & Alexopoulos, 2013). These changes could also stem from early developments triggered by Alzheimer's disease or the initial stages of vascular dementia (Korczyn & Halperin, 2009).

12. ***Impact of psychologically issues on medical conditions:*** In the elderly geriatric patients frequently contend with a spectrum of ailments encompassing both non-cognitive physical and psychiatric illness, each bearing psychological symptoms (Prakash *et al.*, 2007). The prevalence of concurrent illnesses vividly underscores the intricate relationship between physical and mental health, shaped by a myriad of interacting factors. Overlooking an underlying organic basis for psychopathological condition can result in considerable health complications and even mortality when individuals are inappropriately placed in psychiatric care. Therefore, possessing a foundational comprehension of psychiatric disorders is imperative for medical practitioners, facilitating accurate diagnosis and effective intervention strategies (Sharma *et al.*, 2016).
13. ***Addressing substance abuse in the elderly and its management:*** In individuals aged 60 to 64, the prevalence of alcohol consumption stood at 25.4 per cent (Murthy *et al.*, 2007; Benegal, 2005). Late onset abusers, who begin alcohol use after turning 65 due to adverse life events such as retirement and loss of loved ones (Das, Pal & Ghosal, 2012) constitute a significant group. These events, prevalent in old age, often connect with psychological and psychopathological coexisting conditions, particularly mood and anxiety disorders (Blazer & WU, 2009). Similarly, the prevalence of heavy smokers decreases with age; the proportion falls from 22.7 per cent between 60 and 64 years to 8.2 per cent between 65 and 75 years (Goswami *et al.*, 2005). Notably, the treatment approach for these patients differs substantially from that of adult substance abusers, as their requirements and underlying factors diverge considerably (Cho, 2012).
14. ***Addressing sexual concerns in the elderly:*** In India, sexuality is often viewed as a taboo, perpetuating myths that older individuals and asexual and lack of interest in or engagement with sexual activities (Rao, Ismail, Darshan & Tandon, 2015). In contrast, a majority of individuals aged 60 and above remain actively involved in and derive pleasure from their sexual lives. Unfortunately, elderly individuals frequently become targets of jokes related to physical cognitive and sexual limitations (Merghati-Khoei, Pirak, Yazdkhasti & Rezasoltani, 2016). Several common age related health conditions like dementia, impaired vision or hearing, erectile dysfunction and the use of medical devices such as catheters can adversely affect self-perception and hinder sexual expression

(Lalitha, 2012; De Sousa, 2015). Furthermore, additional factors like controlling entities such as care facilities or caregivers, stereotypical portrayals in media, and the lack of recognition of the sexual identities of LGBT and queer older adults contribute to the suppression of sexual agency in the elderly (Sears, 2013).

15. ***Understanding elder abuse:*** Contemporary research indicates that one out of every ten seniors experiences elder abuse. The interplay between elder abuse and mental health is intricate and significant, warranting careful attention. Notably, evidence highlights a heightened prevalence of depression and anxiety among victims of elder abuse, contributing to social isolation, escalated suicide risk and emotional turmoil (Anand, 2016; Grover, 2015). Individuals subjected to abuse frequently report a range of ailments, encompassing chronic pain, arthritis, neurological issues and gynaecological disorders. Among elder abuse victims who grapple with additional debilitating mental health conditions, premature mortality is not uncommon, as their ability to defend themselves is often compromised. Some may even exhibit a multitude of physical or somatic complaints without an easily identifiable diagnosis (Kaur *et al.*, 2015).
16. ***Geriatric psychiatry research:*** Prior to implementing any relief mechanisms for the elderly population, rigorous testing is im perative (Collins *et al.*, 2014; Math & Srinivasarju, 2010). However, conducting research in India poses various obstacles, encompassing financial constraints, ethical considerations and issues related to obtaining research permissions. A significant contributing factor to the deficiency in research is the insufficient government funding allocated to support ongoing research endeavours. Presently, the Government of India's investment in research remains limited.

The global population is rapidly ageing. Between 2015 and 2050, the proportion of older adults worldwide is projected to almost double, rising from approximately 12 per cent to 22 per cent (Government of India, 2011). In absolute numbers this signifies an anticipated growth from 900 million to 2 billion individuals aged 60 and above. Elderly individuals encounter unique physical and mental health challenges that require recognition and support (Khandelwal, 2003). Mental health issues are frequently underestimated by healthcare professionals and the elderly themselves, compounded by the stigma surrounding such conditions, which deters people from seeking help. Challenges like inadequate training opportunities, lack of awareness, and scarcity of chronic care disease models and unequal distribution of healthcare resources collectively pose significant hurdles for the field of geriatric psychiatry in India (Joshi *et al.*, 2003). While government policies offer social benefits to the elderly the courage remains insufficient and necessitates reform. To tackle geriatric mental health concerns, it is crucial to bolster training and research, raise awareness, establish community based rehabilitation initiatives, enhance capacity and develop a comprehensive primary healthcare framework. Raising public and professionals' awareness about unmet geriatric mental health needs, fostering cross sector collaboration and building a capable workforce are paramount. Swift implementation of national policies, programmes and laws targeting geriatric mental health, while advocating for empowerment, is urgently needed. Incremental efforts in various domains will greatly contribute to advancing a geriatric mental health in India.

Geriatric rehabilitation encompasses series of clinical measures designed to decrease illness and enhance the mobility, autonomy and self-awareness of older individuals, providing them with the tools to lead a life of high quality. In advance healthcare systems, geriatric care has become an integral component of hospital-based healthcare provision. More frequently, specialized entities have entered this common domain, offering comprehensive and dedicated care for the elderly. Their goal is to enhance overall health and the ability to perform daily tasks. These initiatives involve a multidisciplinary assessment overseen by a geriatric physician. This assessment covers various aspects including medical history, physiotherapy, nutrition, respiratory health and psychological well-being.

Existing infrastructure for geriatric mental healthcare support for older individuals dealing with mental health issues is available across four main settings: General hospital psychiatry facilities encompassing both public and private hospitals/medical colleges, as well as private and public psychiatric hospitals; Non-governmental organizations (NGOs) like HelpAge India and AKDSI; and the informal sector represented by family caregivers. Among these, the primary source of care is provided by families. Notably, India currently hosts just two institutions that provide specialized training in geriatric mental health, providing a modest annual output of four DM-trained geriatric psychiatrist. The services provided encompass a spectrum from acute care management to extended long term care. Acute care predominantly takes place within hospital settings. Urban areas and centres of excellence host specialized memory clinics, which offer clinical support, information and advice to individuals dealing with memory issues. ARSDI has even outlined guidelines for the establishment of such clinics. Options for care include day care centres, residential care facilities catering to long term and short respite care needs, domiciliary care services that extend to caregiver training; formal nursing care by geriatric home nurses and other trained personnel support networks for families are available alongside a dedicated dementia helpline manned by trained staff to address queries related to dementia.

Present Human Resources for Geriatric Mental Health Care

Health care personnel (HCPs) in India span from specialized experts to community health workers and community volunteers. By April 2021, approximately 1,266,942 doctors with an MBBS qualification had registered across various states. In 2018, over 75 per cent of these doctors were engaged as general practitioners (GPs) (Prakash, O. & Rajkumar, 2009). According to NMHS 2015-16 report, India only had 0.3 psychiatrist, 0.07 psychologist and 0.07 social workers available per 1,00,000 individuals (Thirunavukarasu, 2010). By 2019, this number had given to around 9,000 with an annual influx of 700 new psychiatrists. Given these statistics, India's ratio stands at 0.75 psychiatrists per 1,00,000 people, falling short of the recommended threshold of at least 3 psychiatrists per 1,00,000.

Around ten institutions nationwide offer MD-geriatric programmes, which incorporate cognitive assessments and the identification of cognitive and mental disorders within their curriculum. However, these programmes are concentrated primarily in a handful of private medical colleges and institutes of national importance (INIS). Furthermore, the availability of DMGMH (doctor of medicine in geriatric mental health) or DM in geriatric psychiatry is extremely limited, producing only four graduates annually (Shaji *et al.*, 2010).

Future Trajectory

The elderly demographic within mental healthcare has often been categorized as a distinct population whose care typically seems feasible only at more advanced facilities like medical colleges, mental health establishment (MHES) or well regarded institutions. Delivering high quality geriatric mental health (GMH) care necessitates a comprehensive, team based approach that draws on multiple disciplines. The provision of services should consider: (a) Depth, encompassing the range of conditions that can be effectively managed. (b) Breadth involving the variety of conditions, and (c) Length, extending to the population that should have access to these services. At each juncture of the existing healthcare system, it is crucial to incorporate policy insights and strategic approaches to tackle anticipated challenges, while mindful available resources.

The role of the family is paramount in the psychological well-being and rehabilitation of geriatric individuals in India. Indian society places significant emphasis on family bonds and support structures, and these plays a crucial role in the care and rehabilitation of older family members. India's cultural fabric places a strong emphasis on familial and societal bonds and harnessing these resources is essential for ensuring the elderly population's mental health and overall quality of life. Families offer a primary source of emotional support to geriatric individuals. The love, care and companionship provided by family members are vital for combating loneliness, depression and anxiety. Many families take on the responsibility of care giving, assisting with daily activities managing medications and ensuring a safe environment. Families often provide financial support for medical expenses, rehabilitation and daily living costs. This financial security eases the economic burden on older adults. Families' gatherings and celebrations provide opportunities for social interaction and reduce feelings of isolation among older members. Indian families often uphold cultural and traditional values that emphasize respect for elders. This fosters a sense of dignity and self-worth in geriatric individuals, positively impacting their psychological well-being. Encouraging older family members to share their life experiences and wisdom contributes to their cognitive well-being and sense of purposes. Family members can serve as advocates within the healthcare system, ensuring that geriatric individuals receive appropriate medical care and rehabilitation services. During health emergencies or crisis, families are crucial timely medical intervention and rehabilitation.

Societal support networks, including neighbours and friends, can provide additional companionship and emotional support to older adults, especially those who may not have family nearby. Community based programmes and organizations can organize social events, workshops and activities specifically designed for older adults, promoting social engagement and mental being. Society can participate in and support campaigns that combat the stigma surrounding mental health issues in the elderly population, encouraging early intervention and treatment. Creating public spaces and transportation systems that are accessible and safe for older adults contributes to their physical and mental well-being. Encouraging individuals to volunteer their time and skills to help older adults can provide companionship and practical assistance. Advocacy groups and societal organizations can push for policies and rights that protect and promote the well-being of older adults, ensuring their dignity and autonomy.

The psychological well-being and rehabilitation of geriatric individuals in India require a collective effort from families, society and government. Focusing on psychological well-being rehabilitation for the elderly population in India is essential not only for their individual benefit but also for the well-being of families, communities and society as a whole. By investing in geriatric mental health support, India can ensure that its ageing population enjoys a dignified and fulfilling life, while also reducing the strain on healthcare and social system.

20

The Risk Factors Associated with Mental Health Problems in the Elderly

Rupesh Ranjan, Richa Priyamvada and *Suprakash Chaudhury*

Introduction

The process of ageing is associated with different challenges like physical disturbances, loneliness, chronic diseases, emotional weakness, a lack of family support, and financial dependence (Bakhtiyari *et al.*, 2017; Ong *et al.*, 2016; Tastan *et al.*, 2019). One of the major contributing factors to disturbances in mental and physical health is retirement. This makes the person feel unimportant—the feeling of ignorance, unemployment, low self-esteem, and sometimes dependency on basic needs etc. Studies reported that approximate 15 per cent of the elderly population suffered from mental health issues (Organization, 2013). An increase in mental health problems is reported in old age, like anxiety problems, depression, and numerous somatic complaints. Feelings of loneliness and lack of a support system in the family reduce love and happiness in the family and threaten the mental health of the elderly (Brosschot *et al.*, 2006). The happiness concept works for the maintenance of health, including life satisfaction, reducing depression, increasing the range of thinking and abilities etc. (Diener *et al.*, 2018). Whereas distress leads to different psychological problems, the stress level of an individual is easily determined by different biological and psychological factors. Elderly abuse is a significant factor and is recognized as a stressful experience that affects their mental health adversely.

Epidemiology

A relative rise in the elderly population from 12 to 22 per cent has been noticed and will reach around 2 billion people. The rise in cognitive impairment and psychiatric illness is a major problem with active ageing, with increases in mental illness ranging from mild personality change to severe illness. The severity of depressive symptoms is seen in 10-25 per cent of the elderly population above 65 years old (Hesser *et al.*, 2013) and incidence rate increases after the age of 81 years (Giri *et al.*, 2016). In 5.6 per cent of depression cases, severe depressive episodes were also noticed (Reynolds *et al.*, 2015). A recent study done in Korea discovered a rise in cases of depression by up to 17.8 per cent and anxiety disorders by up to 15 per cent in population studies among common psychiatric illnesses (Kim *et al.*, 2018). Other authors also found in their studies that patients suffering from anxiety disorder had a predominance of depression; its prevalence stands at 11.4–12.3 per cent, including 5.8 per cent phobia and 6.8–9.1 per cent mood disorders. 13 per cent of the elderly population suffering from anxiety disorder also has depressive disorder, and 36 per cent of depressive patients had a comorbidity of anxiety disorder (WHO, 2015), with the increase in life events and challenges faced, a high prevalence rate of depression is expected in the present age. Researchers explain the increase in affective disorders with the proportion of U-shaped, which reflects the maximum increase of affective symptoms in young and elderly people.

Biological Markers for Mental Health Risks in the Elderly

The ageing process brings about significant changes in the body and brain, which can influence mental health outcomes in the elderly population. The biological markers are associated with an increased risk of mental health disorders in older adults, from neurochemical imbalances and inflammatory processes to genetic predispositions and structural brain changes. Understanding these biological markers is crucial for early detection, intervention, and personalized treatment approaches to mitigate mental health risks in the elderly. Mental health disorders among the elderly pose a growing concern due to the global ageing population. While psychological, social, and environmental factors play a significant role, an understanding of the underlying biological markers is im perative for a comprehensive approach to mental health risk assessment and management in older adults.

Neurochemical Imbalances

Neurotransmitters are critical for communication within the brain and between nerve cells. Changes in neurotransmitter levels, such as reduced serotonin or dopamine, have been associated with mood disorders like depression and anxiety in the elderly. Neurotransmitter imbalances can affect mood regulation, cognition, and overall mental well-being. Monitoring these imbalances through neuroimaging and biomarker assessments can aid in identifying individuals at risk and tailoring interventions.

Inflammatory Processes

Chronic low-grade inflammation, often referred to as "inflammation", is a hallmark of ageing. Inflammation in the body can have a profound impact on the brain, leading to cognitive decline and an increased susceptibility to mental health disorders. Raised levels of pro-inflammatory markers (e.g. interleukin-6 and C-reactive protein) have been related to depression and neurodegenerative diseases in the elderly. Targeting inflammation through lifestyle changes, diet, and medication may help mitigate mental health risks.

Genetic Predisposition

Genetic factors contribute significantly to an individual's susceptibility to mental health disorders. Certain genetic variations may increase the risk of conditions such as Alzheimer's disease, schizophrenia, and bipolar disorder. Advances in genetic research have identified specific gene variants associated with these disorders, allowing for early detection and personalized interventions. Genetic counselling and testing can provide insights into an individual's risk profile and guide preventive measures.

Structural Brain Changes

Structural changes in the brain accompany ageing, including reduced brain volume, alterations in white matter integrity, and the presence of cerebral microinfarcts. These changes can impact cognitive function and increase the risk of mood disorders and cognitive impairment. Magnetic resonance imaging and positron emission tomography of the brain enable the visualization of these structural changes, aiding in the early detection and management of mental health risks.

Neuroendocrine Dysregulation

The hypothalamic-pituitary-adrenal (HPA) axis can become dysregulated with age. Conditions like depression and anxiety have linked to chronic stress and dysregulation of the HPA axis. Cortisol, a hormone produced during stress, is often used as a biomarker to assess HPA axis activity. Understanding the interplay between stress, hormone levels, and mental health is crucial for identifying at-risk individuals.

Oxidative Stress

Oxidative stress contributes to cellular damage and ageing. This oxidative damage can affect brain cells and increase the risk of cognitive decline and mental health disorders. Biomarkers of oxidative stress, such as malondialdehyde (MDA) and glutathione levels, can provide insights into an individual's susceptibility to mental health risks. Antioxidant-rich diets and lifestyle modifications may help mitigate oxidative stress.

Neuroplasticity and Growth Factors

Neuroplasticity plays a crucial role in cognitive function and mental health. Brain-derived neurotrophic factor (BDNF) promotes neuroplasticity and supports the survival of nerve cells. Reduced BDNF levels have been associated with conditions like depression and neurodegenerative diseases. Assessing BDNF levels and promoting activities that enhance neuroplasticity can contribute to better mental health outcomes.

Sleep Disturbances

For proper functioning of the brain and overall well-being, sleep is very essential. Sleep disturbances, including insomnia and sleep apnea, become more prevalent with age and are associated with an increased risk of mental health disorders. Sleep-related biomarkers, such as melatonin and sleep architecture patterns, can provide insights into an individual's sleep quality and potential mental health risks. Addressing sleep disturbances through behavioural interventions and, if necessary, medication can have positive effects on mental health.

Biological markers associated with mental health risk in the elderly encompass a complex interplay of neurochemical, genetic, inflammatory, and structural factors. Early detection and intervention based on these markers hold the potential to identify individuals at risk and implement personalized strategies to prevent or manage mental health disorders.

Psychological Factors are Associated with Mental Health in the Elderly Population

Various internal and external factors influence the psychological well-being of the elderly. There are psychological factors that impact mental health in the elderly population. From coping strategies and personality traits to resilience and self-esteem, understanding these psychological factors is essential for promoting positive mental health outcomes and designing effective interventions for older adults.

Psychological factors play a pivotal role in shaping the mental health of the elderly population. As people age, their psychological well-being becomes increasingly susceptible to changes influenced by life experiences, personality traits, and coping strategies. The psychological factors are associated with mental health in the elderly.

***Coping Strategies*:** Effective coping strategies are crucial for managing stressors and maintaining mental health. Empirical research has demonstrated that adaptive coping strategies, such as seeking social support and problem-solving, are linked to better mental health outcomes in the elderly. Older adults who utilize positive coping mechanisms are more resilient in the face of challenges, experience lower levels of anxiety and depression, and report greater life satisfaction.

***Personality Traits*:** Personality traits continue to influence mental health well into old age. Studies have identified that traits like extraversion, openness to experience, and conscientiousness are associated with better psychological well-being among the elderly. These traits contribute to a positive outlook on life, greater social engagement, and a reduced risk of mood disorders. Conversely, studies have linked increased mental health vulnerabilities to high neuroticism and low extraversion.

***Resilience*:** Resilience, the ability to bounce back from adversity, is a key psychological factor in maintaining mental health. Empirical evidence suggests that resilient individuals in the elderly population are more likely to adapt positively to life changes and setbacks. Resilience acts as a buffer against stress and contributes to lower rates of depression and anxiety among older adults.

***Self-Esteem and Self-Efficacy*:** These are crucial components of psychological well-being. Research indicates that elderly individuals with higher self-esteem have better mental health outcomes, including reduced depressive symptoms and a better quality of life. Similarly, strong self-efficacy beliefs, which pertain to one's confidence in their ability to accomplish tasks, are associated with lower levels of anxiety and higher levels of life satisfaction.

Emotional Regulation: Emotional regulation skills are vital for managing the ups and downs of life. Empirical findings suggest that older adults who possess effective emotional regulation strategies experience fewer mood disturbances. These individuals are better equipped to handle stress, maintain stable emotions, and exhibit greater psychological resilience.

***Social Support and Loneliness*:** Social connections and support networks have a profound impact on mental health in the elderly. Research demonstrates that strong social ties are associated with lower rates of depression and anxiety. On the other hand, poor mental health outcomes are associated with feelings of loneliness and social isolation. Elderly individuals with ample social support are more likely to experience positive emotions and reduce psychological distress.

***Cognitive Function and Engagement*:** Cognitive function and engagement in intellectually stimulating activities contribute to psychological well-being. Empirical studies show that participating in cognitive activities, such as reading, puzzles, and learning new skills, can enhance cognitive vitality and reduce the risk of cognitive decline. Such engagement fosters a sense of purpose and accomplishment, leading to improved mental health outcomes.

Meaning and Purpose: Finding meaning and purpose in life is a psychological factor that significantly influences mental health. Elderly individuals who maintain a sense of purpose have lower rates of depression and elevated levels of life satisfaction. Engaging in activities that provide a sense of fulfilment, whether through volunteer work or hobbies, contributes to a positive outlook on life.

Empirical research underscores the significance of psychological factors in influencing mental health outcomes in the elderly population. Coping strategies, personality traits, resilience, self-esteem, emotional regulation, social support, cognitive engagement, and a sense of meaning all contribute to psychological well-being. A holistic approach that considers the multifaceted interactions between biological, psychological, and environmental factors is essential for promoting optimal mental health outcomes in the elderly population.

Challenges Faced in Old Age

Effects of Psychological Problems on Medical Illness

It is a known fact that the elderly have both physical and psychiatric illnesses, and the comorbidity of both physical and psychological disorders clearly defines the link between them. Therefore, the diagnosis of organic and non-organic disorders is made clear, as is, sometimes, physical illness.

The presence of psychological problems makes them more vulnerable. It is important to note that a focus should be placed on understanding the psychiatric and medical problems of patients, which will further help in diagnosis and management.

Social Factors Play a Role in Psychiatric Problems in the Elderly

Major stressors that older people face after retirement are a drop in financial status, loneliness, indecisiveness, feelings of ignorance, a lack of family support etc. 80 per cent of the elderly population lives in rural areas, where minimum services are available, including their medical facilities, which suffer the most. Government schemes like the elderly pension helped almost 2.76 million out of 28 million.

The Management of Cancer in the Elderly Presents Unique Challenges

Lack of awareness of psycho-oncology in old age leads to serious medical problems as well as psychological problems like depression, anxiety, and fatigue, which is a major concern. Problems related to life care for the elderly involve a lack of decision-making for medical management, which requires proper guidance from family members. Sometimes, they are forced to take patients back home due to time constraints, communication with medical teams, financial problems, and the availability of specialized interventions.

Delirium Management in the Elderly

A very common psychiatric problem seen in the geriatric population is dementia, where most of the patients require regular monitoring and intensive care. Due to fluctuations in orientation, the attention of the patient becomes difficult to manage, which might create a problem for dementia patients. Sometimes, ignorance may cause death, and hence it becomes a challenge and a pressure for caregivers who deal with patients regularly.

The Management of Substance Abuse in the Elderly is a Complex Issue

Alcohol consumption is often reported in the elderly; the prevalence of consumption is found to be almost 25.4 per cent. The reasons for taking alcohol at a late age are their response to negative life events such as loneliness, death, and retirement life stressors. These negative lives are very common in old age, further linked to different psychopathologies and comorbid disorders, anxiety, and depression. Treatment of these patients becomes difficult as the causes and needs of these patients are different, and treatment differs from that of adult patients.

Abuse Faced by the Elderly

Evidence reported that among 10 old people, 1 person faces abuse, which affects their mental health. The elderly suffering from abuse have a high prevalence of anxiety and depression stress, which increases the risk of suicide and emotional distress. Death reports are very common in elderly people facing mental health issues, and many of them showed their reactions in the form of numerous somatic complaints.

Suicide in the Elderly

Suicide is common among the elderly, compared to other groups' estimations of suicidal ideation in old-age people of around 9 per cent–12 per cent. About 1 per cent of psychiatric patients in primary care had suicidal ideation, as did 42 per cent of geriatric patients with major depression (Dombrovski, Szanto & Reynolds, 2005). It was reported that 1.9 per cent of adults experience their first suicidal thoughts after the age of 55 years, and it increases when they have a serious illness or accident (Beristianos, Maguen, Neylan & Byers, 2016).

Risk Factors

The risk factors associated with this condition are social isolation, lack of social support, substance abuse, depression, anxiety, poor physical health, death, and financial loss. The prevention of suicide among elderly people is very important, and efforts are being made in this context. Elderly people show less resilience and are more vulnerable to stress-related issues as their coping mechanisms fail with age, which results in depression. The idea of helplessness, hopelessness, stress, and anxiety decreases self-concept and lowers self-esteem; loneliness accompanies sadness (Mann, 2005; Osgood, 1985) and leads to life crises and unacceptable pain. With the increase in domestic violence, for property, house, and family history of substance abuse and suicide risks, factors increase for suicidal behaviour. (Mann *et al.*, 2005; NIMH, 2010).

Preventive Measures

A regular screening for suicide and depression in the elderly at every instance, as well as effective treatment for depression, can help in the prevention of suicide (Cheung *et al.*, 2007; Heisel *et al.*, 2010; Mann *et al.*, 2005; Plaweski & Amrhein, 2010). It was reported that approximately. 80 per cent of depressed elderly showed a good response to a combination of antidepressants and psychotherapy, hence helping in relapse prevention (NIMH, 2007).

Secondly, the involvement of the elderly in different activities of their interest, including family and community support, can reduce social isolation. However, experts say that in the theory of disengagement, sometimes the elderly think that they are retired and voluntarily avoid social gatherings. Activity theory defines that older people are healthier and more satisfied when they remain active.

The strategies made for the prevention of suicide and loneliness for the elderly population should be according to their needs, interests, and involvement. This helps reduce the risk of suicide due to social isolation. Different community-level programmes and workers have noticed the change in their behaviour with the elderly and must be trained for the identification of symptoms.

Stress has a Significant Impact on the Quality of Life of Elderly Individuals

According to WHO (1995), quality of life is defined as one's perceptions towards their life, culture, values, beliefs, goals, standards, and expectations in life.

Stress showed an impact on the day-to-day functioning of older adults, like basic self-care, personal hygiene, daily living activities, and other difficult tasks like medicine taking, managing finances, and different instrumental activities for carrying out daily living, following social customs and relationships etc. It affects every other aspect of life. Stress also shows its impact on the cognitive functions of the elderly, affecting some of the other ways that affect their everyday lives' functions. The impact of stress on the cognitive functioning of an individual brings about changes in one's daily functioning. A study reported more cognitive decline in middle age and old age, which is mainly associated with a daily stress routine that leads to memory problems (Rickenbach *et al.*, 2014). The relationship between chronic physical health and old age showed significant effects on their quality of life, both physically and mentally. It was noted in a few studies that poor resilience and a lack of social support reduce their copying and prevent them from utilizing their resources effectively, contributing to poor quality of life. Also, with the diagnosis of mental illness, the severity of its adverse effects is seen on the mental health of an individual. Numerous disorders have been diagnosed that have shown an impact on quality of life in old age, including anxiety, schizophrenia, PTSD, and depression. However, it cannot be overlooked that, other than stress, numerous other factors play an important contributing factor in disturbing the quality of life of an individual. Exposure to trauma throughout life is also associated with a poor quality of life. Adults suffering from PTSD showed worse effects than adults without any trauma exposure. The comorbidity of PTSD showed worse effects on mental health and quality of life.

Researchers have initiated investigating whether mental health interventions help in alleviating symptom distress and also enhance quality of life (QOL) in elderly individuals. (Forsman *et al.*, 2011). Numerous studies suggested that CBT is linked with the quality of life (QOL) in older adults and showed positive effects in conditions like generalized anxiety disorders (Brenes *et al.*, 2012; Scogin *et al.*, 2007; Shrestha *et al.*, 2015). Individuals with higher levels of mindfulness experienced a mitigated impact of stress on their quality of life. Collectively, these findings propose that mental health interventions could be effective in changing the quality of life among older adults.

Psychological Management

Conducting comprehensive mental health assessments during primary care visits constitutes the initial step in identifying individuals who require further services. First and foremost, it is crucial to provide comprehensive training to all healthcare providers in addressing age-related issues and disorders. Implementing programmes that promote healthy lifestyles in older adults, proven to reduce stress and enhance mental health, can be relatively straightforward in standard healthcare settings. Offering education, training, and avenues for social support to older adults can significantly improve their quality of life.

Approaches in Psychotherapy

Psychodynamic approach: The key characteristics that differentiate the psychodynamic approach from other therapeutic modalities are: emphasis on affect and emotional expression; examination of strategies to shun upsetting feelings and thoughts; recognition of recurring topics and patterns; consideration of past developmental experiences; emphasis on interpersonal relationships; emphasis on the therapeutic relationship itself; and examination of fantasy life. A seminal study in this area (Thompson *et al.*, 1987) demonstrated that behavioural, cognitive, or brief psychodynamic therapy resulted in improvements in the symptoms of major depression in older adults, with no significant distinctions between these treatment methods. In a subsequent study, Gallagher-Thompson and Steffen (1994) compared CBT with psychodynamic therapy for alleviating depression in family caregivers. The study found both approaches to be effective, with no clear su periority of one over the other. More recently, a longitudinal study assessing the efficacy of brief psychodynamic therapy in older adults identified statistically significant changes, indicating the therapy's effectiveness (Rosebourough *et al.*, 2013).

Cognitive-Behaviour Therapy (CBT): CBT possesses an extensive and robust evidence base that encompasses patients of various age groups and a wide range of mental and physical health conditions. CBT primarily aims to modify dysfunctional thinking and behaviour (Beck, 1964). It shows better outcomes in terms of relapse prevention. Depression and anxiety are very common features of old age and work as cofounding factors in the deterioration of their quality of life, as CBT focuses more on the change of maladaptive thoughts, hence change in cognition, emotion, and behaviour, and equilibrium in these components reduces one's anxiety. Johnco *et al.* (2014) found that individuals with poor cognitive flexibility had difficulties engaging successfully in cognitive restructuring, highlighting the importance of considering older adults' cognitive abilities when applying a CBT approach to ensure optimal outcomes. Among the therapeutic modalities, CBT stands out as the most extensively researched. As a result, it offers a robust evidence base. However, caution is necessary when extending these findings to less-studied subpopulations, particularly among older individuals.

Interpersonal Psychotherapy (IPT): Interpersonal psychotherapy (IPT) focuses on understanding how interpersonal difficulties impact an individual's psychological well-being. It draws its theoretical foundation from attachment theory and aims to address interpersonal challenges affecting mental health. IPT focuses on four main interpersonal stressors: role transitions, grief and loss, inter personal sensitivity, and inter personal disputes. Weisman *et al.* (1979) compared the efficacy of psychiatric drugs and IPT. They observed that both treatments were individually effective, but their combination yielded better results for treating acute depression in adults. Researchers have extensively researched IPT in older adults, particularly in the context of depression (Hinrichsen & Clougherty, 2006). Recent studies have continued to explore its effectiveness, including its use in addressing suicidality. Older adults at risk of suicide widely use IPT, which significantly reduces suicidal ideation, death ideation, and depression severity. While this study lacked a control group, the positive impact on participants' psychological well-being adds to the evidence supporting IPT as a valuable intervention in later life. IPT offers a therapeutic approach that emphasizes the inter personal context, providing a different perspective on factors contributing to psychiatric disorders in older adults.

Motivational Interviewing: Motivational Interviewing (MI) focuses on facilitating structured conversations about change to motivate clients. Various contexts widely use it to promote behaviour change, including substance abuse treatment and other health-related behaviours. Studies in this field have demonstrated the efficacy of MI in promoting behaviour change among older adult populations, particularly in areas such as diet, physical activity, and smoking cessation. The impact of MI reduces risks for misuse of opioids and chronic pain; moreover, older adults, despite the well-documented benefits of exercise and a healthy diet in protecting from cardiovascular disease and other medical conditions, may hesitate to engage in physical activity due to fears of falling, worsening their condition, or low self-efficacy. MI was effective at increasing physical activity and lowering cholesterol levels, particularly among older adults with higher cardiovascular disease risk factors. While MI has shown effectiveness with older adults, questions remain about relapse and the maintenance of effects.

Third-wave therapeutic approaches: These approaches centre on how individuals relate to their thoughts and emotions.

1. **Mindfulness:** Meditation and psycho-education often practice mindfulness, which involves observing thoughts and emotions without judgment. Mindfulness-based stress reduction (MBSR) and mindfulness-based cognitive therapy (MBCT) are notable programmes in this realm. Mindfulness programmes help to reduce pain in the lower back, improve pain acceptance, and improve physical function in older adults. Cresswell *et al.* (2012) used a similar approach to reduce loneliness and pro-inflammatory gene expression in older adults, showing positive outcomes in both areas. The impact of mindfulness on stress and neurocognitive difficulties includes finding improvements in memory, worry, depression, and anxiety, with sustained benefits at follow-up. Overall, while mindfulness has a long history as a therapeutic intervention, empirical support is modest but promising. Robust research is necessary to further establish its effectiveness, particularly in the context of ageing.
2. **Acceptance and Commitment Therapy (ACT):** ACT represents a therapeutic approach geared towards addressing mental health challenges stemming from psychological inflexibility, as outlined by Hayes, Strosahl, and Wilson in their seminal work from 1999. ACT integrates various components aimed at mitigating psychological rigidity. These components involve orienting the client towards the present moment, identifying and clarifying core personal values, nurturing a stance of acceptance, promoting defusion (as opposed to fusion) from cognitions, cultivating a dedication to meaningful actions, and fostering self-compassion and self-acceptance. In contrast to approaches like Cognitive Behavioural Therapy (CBT), ACT emphasizes the importance of recognizing and embracing the self in the current context, refraining from attempts to negate thoughts that may hold validity in certain circumstances, such as the distress resulting from the loss of a lifelong partner, which may understandably lead to symptoms of depression. Consequently, ACT advocates the ability to sit with such thoughts and accompanying emotions, acknowledging their presence without the need to actively counter them, given the reality of specific life situations. ACT emerges as a highly acceptable form of therapy for older adults, particularly those grappling with mental health challenges that may be inherently unchangeable and could benefit significantly from fostering an attitude of acceptance. Importantly, there is an encouraging

indication that the positive effects of ACT can be sustained over time, as observed during follow-up assessments (Hayes *et al.*, 1999; Wetherell, Afari, Rutledge, *et al.*, 2011; Wetherell, Afari, Ayers, *et al.*, 2011; McCracken and Jones, 2012; Veehof, Oskam, Schreurs, and Bohlmeiher, 2011; Karlin *et al.*, 2013; Davison, Eppingstall, Runci, and O'Connor, 2017).

3. **Dialectical Behaviour Therapy (DBT):** Linehan (1981) introduced DBT primarily for individuals exhibiting highly suicidal behaviour. DBT seeks to find a balance between accepting and tolerating distress rather than solely focusing on change (Linehan & Wilks, 2015). Linehan & Wilks (2015) designed DBT in a modular form, allowing for customization based on individual client needs, despite the presence of a treatment protocol. Lynch *et al.*'s work focused on using DBT to treat comorbid personality disorders and depression in older adults. Another difficulty in evaluating the effectiveness of DBT with geriatric subjects lies in the paucity of research on this topic. Earlier studies, which examined the treatment of personality disorders in older adults, identified only four treatment studies, one of which utilized DBT (Lynch *et al.*, 2007). Not surprisingly, they arrived at a similar conclusion as Lynch *et al.*, affirming that DBT was a feasible treatment approach for older adults.
4. **Problem-solving therapy:** PST is a therapeutic approach that focuses on enhancing a client's problem-solving skills to alleviate psychosocial distress. It encompasses two key components outlined by Nezu, Maguth Nezu, and D'Zurilla (2013): a general orientation towards viewing problems as solvable, coupled with self-efficacy in problem-solving, and the actual application of problem-solving skills in identifying and executing effective solutions. PST has also proven effective in cases involving executive dysfunction, showing positive outcomes in terms of treatment response and remission (Areán *et al.*, 2010). When applied in the context of cardiovascular disease, Gellis & Bruce (2010) observed a decrease in depression, though not in anxiety. Additionally, PST reduced suicide risk in older adults at both 12-week and 36-week post-treatment intervals (Gustavson *et al.*, 2016). PST may also be a useful intervention for late-life anxiety (Beaudreau *et al.*, 2019). PST is heralded as a practical therapeutic approach, making it appealing to clients who prefer a more concrete, targeted form of therapy. Overall, the evidence supports its effectiveness and sustained benefits over time when working with older adults.

5. **Strengths-based Approaches:** Older adults often bring a wealth of knowledge and life experience to various situations they encounter. Unfortunately, prevailing ageing stereotypes sometimes overlook this valuable asset, assuming that age implies a lack of competence. This viewpoint is more pronounced in Western cultures. Observations show that even in Eastern cultures, where there is greater reverence for older adults, children are relocating from rural areas, leaving ageing parents without familial support (Liu, 2014). However, in psychotherapy, leveraging the wisdom, life experiences, and knowledge of older adults can significantly enhance therapeutic outcomes and lead to enduring benefits (Daniels, Boehnlein & McCallion, 2015; Linden, Baumann, Lieberei, Lorenz & Rotter, 2011).
6. **Positive Psychology:** Positive psychology emphasizes achieving optimal levels of functioning and overall well-being. Seligman and Csikszentmihalyi (2000) emphasize elements such as contentment, well-being, and satisfaction in the past; optimism and hope for the future; and experiencing happiness in the present. They also highlight positive individual traits like perseverance, courage, forgiveness, and wisdom. Positive psychology interventions aim to cultivate happiness, as defined by Seligman (2002) as a life that is pleasant, engaged, and meaningful. These interventions include practices like fostering gratitude, enhancing awareness of positive aspects of one's life, and identifying one's strengths and virtues (Seligman *et al.*, 2005). The intervention focused on themes such as optimism, gratitude, savouring positive experiences, cultivating happiness, nurturing curiosity, demonstrating courage, expressing altruism, and finding meaning in life. The results showed a reduction in depressive symptoms as well as an increase in overall life satisfaction and happiness. Similarly, Ramirez *et al.* (2014) implemented a positive psychology intervention, which resulted in lower levels of state anxiety and depression, accompanied by an elevated sense of life satisfaction. A review suggested that individuals who already possess a positive outlook tend to derive the greatest benefits from positive psychology-based therapy (Sin and Lyubomirsky, 2009). Additionally, Sin and Lyubomirsky (2009) proposed that the presence of wisdom and enhanced emotion regulation in positive psychology interventions, particularly with older adults, may yield better outcomes. While positive psychology holds promise for enhancing well-being among older adults, it is

important to consider when it should be employed in comparison to other therapeutic approaches (Seligman, 2002; Seligman & Csikszentmihalyi, 2000; Sin & Lyubomirsky, 2009).

7. **Reminiscence:** Reminiscence, defined by Bluck and Levine (1998), involves reflecting on one's past life experiences. Butler (1963) characterizes reminiscence as a universal mental process characterized by the resurgence of past experiences and conflicts. Reminiscence not only involves reflection but also active engagement in consolidating memories, learning from the past, and fostering personal growth (Bohlmeijer, Roemer, Cuij pers & Smit, 2007). Cappeliez and O'Rourke (2006) highlight that self-negative reminiscence impacts psychological well-being negatively, while meaningful reminiscence has a positive effect.
8. **Wisdom:** Baltes & Smith (1990) describe wisdom as a multi-dimensional trait that encompasses ex pertise in life's fundamental practicalities, the capacity to navigate uncertainty, and the ability to offer sound judgment and advice across life's spectrum. According to Linley (2003), the adaptation and wisdom that arise from facing stressful life events are termed post-traumatic positive adaptation. Linden *et al.* (2011) assert that wisdom can assist in effectively coping with negative life events, linking it with resilience. However, the relationship between wisdom and resilience goes beyond mere bouncing back after a negative event. Sternberg (1990) further associates wisdom with problem-solving, particularly in situations lacking a clear-cut response or definitive outcome, as well as those necessitating a more metacognitive approach. Hanna and Ottens (1995) argue that we should view wisdom not only as a valuable technique in therapy, but also as a desired outcome of therapy. Under CBT, wisdom psychotherapy focuses on cultivating qualities associated with wisdom as the therapy's objective (Linden *et al.*, 2011). Sternberg (1990) emphasizes that a wise individual possesses the capacity for independent thought, free from automatic cognitive patterns, aligning with a common goal in CBT. Linden *et al.*'s (2011) work underscores the potential of wisdom psychotherapy, particularly in addressing post-traumatic stress disorder (PTSD). This form of therapy aims to build factual knowledge about the issue at hand, enhance coping with uncertainty, and view the problem from a broader perspective. This form of therapy may be particularly useful for older adults since the likelihood of experiencing some form of trauma or challenging life event increases with age.

9. **Resilience:** Resilience, the ability to rebound after encountering difficult life events, is a crucial attribute, particularly in later life. Older adults often draw from their life experiences to navigate and adapt to challenges. MacLeod *et al.* (2016) identify factors like adaptive coping, optimism, positive emotion, and social connectedness as pivotal in building and maintaining resilience.

Technology and Psychotherapy

The integration of technology with psychotherapy offers innovative opportunities to extend therapeutic reach, especially for those facing barriers to in-person sessions. Telehealth, web-based interventions, and virtual reality have shown promise in enhancing mental health support. However, more comprehensive research is necessary to establish their effectiveness, particularly with older adult populations.

Conclusion

Finally, numerous forms of psychotherapy have demonstrated modest effectiveness in the existing literature, and the emergence of e-health adaptations is also gaining traction with growing research support and significant clinical applications. However, research on therapeutic interventions for older adults, especially those dealing with multiple comorbidities or at an advanced age, remains relatively limited. The available research provides some support for positive outcomes and underscores the potential and feasibility of employing a range of therapeutic approaches with older individuals. The rapid pace of technological advancement presents an opportunity to expand upon existing research by integrating telehealth and online therapy methods. Although studies specific to older adults in this domain are still scarce, the existing scientific evidence holds considerable promise. This is particularly significant for underserved populations, including those residing in remote rural areas and individuals with limited mobility. While CBT variants boast the most extensive empirical foundation, other therapeutic modalities such as ACT and mindfulness-based approaches have proven beneficial for addressing a growing array of presenting issues. Furthermore, affording older adults the option to choose from various therapy modalities and refining research to determine which therapies are most effective for specific older adult populations in diverse contexts are both crucial steps in delivering optimal mental health outcomes for older individuals.

References

Areán, P.A., Raue, P., Mackin, R.S., Kanellopoulos, D., McCulloch, C. & Alexopoulos, G.S. (2010). "Problem-solving Therapy and Supportive Therapy in Older Adults with Major Depression and Executive Dysfunction". *American Journal of Psychiatry*, *167*(11): 1391-1398. https://doi.org/10.1176/appi.ajp.2010.09091327

Bakhtiyari, M., Emaminaeini, M., Hatami, H., Khodakarim, S. & Sahaf, R. (2017). "Depression and Perceived Social Support in the Elderly". *Salmand*, *12*(2): 192-207. https://doi.org/10.21859/sija-1202192

Beaudreau, S.A., Gould, C.E., Mashal, N.M., Terri Huh, J.W. & Kaci Fairchild, J. (2019). "Application of Problem-Solving Therapy for Late-Life Anxiety". *Cognitive and Behavioural Practice*, *26*(2): 381-394. https://doi.org/10.1016/j.cbpra.2018.05.003

Beck, A.T. (1964). "Thinking and Depression. II. Theory and Therapy". *Archives of General Psychiatry*, *10*(6): 561-571. https://doi.org/10.1001/archpsyc.1964.01720240015003

Beristianos, M.H., Maguen, S., Neylan, T.C. & Byers, A.L. (2016). "Trauma Exposure and Risk of Suicidal Ideation Among Older Adults". *American Journal of Geriatric Psychiatry*, *24*(8): 639-643. https://doi.org/10.1016/j.jagp.2016.02.055

Bluck, S., Levine, L.J. & Laulhere, T.M. (1999). "Autobiographical Remembering and Hypermnesia: A Comparison of Older and Younger Adults". *Psychology and Ageing*, *14*(4): 671-682. https://doi.org/10.1037//0882-7974.14.4.671

Bohlmeijer, E., Roemer, M., Cuijpers, P. & Smit, F. (2007). "The Effects of Reminiscence on Psychological Well-being in Older Adults: A Meta-analysis". *Ageing and Mental Health*, *11*(3): 291-300. https://doi.org/10.1080/13607860600963547

Brenes, G.A., Miller, M.E., Williamson, J.D., McCall, W.V., Knudson, M. & Stanley, M.A. (2012). "A Randomized Controlled Trial of Telephone-Delivered Cognitive-Behavioural Therapy for Late-Life Anxiety Disorders". *American Journal of Geriatric Psychiatry*, *20*(8): 707-716. https://doi.org/10.1097/JGP.0b013e31822ccd3e

Brosschot, J.F., Gerin, W. & Thayer, J.F. (2006). "The Perseverative Cognition Hypothesis: A Review of Worry, Prolonged Stressrelated Physiological Activation, and Health". *Journal of Psychosomatic Research*, *60*(2): 113-124. https://doi.org/10.1016/j.jpsychores.2005.06.074

Butler, R.N. (1963). "The Life Review: An Interpretation of Reminiscence in the Aged". *Psychiatry*, *26*, 65-76. https://doi.org/10.1080/00332747.1963.11023339

Cappeliez, P., O'Rourke, N. & Chaudhury, H. (2005). "Functions of Reminiscence and Mental Health in Later Life". *Ageing and Mental Health*, *9*(4): 295-301. https://doi.org/10.1080/13607860500131427

Cheung, Y.B., Liu, K.Y. & Yip, P.S.F. (2007). "Performance of the CES-D and Its Short Forms in Screening Suicidality and Hopelessness in the Community". *Suicide and Life-Threatening Behaviour*, *37*(1): 79-88. https://doi.org/10.1521/suli.2007.37.1.79

Creswell, J.D., Irwin, M.R., Burklund, L.J., Lieberman, M.D., Arevalo, J.M.G., Ma, J., Breen, E.C. & Cole, S.W. (2012). "Mindfulness-based Stress Reduction Training Reduces Loneliness and Pro-Inflammatory Gene Expression in Older Adults: A Small Randomized Controlled Trial". *Brain, Behaviour, and Immunity*, *26*(7): 1095-1101. https://doi.org/10.1016/j.bbi.2012.07.006

Daniels, L.R., Boehnlein, J.K. & McCallion, P. (2015). "Life Review and PTSD Community Counselling with Two Groups of Vietnam War Veterans. *Traumatology*, *21*(3): 161-171. https://doi.org/10.1037/trm0000045

Davison, T.E., Snowdon, J., Castle, N., McCabe, M.P., Mellor, D., Karantzas, G. & Allan, J. (2012). "An Evaluation of a National Programme to Implement the Cornell Scale for Depression in Dementia into Routine Practice in Aged Care Facilities". *International Psychogeriatrics*, *24*(4): 631-641. https://doi.org/10.1017/S1041610211002146

Diener, E., Lucas, R.E. & Oishi, S. (2018). "Advances and Open Questions in the Science of Subjective Well-being". *Collaborate. Psychology*, *4*(1). https://doi.org/10.1525/collabra.115

Dombrovski, A.Y., Szanto, K. & Reynolds, C.F. (2005). "Epidemiology and Risk Factors for Suicide in the Elderly: 10-Year Update". *Ageing Health*, *1*(1): 135-145. https://doi.org/10.2217/1745509X.1.1.135

Forlani, C., Morri, M., Ferrari, B., Dalmonte, E., Menchetti, M., DeRonchi, D. & Atti, A.R. (2014). "Prevalence and Gender Differences in Late-Life Depression: A Population-based Study". *American Journal of Geriatric Psychiatry*, *22*(4): 370-380. https://doi.org/10.1016/j.jagp.2012.08.015

Forsman, A.K., Nordmyr, J. & Wahlbeck, K. (2011). "Psychosocial Interventions for the Promotion of Mental Health and the Prevention of Depression among Older Adults". *Health Promotion International*, *26*(Suppl. 1): i85-i107. https://doi.org/10.1093/heapro/dar074

Gallagher-Thompson, D. & Steffen, A.M. (1994). "Comparative Effects of Cognitive-Behavioural and Brief Psychodynamic Psychotherapies for Depressed Family Caregivers". *Journal of Consulting and Clinical Psychology*, *62*(3): 543-549. https://doi.org/10.1037//0022-006x.62.3.543

Gellis, Z.D. & Bruce, M.L. (2010). "Problem-Solving Therapy for Subthreshold Depression in home Healthcare Patients with Cardiovascular Disease". *American Journal of Geriatric Psychiatry*, *18*(6): 464-474. https://doi.org/10.1097/jgp.0b013e3181b21442

Gustavson, K.A., Alexopoulos, G.S., Niu, G.C., McCulloch, C., Meade, T. & Areán, P.A. (2016). "Problem-solving Therapy Reduces Suicidal Ideation in Depressed Older Adults with Executive Dysfunction". *American Journal of Geriatric Psychiatry*, *24*(1): 11-17. https://doi.org/10.1016/j.jagp.2015.07.010

Hayes, S.C., Strosahl, K. & Wilson, K.G. (1999). "*Acceptance and commitment therapy: Understanding and treating human suffering*. Guilford Press.

Heisel, M.J., Duberstein, P.R., Lyness, J.M. & Feldman, M.D. (2010). "Screening for Suicide Ideation Among Older Primary Care Patients". *Journal of the American Board of Family Medicine*, *23*(2): 260-269. https://doi.org/10.3122/jabfm.2010.02.080163

Heser, K., Tebarth, F., Wiese, B., Eisele, M., Bickel, H., Köhler, M., Mösch, E., Weyerer, S., Werle, J., König, H.H., Leicht, H., Pentzek, M., Fuchs, A., Riedel-Heller, S.G., Luppa, M., Prokein, J., Scherer, M., Maier, W., Wagner, M. & Age CoDe Study Group. (2013). "Age of Major Depression onset, Depressive Symptoms, and Risk for Subsequent Dementia: Results of the German Study on Ageing, Cognition, and Dementia in Primary Care Patients (AgeCoDe)". *Psychological Medicine*, *43*(8): 1597-1610. https://doi.org/10.1017/S0033291712002449

Hinrichsen, G.A. & Clougherty, K.F. (2006). "Interpersonal Psychotherapy for Depressed Older Adults". *American Psychological Association*. https://doi.org/10.1037/11429-000

Johnco, C., Wuthrich, V.M. & Rapee, R.M. (2014). "The Influence of Cognitive Flexibility on Treatment Outcome and Cognitive Restructuring Skill Acquisition During Cognitive Behavioural Treatment for Anxiety and Depression in Older Adults: Results of a Pilot Study". *Behaviour Research and Therapy*, *57*, 55-64. https://doi.org/10.1016/j.brat.2014.04.005

Karlin, B.E., Walser, R.D., Yesavage, J., Zhang, A., Trockel, M. & Taylor, C.B. (2013). "Effectiveness of Acceptance and Commitment Therapy for Depression: Comparison among Older and Younger Veterans". *Ageing and Mental Health*, *17*(5): 555-563. https://doi.org/10.1080/13607863.2013.789002

Linden, M., Baumann, K., Lieberei, B., Lorenz, C. & Rotter, M. (2011). "Treatment of Post-traumatic Embitterment Disorder with Cognitive Behaviour Therapy Based on Wisdom Psychology and Hedonia Strategies". *Psychotherapy and Psychosomatics*, *80*(4): 199-205. https://doi.org/10.1159/000321580

Linehan, M.M. (1981). "A Social-Behavioural Analysis of Suicide and Parasuicide: Implications for Clinical Assessment and Treatment". In H. Glazer (Ed.) J.F. Clarkin (Eds.): *Depression, Behavioural and Directive Intervention Strategies* (pp. 229-294). New York: Garland Press.

Linehan, M.M. & Wilks, C.R. (2015). "The Course and Evolution of Dialectical Behaviour Therapy". *American Journal of Psychotherapy*, *69*(2): 97-110. https://doi.org/10.1176/appi.psychotherapy.2015.69.2.97

Lynch, T.R., Cheavens, J.S., Cukrowicz, K.C., Thorp, S.R., Bronner, L. & Beyer, J. (2007). "Treatment of Older Adults with Co-Morbid Personality Disorder and Depression: A Dialectical Behaviour Therapy Approach". *International Journal of Geriatric Psychiatry*, *22*(2): 131-143. https://doi.org/10.1002/gps.1703

MacLeod, A., Skinner, M.W., Wilkinson, F. & Reid, H. (2016). "Connecting Socially Isolated Older Rural Adults with Older Volunteers through Expressive Arts". *Canadian Journal on Ageing*, *35*(1): 14-27. https://doi.org/10.1017/S071498081500063X

Mann, J.J., Apter, A., Bertolote, J., Beautrais, A., Currier, D., Haas, A., Hegerl, U., Lonnqvist, J., Malone, K., Marusic, A., Mehlum, L., Patton, G., Phillips, M., Rutz, W., Rihmer, Z., Schmidtke, A., Shaffer, D., Silverman, M., Takahashi, Y., Hendin, H. (2005). "Suicide Prevention Strategies: A Systematic Review". *JAMA*, *294*(16): 2064-2074. https://doi.org/10.1001/jama.294.16.2064

McCracken, L.M. & Jones, R. (2012). "Treatment for Chronic Pain for Adults in the Seventh and Eighth Decades of Life: A Preliminary Study of Acceptance and Commitment Therapy (ACT)". *Pain Medicine*, *13*(7): 860-867. https://doi.org/10.1111/j.1526-4637.2012.01407.x

Mirowsky, J. & Reynolds, J.R. (2000). "Age, Depression, and Attrition in the National Survey of Families and Households". *Sociological Methods and Research*, *28*(4): 476-504. https://doi.org/10.1177/0049124100028004004

Nezu, Nezu, M. & D'Zurilla. (2013). *Problem-solving Therapy: A Treatment Manual*. Springer Publishing Co.

National Institute of Mental Health. (2010). *Suicide in the U.S.: Statistics and Prevention*. http://www.nimh.nih.gov/health/publications/suicide—in—the—us—statistics—and—prevention/index.shtml

Ong, A.D., Uchino, B.N. & Wethington, E. (2016). "Loneliness and Health in Older Adults: A Mini-Review and Synthesis". *Gerontology*, *62*(4): 443-449. https://doi.org/10.1159/000441651

Ottens, A.J. & Hanna, F.J. (1998). "Cognitive and Existential Therapies: Towards an Integration". *Psychotherapy: Theory, Research, Practice, Training*, *35*(3): 312-324. https://doi.org/10.1037/h0087832

Linley, P.A. (2003). "Positive Adaptation to Trauma: Wisdom as Both Process and Outcome". *Journal of Traumatic Stress*, *16*(6): 601-610. https://doi.org/10.1023/B:JOTS.0000004086.64509.09

Plawecki, L.H. & Amrhein, D.W. (2010). "Someone to Talk to. The Nurse and the Depressed or Suicidal Older Patient". *Journal of Gerontological Nursing*, *36*(5): 15-18. https://doi.org/10.3928/00989134-20100330-11

Sternberg, R.J. (Ed.). (1990). *Wisdom: Its Nature, Origins, and Development*. Cambridge University Press.

Ramírez, E., Ortega, A.R., Chamorro, A. & Colmenero, J.M. (2014). "A Programme of Positive Intervention in the Elderly: Memories, Gratitude and Forgiveness". *Ageing and Mental Health*, *18*(4): 463-470. https://doi.org/ 10.1080/13607863.2013.856858

Rickenbach, E.H., Agrigoroaei, S. & Lachman, M.E. (2015). "Awareness of Memory Ability and Change: (In)Accuracy of Memory Self-Assessments in Relation to Performance". *Journal of Population Ageing*, *8*(1-2): 71-99. https://doi.org/10.1007/s12062-014-9108-5

Roseborough, D. J., Luptak, M., McLeod, J. & Bradshaw, W. (2013). "Effectiveness of Psychodynamic Psychotherapy with Older Adults: A Longitudinal Study.

Clinical Gerontologist, 36(1): 1-16. https://doi.org/10.1080/07317115.2012.731476

Satnely, M.A., Wilson, N., Shrestha, S., Amspoker, A.B. & Armento, M.M. (Advance online publication). Cummings, J.P., Kunik, M.E. (2016). "Calmer Life: A Culturally Older Adults". *American Journal of Geriatric Psychiatry*. https://doi.org/10.1016/j.japi2016.03.008

Scogin, F., Morthland, M., Kaufman, A., Burgio, L., Chaplin, W. & Kong, G. (2007). "Improving Quality of Life in Diverse Rural Older Adults: A Randomized Trial of a Psychological Treatment". *Psychology and Ageing, 22*(4): 657-665, https://doi.org/10.1037/0882-7974.22.4.657

Seligman, M.E.P. (2002). "Positive Psychology, Positive Prevention, and Positive Therapy". In C.R. Snyder & S.J. Lopez (Eds.): *Handbook of Positive Psychology* (pp. 3-9). Oxford University Press.

Seligman, M.E.P. & Csikszentmihalyi, M. (2000). "Positive Psychology: An Introduction". *American Psychologist, 55*(1): 5-14. https://doi.org/10.1037//0003-066x.55.1.5

Seligman, M.E.P., Steen, T.A., Park, N. & Peterson, C. (2005). "Positive Psychology Progress: Empirical Validation of Interventions". *American Psychologist, 60*(5): 410-421. https://doi.org/10.1037/0003-066X.60.5.410

Sin, N.L. & Lyubomirsky, S. (2009). "Enhancing Well-being and Alleviating Depressive Symptoms with Positive Psychology Interventions: A Practice-Friendly Meta-analysis". *Journal of Clinical Psychology, 65*(5): 467-487. https://doi.org/10.1002/jclp.20593

Smith, J. & Baltes, P.B. (1990). "Wisdom-Related Knowledge: Age/Cohort Differences in Response to Life-Planning Problems". *Developmental Psychology, 26*(3): 494-505. https://doi.org/10.1037/0012-1649.26.3.494

Tastan, S., Ayhan, H., Kose, G., Iyigun, E. & Gokcul, S. (2019). "Analysis of the Relationship Between the Autonomy of Turkish Elderly People and their Happiness and Anxiety Depression Status: A Cross-sectional Study". *International Psychogeriatrics, 31*(12): 1841-1842. https://doi.org/10.1017/S1041610219000164

Thompson, L.W., Gallagher, D. & Breckenridge, J.S. (1987). "Comparative Effectiveness of Psychotherapics for Depressed Elders". *Journal of Consulting and Clinical Psychology, 55*(3): 385-390. https://doi.org/10.1037//0022-006x.55.3.385

Veehof, M.M., Oskam, M.J., Schreurs, K.M.G. & Bohlmeijer, E.T. (2011). "Acceptance-based Interventions for the Treatment of Chronic Pain: A Systematic Review and Meta-Analysis". *Pain, 152*(3): 533-542. https://doi.org/10.1016/j.pain.2010.11.002

Weissman, M.M., Prusoff, B.A., DiMascio, A., Neu, C., Goklaney, M. & Klerman, G.L. (1979). "The Efficacy of Drugs and Psychotherapy in the Treatment of Acute Depressive Episodes". *American Journal of Psychiatry, 136*(4B): 555-558. https://doi.org/10.1176/ajp.1979.136.4b.555, PubMed: 371421, Google Scholar.

Wetherell, J.L., Afari, N., Rutledge, T., Sorrell, J.T., Stoddard, J.A., Petkus, A.J., Solomon, B.C., Lehman, D.H., Liu, L., Lang, A.J. & Atkinson, H.J. (2011). "A Randomized, Controlled Trial of Acceptance and Commitment Therapy and Cognitive-Behavioural Therapy for Chronic Pain". *Pain*, *152*(9): 2098-2107. https://doi.org/10.1016/j.pain.2011.05.016

World Report on Ageing and Health. (2015). https://www.who.int/ageing/events/world-report2015-launch/en/. Retrieved December 17, 2019.

21

Concept of Ageing

Prospects and Retrospects

Kiran Karnatak

Introduction

Today, people are living longer than ever before due to advances in education, technology, medicine, food distribution, and sanitary conditions. So, now-a-days, it is not unusual to meet people who are in their 70s, 80s, 90s, and some who are close to 100 years old. However, "adding the years to life", does not mean that we are also able to "add more life to the extra years." In other words, living longer does not always mean we will also have better or a good quality of life in later years. Some older adults in late life are healthy and independent and are still very involved in their family and community lives. Then again, it is not unusual to see older persons who can get very ill and are not able to get themselves out of bed.

Ageing is a lifelong process of growing up and growing old. It begins at conception and ends with death. So, in this sense, we are all ageing from the time of birth. In our younger years, ageing is called by other names. For example, in our infant years, we call ageing "growth and development". In our teenage and young adult years, we refer to ageing as "maturation". After age 30, our physical body begins to wear out and our functioning declines. This is called "senescence".

Ageing includes three parts:

A. Growth and development: In our infant years,
B. Maturation: In our teenage and young adult years, and
C. Senescence: After age 30. So, ageing should be explained based on these three parts.

The human body changes in many noticeable ways with age, and ageing is often accompanied by decline in bodily functions. However, a decline in function is different from loss of function that results from disease. Perhaps the first sign of ageing occurs when the eye cannot focus easily on close objects. Often by age 40, many people find it difficult to read without using glasses. Hearing also changes with age. People tend to lose some ability to hear the highest pitched tones. Therefore, older people may find that violin music no longer sounds as exciting as it did when they were younger. Our skin wrinkles and our hair turn gray or white.

The functioning of our internal organs—the heart, lungs, liver, and kidneys—also declines with age. These functions generally peak at about age 30 and then begin a gradual decline. The decline in the functioning of internal organs means that older people are more likely to experience adverse effects from drugs, changes in the environment, toxins, and illness.

All vital organs begin to lose some function as you age during adulthood. Ageing changes occur in all of the body's cells, tissues, and organs and these changes affect the functioning of all body systems. Living tissue is made up of cells. There are many different types of cells, but all have the same basic structure. Tissues are slayers of similar cells that perform a specific function.

Cells are the basic building blocks of tissues. All cells experience changes with ageing. They become larger and are less able to divide and multiply. Among other changes, there is an increase in pigments and fatty substances inside the cell (lipids). Many cells lose their ability to function, or they begin to function abnormally.

Despite this decline, most functions remain adequate throughout life, because most organs have considerably more functional capacity (functional reserve) than the body needs. For example, even if half the liver is destroyed, more than enough liver tissue remains to maintain normal function.

It is important to remember that disease, rather than normal ageing, usually accounts for loss of function in old age. Therefore, it is important to be able to distinguish between normal ageing and disease, so that diseases can be diagnosed and treated in their early stages.

Different Types of Ageing

Ageing can be viewed in different way. We need broader eyes, views to understand the ageing related issues. In this context, ageing is classified as biological ageing, psychological ageing, social ageing, chronological ageing and functional ageing.

Chronological Ageing

Chronological Ageing is the number of years a person has lived so far. An 85-year-old lady is chronologically older than a man who is 75 years old. However, chronological age may not match a person's biological, psychological, or social age. For example, the 85-year-old woman may be an active volunteer, while the 75-year-old man could be homebound. Sometimes we say, "he looks younger than his age", or "she does not act her age." In these cases, the biological, psychological, and social age do not match the chronological age.

Biological Ageing

Biological Ageing involves the loss of cells over time. With biological ageing, tissues and organs are less likely to function efficiently, the body's ability to repair itself slows down, and the immune functions decline, making the body more prone to infection. Biological ageing is sometimes referred to as Physical Ageing. A person who keeps fit and gets regular check-ups can appear biologically younger than someone who has the same age but does not keep fit.

Psychological Ageing

Psychological Ageing involves changes in memory, learning intelligence, personality, and coping. An older person who is mentally active and is able to deal with new situations can be said to be psychologically young.

Social Ageing

Social Ageing refers to changes in roles and relationships as we age. For example, it is not unusual for older people to gain new roles, like becoming grandparents. Or they may change roles, from an employee to a retiree. With role changes in later years, society may expect people to behave in certain ways. So, for some people, it may not be proper for "grandma" to go roller skating or bungee jumping because "these are things that young people do." The social age of a person in a given context can be very important because it shapes the meaning of ageing for the person, and this can make ageing a positive or negative experience.

Functional Ageing

It is related to how people compare psychologically to others to similar age.

Category of Older Persons

With increasing life expectancy and number of people increasing day by day in the 60+ category, age 60 years and above is also further classified for the demographic data collection and for other purposes also. In the Western and developed countries chronologically 65 years is considered as beginning of ageing and accordingly the ageing can be classified as:

(a) Young old: Year (65 to 74)
(b) Middle Old: Year (75 to 84)
(c) Old-Old: Years (85+)
(d) Centenarians (100+).

Changes that Occur with Ageing

As people age, they experience biological, psychological, and social changes. These changes are normal, but there are a lot of things that can be done to help older adults adjust to and compensate for these changes.

Biological Changes

External Changes: External changes are some of the most obvious changes with ageing. These include changes to one's hair, nails, and skin.

(a) Changes to the Hair

As people age, their hair loses its pigment and turns gray or white. As people get older, their hair thins. Many men become bald or have a "receding hairline", but even women notice that their hair becomes less thick. Because the hair disappears or thins, older people are more likely to get sunburned on their heads.

(b) Changes to the Nails

Nails thicken and become rigid and more brittle.

(c) Changes to the Skin

As people get older, skin loses elasticity. It becomes thin and fragile. The blood flow and oil production in the skin decrease. And the skin tends to become dry and wrinkled. "Liver spots" often appear on the hands and face. The skin may look pale and translucent. Sweat glands decrease, and there is an increased risk for heat stroke. Wounds take a longer time to heal in older persons.

When these changes happen, older adults are at risk of getting decubitus ulcers (sores that are hard to heal).

Sensory Changes

Sensory changes include changes to taste, smell, sight, and hearing.

Changes to Taste and Smell

The senses of taste and smell decline in later years. The danger is that the loss of taste and smell can make it difficult to tell if food is spoiled or if there is a gas leak in the kitchen stove.

The decline in senses of taste and smell can also have serious nutritional outcomes. Tasteless, bland foods can make eating less enjoyable.

Changes in Vision

As a person gets older, the lens in the eye becomes yellow and thickens. This means that the older eye needs more light than a younger eye. The lens of the eye can grow unevenly. This may cause glare problems. A small amount of glare may cause great difficulties for an older adult, and it may cause anxiety or affect their ability to concentrate.

Changes in the lens also make colour perception more difficult. It may be hard for older adults to clearly see pastel colours like pale blue, light green, pale yellow, and pale pink. It becomes hard to tell the difference between dark brown, dark blue, and black. Red is the easiest colour to see in old age. The older eye does not adjust quickly to changes in levels of light. Sudden changes in lighting may be dangerous and may cause accidents and falls. Conditions of the eye can cause vision loss. More than half of severe visual impairment occurs in people 65 and older. However, this does not always make older people totally blind. Many people can still function with moderate vision loss.

Changes in Hearing

There is a decline in the hearing ability of older persons.

Hearing loss is worse at high frequencies. So, high pitched sounds may be more difficult to hear than low-pitched sounds. Changes in hearing may mean that:

(a) Some sounds will be heard and others may not,
(b) Some sounds may be distorted or heard incorrectly, and
(c) Things are heard incorrectly and misinterpreted.

Many people do not want to admit that they can not hear and might "cover up" by just smiling or nodding at whatever you say.

Organ System Changes: These include changes to the heart and cardiovascular system, the lungs and respiratory system, the gastrointestinal system, the urinary tract system, and the musculoskeletal system.

Changes to the Heart and Cardiovascular System

With age, the heart pumps with less force, and there is a decrease in cardiac output. More time is required for the heart to return to normal after exertion.

Changes to the Lungs and Respiratory System

Deep breathing may become difficult because the skeletal muscles become more rigid. The cough mechanism becomes less effective due to anatomic and muscle changes. Breathing moves to the upper part of the chest. The lungs become less elastic and decrease in size.

Changes to the Musculoskeletal System

We reach our maximum height at age 25. After that, height declines an average of 3 inches over the life span, due to loss of bone. With age, the width of the shoulders declines. There is bone loss, weakened muscles, and loss of elasticity in ligaments. Cartilage between joints wears thin, and lubricating fluid decreases, causing stiffness in the joints. Joint stiffness limits physical activity and mobility. This affects gait and posture. With declines in physical activity, strength and stamina will also be affected.

Changes to the Gastrointestinal System

With age, there is a decrease in the contraction of muscles in the esophagus, so it takes more time for food to get to the stomach. This explains why many older adults have the sensation of being full before finishing a full meal. This can result in inadequate nutrient intake.

Changes to the Urinary Tract

With age, kidneys decrease in size and volume, this affects renal function. This makes the need to urinate more frequent. The bladder may not empty completely after voiding. This can lead to urinary tract infections. Weak muscles of the bladder can lead to incontinence (the inability to control bladder functions).

Psychological Changes

In normal ageing, people become slower at "recalling" facts. It takes them a longer time to "react" to things. However, if given enough time, they may be very functional. Learning can be a challenge if elders have problems with their hearing or eyesight. Learning and memory can be impaired if the environment is noisy, uncomfortable, or unpleasant. Learning and memory can be impaired due to illness, overmedication, depression, and stress.

Social Changes

Elders experience many losses. Their children grow up and leave home, they retire from work, they experience physical declines, and their older friends start to die. Most elders live on fixed incomes. When elders can not live on their own, they have to live with others, for example with family or friends or in nursing homes. When elders are lonely and frail, they can become victims of fraud and abuse.

Common Health Conditions Associated with Ageing

Common conditions in older age include hearing loss, cataracts and refractive errors, back and neck pain and osteoarthritis, chronic obstructive pulmonary disease, diabetes, depression and dementia. As people age, they are more likely to experience several conditions at the same time.

Older age is also characterized by the emergence of several complex health states commonly called geriatric syndromes. They are often the consequence of multiple underlying factors and include frailty, urinary incontinence, falls, delirium and pressure ulcers.

Factors Influencing Healthy Ageing

A longer life brings with it opportunities, not only for older people and their families, but also for societies as a whole. Additional years provide the chance to pursue new activities such as further education, a new career or a long-neglected passion. Older people also contribute in many ways to their families and communities. Yet the extent of these opportunities and contributions depends heavily on one factor: health.

Evidence suggests that the proportion of life in good health has remained broadly constant, implying that the additional years are in poor health. If people can experience these extra years of life in good health and if they live in a supportive environment, their ability to do the things they value will be little different from that of a younger person. If these added years are dominated by declines in physical and mental capacity, the implications for older people and for society are more negative.

Although some of the variations in older people's health are genetic, most is due to people's physical and social environments—including their homes, neighbourhoods, and communities, as well as their personal characteristics—such as their sex, ethnicity, or socio-economic status. The environments that people live in as children – or even as developing fetuses—combined with their personal characteristics, have long-term effects on how they age.

Physical and social environments can affect health directly or through barriers or incentives that affect opportunities, decisions and health behaviour. Maintaining healthy behaviours throughout life, particularly eating a balanced diet, engaging in regular physical activity and refraining from tobacco use, all contribute to reducing the risk of non-communicable diseases, improving physical and mental capacity and delaying care dependency.

Supportive physical and social environments also enable people to do what is important to them, despite losses in capacity. The availability of safe and accessible public buildings and transport, and places that are easy to walk around, are examples of supportive environments. In developing a public-health response to ageing, it is important not just to consider individual and environmental approaches that ameliorate the losses associated with older age, but also those that may reinforce recovery, adaptation and psychosocial growth.

Challenges in Responding to Population Ageing

There is no typical older person. Some 80-year-olds have physical and mental capacities similar to many 30-year-olds. Other people experience significant declines in capacities at much younger ages. A comprehensive public health response must address this wide range of older people's experiences and needs.

The diversity seen in older age is not random. A large part arises from people's physical and social environments and the impact of these environments on their opportunities and health behaviour. The relationship we have with our environments is skewed by personal characteristics such as the family we were born into, our sex and our ethnicity, leading to inequalities in health.

Older people are often assumed to be frail or dependent and a burden to society. Public health professionals, and society as a whole, need to address these and other ageist attitudes, which can lead to discrimination, affect the way policies are developed and the opportunities older people have to experience healthy ageing.

Globalization, technological developments (e.g. in transport and communication), urbanization, migration and changing gender norms are influencing the lives of older people in direct and indirect ways. A public health response must take stock of these current and projected trends and frame policies accordingly.

The concept of Quality of Life is a pervasive and dynamic term. There are so many ways by which quality of life has been defined in the literature. But all has considering the fact related to socio-cultural and environmental aspects of life. According to World Health Organization, it is the perception of the individual's position in life, expectations, standards, and concerns (WHOQOL Group, 1998). Quality of life has multidimensional parameters which consider the individualistic perception of their physical, psychological, social as well as environmental aspects taken into account while commenting on people's quality of life. It has four major domains—physical, psychological, social relationships, and environment (Dykstra, 2009).

"Spirituality" is mainly concerned with individualistic inner life experiences and about their spirit mind and how he or she relates them with the world. A spiritual person generally seeks inner peace of mind, harmony, optimism, and mercy for themselves as well as for others. Spirituality gives an attitude to see the world from different but positive perspectives. The term spirituality has come from the Latin word 'spiritus' which means 'the breath' and breath is a most vital aspect of life. The major connection of spirituality was found with the person's inner world, mind, soul, and its connection with the world. Spirituality provides a deep inner sense to solve existential questions and awareness of multiple levels of consciousness. It also develops insight into the spirit and soul as the creative life force of evolution.

There is a difference in an individual's spiritual, emotional, and intellectual intelligence. Intellectual ability generally answers 'what', emotional ability answers 'how' but spiritual intelligence answers 'why' related questions of an individual's phenomenological world. Spiritual intelligence converts the personal to the trans personal and the self to the spirit (Vaughan, 2002).

Spiritual intelligence has also been defined as the highest levels of development of cognitive, moral, emotional, and interpersonal ability, as a separate developmental line, an attitude of openness to love at any stage, and as a peak experience (Wilber, 2000). According to King, spiritual intelligence makes an individual able to understand existential and non-existential metaphysical issues and the reality of the universe. Spirituality also gives deep knowledge and awareness about the meaning and purpose of life and develops the capacity to identify the beaneries of self and the ability to connect one's past and future to the present. Spiritual intelligence makes an individual able to enter and exit in the higher states of conscious awareness at one's direction (King, DeCicco, 2009). Spiritual intelligence is an outcome of an individual's highest growth in terms of higher mental function, knowledge of the meaning and purpose of life, and awareness about the boundaries of the self. Therefore, spiritual intelligence can be a significant tool in the individual's adjustment and adaptability to the surroundings and improvement of quality of life (Amram, 2009). Spirituality helps elderly people in stress management through ways of adaptive coping, controlling unhealthy emotions, handling relationship issues, and promote for health-seeking behaviour (Koeing,

2006). The elderly who were higher in spirituality were usually found with overall good health because spirituality strongly promotes their daily life functioning and level of satisfaction (Saad *et al.*, 2010). The previous study postulated a significant connection between living conditions and spirituality as important factors in maintaining general health conditions among the older population (Philip Sijuwade, 2013). Spirituality plays an important and positive role in various aspects related to physical, psychological, self, and environmental deals, such as it helps to deal with stressful situations, developing self-resilience and improving self-esteem, creating a positive perception of one's environment, mental health, quality of life, well-being, promotes good adjustments and adaptability to the adverse situations, helps to maintain meaningful and healthy inter-personal relationships. Higher spiritual intelligence and good mental health influence the individual's flexibility of actions positively.

In India, however, the retirement age is between 58 to 60 years in the private sector. For Central Government employees, it is 60 years. Retirement itself give a very negative experience to the elderly because it set a narrative of being unproductive among people's mind, and elderly are treated as out of the centre of society and life. While the duration of absolute dependency of elderly is seen only in the last few years of their life, but they have been usually tagged as unproductive and marginalized starting from the 60 years of age. While they can, and want to be productive, but there is no provision in the Government policies for their empowerment. Our elderly needs empowerment and respect not only sympathy or pity. In 2022, near about 400 studies analysis is saying that, those who are having positive attitude towards life live 7 years more than those who carry a negative outlook.

References

Amram, Y. (2009). *The Contribution of Emotional and Spiritual Intelligence to Effective Business Leadership*. Doctoral Dissertation, Institute of Transpersonal Psychology, California, Palo Alto.

Dykstra, P. (2009). "Older Adult Loneliness: Myths and Realities". *European Journal of Ageing, 6*: 91-100.

King, D.B., DeCicco, T.L. (2009). "A Viable Model and Self-Report Measure of Fair Deal Inteligence". *International Journal of Transpire Studies*, 28.68.85.

Koeing, G. (2006). "Religion, Spirituality and Ageing". *Ageing and Mental Health, 10*(1).

Saad *et al.,* (2010). "The Impact of Spiritual Intelligence on the Health of the Elderly in Malaysia". *Asian Social Work and Policy. 4*(2): 84-97. https://doi.org/10.1111/j.17531411.2010.00039.x

Sijuwade, P.O. (2013). "Spiritual Intelligence, Living Status and General Health of the Elderly". *Pakistan Journal of Social Sciences, 10*(3): 135-138.

Vaughan, D. (2002). *Media Launch Contexts. 1*: 68-69. DOI: 10.1525/ctx.2002.1.2.68.

WHOQOL Group, (1998). "The World Health Organization Quality of Life Assessment (WHOQOL): *Development and General Psychometric Properties. Social Science & Medicine, 46*: 1569-1585.

Wilber, K. (2000). *Integral Psychology*. Boston: Shambhala, pp. 197-217.

22

Successful Ageing

Old is Gold

Aradhana Shukla

Introduction

"It's not how old you are. It's how you are old."—*Jules Renard*

Brief Summary of the History of the "Ageing Concept": The first key element in this short history is 1948 when WHO Member States adopted a new definition of health as "a state of complete physical, mental and social well-being and not merely the absence of disease or infirmity" (World Health Organization, 2015). The 1986 Ottawa Charter for Health Promotion, built on the progress made through the Declaration on Primary Health Care at *Alma-Ata*, and further specified that to "reach a state of complete physical, mental, and social well-being, an individual or group must be able to identify and to realize aspirations, to satisfy needs, and to change or cope with the environment" (World Health Organization, 1986). These fundamentals should be understood in the context of "health as the capacity to love and work" (Smith, 2008); and the importance of "happiness, harmonious relations and security of all peoples" (World Health Organization, 2015). A second element is that health at both ends of the spectrum of life may be more closely related than previously thought. The Life Course Approach (Hanson, 2016) connects broader social, political, and environmental determinants of health, including the organization and effectiveness of health and other social systems, to health outcomes, across all critical life stages [refer to D. Kuh's Chap. (Kusumastutia, 2016)]. Along with genetic variation, the impact can explain the wide variations in the rate of ageing (Sadana, Blas, Budhwani, Koller & Paraje, 2016), in terms of declining capacities (Hanson, Cooper,

Aihie Sayer, Eendebak, Clough & Beard, 2016), eventually resulting in frailty, disease, disability, and death (Mount, Lara, Schols & Mathers, 2016). Although the promoting and maintaining of intrinsic capacity is a priority from a medical perspective, evidence indicates that what is more important to the individual, particularly older adults, is functional ability that enables a person to do what he or she values, the essence of well-being (World Health Organization, 1986; Smith, 2008), the third element. Specifically, WHO defines functional ability as "the health related attributes that enable people to be and to do what they have reason to value. It is determined by the intrinsic capacity of the individual (i.e., the combination of all the individual's physical and mental capacities). Intrinsic capacity at any point in time is determined by many factors, including underlying physiological and psychological changes, health-related behaviours, and the presence or absence of disease.

Objective well-being includes people's living conditions and their opportunities to realize their potential, which in principle should be equitably distributed among all people, including older adults. Moreover, three components make up subjective well-being: eudemonic well-being—self-perceptions of autonomy, competence, purpose of life, locus of control; positive and negative states—experience of joy, happiness, anxiety, sadness; and life evaluation—a reflective assessment (World Health Organization Regional Office for Europe, 2012). Well-being is more than just physical health or objective living conditions, as it carries strong connotations of happiness, but also of hedonism (Brussow, 2013). Moreover, the benefits of maintaining "good health" well into old age include reduced dependency and healthcare costs (Rowe & Kahn, 2015). "Good health" will allow older people to continue participating productively in society, and to put to good use the many advantages older adults can offer, such as their stability, a heightened ability to manage conflicts, and their consideration for other age groups (Brussow, 2013). Since mid-twentieth century, the number of attempts to name, define, conceive, and measure the process of ageing across the life span has been impressively diverse (see Table 22.1). Even when limited to literature mostly from Western and higher income country settings, different concepts and definitions reflect distinct viewpoints, norms, and values, as well as differences in the approach to measurement and interpretation (Kusumastutia, Derksb, Tellier, Di Nucci, Lund, Mortensen & Westendorp, 2016).

Table 2.1: Key concepts in a brief history of the ageing concept (see also Martin *et al.*)

Basic healthy ageing definition	**General condition of ageing of a person's mind and body, usually meaning freedom from illness, injury, or pain**	
Ego integrity *vs.* despair (1950)	Subjective evaluation of one's life as having been a fulfilling and satisfying one	(Erickson, 1950)
Activity theory (1961)	Maintaining middle-aged activities and attitudes into later adulthood	(Cumming and Henry, 1961)
Disengagement theory (1961)	Desire and ability of older people to disengage from active life in order to prepare themselves for death	(Cumming and Henry, 1961)
Successful ageing (1961)	Conditions promoting a maximum satisfaction and happiness	(Havighurst, 1961)
Successful ageing (1963)	Having inner feelings of happiness and satisfaction with one's present and past life	(Havighurst, 1963)
Index of activities of daily living (ADL) (1963)	Systematic approach to measuring physical performance in a population of older or chronically ill persons	(Katz *et al.*, 1963)
Ageing successfully (1972)	Coping style, prior ability to adapt, and expectations of life, as well as income, health, social interactions, freedoms, and constraints; coalescence of personality which plays into the enormous complexity of successful ageing	(Neugarten, 1972)
Successful ageing (1987; 1998)	Interplay between social engagement with life, health, and functioning for a positive ageing experience (low probability of disease and disease-related disability)	(Rowe, 1987 and Kahn, 1998)
Selective optimization with compensation (1990)	(a) Selective adaptation and transformation of internal and external resources (b) Optimization and compensation (c) Maintenance of function, maximizing gains and minimizing losses	(Baltes and Baltes, 1990)
Productive ageing (1990)	Any activity by an older individual that contributes to producing goods or services, or develops the capacity to produce them (whether or not the individual is paid for this activity)	(Butler *et al.*, 1990)

(*Contd.*)

Active ageing (2002)	Active ageing is the process of optimizing opportunities for health, participation, and security in order to enhance quality of life as people age	(WHO, 2002)
Civic engagement (2004)	Need to involve older adults in the community, create opportunities for participation, and generate further interest in the mutual benefit of participation for community beneficiaries and participants	(GSA, 2004; Martinson *et al.*, 2006)
Gerotranscendence (2005)	Legacy building and existential concerns allowing old age to possess its own meaning and character	(Tornstam, 2005)
Healthy ageing (2006)	Optimizing opportunities for good health, so that older people can take an active part in society and enjoy an independent and high quality of life	(Swedish National Institute of Public Health, 2006)
Cultural aspects of "good ageing"(2007)	Different cultures have different understandings and interact in different ways to promote or detract from a "good old age"	(Fry *et al.*, 2007)
Successful ageing and diseases (2009)	Successful ageing may coexist with diseases and functional limitations *if* compensatory psychological and/or social mechanisms are used	(Young *et al.*, 2009)
Cognitive and emotional aspects of successful ageing (2010)	There is a gulf between researcher and lay definitions—the former describes freedom from disease and disability, and the latter focuses on adaptation, meaningfulness, and connection	(Jeste *et al.*, 2010)
Healthy and active ageing (2011)	The process of optimizing opportunities for health to enhance quality of life as people age and grow old	(European Commission, 2011)
Resilient ageing (2014)	The process an older person endures beyond physical, psychosocial, or cognitive adversity, through protective factors that influence the attributes of coping, hardiness, and self-concept, in the person's quest towards quality of life	(Hicks and Conner, 2014)
Healthy ageing (2015)	Healthy ageing is more than just the absence of disease; it is the process of developing and maintaining the functional ability that enables well-being in older age	(WHO, 2015)

Bearing in mind all these interacting factors, approaches to the concept of ageing have evolved from the disengagement theory promoted in the 1960s (Cumming E, Henry, 1961), towards a more "positive gerontology" approach, which really took off in the late 1980s (Rowe & Kahn,1987). Currently, the WHO's 2015 definition of "Healthy Ageing" (World Health Organization, 2015) appears to be most realistic, and considers continuous, trajectories of health across the life course, rather than a focus on chronologic age or a threshold for good ageing (Sadana, Blas, Budhwani, Koller & Paraje, 2016). It is also more realistic as it is inclusive of all older adults, in contrast to "successful ageing" or "anti-ageing" discourses that focus on elimination of disease or ageing processes. It is also more visionary, as it recognizes all older adults, irrespective of their level of intrinsic capacities, can be supported to have a good level of functional ability.

Successful ageing has been receiving much attention in recent years due to the longevity, growing elderly population and high risk for having various physical and mental health problems. Successful ageing is a state of health (physical and psychological) and vitality throughout one's life span. It simply denotes health and well-being in later decades of life. It has been so significant that the year 1999 was called as "Year of the Older Persons" by the World Health Organization. It gave an impetus to look for the factors and conditions that would develop an understanding of the problems of ageing and identifying the strategies for facilitating successful ageing. It is also worth knowing that there is diversity in the ageing process. Advancement in medicines and technological usage in health have led to increase in life expectancy, thus leading to a greater surge in the older population in both developed and developing countries. This increase in the elderly population has brought several issues related to physical and psychosocial problems. Increase in the longevity has brought the focus on how to old, with greater impetus to age well.

In recent years, the concept of successful ageing has induced much debate (Calasanti, 2016; Bulow & Soderqvist, 2015), and various definitions of the concept have been introduced in various studies (Cosco. *et al.,* 2014).

- According to the classic concept of Rowe and Kahn, successful ageing is defined as high physical, psychological, and social functioning in old age without major diseases (Rowe & Kahn,1987; Rowe & Kahn, 1997). Here, we use the classic name, although several terms of this concept, such as healthy ageing, active ageing, productive ageing, and ageing well etc. have been used in the field (Fernandez-Ballesteros, 2019). The relationship of these terms, and the dimensions of successful ageing are presented in Fig. 22.1. This figure clearly denotes profile of successful ageing and reflects it is all possible components that make the aging successful.

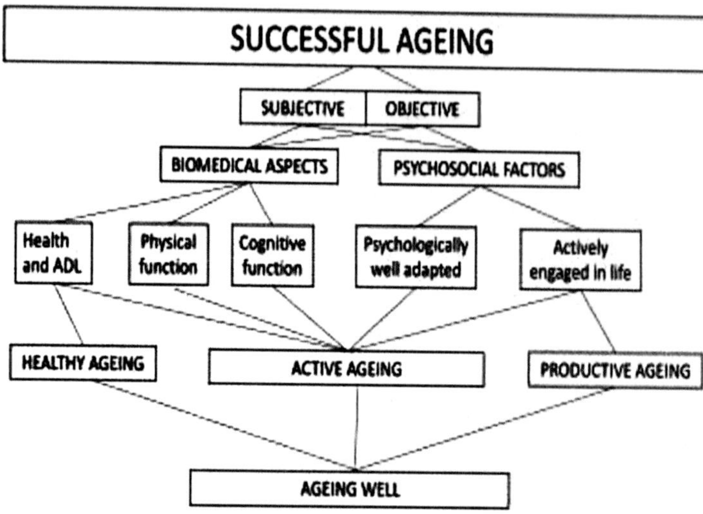

Fig. 22.1

Source: The dimensions of successful ageing. Modified from Fernandez-Ballesteros (2019).

The main focus in the concept of successful ageing is how to expand healthy and functional years throughout the life span (Fries,1980; Kivimäki,Ferrie, 2011). The phenomenon of successful ageing can be viewed from a population or an individual perspective (Fernandez-Ballesteros, R., 2019). At the population level, definition includes determinants of health and participation for the purpose of promoting policies, whereas at the individual level it is defined by outcomes of health, physical, and cognitive function, and life involvement (Fernandez-Ballesteros, 2019). Because, successful ageing is a multidimensional concept encompassing domains of physical, functional, social, and psychological health, all of these dimensions should be taken into account, both with objective and subjective conditions, while studying the phenomenon (Cosco, Prina, Perales, Stephan, Brayne, 2014; Fries, 1980; Martin, Kelly, Kahana, *et al.,* 2014; Depp, Jeste, 2006).

Kim and Park (2016) conducted a meta-analysis of the correlates of successful ageing and they identified that four domains describing successful ageing were—avoiding disease and disability, having high cognitive, mental and physical function, being actively engaged in life, and being psychologically well adapted in later life. Similarly, in the model of "Aging well" by Fernandez-Ballesteros *et al.* (Fernández-Ballesteros, Garcia, Abarra, *et al.,* 2008; Fernández-Ballesteros, Robine, Walker, Kalache, 2013), successful ageing is defined by the domains of health and activities of daily living (ADL), physical and cognitive functioning, social participation and engagement, and also positive affect and control, when the definition by Baltes and colleagues (Baltes, Baltes,1990; Baltes, 1997) is also considered. Kok *et al.* (Kok, Aartsen, Deeg and Huisman, 2015) found in their study that many older adults were ageing relatively successfully, but there was a variation between indicators of characteristics of successful ageing, and the combinations of successful indicators that may vary between individuals.

Most definitions of successful ageing include such outcomes which can be described as the operational definitions of the concept (Fernandez-Ballesteros, 2019). The operational definitions are generally based on objective measurements of health and functionality and do not necessarily take into account individual's perceptions of their own health and well-being which would give more comprehensive view of ageing (Cosco, Prina, Perales, Stephan and Brayne, 2014). Kleinedam and colleagues (Kleinedam, Thoma, Maercker *et al.,* 2018) have suggested that well-constructed operationalisation of successful ageing includes measurements of physiological health, well-being and social engagement, with subjective and objective aspects.

Successful aging is an important concept, and one that has been the subject of much research. During the last 15 years, this research has shifted from formulating criteria for successful aging to describing the processes involved in successful ageing. The model of Selective Option with Compensation (SOC-model) proves to be one of the leading models in this field. Although evidences about its value is accumulating, we argue that this model mainly focuses on how people react to losses and that proactive coping aimed at potential threats to goals may also be a valuable strategy. We propose that proactive coping may be important for success since it results in a prolonged availability of resources for optimization and compensation processes and a delay in disengagement from important goals.

Important Goals

Models of successful aging that are purely objective as well as those that are purely subjective inhibit advancement of the (Cosco, Prina, Perales, Stephan, *et al.,* 2014). Biomedical models are unrealistic, as studies of the oldest old and centenarians find that nearly all people experience chronic health problems and functional disability in very old age (Ranberg, Schroll, & Jeune, 2001; Cho, Martin, & Poon, 2012; Von Faber *et al.,* 2001). Given the plasticity and adaptability nature, according to Baltes and Baltes (1990), purely subjective conceptualizations of successful aging, with their inherent individual biases, are also insufficient. While Baltes and Baltes (1990) have contended that both objective and subjective aspects for successful aging were important, they said, "the objective aspects of medical, psychological, and social functioning and the subjective aspects of life.quality and life meaning seem to form a Gordian knot that no one is prepared to untie at the pres. However, if we integrate knowledge gained about successful aging over the past several decades with the roots established by Havighurst (1961) and by Katz *et al.* (1963), it may be possible to cut through the knot and gain new appreciation for the construct.

One of the main conceptual challenges of the successful aging literature is disentangling aging, marked by the passage of successful ageing. Depp and Jeste's (2006) review found that across a host of studies, the most consistent predictor of successful aging was age. Similarly, using the Health and Retirement Study, McLaughlin *et al.* (2010) found that between the young and old group participants aged 75 years and older were 70 per cent less likely to experience successful ageing. However, when ageing was assessed using self-ratings, Jeste *et al.* (2013) reported that older age was associated with higher ratings of successful even after accounting for declining physical and cognitive functioning.

What are the Major Challenges Faced by the Elderly People

Problems of the elderly can be attributed to a number of factors. Everyday problems for the elderly include physical health, mental health, ageism, and financial insecurity. Below, we will take a look at problems faced by senior citizens and solutions.

Physical Health Problems of the Elderly

The biggest challenge to older adults can often be their health. To monitor these old-age problems, it's best to get regular check-ups and monitor your body for changes. Depending on the health concerns, possible solutions to these problems can include a healthy diet, exercise, possible medicines and/or yogic exercises. Some of these health concerns include:

- Heart disease
- Diabetes
- Hearing loss
- Cataracts
- Chronic obstructive pulmonary disease
- Heart attack and/or stroke
- Extra susceptibility to sexually transmitted diseases
- Muscle weakness
- Fatigue
- Loss of balance, which can result in falls
- Malnutrition
- Oral health issues, such as dry mouth and gum disease
- Incontinence and constipation.

Age related system change in physical activity.

Predictors of Successful Ageing: Physical Observation

Several factors have been found to be important predictors of successful ageing. Understanding of the predictive factors help in guiding interventions for promotion of successful ageing. They help in enhancing quality of life, decreasing mortality and morbidity.

Subjective Well-being

Subjective experience of happiness or well-being is regarded as crucial for successful ageing. High subjective well-being is considered beneficial as it enhances our ability to cope and deal with challenges. Subjective well-being can be conceptualized in terms of an affective component (presence of positive affect and absence of or low negative affect) and (a cognitive-evaluative component sense of satisfaction in life) (Diener, 1984). Higher subjective well-being is associated with better health and longevity, cardiovascular health and good immune system.

One's physical and mental well-being have also been found to be affected by resilience. Resilience buffers and protects against traumas, losses, deprivation and threats. Researches on resilience initially was carried out on children with deprivation but later on it has been spread to other areas as well and its role in successful ageing is now well established. Several demographic factors (socio-economic status, financial well-being factors, life satisfaction, health status, socio-psychological factor, health risk behaviour, psychometric factors, productive engagement and personal resources) have also been found to affect our subjective well-being and correlate with successful ageing. It has been noticed that people with higher education have a better sense of well-being during old age. Theng *et al.,* (2022) did a global research to study the trend in the subjective well-being of older adult from 2001-2021 following a biometric approach and noted that the mechanism, especially in the bidirectional effect, between the subjective well-being of older adults and its influencing factors is still worthy of further exploration. They did more studies to wide the comprehensive file of older people. Higher education leading to better job opportunities and in turn resulting in increased income, enables elderly to have better access to resources and hence, have better chances of successful ageing. Marital status and good social support also play an important role in predicting successful ageing. Jimmy Young (2014) showed a close knit between successful ageing and well-being and developed an adaptation model to empirically define the direct and indirect effects of two distal (education and past life expectation) and five proximal influences (physical functioning, cognitive functioning, physical health impairment, social research and perceived economic status).

Cognitive Functioning

Cognitive functioning refers to higher mental processes including attention, executive function, speed of processing, linguistic ability, learning, memory and visuo-spatial function. Higher cognitive functioning is another crucial component for successful ageing. Better cognitive abilities such as planning, problem solving and memory can help us to deal with our day-to-day challenges and enable us to function independently. Better cognition could enhance our confidence, self-esteem and well-being. On the other hand, cognitive impairment affected our physical and psychological well-being.

It may be noted here that normal ageing affects our cognition especially decline in processing speed and memory. However, such decline is considered normal and does not require professional help or support. On the other hand, many times memory problems could start affecting our decision making and activities of daily life. And such condition might be called dementia. Dementia is a general term for loss of memory, and other thinking abilities that are severe enough to interfere with daily life. According to World Health Organization, "dementia is a syndrome due to disease of the brain, usually of chronic or progressive nature, in which there is impairment of multiple higher cortical functions, including memory, thinking, thinking orientation, mathematical ability, learning capacity, language and judgement" (ICD-10). Dementia is associated with significant medical, psychological and social burden. There are 3.7 million Indians with dementia and the total societal cost is about 14,700 crore and the numbers are expected to take doubled by 2030 (Gela, Fekadu and Mengistie, 2022).

Physical Functioning

Health is usually considered as wealth. Better health is associated with happiness and ageing successfully. Ageing can attract a host of physical and mental health problems such as arthritis, hypertension, hearing problems, anxiety and depression. Presence of physical or psychological problems could adversely affect our well-being and psychosocial functioning including quality of life. Moreover, bone shrinkage, muscular shrinkage, spinal discs, visual and hearing loss, chronic condition, falls, unitary in continence, osteoarthritis and other health problems are commonly seen in the people of old age (Fried & Guralnik, 1997). Muhammad *et al.* (2023) studied multiple socio-economic risks and cognitive impairment among older men and women in India and found that in older men, the cognitive impairment was higher than women. Poor quality of life is associated with low subjective experience of successful ageing. On the other hand, absence of disease and disability enables us to function independently and enhances our subjective experience of successful ageing (as proposed by Rowe and Kahn, 1987). Physical and mental illness can adversely affect our independence, social activities, leisure activitics as well as instrumental activities of daily living and such interruption might compromise successful ageing. Therefore, physical and psychological health and well-being both are necessary components of successful ageing.

Age-associated Body System Changes

Age impacts widespread changes, in various body tissues and systems, at variable rates. Despite all these changes, elderly individuals may significantly expand their productive life at home, in society and the workplace, by engaging in social, physical and cognitive activities. In healthy older volunteers, cognitive training can lead to increase in brain grey matter volume in the "exercised" areas (MacLaughlin, J. & Holick, M.F., 1985).

Lifestyle and behavioural measures, with specific carefully designed, age-oriented medicalcare and specific devices wherever needed, are instrumental to achieve successful aging. Remaining active physically, cognitively, and socially, with continued generativity and making a contribution, are the main parameters of successful aging (Fried, L.P., Freedman, M., Endres, T.E. *et al.,* 1997; Pattanaungkul, S., Riggs, B.L., Yergey, A.L. *et al.,* 2000). Remaining active has specific health benefits, both in the physical and cognitive domains. There is evidence to support the old saying "use it or lose it": to live longer and also healthier.

There is abundance of evidence suggesting that mental health diverges from physical health, in that coping, adaptation and resilience functions are surprisingly well preserved throughout most of the human life span. This important aspect of aging has very significant implications in various roles that older people can perform in various aspects of their societies. Their input could be extremely fruitful in many areas that need cognitive capability. The physical aging should not bar them from providing this crucial input. This may add to various shortcomings and fallacies of the arbitrary retirement age of 65 years.

Additional benefits include:

- Improved bone health with reduction in risk of fractures.
- Improved postural stability, with reduction in falls.
- Increased coordination, flexibility and range of motion.
- Psychological benefits: related to preserved cognitive function and alleviation of depression.
- Improved concept of personal control and self-efficacy, independent lifestyle, functional capacity and quality of life.

A good number of clinical studies showed significant benefits of exercise and community involvement (American College of Sports Medicine Position Stand, 1998; Depp CA&Jestc DV, 2006).Those who live longer lives, and are vibrant until shortly before death, may provide the best possible example of successful ageing. From the psychological domain, ageing is seen as a life-long adaptive process, an ongoing dynamic of selective optimization with compensation, involving the following three elements, which provide a general framework for understanding the developmental changes and resilience across the life span:

1. **Selection:** As a result of physical and cognitive limitations, individuals select, or optimize, their efforts into areas of high priority.
2. **Optimization:** Individuals continue to engage in behaviours that enrich and augment their physical and mental reserves.
3. **Compensation:** Individuals compensate by using psychological and technological strategies.

Psychological strategies may involve using external memory aids. Technological strategies may include a hearing aid. The three elements interplay with one another so that a person may suffer from a reduction in general capacity and losses in specific functions, but creates a transformed and effective life, and thereby the older person maximizes and attains positive or desired outcomes, and minimizes or avoids negative or undesired ones.

Positive Personality Traits

The role of personality cannot be denied in the process of successful ageing. Several personality characteristics have been found to be positively related to well-being and longevity. The big five personality traits (Fiske, 1949; McCrae & Costa, 1987)—openness to experience, agreeableness, extra version, conscientiousness and neuroticism, have been found to be associated with environmental mastery, purpose in life and self-acceptance. Several researches have been carried out and established the inevitable role of personality traits in ageing successfully. Having a meaning or purpose in life makes one's life objective and significant. It also helps in understanding the negative or stressful events in more positive way.

Resilience, optimism, perseverance, self-efficacy, hardiness, ego-resiliency are some of the other characteristics found to be related to well-being and in ageing successfully. Resilience is an important component in subjective well-being and is considered both as a process and an outcome as well.

Research studies consider resilience to be a dynamic developmental process rather than resilience as a personality trait. Resilience can be enhanced and strengthened, however, presence of certain other traits can affect the outcome such as, optimism, which is having a strong conviction that good rather than bad will only happen; perseverance, which is undertaking tasks and challenges and finishing them; self-efficacy plays a strong protective role in handling challenges and stresses in life. As defined by Bandura, "self-efficacy is people's beliefs in their capabilities to produce desired effects by their own actions".

Another term which is often used with resilience is "ego-resiliency." It is the capacity to overcome, and bounce back from adversity, and has been considered to be a stable personality trait. It has been found that adults high on ego-resiliency exhibited greater physiological and emotional recovery from stress. Similarly, another trait which is psychological hardiness, is also associated with resilience, as it enables older adults to handle difficulties and challenges in later years. Psychological hardiness consists of three Interrelated dispositions: commitment (not alienation), control (not powerlessness), and challenge (not (threat). Another personality characteristic which is very important is hope, that is having positive expectation from future and also working towards it.

Living Life Fullest

There are several intentional and effortful activities that we do in our life order to make our life more productive and healthy. Indulging in a variety of such activities is useful such as drawing, gardening, reading, painting, stitching, embroidery, cooking or learning new skills, engaging in physical activities, making effort to enhance quality relationship, donating and helping people, spending time with nature and so on. It is worth mentioning here that active participation in effortful activities could have far reaching beneficial impact on our physical, psychological and social health. For example, leisure or social activities involve some form of physical, mental or social stimulation which in turn improves our physical and psychosocial well-being. Similarly, participation in social activities is known to enhance interactive skills, sense of belonging, purpose, support as well as physical and mental stimulation. To summarize, engaging in the health behaviours such as having good eating habits, exercising or doing some physical activity, getting health check-ups regularly, avoiding smoking and alcohol, maintaining a regular routine and sleeping well, reduce the chances of physical health problems. Social activities, recreational activities and creative activities also affect one's physical, mental and cognitive well-being.

Strategies to Promote Successful Ageing

Over the years various strategies have been found to be effective in promoting successful ageing. Such activities comprise active participation in regular physical activities such as walking and *yoga*, eating a balanced diet, self- monitoring of one's own health, following a healthy lifestyle, engaging in social relations, having a positive attitude towards self and others, doing things that gives happiness, staying mentally active by doing activities such as reading newspaper, solving quizzes, learning new skills, improving knowledge about latest technology.

Lifestyle Matters

Age related decline in physical and cognitive functions are often associated with lifestyle and related factors. Lifestyle factors are our own learned habits and behaviours, and hence, it is modifiable in nature. Exercise, sleep patterns, cigarette smoking, drugs use, medications, alcohol use, caffeine consumption, eating habits, use of seat belt, helmets are some of the examples of lifestyle factors. Successful ageing can be achieved by keeping in mind the above things and following a healthy lifestyle such as abstaining from smoking and drug use, doing physical activity and regular exercise and sustaining quality dietary habits.

Beneficial role of physical activities/exercise and quality dietary habits is widely reported in scientific literature. It is well proven that physical activity is associated with better health, memory and cognition. Further it reduces our risk to develop ageing related health problems such as cardiovascular disease, hypertension, diabetes and other physical and brain related problems.

Social Support Helps

Quality social support is considered important for successful ageing. Our social ties, relationship and related support are known to enhance our well-being. It is basically network of people, such as friends, relatives, neighbours or significant others who are accessible or available for support and help. Social support can be available in terms of structure (size of network) and function (emotional or instrumental) it serves. Having quality support system is associated with healthy and successful ageing. High quality social support is known to enhance our coping to deal with the stress as well as illness through perceived support and assistance.

Benefits of social support are as follows:

- Longevity.

- Better physical health.
- Better emotional health and well-being.
- Tangible assistance.
- Information and guidance.

Keep Learning

Constantly engaging in varieties of stimulating activities like learning new things, reading, exploring new things, doing creative activities, playing stimulating games are known to improve our cognitive functions. Cognitive or mental stimulation helps keep our brain healthy. Beneficial effects of such activities are widely reported in successful ageing literature. Cognitive activity enhances our brain resilience and therefore, helps to achieve successful ageing. Participation in these activities can stimulate as well as enhance our physical, social and cognitive functions.

Tips for Successful Ageing : Ways to go Ahead

Being old is not a sin nor a person having old age should feel a guilt. It is not the sunset of life but to start the new inning with full pride, spirit, pleasure and endeavour. There are some ways to be followed which make an old man a golden man. Dr. Bada has named them "lucky people". He has stated some strategies to deal the old age in successful mode.They are as follows:

1. Don't stop moving.
2. When you feel irritated take a deep breath.
3. Do exercises regularly to avoid muscular aches.
4. Drink more water when you live in active air conditioner.
5. Chewing the food is very necessary. It makes the mind and body energetic.
6. Memory declination is not particularly caused due to increase in age but it is due to least usage of brain.
7. There is no need to take more medicine.
8. There is no need to minimise deliberately the blood pressure or blood sugar. They are the need of the age.
9. Do the work which you adore.
10. Daily movement out from home and be with the loved ones at there is necessary. Therefore, go out of the home everyday and make friends and sides.

11. Take nurturing and balanced diet.
12. Do every work with responsibility.
13. Be empathetic by nature.
14. Take care of yourself and those who love you.
15. In spite of fighting with diseases try to live with.
16. Come forth in the tough time of the others and help them. Make regular connections with those who love and regard you.
17. Use lukewarm water after every food intake.
18. Take maximum use of water.
19. Don't try to please your sleep. It is a natural process.
20. Try to do the things that make you happy. Sharpening the mind is the best exercise.
21. Don't stop conversation to those whom you have a good reciprocal relationship. Be in the contact with them either by phone or by physical presence
22. Patience is a good habit but don't seek favour always.
23. Search a family doctor nearby you and make a positive relationship with him/her.
24. Leave the habit of acquisition.
25. Do the work that is beneficial for you and others.
26. Live in your presence don't repent on past and expect more in future. Be optimistic and make your own rules of life.

References

American College of Sports Medicine Position Stand (1998). "Exercise and physical activity for older adults". *Med Sci Sports Exerc*, *30*(6): 992-1008. https://doi. Org/10.1249/00005768-199806000-00033.https:// doi. org/10.1097/00005768-199806000-00033. PMid:9624662

Baltes, P.B. (1997). "On the Incomplete Architecture of Human Ontogeny: Selection, Optimization, and Compensation as Foundation of Developmental Theory". *The American Psychologist*, *52*: 366-380. Doi:10.1037//0003-066X.52.4.366. [PubMed] [Google Scholar]

Baltes, P.B. and Baltes, M.M. (1990). "Psychological Perspectives on Successful Ageing: The Model of Selective Optimization with Compensation. Successful Ageing: Perspectives from the Behavioural Sciences". In: Baltes, P.B., Baltes M.M. editors. New York: Cambridge University Press: pp. 1-34. [Google Scholar]

Brussow, H. (2013). "What is Health?", *Microb Biotechnol, 6*:341-348.

Bülow, M.H., Söderqvist, T. (2014). "Successful Ageing: A Historical Overview And Critical Analysis of A Successful Concept". *Journal of Ageing Studies*,

31:139-149. http://dx.doi.org/10.1016/jamine.08.009-0890-4065-[PubMed] (Google Scholar).

Butler, R., Oberlink, M, Schecter, M. (1990). *The Promise of Productive Ageing*. Springer, New York.

Calasanti, T. (2016). "Combating Ageism: How Successful is Successful Ageing?" *The Gerontologist*, *56*:1093-1101. Doi:10.1093/geront/gv076. [PubMed] (Google Scholar).

Cho, J., Martins, I., and Poors, L.W. (2015). "Successful Ageing and Subjective Well-being Among Oldest-Old Adult". *Gerontologist 55*. 132-143, doi 10.1093/geront/gn0074

Cosco, T.D., Prina, A.M., Perales, I., Stephan, B.C., Brayne, C. (2014). "Operational Definitions of Successful Ageing: A Systematic Review". *International Psychogeriatrics*, *26*: 373-381. Doi:10.1017/51041610213002287 [PubMed] (Google Scholar).

Cumming, E., Henry, W.E. (1961). *Growing Old: The Process of Disengagement*. New York: Basic Books.

Depp, C.A. and Jeste, D.V. (2006). "Definitions and Predictors of Successful Ageing: A Comprehensive Review of Larger Quantitative Studies". *Am J Geriatr Psychiatry, 14*(1): 2-5. https://doi.org/10.1097/01. JGP.0000192501.03069. bc, PMid:16407577

_______(2006). "Definitions and Predictors of Successful Ageing: A Comprehensive Review of Larger Quantitative Studies". *The American Journal of Geriatric Psychiatry*, *14*: 6-doi:10.1097/01.JGP.0000192501.03069.bc. [PubMed] [Google Scholar].

Diener, E.D. (1984). "Subjective Well-being". *Psychological Bulletin*, *95*(3): 542-575.https : doi.org 10.1037/0033.2909.95.3.542.

Erikson, E.H. (1950). *Childhood and Society*. New York: Norton.

European Commission (2011). How to Promote Active Ageing in Europe: EU Support to Local and Regional Actors. European Commission, European Union-Committee of the Regions & Age Platform Europe, Brussels.

Fernandez-Ballesteros, R. (2019). *The Concept of Successful Ageing and Related Terms. The Cambridge Handbook of Successful Ageing*. In: Fernandez-Ballesteros, R., Benetos, A., Robine, J.M. (eds.). Cambridge University Press, pp. 6-22. [Google Scholar].

Fernández-Ballesteros, R., Robine, J.M., Walker, A., Kalache, A. (2013). *Active Ageing: A Global Goal. Current Gerontology and Geriatrics Research*. Article ID 298012, doi.org/10.1155/2013/290012 [PMC free article] [PubMed] [Google Scholar].

Fernández-Ballesterus R, García, L.F., Abarra, D., *et al.* (2008). "Lay Concept of Ageing Well: Cross-cultural Comparions". *Journal of the American Geriatrics Society*, *56*: 950-952. Doi:10.1111/j.1532-5415.2008.01654x [PubMed] [Google Scholar].

Fiske, D.W. (1949). "Consistency of the Factorial Structure of Personality Ratings from Different Sources". *The Journal of Abnormal and Social Psychology*, *44*(3). 329-344 https: doi.org/10.1037/h0057198

Foster, J.R. (1997). "Successful Coping, Adaptation and Resilience in the Elderly: An Interpretation of Epidemiologic Data". *Psychiatr Q 1997, 68*(30): 189-219.

Fried, L.P., & Guralnik, J.M. (1997). "Disability in Older Adults: Evidence Regarding Significance, Etiology and Risk". *Journal of American Geriatrics Society. 45*(1): 92-100 doi : 10.1111/j. 1532-5415.1997.tbo. 0986.x.PMID: 8994496.

Fried, L.P., Freedman, M., Endres, T.E, *et al.,* (1997). "Building Communities That Promote Successful Ageing". *West Med, 167*: 216-219.

Fries, J.F. (1980). "Ageing, Natural Death, and the Compression of Morbidity". *New England Journal of Medicine, 303*: 130-135. [PubMed] [Google Scholar]

Fry, C.L., Dickerson-Putman, J., Draper, P., Ikels, C., Keith, J., Glascock, P, Harpending, H.C. (2007). "Culture and the Meaning of a Good Old Age". In Sokolovsky, J. (ed.) *The Cultural Context of Ageing: Worldwide Perspectives.* Bergin & Garvey, Westport, CT, p. 104.

Gela, Y.Y., Addis, F. and Fekadu, M. (2022). "Cognitive Impairment and Associated Factors among Mature and Older Adults Living in the Community of Gender Town Ethiopia 2020". *Scientific Reports, 12*, 7545. https:/doi. org/1.1038/541598-02211735-2

Hanson, M.A., Cooper, C., Aihie Sayer, A., Eendebak, R.J., Clough, G.F., Beard, J.R. (2016). "Developmental Aspects of a Life Course Approach to Healthy Ageing". *J Physiol., 594*: 2147–2160.

Havighurst, R.J. (1961). "Successful Ageing". *The Gerontologist, 1*: 8-13.

_______ (1963). "Successful Ageing". In Williams, R.H., Tibbitts, C., Donahue, W. (eds,) *Processes of Ageing.* Atherton Press, New York, pp. 299-320.

Huang, D., Wang, J., Fang, H., Zang, Y. and Cao, S. (2022). *Global Research Trends in the Subjective Well-being of Older Adults from 2002 to 2022 : A Bibliography Analysis Frontiers in Psychology*, p. 13, https: 11doi. org/10.3389/f psyg. 2022.972515

Jeste, D.V., Savla, G.N. and Thompson, W.K. Depp, C.A. (2013). Association Between Older Age and More Successful Ageing". *American Journal of Psychiatry*, doi 10.1176/appi.ajp.2012.12030386

Jimmy Young, C. (2015). "Successful Ageing and Subjective Well-being among Oldest Old Adult". *The Gerontologist, 55*(1): 132-143.

Katz, S., Ford, A.B., Moskowitz, R.W., Jackson, B.A., Jaffe, M.W. (1963). "Studies of Illness in the Aged. The Index of Adl: A Standardized Measure of Biological and Psychosocial Function". *JAMA, 185*: 914-919.

Kim, S.H. and Park, S.A. (2016). "Meta-analysis of the Correlates of Successful Ageing in Older Adults". *Research on Ageing 39*(5): 657-677. Doi: 10.1177/0164027516656040 [PubMed] [Google Scholar].

Kivimäki, M. and Ferrie, J.E. (2011). "Epidemiology of Healthy Ageing and the Idea of more Refined Outcome Measures". *International Journal of Epidemiology, 40*: 845-847. [PubMed] [Google Scholar].

Kleinedam, L., Thoma, M., Maercker, A., *et al.* (2018). "What is Successful Ageing? A Psychometric Validation Study of Different Construct Definitions". *The Gerontologist. 20*: 1-11. Doi:10.1093/geront/gny083. [PubMed] [Google Scholar].

Kok, A.A, Aartsen, M.J., Deeg, D.J., Huisman, M. (2015). "Capturing the Diversity of Successful Ageing: An Operational Definition Based on 16-Year Trajectories of Functioning". *The Gerontologist, 57*(2): 240-251. Doi:10.1093/geront/gnv127. [PubMed] [Google Scholar].

Kusumastutia, S., Derksb, M.G.L., Tellier, S., Di Nucci, E., Lund, R., Mortensen, E.L., Westendorp, R.G.J. (2016). "Successful Ageing: A Study of the Literature Using Citation Network Analysis". *Maturitas, 93*: 4-12.

MacLaughlin, J., Holick, M.F. (1985). "Ageing Decreases the Capacity of Human Skin to Produce Vitamin D3". *J Clin Invest, 76*:1536. https://doi.org/10.1172/JC1112134

Martin, P., Kelly. N., Kahana, B., *et al.* (2014). "Defining Successful Ageing: A Tangible or Elusive Concept?" *The Gerontologist, 55*(1):14-25. Doi:10.1093/geront/gnu044 [PMC free article] [PubMed] [Google Scholar]

Mattson, M., Chan, S., Duan, W. (2002). "Modification of Brain Ageing and Neurodegenerative Disorders by Genes, Diet and Behaviour". *Physiol Rev, 82*: 637-672. https://doi.org/10.1152/physrev.00004.PMid:12087131

McCrae & Costa (1987). "Validation of the Five Factor Model of Personality Across Instrument and Observers". *Journal of Personality and Social Psychology, 52*(1) 81-90 https:/doi.org 10.1037/0022-3514.52.1.81

McLaughlin, S.J., Connel, C.M., Heeringa, S.G., Li, L.W. and Roberts, J.S. (2010): "Successful Ageing in United States: Prevalence Estimates from a National Sample of Older Adults". *The Journal of Gerontologist, Series B Psychological Sciences and Social Sciences, 65*, 216-226.10.1093. (Geronb/g bp 101).

Mount, S., Lara, J., Schols, A.M., Mathers, J.C. (2016). "Towards a Multidimensional Healthy Ageing Phenotype". *Curr Opin Clin Nutr Metab Care, 19*: 418-426.

Neugarten, B.L. (1972). "Personality and the Ageing Process". *Gerontologist 12*: 9-15.

Pattanaungkul, S., Riggs, B.L., Yergey, A.L., *et al.* (2000). "Relationship of Intestinal Calcium Absorption to 1.25-dihydroxyvitamin D [1.25 (OH)2D] Levels in Young Versus Elderly Women: Evidence for Age-Related Intestinal Resistance to 1.25 (OH)2D) action". *J Clin Endocrinol Metab, 85*: 4023. Press release: civic engagemnent of in an older America. 2004. http://www.civicengagement. org/agingsociety/Pages%20from%20Geron-NLSept05.pdf. Accessed on 4 February 2017.

Ranberg, K.A., Schroll, M. and & Jeune, B. (2015). "Healthy Centenarian's Do Not Exist But Automans Centenarian's Door Population Based Study of Morbidely among Danish Centenarians". *Journal of American Geriatrics.* Doi : 10.10445, 1532-5415.2001.49180

Rowe, J.E. and Kahn, R.L. (1987). "Human Ageing : Usual and Successful". *Science, 237* : 143-149. [PubMed] [Google Scholar].

Rowe, J.E. & Kahn, R.L. (1997), "Successful Ageing". *The Gerontologist. 37*: 433-440. [PubMed] [Google Scholar].

Rowe, J.W., Kahn, R.L. (1998). "Successful Ageing". *Ageing (Milano), 10*: 142-144.

Rowe, J.W., Kahn, R.L. (2015). "Successful Aging 2.0: Conceptual Expansions for the 21st Century". *J Gerontol B Psychol Sci Soc Sci, 70*: 593-596.

Sadana, R., Blas, E., Budhwani, S., Koller, T., Paraje, G. (2016). Healthy Ageing: Raising Awareness of Inequalities, Determinants, and What could be Done to Improve Health Equity". *Gerontologist, 56* (Suppl 2): S178-S193.

Sherman, S.S., Hollis, B.W., Tobin, J.D. (1990). "Vitamin D Status and Related Parameters in a Healthy Population: The Effects of Age, Sex, and Season". *J Clin Endocrinol Metab, 71*: 405. https://doi.org/10.1210/jcem-71-2-405

Smith, R. (2008). "The End of Disease and the Beginning of Health". *The BMJ Opinion*. https://blogs.bmj.com/bmj/2008/07/08/richard-smith-the-end-of-disease-and-the-beginning-of-health/. Accessed on 17 April 2017.

Swedish National Institute of Public Health. *Healthy Ageing: A challenge for Europe*, 2006.

Tornstam, L. (2005), *Gerotranscendence: A Developmental Theory of Positive Ageing*. New York: Springer Publishing Company.

Walston, J., Hardley, E.C., Ferrunic, L. *et al.* (2006). "Research agenda for Frailty in Older Adults: Toward a Better Understanding of Physiology and Etiology: Summary from the American Geriatric Society / National Institute on Ageing Research Conference on Frailty in Older Adults". *J AM Geriatr Soc, 54*: 991-1001 https://doi.org/10.1111/j.1532-5415.2006.00745.x

World Health Organization (1948). *Constitution of the World Health Organization*. WHO, Geneva.

World Health Organization (1986). *Ottawa Charter for Health Promotion*. WHO, Geneva.

World Health Organization (2015). *World Report on Ageing and Health*. WHO, Geneva.

World Health Organization (WHO) (2002). *Active ageing: a policy framework*. World Health Organization, Geneva.

World Health Organization Regional Office for Europe (2012). *Charting the Way to Well-being*. World Health Organization Regional Office for Europe, Copenhagen.

Young, Y., Frick, K.D., Phelan, E.A. (2009). "Can Successful Aging and Chronic Illness Coexist in the Same Individual? A Multidimensional Concept of Successful Ageing". *J Am Med Dir Assoc, 10*: 87-92.

Index

1986 Ottawa Charter for Health Promotion, 345

Activities of daily living (ADL), 36
Ageing population,
palliative and end-of-life care for, 61-70
complex decision-making at end of life, 63
focus on dignity and comfort, 64
holistic support and quality of life, 63
management of chronic illnesses, 63
psychological challenges in, 66
support for families and caregivers, 64
Ageing process, 123
Ageing women, psycho-social dynamics of, 82
Ageing, 1, 207
ageing self, 72
and well-being, 81
challenges in responding to population, 341
changes occurring with, 336
common health conditions associated with, 340
concept of (prospects and retrospects), 333-344
different types, 334
biological, 335
chronological, 335
functional, 336
psychological, 335
social, 335
factors influencing healthy, 340
social psychology of, 72
Ageism, 75
AKDSI, 306
Alzheimer's and Related Disorders Society of India (ARDSI), 85
AYUSH, 100

Behavioural factors, 281
Biological factors, 280
Blood sugar charts, 281
Brain-derived neurotrophic factor (BDNF), 313
Brain-drain, 246

Caregiver's healing,
a life story study of healing from..., 30 -60
challenges immediately following accident, 40
coming to terms with different possibilities of recovery, 45
coming to terms with disability, 46
creation of an experiential vacuum, 41
healing journey, 53
life beyond disability, 50

loss of hope, 42
mental strength and vision through support, 48
Caregiving and care-receiving, 35
Centre for Research on Ageing (CEFRA), 84
Cognitive functioning, 354
Cognitive Reserve Theory, 217
Cognitive-Behaviour Therapy (CBT), 320
Community health worker (CHW), 101
Compassion and empathy, 213
COVID-19 pandemic, 131

Death anxiety, 125
Dementia, 293
Depression, 156
among elderly population in Rasuwa, Nepal,
prevalence and associated factor of, 245-263
prevalence of, 254
and quality of life among Indian older adults, 155-174
Depression Assessment tool, 253
Diabetes, 276
and mental health challenges in the elderly, 278
biological interplay of, 277
classification of, 277
diabetes care teams, 287
features of psychological insulin resistance, 285
geriatric conditions and, 277
management and treatment of, 283
methods for diagnosing, 281
prevalence in India, 276
psychotherapy for treatment of, 284
relationship with mental health, 280
Disability, 33
cross-cultural variations in, 37

Elderly people, 4
Elderly persons of India, understanding diabetes and mental well-being in the, 276-290
Elderly--characteristics of, 192
emotional challenges in later life, 193
physical changes associated with ageing, 192
Emotion Regulation (ER), 8
End-of-life care, 61
Experiential vacuum, 55

Family and caregiver support, 237
Functional ability (FA), 116

Generalized Anxiety Disorder (GAD), 7
Geriatric Depression Scale (GDS), 246, 249
Geriatric mental health in India, challenges in, 298
present human resources for, 307
Geriatric Mental Health,
approaches to, 218
biopsychosocial approach, 221
significance of, 223
holistic care, 218
evidence-based effectiveness, 239
impact on services, 224
intervention strategies for elderly, 229
family and caregiver support, 236
physical health and nutrition, 234
social engagement, 232
models for enhancing, 225
ecological model, 225
social convoy model, 227
positive ageing, 223
Geriatric population, 216
Geriatric rehabilitation, 306
Geriatrics, 71
Gerontology, 71, 81
Gero-psychology and its researches, exploring field of, 71-94

developments in research, education and training, 82
biological gerontology, 83
education and training, 84
medical/geriatric research, 83
qualitative research, 85
social and behavioural gerontology, 83
Global population, 61
Global Strategy and Action Plan for Ageing and Health for 2016–2020, 19
Globalization, 341

Happiness and life satisfaction predictors,
physical and psychological well-being, 271
socio-demographic variables, 271
age, 271
cognitive health, 273
education, 272
financial resources, 272
physical health, 272
psychological health, 273
quality of life, 274
self-esteem, 273
social support, 273
Healing, 37
Health, 291
and mental health, 292
importance of in old age, 291
Health-related quality of life (HQOL), 165
Healthy ageing, new WHO definition of, 115
HelpAge India, 306
Holistic care, 218

Identity assimilation, 73
India ageing Report 2023, 207
India,
current state of geriatric mental health in, 96
access to mental health services, 99
initiatives and interventions, 99
stigma and cultural factors, 97
Indian Association of Palliative Care, 132
Indian older adults,
psychosocial and emotional challenges facing, 4
strategies/ways to handle psychosocial and emotional distress, 8
struggle in handling emotional and psychological challenges, 4-15
Intergenerational activities, 195
International Classification of Functioning (ICF), 115
Interpersonal Psychotherapy (IPT), 321

Journeying through mental landscapes (overcoming loneliness, easing distress, and managing anxiety for optimal wellness), 141-154
distress and anxiety,
consequences of unmanaged on mental wellness, 146
detrimental impact, 145
loneliness, 142, 144
as a precursor to mental Health challenges, 143
mental health, 141
beyond absence of illness, 142
mental well-being,
empowering, 150
preventive measures for, 147
Joy and contentment, 265

Kathmandu valley, 247

Later life,
importance of addressing mental health in 95
functional implications, 96

impact on overall well-being, 95
quality of life, 95

Life satisfaction, 265
Life story research, 38
Life, 175
Loneliness unveiled, mindset matters in geriatric wellness, 189-206
Loneliness,
case studies and successful programmes, 197
community-based initiatives and policies, 196
cultural considerations and tailored interventions, 197
encouraging emotional health and social connectivity, 195
factors contributing to, 193
intervention strategies and holistic approach, 194
leverageing technology to combat, 196
mind-set approaches in loneliness therapies, 195
psychological effects of, 192
understanding in elderly, 191

Meditation, 212
Mental health and ageing in India, understanding the complex nexus of, 291-309
Mental health for geriatric population, creating a positive environment for elderly, 216-244
Mental health in later life, current state and future directions of geriatric mental health care in India, 94-108
Mental health problems in the elderly,
approaches in psychotherapy, 320
biological markers for mental health risks in elderly, 311
genetic predisposition, 312
inflammatory processes, 312
neurochemical imbalances, 311
neuroendocrine dysregulation, 313
neuroplasticity and growth factors, 313
oxidative stress, 313
sleep disturbances, 313
structural brain changes, 312
challenges faced in old age, 316
epidemiology, 310
preventive measures, 318
psychological factors associated with, 314
psychological management, 319
risk factors associated with, 310-332
risk factors, 317
Mental health, 2, 8, 141, 284
common causes of poor mental health in old age, 297
future trajectory, 307
importance of in geriatric population, 294
Motivational Interviewing (MI), 321

National Council on Ageing,, 112
National Policy for Older Persons (NPOP, 1999), 176
National Policy on Older Persons in India, 80
National Programme for Health Care of the Elderly (NPHCE), 133
Non-Governmental Organisations (NGOs), 202
North American Nursing Diagnosis (2007), 123

Objective well-being, 346
Old Age Pension Scheme, 117
Old age,
cognitive gerontology and cognitive development in, 76
personality development in, 77
social relationships in, 79

Older adults,
role of spirituality in assuaging death anxiety among, 123-140
scoping review on predictors of happiness and life satisfaction among the, 264-275
Older persons, category of, 336

Palliative care, 61, 62
Peer support initiatives, 195
PERMA, 20
Person with disability (PwD), 30, 31, 32, 34
Physical morbidities, 94
Positive ageing, 16, 210
building eco-system for fostering well-being of elderly people, 16-29
challenges to be addressed, 23
ecosystem of life, 23
perspectives on well-being of elderly, 20
population ageing, 16
strategies for fostering well-being, 22
successful ageing, 17
Primary mental healthcare (PMHC), 99, 102, 103
Psychological care for older adults, therapeutic interventions in, 68
Psychological distress, 146
PTSD, 37

Quality of life, 156, 166, 319, 341

Reflective practices, 10
Rejuvenation therapy, 111
Reminiscence, 325
Resilience, 326

Social power, concept of, 74
Spinal Cord Injury (SCI), 36
Spirituality, 208, 209, 342
conceptual understandings of spirituality and positive ageing, 209
practicing spirituality in daily life, 212
role of in positive ageing for older adults, 207-215
theoretical basis for research on spirituality and ageing, 211
Stress, 318
Successful ageing, 345-365
age-associated body system changes, 354
important goals, 352
living life fullest, 358
major challenges faced by elderly people, 352
positive personality traits, 357
predictors of, 353
strategies to promote, 358
subjective well-being, 353
tips for, 360

Technology and psychotherapy, 326
Terror management theory (TMT), 124

United Nations Population Fund (UNFPA), 207
Uttarakhand --cultural practices in towards healthy ageing, 109-122
cultural practices in Uttarakhand, 119
dietary practices and nutritional habits in Uttarakhand, 113
indigenous healthcare practices for old aged people, 118
old age in Indian culture, 110
physical activity and labour, 114
problems faced by old age people, 112
social and community support, 11

Uttarakhand, 109

Vanaprastha-detachment, 10, 207
Volunteer programmes, 195

Well-being, 16
Wellness among elderly, promoting the, 175-188
Wellness, 177
  emotional, 180
  environmental, 182
  intellectual, 181
  physical, 177
  promoting wellness among elderly, 183
  social, 179
  spiritual, 180
WHO Global Strategy and Action Plan, 117
World Health Organization (WHO), 19, 34, 71, 94, 142, 176, 216, 345